10th
CANADIAN EDITION

Study Guide for use
Microeconomics

McCONNELL
BRUE
BARBIERO

Prepared by
Torben Andersen
Red Deer College

William B. Walstad
University of Nebraska, Lincoln

Robert C. Bingham

McGraw-Hill
Ryerson

Toronto   Montréal   Boston   Burr Ridge, IL   Dubuque, IA   Madison, WI   New York
San Francisco   St. Louis   Bangkok   Bogotá   Caracas   Kuala Lumpur   Lisbon
London   Madrid   Mexico City   Milan   New Delhi   Santiago   Seoul   Singapore
Sydney   Taipei

**McGraw-Hill
Ryerson**

**Study Guide for use with
Microeconomics,
Tenth Canadian Edition**

ISBN: 0-07-092239-X

1 2 3 4 5 6 7 8 9 10 MP 0 9 8 7 6 5

Printed and bound in Canada.

Vice President, Editorial and Media Technology: Patrick Ferrier
Executive Sponsoring Editor: Lynn Fisher
Economics Editor: Ron Doleman
Developmental Editor: Daphne Scriabin
Marketing Manager: Kelly Smyth
Supervising Editor: Joanne Murray
Production Coordinator: Janie Deneau
Formatter: Jay Tee Graphics Ltd
Printer: Maracle Press Ltd.

Contents

Preface

Welcome to the study of economics. This **Study Guide** complements the course textbook, **Microeconomics**, 10th Canadian edition, by McConnell, Brue and Barbiero. The design of the **Study Guide** is based on the conviction that active study beats passive study. To benefit from an aerobics class, it is not enough to watch the instructor demonstrate—you must also do the exercises yourself. To learn carpentry you cannot merely read a book—you must practice using the tools. And so it is with economics; you must actively do exercises and work with the tools.

The **Study Guide** provides you opportunities for this practice and gives you feedback along the way. Here you will find a range of questions that require verbal, numerical, and graphical answers. These are the three main modes of analysis in economics, and skill in all three areas will likely be expected of you in your exams.

I hope that you will use this **Study Guide** often, and that it will help you to have more success and more fun in your economics course.

Study Guide Organization

For each chapter in the text there is a chapter in the **Study Guide** with a set of common features as follows.

The **Overview** puts the chapter in context and briefly highlights and summarizes the key ideas.

The **Chapter Outline** is divided into the same main sections as the text chapter and for each one provides: specific learning objectives (indicated by ◈), a summary of the main points, a **Quick Quiz** (two or three multiple choice questions dealing specifically with each section), and sometimes special hints or tips (indicated by ➲).

A list of **Terms and Concepts** shows which new terms and concepts are introduced in the chapter.

The remainder of the chapter consists of practice questions and answers. **Fill-In** and **True-False** questions mainly test your recall of

the reading. There are more questions of the **Multiple-Choice** variety because such questions are most common on exams in most colleges and universities. Many of these questions involve analysis and application of concepts (including graphs, calculations, and other technical aspects). **Problems and Projects** require analysis and application, frequently with graphs, charts and calculations. The **Discussion Questions** may serve as review questions for study groups, and give some suggestion of possible short essay questions for exams. The **Answers** section provides solutions, often with a bit of explanation, for all questions except the **Discussion Questions**.

The last section of the Study Guide provides detailed answers to the **Key Questions** found at the end of chapters in the text.

A Bit of Advice

Try to work several times each week with your text and the **Study Guide**. Economics is absorbed most effectively in small, frequent doses.

It may be useful to preview the **Overview** and **Chapter Outline** sections before tackling a new chapter in the textbook. However, most of your time with the **Study Guide** should come after reading the chapter in the textbook, and probably after your instructor has addressed the material in class.

Make a serious attempt to answer a question before looking at its solution. Evaluate your results to identify your strengths and weaknesses. Especially if you don't have time to do all of the questions, stress those that seem more important given your instructor's emphasis of topics and style of exam questions. If you are thinking like an economist, you will strive to know the most important things extremely well and the less important things not so well!

When reviewing for exams, you may not have time to re-read all of the textbook chapters. Use the **Overview** and **Chapter Outline** sections for quick review and to zero in on key areas that will require more detailed review of the textbook.

Acknowledgments

Thanks to Tom Barbiero for the encouragement and advice, and for writing such a fine textbook for Canadian students. I owe a great deal also to the authors of previous editions of the **Study Guide**: Cyril Grant, William Walstad, and Robert Bingham. I am grateful for helpful comments from my colleague, Chandan Shirvaikar, and from numerous students. Once again I have enjoyed working with the good people at McGraw-Hill Ryerson, especially Ron Doleman and Daphne Scriabin.

If you have any comments on the **Study Guide** I would be delighted to hear from you. Please email me at torben.andersen@rdc.ab.ca.

--- Torben Andersen
    Red Deer, Alberta

Chapter 1 — The Nature and Method of Economics

Overview

Economics is the social science concerned with the efficient use of scarce resources to achieve maximum satisfaction of wants. Chapter 1 introduces you to the kinds of topics economists study, how economists analyze these topics, and why economics is useful and important. You also learn about eight widely accepted economic goals that are important to our society.

The central idea in economics is scarcity of resources. Our resources are limited, but our wants are unlimited, so we must choose how to allocate our resources. In these choices we face tradeoffs. When we choose to spend resources to produce one thing we sacrifice the production of something else. This sacrifice is known as an opportunity cost. Economics consists of analyzing how humans behave in response to the problem of scarcity. The analysis is based on the assumptions of "rational self-interest" and on "marginal analysis."

The field of economics uses the scientific method. Based on observations of human behaviour (facts or data), we formulate hypotheses that are possible explanations of the causes and effects of these behaviours. Therefore, we test the predictions of our hypotheses to see whether they are supported by the data. Explanations that produce predictions that are highly consistent with the data become accepted theories. Policy economics applies theories and data to formulate policies to solve economic problems or achieve our economic goals. Policy controversies often centre on the interpretation and relative importance of goals that may be in conflict with each other. Such issues move us from positive economics (which investigates *what is*) to normative economics (which incorporates subjective views of *what ought to be*).

Economics is divided into two main categories. Microeconomics studies individual or specific economic units. Macroeconomics studies economy-wide aggregates.

Clear thinking requires that we avoid many common pitfalls or errors in thinking. These include: bias, loaded terminology, imprecise definitions, fallacies of composition, and causation fallacies.

Chapter Outline

◇ What is the definition of economics?
• Economics is the social science concerned with the efficient use of scarce resources to obtain the maximum satisfaction of society's unlimited wants.

1.1 Ten Key Concepts to Retain for a Lifetime

◇ What are the ten key concepts?
• There are ten key concepts that we hope you will recall long after this course is over. These concepts are merely listed in this chapter, but they recur throughout the text. Wherever one appears it is identified with the "key" icon.
• The ten key concepts fall into three categories: (a) those that pertain to the individual; (b) those that explain the interaction among individuals; and (c) those that deal with the economy as a whole and the standard of living.

Quick Quiz

1. Which of the following is not among the key concepts related to the individual?
   (a) the effectiveness of markets
   (b) facing tradeoffs
   (c) choosing a little more or a little less
   (d) the influence of incentives

2. To say that "choices are made at the margin" means that:
   (a) we choose the best option
   (b) we choose a little more or a little less
   (c) government makes the choices for us
   (d) we sometimes make incorrect choices

1

3. In the economy as a whole, the standard of living improves when there is more:
  (a)   inflation
  (b)   unemployment
  (c)   government involvement
  (d)   production of goods and services

1.2 The Economic Perspective

◇ What is the economic way of thinking?
  o   What is scarcity?
  o   What is an opportunity cost?
  o   What is rational behaviour?
  o   How does marginal analysis work?

• The economic perspective on human behaviour is described in three interrelated ideas: scarcity, rational behaviour, and marginal analysis.
• Scarcity of resources forces people to make choices and incur opportunity costs. The opportunity cost of a choice is the value of the next best alternative forgone.
• People make rational decisions based on their own self-interest. Whatever gives a person maximum satisfaction (or utility) is deemed to be in that person's self-interest.
• People make choices by comparing marginal costs and marginal benefits.

Quick Quiz

4. A major feature of the economic perspective is:
  (a)   equating rational self-interest with selfishness
  (b)   comparing marginal benefits with marginal costs
  (c)   the validity of normative economics for decision making
  (d)   the recognition of the abundance of economic resources

5. Because our resources are limited:
  (a)   we face the problem of scarcity
  (b)   we must make choices
  (c)   we must incur opportunity costs
  (d)   all of the above

6. People are behaving rationally only if:
  (a)   they behave selfishly
  (b)   they consistently pursue their own self-interest
  (c)   government makes the choices for us
  (d)   they never make any choices they later regret

1.3 Economic Methodology

◇ How do economists construct theories?
  o   What are the five elements of the scientific method?
  o   What constitutes a good economic theory?
  o   Why do economists use the other-things-are-equal assumption?

• The scientific method consists of: (1) observing facts (data); (2) formulating possible cause-effect explanations (hypotheses); (3) testing hypotheses by comparing their predictions with data from specific real world events: (4) accepting, rejecting or modifying hypotheses based on test results; (5) continued testing.
• Economists develop economic principles (also called theories, laws or models) to explain the economy and formulate policies to solve economic problems.
• Economic principles are expressed as generalizations or tendencies. Good theories are those that explain and predict well. Predictions of a theory need not hold true in every single case in order for the theory to be useful.
• The *ceteris paribus* or other-things-equal assumption is used in order to focus on only the variables of main interest in a theory.
• Economic theories are abstractions from reality because they are intentionally simplified to omit irrelevant facts.
• An explanation that has not yet been tested is often called a hypothesis; one that has been tested and supported by the data is often called a theory; one that has been tested many times, and is regularly supported by the data, is often called an economic law or principle.

➲ You may have difficulty accepting that economics is a science, especially because economic theories are inexact. Economics is a science by virtue of the methodology it uses to arrive at generalizations. Think of generalizations from cancer research or meteorology. Scientists have proven a link between smoking and lung cancer, even though their knowledge is not exact enough to identify which specific smokers will get cancer. Meteorologists' weather forecasts are not always correct, yet we rely on these forecasts because they are generally better than the forecasts we could generate ourselves without the benefit of the inexact science of meteorology.

◇ What is policy economics?

o Distinguish between policy economics and theoretical economics.

o What are the basic steps in policy-making?

o List the eight widely accepted goals of economic policy in Canada.

• Policy economics involves the application of economic theories and data to formulate policies designed to achieve specific goals.

• The three steps in policy-making are: (1) stating the goals; (2) determining the policy options for achieving the chosen goals; and (3) implementing the chosen policy and evaluating its effects.

• Eight major economic goals are widely accepted in Canada: economic growth, full employment, economic efficiency, price-level stability, economic freedom, equitable distribution of income, economic security, and balance of trade.

• Economic goals may be complementary or conflicting. When goals conflict, the tradeoffs must be assessed and value judgments made about how to balance them.

Quick Quiz

7. When economists state that "consumer spending rises when personal income increases," this is an example of:

(a) a generalization

(b) loaded terminology

(c) a normative statement

(d) a fallacy of composition

8. Economists usually test their theories by:

(a) mathematical calculations and proofs

(b) making assumptions

(c) comparing their predictions with data from the real world

(d) doing experiments in a laboratory

9. The three basic steps in economic policy making are:

(a) gather facts, make abstractions, show findings

(b) state the goal, determine the options, evaluate results

(c) create the theory, analyze assumptions, derive conclusions

(d) form hypothesis, simplify the model, assume other things are equal

1.4 Macroeconomics and Microeconomics

◇ What is the difference between macroeconomics and microeconomics?

• Macroeconomics deals with the nation's economy as a whole by examining aggregate measures (such as the overall price level in Canada). Microeconomics looks at specific economic units (such as the price of houses in one city).

◇ What is the difference between positive and normative economics?

• Positive economics concerns the study of facts to determine *what is*, whereas normative economics involves value judgments to determine *what ought to be*. Theoretical economics is positive in nature, whereas policy economics must involve both positive and normative.

Quick Quiz

10. When we look at the whole economy or its major aggregates, our analysis would be at the level of:

(a) microeconomics

(b) macroeconomics

(c) positive economics

(d) normative economics

11. Which would be studied in microeconomics:

(a) the output of the entire community

(b) the total number of workers employed in Canada

(c) the general level of the prices in the Canadian economy

(d) the output and price of wheat in Canada

12. Which is a normative statement?

(a) the consumer price index rose 5.6% last month

(b) an unemployment rate of 6.8% is too high

(c) the average rate of interest on loans is 8.6%

(d) the economy will grow by 2.6% next year

1.5 Pitfalls to Objective Thinking

◇ What are six common pitfalls to objective thinking?

o Give examples of: the fallacy of composition, the post hoc fallacy, and confusion between correlation and causation.

- Common pitfalls to avoid in order to think clearly and logically using the economic perspective include:
  o bias or preconceptions not warranted by facts
  o loaded terminology that appeals to emotions
  o careless use of terms whose precise technical definitions differ from common usage
  o the fallacy of composition, or the assumption that what is true for one is necessarily true for the group
  o the *post hoc* fallacy, or the mistaken belief that if event A precedes event B, A is the cause of B
  o confusion of correlation with causation, or the mistaken belief that if A and B are correlated that must be a cause and effect relationship between A and B

➲ To remember them more easily, associate each pitfall with a specific example: perhaps one that is funny or has personal meaning for you. For example: "Last summer when it was really hot I ate lots of ice cream, so if I eat more ice cream now the weather will warm up." Which fallacy does this example illustrate?

Quick Quiz

13. If one fan can get a better view of a hockey game by standing up, then every fan can get a better view of the game by standing up. This is a case of:
- (a)   the after this, therefore because of this fallacy
- (b)   the fallacy of composition
- (c)   economic bias
- (d)   using loaded terminology

14. What pitfall to objective thinking is reflected in a person's view that corporate profits are always excessive?
- (a)   bias
- (b)   definition
- (c)   the fallacy of composition
- (d)   confusing correlation and causation

15. During World War II, price controls were used to prevent inflation; some people called this "a fascist and arbitrary restriction of economic freedom," while others said it was a "necessary and democratic means of preventing ruinous inflation." Both labels are examples of:
- (a)   economic bias
- (b)   the fallacy of composition
- (c)   misuse of commonsense definitions
- (d)   loaded terminology

Terms and Concepts

economics	policy economics
economic perspective	tradeoffs
utility	macroeconomics
marginal analysis	aggregate
scientific method	microeconomics
theoretical economics	positive economics
principles	normative economics
generalizations	fallacy of composition
"other-things-equal" assumption	post hoc, ergo propter hoc fallacy

Fill-In Questions

1. Economics is concerned with the _____ use of _____ resources to attain the _____ satisfaction of human wants.

2. Deriving principles or theories is called _____ economics, whereas applying economic principles to solve problems is called _____ economics.

3. The three steps involved in the formulation of economic policy are:
- (a)   _____
- (b)   _____
- (c)   _____

4. Eight economic goals that are widely accepted in Canada include:
- (a)   _____
- (b)   _____
- (c)   _____
- (d)   _____
- (e)   _____
- (f)   _____
- (g)   _____
- (h)   _____

5. The economic perspective has three interrelated features: It recognizes that (a) scarcity requires _____; (b) that people make decisions in a _____ manner based on their _____; and (c) that weighing the costs and benefits of a decision is based on _____ analysis.

True-False

Circle T if the statement is true, F if it is false.

1. We use the "other things equal" or ceteris paribus assumption in order to simplify the reasoning process.   **T F**

2. Abstraction in economic theory is useful because it eliminates unnecessary complexity and irrelevant facts.   **T F**

3. A common reason that individuals disagree on what economic policy should be chosen is that they disagree on the goal or desired result.   **T F**

4. Making value judgments as to preferred goals of an economy is known as positive economic analysis.   **T F**

5. The statement: "Increased patent protection for the Canadian pharmaceutical industry will result in increased research and development activity in Canada" is a positive statement.   **T F**

6. If two variables are correlated with one another, changes in one must be causing changes in the other.   **T F**

7. Scarcity is caused by the fact that people make choices.   **T F**

8. In economics the word "marginal" means additional, or extra.   **T F**

Multiple-Choice

Circle the letter that corresponds to the best answer.

1. Which statement is the best one to complete a short definition of economics? "Economics is the study of:
 (a) profit maximization by businesses."
 (b) the triumph of the capitalistic system over communism."
 (c) monetary transactions."
 (d) the efficient use of scarce resources."

2. The statement that "there is no free lunch" refers to what economic concept?
 (a) correlation does not imply causality
 (b) everything has an opportunity cost
 (c) nothing is free because government taxes everything
 (d) individuals have different tastes and preferences

3. If Ben is rational, when he buys soup he will:
 (a) never donate any cans of soup to the food bank
 (b) always choose the same brand of soup
 (c) always choose the cheapest brand of soup
 (d) choose the brand of soup that offers the most utility in relation to the price

4. One economic principle states that, *ceteris paribus*, the lower the price of a commodity the greater will be the quantity of the commodity consumers will wish to purchase. On the basis of this principle alone, it can be concluded that:
 (a) if the price of mink coats falls, consumers will purchase more mink coats
 (b) if the price of mink coats falls, there must have been a decrease in the demand for clothes made of fur
 (c) if the price of mink coats falls and there are no important changes in the other factors affecting their demand, consumers will purchase more mink coats
 (d) if more mink coats are purchased this month than last month, it is because the price of mink coats has fallen

5. An economic model is *not*:
 (a) an ideal type of economy or economic policy that we should strive to achieve
 (b) a tool economists employ to enable them to predict
 (c) an abstract representation of the economy or some part of the economy

(d)   an explanation of how the economy or a part of the economy functions in its essential details

6.   Which of the following is *not* among the dangers encountered when constructing or applying an economic model?
(a)   it may contain irrelevant facts and be more complex than necessary
(b)   it may come to be accepted as "what ought to be" rather than as "what is"
(c)   it may be overly simplified and so be a very poor approximation of the reality it explains
(d)   it may result in a conclusion that is unacceptable to people

7.   A theory in economics:
(a)   is useless if it uses simplifying assumptions
(b)   is of little use if it is abstract
(c)   is useful if the predictions of the theory usually correspond to actual economic occurrences
(d)   is useless if its predictions are not always correct

8.   Which of the following would not be contained in an economic theory?
(a)   predictions that follow from that theory
(b)   definitions that clearly set out the variables included in the model
(c)   statements of the relationships among the variables in the model
(d)   normative statements about the most preferred outcomes

9.   If one individual decides to consume less beef, there will be little or no effect on beef prices. To argue, therefore, that if all individuals consume less beef there will be little or no effect on beef prices is an example of:
(a)   the post hoc, ergo propter hoc fallacy
(b)   the fallacy of composition
(c)   an oversimplified generalization
(d)   using loaded terminology

10.   The Great Depression that began in 1929 was preceded by a stock market crash. To conclude that the Depression was therefore caused by the stock market crash is an example of:
(a)   the post hoc, ergo propter hoc fallacy
(b)   the fallacy of composition

(c)   the ceteris paribus assumption
(d)   using loaded terminology

11.   Which of the following is not a widely accepted economic goal?
(a)   price-level stability
(b)   zero taxation
(c)   economic efficiency
(d)   economic freedom

12.   Which economic goal is associated with the idea that we want to get the maximum benefit at the minimum cost from the limited productive resources available?
(a)   economic security
(b)   economic growth
(c)   economic efficiency
(d)   economic freedom

13.   Which of the following might be studied in microeconomics?
(a)   the output of the entire economy
(b)   the national unemployment rate
(c)   the effect of money supply changes on the Consumer Price Index
(d)   the price and output of apples from the Annapolis Valley

14.   If economic growth tends to produce a more equitable distribution of income among people in a nation, then the goals of growth and equitable income distribution seem to be:
(a)   a tradeoff
(b)   conflicting
(c)   complementary
(d)   mutually exclusive

15.   To say that two economic goals are conflicting means that:
(a)   there is a tradeoff in the achievement of the goals
(b)   some people do not agree with these goals
(c)   the achievement of one goal results in achievement of the other goal
(d)   it is impossible to quantify both goals

16.   Which of the following is a macroeconomic topic?
(a)   the effect of cigarette tax reductions on cigarette smoking
(b)   the effect of government set stumpage fees on the amount of lumber exported to the United States

(c)   the effect of the cod fishery closure on the unemployment rate in Halifax

(d)   the effect of the falling Canadian dollar on Canada's exports and imports

Problems and Projects

1. Opportunity Cost
Use the idea of opportunity cost to provide some possible explanations for these observations:

(a) Ashley turned down an "all-expenses-paid" trip to California because the trip was the week before her midterms.

(b) Dennis decided to use a realtor to sell his house, even though he could have avoided the realtor's fee by selling it himself.

(c) The St. Amand family buys a dishwasher from Sears because they didn't know that the same model was available at a lower price at a discount warehouse store.

2. Marginal Analysis
Kim Mitchell is at Canadian Tire shopping for patio lanterns. He must choose between a pack of 10 lights for $50 and a pack of 20 lights for $75. Explain the thought process he might use if he applies marginal analysis.

3. Positive and Normative Statements
Indicate in the space beside each statement whether it is positive (P) or normative (N).

(a) Tuition fee increases are causing university enrolments to decrease. _____

(b) Agricultural subsidies in Europe are killing small towns in Saskatchewan. _____

(c) Higher automobile insurance premiums increase the number of people willing to drive without insurance. _____

(d) The Employment Insurance program is too generous because it gives people the incentive to quit their jobs. _____

(e) It is unfair for the government to tax scholarship income. _____

(f) The federal government should do more to eliminate regional disparities in Canada. _____

4. Economic Methodology
Match the terms on the left-hand list with the descriptions on the right-hand list.

(a) hypothesis   (i)   explanation supported by data

(b) law   (ii)   proposed explanation

(c) theory   (iii) explanation supported by data many times

5. Pitfalls to Objective Thinking
Below are five statements, each containing an example of a common pitfall in thinking about economics. Indicate, in the space following each statement, the type of pitfall involved.

(a) The Second World War resulted in forty-five years of economic expansion in Canada. _____

(b) "An unemployed worker can find a job if he or she looks diligently and conscientiously for employment; therefore, all unemployed workers can find employment if they search diligently and conscientiously." _____

(c) "Just tell me when rain will be needed and I will schedule my vacation for that week." _____

(d) "The players, not the team owners, deserve to benefit from the recent jump in revenues earned by the National Basketball Association; after all, it is the players that fans pay to see." _____

(e) "The North American Free Trade Agreement is making Canadian workers pawns of the powerful corporations who can move their sweat shops to Mexico."

Discussion Questions

1. What are some issues that you face in your personal or work life for which some knowledge of economics could provide useful skills?

2. What is a "laboratory experiment under controlled conditions?" Why are such experiments not normally possible in economics? What does economics have instead of a laboratory?

3. What is the relationship between facts and theory?

4. Why are economic principles and models necessarily generalizations and abstractions?

5. Sketch a map showing me how to get from your home to the nearest grocery store. In what ways is your map realistic, and in what ways is it unrealistic (abstract)? Would your map necessarily be more helpful to me in finding the store if it was more realistic? Would it be worth making it more realistic? How do these issues concerning your map relate to issues concerning economic theories?

6. Explain each of the following: (a) fallacy of composition; (b) loaded terminology; (c) the *post hoc, ergo propter hoc* fallacy.

7. Explain briefly the difference between: (a) macroeconomics and microeconomics; (b) correlation and causation

Answers

Quick Quiz
1. p. 3
2. p. 5
3. p. 9
4. pp. 4-6
5. p. 4
6. pp. 4-5
7. p. 8
8. p. 7
9. p. 9
10. (b) pp. 10-11
11. p. 11
12. (b) p. 11
13. (b) pp. 12-13
14. p. 12
15. p. 12

Fill-In Questions
1. efficient, scarce, maximum
2. theoretical, policy
3. stating goals; analyzing policy options; evaluating policy effectiveness
4. full employment; economic growth; price-level stability; balance of trade; equitable distribution of income; economic efficiency; economic security; economic freedom
5. choices; rational; self-interest; marginal

True-False
1. T
2. T
3. T
4. F   Value judgments imply normative economics
5. T   The statement is positive, whether true or false
6. F   Don't confuse correlation with causation
7. F   The other way around
8. T

Multiple-Choice
1. (d)   This one is the most comprehensive
2. (b)   Everything has a cost in some form
3. (d)   He may have charitable motives, he may buy different brands due to price changes, and he may buy more expensive soup because it gives him more utility
4. (c)   *Ceteris paribus* means "other things remaining constant"
5. (a)   An economic model explains how the world is, not how we want it to be
6. (d)   Perhaps the conclusion will be unacceptable to some people, but this does not affect the validity of the theory
7. (c)   Good theories always involve assumptions and abstractions, and may not predict correctly in *every* case.
8. (d)   Theories are limited to positive aspects
9. (b)   What is true for one need not be true for all
10. (a) Because B happened *after* A does not prove that B *caused* A
11. (b) Zero taxation is not on the list of eight goals
12. (c)
13. (d) This topic deals with a single market rather than with the economy in aggregate
14. (c) Complementary because they can be achieved together, without tradeoff
15. (a) To move towards one goal entails moving away from the other
16. (d) All the others deal with specific markets

Problems and Projects
1. Each of these decisions was presumably made because the opportunity cost was too high: (a) by going to Disneyland, Ashley would lose study time and her exam results would suffer; (b) selling his own house would have cost Dennis some time, and perhaps some money if a realtor could get a higher price; (c) shopping at every store to find the absolute lowest price is not usually worth the cost of time and travel.
2. Mitchell would compare the extra enjoyment or use he would get from the 10 extra lights in the larger pack with what other enjoyment he could get by spending on something else the $25 extra cost for the larger pack. That is, he would compare marginal benefit and marginal cost.
3. (a) P; (b) P; (c) P; (d) N; (e) N; (f) N. In principle it is possible to test whether positive statements are true or false, while normative statements depend on values.
4. (a)-(ii); (b)-(iii); (c)-(i)
5. (a) *post hoc ergo propter hoc* fallacy; (b) the fallacy of composition; (c) confusing correlation and causation; (d) bias; (e) loaded terminology

Graphs and Their Meaning

Appendix to Chapter 1

Overview

The old saying that "a picture is worth a thousand words" is true in economics because economists use graphs to "picture" relationships between variables. A graph can display a lot of information in a manner that is precise yet quick to comprehend. Because we rely so much on these "pictures," you need to be skilled in constructing and interpreting graphs. If you are already skilled with the basics of graphing, you may only need to review this appendix quickly. On the other hand, if this material seems unfamiliar, relax and work carefully through the appendix; all of the basics you need are here.

The appendix shows how to construct a graph from a table of data on two variables (using the example of income and consumption). Each variable is represented on one of the two axes, so each axis should be labelled with the variable name, its units of measurement, and marked off with a consistent measurement scale. We often plot data to determine whether two variable are related, and if so, whether directly or inversely.

Economists usually, but not always, measure the independent variable on the horizontal axis and the dependent variable on the vertical axis of a graph. The curve plotted to illustrate the relationship between the two variables is drawn based on the ceteris paribus condition. If any other variable affecting the dependent variable happens to change, then we must plot a whole new curve passing through a different set of points. This is called a shift in the curve.

A relationship that is linear (a straight line) can be defined by two simple elements: the slope and the vertical intercept of the line. A linear relationship is easily expressed in equation form once the slope and the vertical intercept are found from a graph or table of data. Slope often has economic meaning, because slopes measure how a marginal change in the independent variable causes a marginal change in the dependent. For a nonlinear curve the slope is not constant; it varies as one moves along the curve.

Appendix Outline

◇ What is a graph?

◇ How is a graph constructed?

• A graph is a visual representation of the relationship between variables and is helpful in describing economic theories and models.

• To construct a simple graph, plot numerical data about two variables from a table. Sometimes the tabular data must be found first by using an equation relating the two variables.

- o Each graph has a horizontal and a vertical axis that is labelled for each variable and then scaled for the range of the data points that will be measured on the axis. Along a given axis a certain increment of distance represents a consistent increment in the variable.
- o Data points are plotted on the graph by drawing perpendiculars from the scaled points on the two axes to the place on the graph where the perpendiculars intersect.
- o A line or curve can then be drawn to connect the points plotted on the graph. If the line is straight the relationship is "linear."

➲ Some students are comfortable with economic graphs right away, but others initially have an aversion to graphs. If you are in the first group, you are fortunate because economics will come more easily to you. If you are in the second group, do not run because you cannot hide! It is incredibly important that you quickly develop basic skills with graphing. If you find this appendix very difficult you should seek extra help with these tools.

➲ All graphs in this appendix have actual numerical values marked on the axes. Later in the text you will see graphs without any numbers on the axes. In such cases the specific numbers are not necessary for the explanation, but you should recognize that there are numbers implicit on the axes. If at first you have difficulty comprehending such abstract graphs, you could pencil in arbitrary values on the axes until you get used to such graphs.

◇ What are direct and inverse relationships?

◇ What are dependent and independent variables?

• The slope of the line on a graph indicates the relationship between the two variables.

   o A line that is upsloping to the right indicates a positive or direct relationship between the two variables: an increase (a decrease) in one is associated with an increase (a decrease) in the other.

   o A line that is downsloping to the right indicates a negative or inverse relationship between the two variables because the variables are changing in opposite directions: an increase (a decrease) in one is associated with a decrease (an increase) in the other.

• Economists are concerned with determining cause and effect in economic events.

   o An independent variable is the variable that changes first, and causes another variable to change.

   o A dependent variable is one that changes as a result of a change in another variable.

   o Economists do not always follow the convention used in mathematics whereby an independent variable is placed on the horizontal axis and a dependent variable on the vertical axis.

• A two-variable graph is a simplified representation of an economic relationship. In such a graph there is an implicit assumption that all other factors are being held constant.

• This "other things equal" or ceteris paribus assumption is a simplification that helps us focus on the two variables of interest. If another variable that influences the dependent variable does change, then the curve on the graph will shift to a new position.

◇ How is a relationship defined by a line defined in algebraic terms?

   o What is the slope of a line?

   o What is the vertical intercept of a line?

• A slope and vertical intercept can be calculated for a linear relationship (straight line

graph). These values also define the equation of the line.

   o The slope of a straight line is the ratio of the vertical change to the horizontal change between two points.

   o The slope measures the marginal effect on one variable of a small change in the other.

   o A positive (negative) slope indicates a direct (inverse) relationship between the two variables.

• The vertical intercept is the value where the line intersects the vertical axis of the graph.

• A linear equation is written as $y = a + bx$. If the values for the intercept a and the slope b are known, then given any value of variable x, the value of variable y can be determined.

• A straight line has a constant slope, but a nonlinear curve has a continually changing slope. To estimate the slope of a nonlinear curve at a point, calculate the slope of a line tangent to the curve at that point.

➲ Some graphs in the text use real world data showing relationships between two variables. Such graphs often take the form of a "scatter diagram" with a "best-fitting line." That is, the data points may be somewhat scattered, rather than lying exactly on a curve. Therefore, no **precise** relationship is evident in the data, but there is a discernible tendency or pattern in the data, indicating that the variables are related. A "best-fitting line" through the data points indicates this pattern. If you take a statistics course you will learn the proper techniques for determining best-fitting lines, and for judging when you can be confident that the points in a scatter diagram do indicate some relationship. To understand this textbook you need only have a rough idea of a "best-fitting line."

Quick Quiz

1. If an increase in variable A is associated with a decrease in variable B, then we can conclude that A and B are:

   (a)   nonlinear
   (b)   directly related
   (c)   inversely related
   (d)   positively related

2. In the relationship between average birthweight of babies and the rate of cigarette smoking of their mothers, we would expect:

(a)   birthweight to be dependent
(b)   rate of smoking to be dependent
(c)   both variables to be dependent
(d)   both variables to be independent

3.   Given the equation of a line as $y = 100 - 5x$. Then the point with the horizontal coordinate of 12 will have a vertical coordinate of:
(a)   160
(b)   112
(c)   88
(d)   40

Terms and Concepts

horizontal axis   independent variable
vertical axis   dependent variable
direct relationship   slope of a straight line
inverse relationship   vertical intercept

Fill-In Questions

1.   The relationship between two variables can be visualized with a two-dimensional graph.
(a)   The (dependent, independent) _____ variable is said to change because of a change in the _____ variable.
(b)   The vertical and horizontal (scales, ranges) _____ on the graph are calibrated to reflect the _____ of values in a table of data points on which the graph is based.

2. The graph of a straight line that slopes downward to the right indicates that there is (a direct, an inverse) _____ relationship between the two variables. A graph of a straight line that slopes upward to the right tells us that the relationship is (direct, inverse) _____. When the value of one variable increases and the value of the other variable increases, then the relationship is _____; when the value of one increases, and the other decreases, the relationship is _____.

3. The slope of a straight line between two points is defined as the ratio of the (horizontal, vertical) _____ change over the _____ change. The point at which the line meets the vertical axis is called the _____.

4.   We can express the graph of a straight line with a linear equation written as y = a + bx

(a)   a is the (slope, intercept) _____ and b is the _____.
(b)   If a = 2, b = 4, and x = 5, then y would be _____.

5.   The slope of a (straight line, nonlinear curve) _____ is constant throughout; the slope of a _____ varies from point to point. The slope of a nonlinear curve at a point can be estimated by calculating the slope of a straight line that is _____ to the point on the curve.

True-False

Circle T if the statement is true, F if it is false.

1.   If the straight line on a two-variable graph is upward sloping to the right, then there is a positive relationship between the two variables.   **T F**

2.   A variable that changes as a consequence of a change in another variable is considered to be a dependent variable.   **T F**

3.   *Ceteris paribus* means that the value of all other variables is set equal to zero.   **T F**

4.   In the ratio for the calculation of the slope of a straight line, the horizontal change is divided by the vertical change.   **T F**

5.   If the slope of the linear relationship between consumption (on the vertical axis) and income (on the horizontal axis) is 0.90, then it tells us that for every $1 increase in income there will be a $0.90 increase in consumption.   **T F**

6.   If the slope of a straight line on a two-variable (x, y) graph is 2 and the vertical intercept is 6, then if the value for x is 10, the value for y is 22.   **T F**

7.   If there is an inverse relation between price and quantity demanded, the graph of this function will be downward-sloping.   **T F**

8.   In the relationship between snowfall and demand for snowblowers, snowfall is the dependent variable.   **T F**

9. If the line tangent to a nonlinear curve is up-sloping, this indicates that the slope of the curve is positive at that point.   **T F**

10. If two points described by the (x, y) combinations of (13, 10) and (8, 20) lie on a straight line, then the slope is 2.   **T F**

11. On a graph relating the number of visitors to Canada's national parks to the price of admission to the parks, an increase in levels of rainfall would likely shift the curve to the left.   **T F**

Multiple-Choice

Circle the letter that corresponds to the best answer.

1. If an increase in variable A is associated with a decrease in variable B, then we can conclude that A and B are:
- (a)   nonlinear
- (b)   directly related
- (c)   inversely related
- (d)   positively related

2. Economists:
- (a)   always put the independent variable on the vertical axis
- (b)   always put the independent variable on the horizontal axis
- (c)   sometimes put the dependent variable on the horizontal axis
- (d)   use only linear functions

3. If y is plotted on the vertical axis and x is on the horizontal axis, which of the following is a false statement regarding the equation $y = 100 + 0.4 x$?
- (a)   the vertical intercept is 100
- (b)   the slope is 0.4
- (c)   when x is 20, y is 108
- (d)   the graph is nonlinear

4. The equation of a line is: $y = 10 + 5x$. If the value of $x = 6$, then what is the value of y?
- (a)   30
- (b)   40
- (c)   50
- (d)   none of the above

5. Which of the following has a slope of zero at all points?

- (a)   a vertical line
- (b)   a horizontal line
- (c)   a curved line
- (d)   a straight line

6. If a straight line drawn tangent to a nonlinear curve has a slope of zero, then at the point of tangency the curve is:
- (a)   vertical
- (b)   horizontal
- (c)   upsloping
- (d)   downsloping

Answer questions 7 through 10 on the basis of the following diagram.

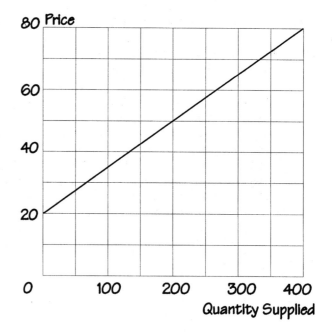

7. The graph indicates that price and quantity supplied are:
- (a)   positively related
- (b)   negatively related
- (c)   indirectly related
- (d)   nonlinear

8. The slope of the line is:
- (a)   0.15
- (b)   0.20
- (c)   1.50
- (d)   6.67

9. The vertical intercept is:
- (a)   0
- (b)   10
- (c)   20

(d)   80

10. The linear equation for the function is:
  (a) $p = 20 + 0.15q$
  (b) $q = 20 + 6.67p$
  (c) $p = 20 + 6.67q$
  (d) $q = 20 + 0.15p$

11. Consider a graph relating gasoline consumption (on the vertical axis) to population (on the horizontal axis). All of the following will affect gasoline consumption, but which one will **not** shift the curve?
  (a)   increased consumer incomes
  (b)   increased availability of public transit
  (c)   increased population
  (d)   more efficient gasoline engines

12. Which of the following statements is true?
  (a)   a vertical line has a slope of zero
  (b)   a horizontal line has a slope of infinity
  (c)   a nonlinear curve has different slopes at different points
  (d)   an upsloping line has a negative slope

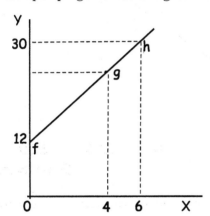

13. The slope of the line is:
  (a)   9
  (b)   3
  (c)   5
  (d)   2

14. The equation of the line is:
  (a) $y = 12 + 3x$
  (b) $y = 30 + 6x$
  (c) $y = 12 + 2x$
  (d) $y = 30 - 3x$

15. The y-axis coordinate of the line at point g is:
  (a)   16
  (b)   18

(c)   22
(d)   24

Problems and Projects

1. Graphing: Dependent and Independent Variables

The data below represent the relationship between the mortgage interest rate and the number of new houses built.

Mortgage Rate (% per year)	Housing Starts (thousands per year)
12	70,000
10	90,000
8	110,000
6	130,000
4	150,000

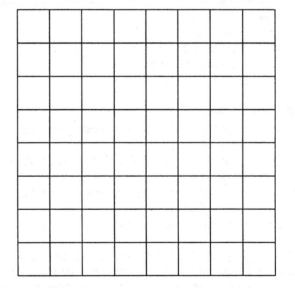

(a) Which variable is dependent? _____ Which is independent? _____
(b) On the axes of the graph below, set up the scales to best suit these data. Label each axis of the graph (including the units of measurement).
(c) Plot the five data points given in the table.
(d) The curve is (up-, down-) _____ sloping, meaning that the relationship between the mortgage interest rate and housing starts is (direct, inverse) _____ .

2. Shifts and Movements Along a Curve

(a) Based on the relationship found in question 1, if the mortgage rate increases by 1%, ceteris paribus, then housing starts will (decrease, increase) _____ by _____ thousands per year.

(b) If household incomes rise, new homes would become more affordable, so there would be more new housing starts at the same interest rate as before. On the graph, this would cause a (leftward, rightward) _____ shift of the curve in question 1.

(c) If lumber prices increase, new homes would become less affordable, so there would be fewer new housing starts at the same interest rate as before. On the graph, this would cause a (leftward, rightward) _____ shift of the initial curve.

3. The Graph and Equation of a Line

The Hammerheads, a very mediocre club band, have just released a CD. They will immediately sell 10 copies to their parents and friends. Thereafter, they can sell 4 copies for each performance they give in a club.

(a) Use this information to complete the table.

Performances	CD Sales
0	_____
5	_____
10	_____
15	_____
20	_____

CD Sales

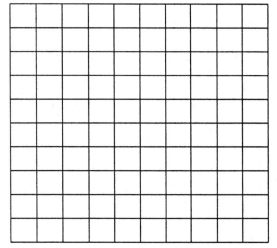

Performances

(b) Which variable is dependent? _____ Which is independent? _____

(c) Plot the data on the graph below.

(d) The vertical intercept value is _____.

(e) The slope value is _____.

(f) Write the equation for this relationship:

_____.

4. The Slope of a Line

(a) The function in the graph below has a negative slope between the X values of _____ and _____. Over this range the relationship between X and Y is (direct, inverse) _____.

(b) Find the slope of the curve at these points:
A: _____, B: _____, C: _____

5. Finding a Best-Fitting Line and Equation

An economist is hired to determine the relationship between real estate value and proximity to the waterfront in a Manitoba lakeshore resort community. The table below gives recent selling prices for undeveloped building lots.

Lot	Distance to Shore (m)	Price ($)
A	200	9,000
B	0	18,000
C	50	16,000
D	100	15,000
E	50	17,000
F	150	10,000
G	200	7,000
H	125	12,000

(a) On the graph provided, create a "scatter diagram" with lot prices on the vertical axis and distance to shore on the horizontal axis.

(b) The scatter diagram suggests that lot prices are (directly, inversely, not) _____ related to their proximity to the waterfront.

(c) With a ruler, draw in what appears to be the "best-fitting" line through these data points.

(d) The value of the vertical intercept is _____. This value indicates price for a lot that is _____.

(e) The value of the slope is _____. This value indicates that price (falls, rises) _____ by $_____ for each metre from the waterfront.

(f) The expression for the equation of this line is: _____.

Price (thousand $)

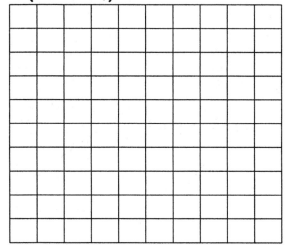

Distance to shore (m)

Discussion Questions

1. Why do economists use graphs?

2. If the vertical intercept increases in value but the slope of a straight line stays the same, what happens to the graph of the line? If the vertical intercept decreases, what happens to the line?

3. If you know that variables X and Y are inversely related, what does this tell you about the slope of a line showing the relationship between these two variables? What do you know about the slope when X and Y are positively related?

4. Identify the dependent and independent variables in the following statement: "A decrease in business taxes gave a big boost to investment spending." How does one tell the difference between a dependent and independent variable when examining economic relationships?

5. Why is it assumed that all other variables are held constant when we construct a two-variable graph of the price and quantity of a product?

6. If you were to plot a two-variable graph of the price of gasoline versus per capita use of gasoline, using the data for various nations, what sort of graph would you expect, and what sort of relationship would this represent? The data points would probably be somewhat scattered, rather than consistently located along a precise line or curve. Give some reasons why the data points might be somewhat scattered.

Answers

Quick Quiz
1. (c) p. 18
2. (a) p. 18
3. (d) pp. 20-21

Fill-in Questions
1. (a) dependent, independent; (b) scales, ranges
2. an inverse; direct; direct, inverse
3. vertical, horizontal; vertical intercept
4. (a) intercept, slope; (b) 22
5. straight line; nonlinear curve; tangent

True-False
1. T   This is also termed a direct relationship
2. T
3. F   It means "other things equal"
4. F   Vertical change divided by horizontal change
5. T
6. F   The equation is $y = 6 + 2x$; at $x = 10$, $y = 26$
7. T
8. F   The amount of snowfall does not depend on how many snowblowers are purchased
9. T   An upsloping curve
10. F $(20-10)/(8-13) = -2$
11. T   Rainfall would likely be one of the variables held constant on the original graph, so if rainfall changes the curve will shift

Multiple-Choice
1. (c) Variables changing in opposite directions are inversely or negatively related
2. (c) There is no consistent convention
3. (d) Because the slope is a fixed number, the graph is a straight line
4. (b)

5. (b) There is no vertical change

6. (b)

7. (a) The curve is upsloping

8. (a) (80-20)/(400-0) = 0.15

9. (c)

10. (a) See the answers to questions 8 and 9

11. (c) Population is held constant along the initial curve

12. (c) The slope of the tangent line keeps changing

13. (b) (30-12)/(6-0) = 3

14. (a)

15. (d) 12+(3)(4) = 24

Problems and Projects

1. (a) housing starts; mortgage interest rates; (d) down; inverse; (b) and (c):

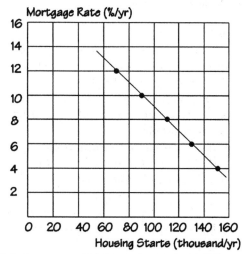

2. (a) decrease, 10; (b) rightward; (c) leftward

3. (a) 10, 30, 50, 70, 90; (b) CD sales; performances; (c) see graph; (d) 10; (e) 4; (f) CD Sales = 10 + 4 Performances

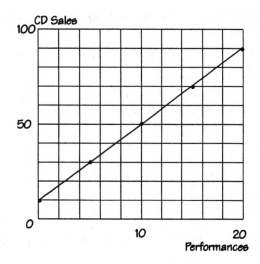

4. (a) 8; 17; inverse; (b) 3.0; 0; -2.1.

5. (a) see graph; (b) inversely; (c) see graph; (d) about $19,000; on the waterfront; (e) vertical change/horizontal difference is approximately = (8,000-19,000)/(200-0) =   -11,000/200 = about -55; falls; about $55. (f) Price = 19,000 – 55 Distance.

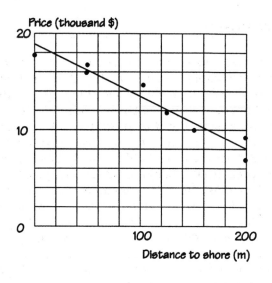

Chapter 2

The Economic Problem: Scarcity, Wants, and Choices

Overview

The field of economics is based on two key facts: our wants are unlimited or insatiable, and the resources available for satisfying these wants are limited, or scarce. Consequently, we face the economic problem: the need to make choices about how to allocate our scarce resources. These resources are land, capital, labour, and entrepreneurial ability. Given scarcity, all resources must be fully employed and used efficiently if we are to satisfy wants to the fullest possible extent. Efficiency has two elements: productive efficiency is achieved if resources are used in the least cost manner, and allocative efficiency is achieved if resources are used to produce those goods society wants most.

The production possibilities table and the production possibilities curve are very basic and important tools that illustrate many concepts in this chapter: scarcity, choice, the law of increasing opportunity cost, allocative and productive efficiency, unemployment, and economic growth.

Every society uses some sort of economic system to address the problem of scarcity. Most use some combination of the two basic types: the market system and the command system. In a market system most resources are owned privately and economic activity is coordinated spontaneously, with little government interference. In a command system government owns most of the property resources and economic activity is centrally planned. Canada uses a market system with some elements of a command system.

Chapter Outline

2.1 The Foundation of Economics

◇ What is the economic problem, and what two key facts create this problem?

• The study of economics rests on two facts:
  o Society's wants are essentially unlimited and insatiable.

  o The resources for producing goods and services to satisfy society's wants are limited or scarce.
• These two facts create the problem of scarcity, whereby we are forced to make choices.
• The four categories of resources are land, capital, labour, and entrepreneurial ability. The payments received by suppliers of these resources are, respectively: rental income, interest income, wages, and profits.

Quick Quiz

1. Which of the following statements is false:
   (a) human wants outstrip the ability of our resources to satisfy our wants
   (b) economists believe that improvements in technology will eventually eliminate the scarcity problem
   (c) scarcity exists in all human societies
   (d) if there was no scarcity problem we would not face opportunity costs

2. Which is the correct match of an economic resource and payment for that resource?
   (a) land and wages
   (b) labour and interest income
   (c) capital and rental income
   (d) entrepreneurial ability and profit

2.2 Efficiency: Getting the Most from Available Resources

◇ What is the nature of economic efficiency?

◇ Distinguish between:
  o full employment and full production
  o productive efficiency and allocative efficiency
• Economics is the social science concerned with the problem of using scarce resources to attain the maximum fulfillment of society's unlimited wants.
• To achieve this goal society must use its resources efficiently, achieving both:
  o full employment (available resources are being used)

- o   full production (the resources are being used as efficiently as possible)
- Two kinds of efficiency must be achieved:
  - o   productive efficiency (goods and services are produced in the least costly way)
  - o   allocative efficiency (the resources are used to produce that particular mix of goods and services most wanted by society)

◈ What is a production possibilities table or curve, and how does it illustrate scarcity, efficiency, choice, and opportunity cost?

◈ What assumptions are made when a production possibilities table or curve is presented?

- The production possibilities table, or production possibilities curve, indicates the alternative combinations of goods and services an economy can produce.
- Four assumptions are made in constructing a production possibilities table or curve:
  - o   full employment and productive efficiency
  - o   fixed resources
  - o   fixed technology
  - o   two goods are being produced

➲ The production possibilities curve is the first of many instances in the textbook where graphing skills are needed. If you have serious difficulty with this graph you probably have a general weakness in graphing that you should remedy immediately. Spend extra time on the graphical questions in this study guide, the relevant sections of the chapter, and on Appendix 1A of the textbook and this study guide. Your instructor may have additional resources or advice for you.

- Any point on the production possibilities curve is attainable, but society must choose one point (one particular combination of goods). If the chosen combination provides the greatest satisfaction, the economy is said to be allocatively efficient.

➲ Many students initially confuse the coordinates of a point on the production possibilities curve with the intercepts of the curve. The intercepts indicate the *maximum*, or *potential*, production for each good (if all resources are dedicated to producing that good), whereas the coordinates

of the production point show *actual* production for each good.

- Points outside the curve are unattainable, so the production possibilities curve illustrates the condition of scarcity.
- Given full employment and full production, society can produce more of one good only by producing less of the other good. This foregone output is termed the opportunity cost and arises because resources must be shifted from one production activity to another.
- The marginal opportunity cost of producing additional units of a product usually increases as more of that product is produced. This generalization is the law of increasing opportunity costs.
  - o   Opportunity costs are increasing because resources are not perfectly adaptable from one production use to another.
  - o   Increasing opportunity costs cause the production possibilities curve to be concave (bowed out from the origin).

◈ How is allocative efficiency related to marginal benefit and marginal cost?

- The amount of resources allocated to the production of a good is optimal where the marginal benefit (MB) received from the last unit produced equals its marginal cost (MC). MC is the opportunity cost in terms of other goods that could have been produced with the same resources.
  - o   The optimal production level on the production possibilities curve corresponds to the point of allocative efficiency.
  - o   MB falls as more is produced.
  - o   MC rises as more is produced.

Quick Quiz

3. When a production possibilities table is written (or a production possibilities curve is drawn), four assumptions are made. Which of the following is one of those assumptions?
  (a)   more than two products are produced
  (b)   the state of technology changes
  (c)   the economy has both full employment and productive efficiency
  (d)   the quantities of all resources available to the economy are variable, not fixed

4. A point outside today's production possibilities curve:
  (a)   represents allocative inefficiency

(b)   represents productive inefficiency
(c)   represents unemployment
(d)   represents a production level unattainable with current resources and technology

5. The changing slope of the production possibilities curve when moving along the curve reflects:
(a)   increasing resource supplies
(b)   increasing production of both goods
(c)   increasing opportunity cost as production of one good increases
(d)   increased productive and allocative efficiency

6. Society is said to be underallocating resoures to the production of a good if for the last unit produced:
(a)   marginal benefit is greater than the marginal cost
(b)   marginal benefit is less than the marginal cost
(c)   opportunity cost of production is rising
(d)   consumption of the product is falling

2.3 Unemployment, Growth, and the Future

◈ How is economic growth achieved?

•   This section examines the effects of dropping some of the assumptions underlying the production possibilities model.

•   An economy experiencing unemployment or productive inefficiency is operating at a point inside its production possibilities curve, and is therefore failing to meet its productive potential.

•   Economic growth occurs through improvements in technology or expansions in resource supplies, causing the production possibilities curve to expand, or shift outward.

➲ A movement from one point on the production possibilities curve to another point on the same curve shows a change in what combination of products society *chooses*. In contrast, a shift of the whole production possibilities curve indicates a change in the *set of choices* available to society.

•   Today's resource allocation decisions shape our future production possibilities; the more capital or future goods that we produce today, the more the production possibilities curve will expand in the future.

•   If a nation specializes and trades with other nations, then the nation is not limited to consuming combinations of products represented by points on the production possibilities curve.

Quick Quiz

7. A nation's production possibilities curve will shift outwards if:
(a)   the nation reduces its unemployment rate
(b)   the nation discovers new mineral resources
(c)   the nation increases its foreign trade
(d)   any of the above occurs

8. Canada could expect to grow faster in the coming years if, *ceteris paribus*, Canada today increases her production of:
(a)   food
(b)   video games
(c)   clothing
(d)   highways

9. When an economy slides into a recession:
(a)   the production possibility curve will shift inwards
(b)   the production possibility curve will become steeper
(c)   the production possibility curve will become flatter
(d)   the production point will fall below the production possibility curve

2.4 Economic Systems

◈ What are the characteristics of the two main types of economic systems?

•   Different societies use different economic systems for addressing the fundamental economic problem of scarcity. Systems differ mainly in the ownership of resources, and in the method used to coordinate and direct economic activity.

•   At one extreme is the market system, or capitalism, which relies upon private ownership of resources, the profit motive, and coordination through the use of prices and markets. The type of capitalism used in Canada also gives government a significant role in the economy.

•   At the other extreme, the command economy uses public ownership of resources and decisions are made by central planning. In recent years a number of command economies have incorporated elements of the market system.

Quick Quiz
10. The private ownership of property resources and use of the market system to direct and coordinate economic activity is characteristic of:
(a)   pure capitalism
(b)   the command economy
(c)   market socialism
(d)   the traditional economy

11. In a centrally planned economy resource allocation decisions are made by the:
(a)   the command system
(b)   the market system
(c)   the capitalist system
(d)   the laissez-faire system

2.5 The Circular Flow Model

◈   What is the circular flow model?
•   The circular flow model illustrates the interaction between businesses and households in resource markets and product markets. In exchange for resources that households supply to firms, firms pay incomes that households in turn use to demand goods and services produced by firms.

Quick Quiz
12. The two kinds of markets found in the circular flow model are:
(a)   real and money markets
(b)   real and traditional markets
(c)   money and authoritarian markets
(d)   product and factor markets

13. In the circular flow model, businesses:
(a)   demand both products and resources
(b)   supply both products and resources
(c)   demand products and supply resources
(d)   supply products and demand resources

Terms and Concepts

economic problem	capital goods
economic resources	production possibilities table
land	
capital	production possibilities curve
investment	
labour	opportunity cost
entrepreneurial ability	law of increasing opportunity cost
factors of production	economic growth

full employment	economic system
full production	market system
productive efficiency	command system
allocative efficiency	factor market
consumer goods	product market
	circular flow model

Fill-In Questions

1. The two fundamental facts that provide the foundation of economics are:
(a)   Society's wants are _____.
(b)   Society's resources are _____.

2. Economic efficiency requires that there be both full _____ of resources and full _____. Full production implies that both _____ efficiency and _____ efficiency are achieved.

3. Below is a production possibilities curve for ropes and ladders.

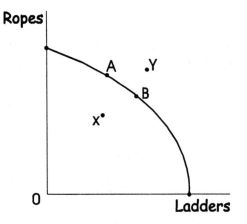

(a) If the economy moves from point *A* to point *B*, it will produce (more, fewer) _____ ropes and (more, fewer) _____ ladders.
(b) If the economy is producing at point *X*, some of the resources of the economy are either _____ or _____.
(c) In order for the economy to produce at point *Y*, it must either expand its supply of _____ or improve its _____.

4. If Canada attempts to expand her apple industry, the opportunity cost per apple will tend to increase because resources are not completely _____ to different uses. This is an example of the generalization known as the law of _____.

True-False

Circle T if the statement is true, F if it is false.

1. If you must stand in line for six hours to get into a free concert by the Rolling Stones, there is no opportunity cost to you for seeing the concert.
   T F

2. Money is a resource and is classified as "capital."
   T F

3. Profit is the reward paid to those who provide the economy with capital.
   T F

4. The opportunity cost of producing wheat tends to increase as more wheat is produced because land less suited to its production must be reallocated from other uses.
   T F

5. A production possibilities curve that is concave to the origin reflects the law of increasing opportunity costs.
   T F

6. The problem of scarcity is likely to be solved someday by technological progress.
   T F

7. An economy that is employing the least cost productive methods has achieved allocative efficiency.
   T F

8. Given full employment and full production, it is impossible for an economy that can produce only two goods to increase production of both.
   T F

9. The more capital goods an economy produces today, the greater will be its ability to produce all goods in the future, ceteris paribus.
   T F

10. Most nations use economic systems somewhere between the extremes of pure capitalism and command economy.
    T F

11. In a command economy most resources are privately owned and are allocated by the market system.
    T F

12. In the circular flow model, households act on the demand side of resource and product markets.
    T F

Multiple-Choice

Circle the letter that corresponds to the best answer.

1. In her role as an "innovator" an entrepreneur:
   (a) makes policy decisions in a business firm
   (b) combines factors of production to produce a good or service
   (c) invents a new production process
   (d) takes risks in the market place

2. An economy is efficient when it has achieved:
   (a) full employment
   (b) full production
   (c) full employment or full production
   (d) full employment and full production

3. When a production possibilities curve is drawn, four assumptions are made. Which is not one of those assumptions?
   (a) only two goods are produced
   (b) wants are unlimited
   (c) the economy has both full employment and full production
   (d) the quantities of all resources available to the economy are fixed

The next three questions are based on the following production possibilities table for Nashia Twang, a singer who can use her time and other resources to perform concerts or write new songs.

Alternative	A	B	C	D	E
Concerts	0	20	40	60	80
Songs	10	9	7	4	0

4. The opportunity cost of writing one more song as Twang moves from alternative C to B is:
   (a) 40 concerts per song
   (b) 20 concerts per song
   (c) 10 concerts per song
   (d) 8 concerts per song

5. The opportunity cost of playing one more concert as Twang moves from alternative C to D is:
   (a) 3/20 song per concert
   (b) 3 songs per concert
   (c) 20 songs per concert
   (d) 6 2/3 songs per concert

6. Twang's highest opportunity cost for producing one more song occurs in the neighbourhood of alternative:
- (a)   A
- (b)   B
- (c)   C
- (d)   D

7. If opportunity costs are constant, instead of increasing, the production possibilities curve will be:
- (a)   concave to the origin
- (b)   convex to the origin
- (c)   a downward sloping straight line
- (d)   parallel to the horizontal axis

Answer the next three questions on the basis of the following diagram.

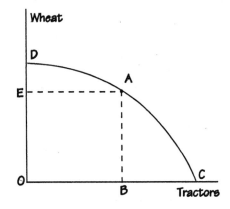

8. At point *A* on the production possibilities curve:
- (a)   less wheat than tractors is being produced
- (b)   fewer tractors than wheat are being produced
- (c)   the economy is employing all its resources
- (d)   the economy is not employing all its resources

9. The opportunity cost of producing *OB* of tractors is:
- (a)   *OD* of wheat
- (b)   *OE* of wheat
- (c)   *ED* of wheat
- (d)   *OC* of tractors

10. If there occurred a technological improvement in the production of tractors but not wheat:

- (a)   point *D* would remain fixed and point *C* shift to the left
- (b)   point *C* would remain fixed and point *D* shift upward
- (c)   point *D* would remain fixed and point *C* shift to the right
- (d)   point *C* would remain fixed and point *D* shift inward

11. From one point to another along the same production possibilities curve:
- (a)   resources remain fixed but are reallocated between the production of the two goods
- (b)   resources are increased and are reallocated between the two goods
- (c)   resources are increased and production of both goods increased
- (d)   idle resources are put to work to increase the production of one good

12. Which of the following would cause a nation's production possibilities curve to shift inward toward the origin?
- (a)   more people in the labour force
- (b)   increased international trade
- (c)   rising unemployment of workers
- (d)   not replacing capital equipment as it wears out

13. Which of the following will slow down the rate at which Canada's production possibilities curve shifts rightward?
- (a)   increasing rate of technological change
- (b)   increased immigration
- (c)   depletion of Canada's oil and gas deposits
- (d)   freer trade between Canada's provinces

14. If there is an increase in the resources available within the economy:
- (a)   more goods and services will be produced in the economy
- (b)   the economy will be capable of producing more goods and services
- (c)   the standard of living in the economy will rise
- (d)   the technological efficiency of the economy will improve

15. The opportunity cost of providing a governmentally financed stadium for a city's baseball team is:

(a)   the interest on the money borrowed to finance the stadium

(b)   the future tax increase the public will be forced to bear to pay for the stadium

(c)   the other goods and services that must be sacrificed so that resources can be used for stadium construction

(d)   there is no opportunity cost since Ottawa will finance the stadium under a regional development program

16. Private ownership of property resources, use of the market system to direct and coordinate economic activity, and the presence of the profit motive are characteristic of:
   (a)   pure capitalism
   (b)   the command economy
   (c)   market socialism
   (d)   communism

17. Central planning is associated with which economic system?
   (a)   pure capitalism
   (b)   laissez-faire capitalism
   (c)   market economy
   (d)   command economy

18. Productive efficiency is attained when:
   (a)   resources are all employed
   (b)   output is produced at least possible cost
   (c)   there is no government involvement in the economy
   (d)   the production possibilities curve is concave

19. The term "laissez-faire" refers to:
   (a)   the absence of government intervention in markets
   (b)   the absence of monopoly
   (c)   the absence of competition in markets
   (d)   efficient use of employed resources

Problems and Projects

1. Resource Incomes
Match the resources on the left with the corresponding resource payments on the right.
   (a)   labour   (i)   rent
   (b)   capital   (ii)   wages
   (c)   land   (iii)   profits
   (d)   entrepreneurial   (iv)   interest
          ability   income

2. Types of Resources
Below is a list of resources. Indicate in the space to the right of each whether the resource is land (Ld), capital (K), labour (L), or entrepreneurial ability (EA).
(a) fishing grounds in the North Atlantic _____
(b) a farmer's inventory of wheat _____
(c) Maple Leaf Gardens in Toronto _____
(d) the work performed by Bill Gates _____
(e) Cavendish beach in Prince Edward Island ____
(f) Stelco's steel plant in Hamilton ___
(g) the tasks accomplished in making the Apple Computer a commercial success _____
(h) the work of a cashier at Zeller's _____

3. Production Possibilities
An economy produces coolers (C) and heaters (H), according to the production possibilities table below. The usual assumptions apply.
(a) Plot the data on the graph provided, and label the curve PPC.

Coolers	Heaters	Heaters (f)
0	6	____
7	5	____
13	4	____
18	3	____
22	2	____
25	1	____
27	0	____

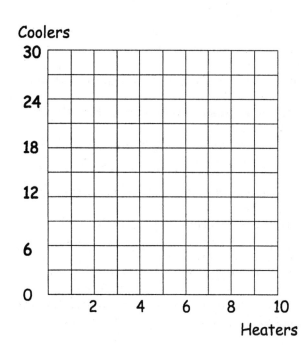

(b) Can the economy produce 4 of H and 22 of C? _____ If not, why? _____ What is the maximum amount of C that can be produced in combination with 4H?_____

(c) If the economy is producing 2H and 15C, what problem is being experienced? _____

(d) Assuming that the economy is productively efficient, what is the opportunity cost of producing 1H instead of none? _____ What is the opportunity cost of the second unit of H? _____ And the third H? _____

(e) As more units of H are produced, what is the trend in the number of units of C that must be given up to get the extra H? _____. Due to this trend, the shape of the production possibilities curve is _____ to the origin.

(f) A technological breakthrough makes it possible to produce 50% more heaters with the same resources as before. Fill in the new values for the column labelled Heaters (f), use this data to plot the new production possibilities curve PPCf.

4. Consumer Goods and Capital Goods

Below is a list of economic goods. Indicate in the space beside each whether the good is a consumer good (C), a capital good (K), or that it depends (D) upon who is using it and for what purpose.

(a) a dairy cow   _____
(b) a tractor   _____
(c) a telephone pole   _____
(d) a telephone   _____
(e) your refrigerator   _____
(f) a refrigerator in a restaurant _____

5. Production Possibilities Curve Shifts

For each case below you are given an initial production possibilities curve between timber and fish. For each event, sketch a new curve to show the result.

(a) Supplies of labour and capital expand.

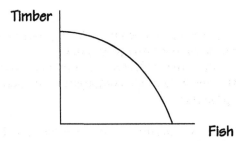

(b) New tree-planting techniques improve the success of reforestation operations.

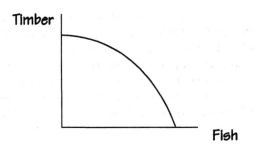

(c) An ecological disaster wipes out a large part of the fish stocks.

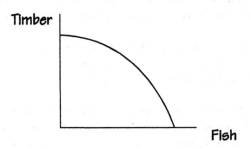

6. The Impact of Technological Change

An economy is achieving full production, producing automobiles and food at point X.

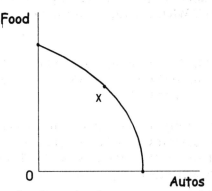

Now a technological advance occurs which enables this economy to produce automobiles with fewer resources than previously. How is it possible for the society to consume more automobiles *and* more food as a result? Illustrate using the production possibilities diagram.

7. Allocative Efficiency

A department store is installing video cameras to reduce shoplifting. The marginal costs and marginal benefits of additional cameras are:

Camera	MB ($/month)	MC ($/month)
1	300	100
2	250	125
3	160	150
4	50	175

(a) If the store must choose one of the options listed in the table, then allocative efficiency is reached by installing __ cameras.

(b) How much better off is the store with the optimal number than with one fewer camera? $__

(c) How much better off is the store with the optimal number than with one more camera? $__

Discussion Questions

1. Explain what is meant by the "economic problem." Why are resources scarce?

2. When is a society economically efficient? What is meant by "full production," and how does it differ from "full employment"?

3. What four assumptions are made in drawing a production possibilities curve? How do technological progress and an increased supply of resources in the economy affect the curve?

4. Why cannot an economist determine which combination in the production possibilities table is "best"? What determines the optimum product-mix?

5. What is opportunity cost? What is the law of increasing opportunity costs? Why do opportunity costs increase?

6. Would the economic problem disappear if the affluent countries, including Canada, offered to pay more for the products of the Third World countries? Explain.

7. During the Cold War, Russia seemed to be quite competitive with the United States in terms of military strength even though Russia's overall production capabilities were much lower than America's. Use the production possibility curve model to resolve this paradox.

8. If resources in an economy are fully employed, what would be the effect on living standards if the government decided to increase the output of goods for the future? Explain using the production possibilities curve.

9. Explain why you agree or disagree with the statement: "The opportunity cost of allocating large numbers of people to clean up Ontario's lakes during a recession is different from the opportunity cost during a period of full employment."

10. Explain the difference between productive and allocative efficiency.

11. What are the roles of households and of businesses in the resource market and the product market?

Answers

Quick Quiz
1. (b) p. 26
2. (d) pp. 27-28
3. (c) pp. 28-29
4. (d) p. 30
5. (c) pp. 30, 32
6. (a) p. 33
7. (b) p. 35
8. (d) pp. 36-37
9. (d) p. 34
10. (a) p. 40
11. (a) p. 40
12. (d) pp. 40-42
13. (d) pp. 41-42

Fill-In Questions
1. (a) unlimited; (b) scarce (or limited)
2. employment, production; productive, allocative
3. (a) fewer, more; (b) unemployed, underemployed; (c) resources, technology
4. adaptable; increasing opportunity costs

True-False
1. F Your time has value
2. F Money is not an economic resource
3. F Profit goes to entrepreneurs; capitalists earn interest income
4. T
5. T
6. F Even as we become able to produce more our wants will continue to expand
7. F Allocative efficiency is not achieved unless the most wanted combination of goods is being produced
8. T
9. T As we produce more capital goods, or goods for the future, our PPC expands more in the future
10. T

11. F The statement describes capitalism or market system

12. F Households are suppliers, not demanders, in resource markets

Multiple-Choice

1. (c) The others are roles of entrepreneurs, but not the innovator role

2. (d) Both are necessary conditions

3. (b) Demands for goods do not determine the position of the PPC

4. (c) (20-40)/(9-7)= -10; 10 concerts are sacrificed per song written

5. (a) (4-7)/(6-40) = -3/20; 3/20 song sacrificed per concert

6. (a) A

7. (c) Such a line would have a constant slope, or trade-off ratio between the two goods

8. (c) Any point on the curve involves full employment

9. (c) Wheat production falls from D to E

10. (c) Maximum tractor output increases; maximum wheat does not change

11. (a) Increased resources would imply a shift; if resources were previously idle the economy was not on the curve

12. (d) The capital stock would shrink, meaning a reduction in the supply of resources

13. (c) Reduction in our supply of resources

14. (b) The PPC will shift out, meaning that the economy is *capable* of producing more, and reaching a higher standard of living; but this potential may not be realized

15. (c) Ultimately the opportunity cost must be measured in other goods given up

16. (a) All are critical to a capitalist or market economy

17. (d) Including socialism and communism

18. (b) Using resources in the most productive way, and minimizing cost of production go hand in hand

19. (a) "Let it be" is government's attitude toward the economy in a "laissez faire" system

Problems and Projects

1. labour/wages; capital/interest income; land/rental income; entrepreneurial ability/ profits

2. (a) Ld; (b) K; (c) K; (d) EA; (e) Ld; (f) K; (g) EA; (h) L

3. (a) see graph below; (b) No; this combination lies outside the PPC (see point b); 13C; (c) productive inefficiency (unemployment or underem-

ployment) (see point C); (d) 2C = 27C – 25C, 3C, 4C; (e) increasing, concave; (f) in the table, add 50% to the values in the Heaters column: 9, 7.5, 6, 4.5, 3, 1.5, 0; the result is PPCf on the graph.

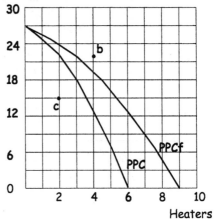

4. (a) K, (b) K, (c) K, (d) D, (e) C, (f) K

5. For each case below, PPC1 is before the event, and PPC2 is after.

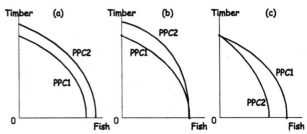

6. More automobiles can now be produced with a given amount of resources, so the automobiles intercept shifts out. If there is no reallocation of resources, production would move from X to X', but by moving some resources from autos to food, the society can produce more food and more automobiles. This is shown by the movement along the new PPC from X' to Y.

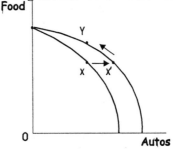

7. (a) 3 cameras, because for each of the first three, the MB > MC; (b) $10/month is the net benefit for the 3rd camera ($160-150); (c) $125/month is the net loss for the 4th camera ($50-175)

Chapter 3 — Individual Markets: Demand and Supply

Overview

This chapter presents the most important tool of economic analysis: the demand and supply model. We use this model to analyze how various events affect the price and quantities of goods and services traded in highly competitive markets with many buyers and sellers trading a standardized product. The model can be expressed in several ways: as algebraic equations, schedules in tables, or graphs.

The law of demand asserts an inverse relationship between price and quantity demanded, *ceteris paribus*. The law of supply states a positive relationship between price and quantity supplied, *ceteris paribus*. Given the demand and supply in a market, equilibrium is found at the one price at which the quantity demanded by consumers exactly equals the quantity supplied by sellers.

Starting from an equilibrium, a change in any demand or supply determinant will shift the demand or supply curve, and throw the market out of equilibrium — creating either a shortage or a surplus. To eliminate the shortage (or surplus) the price must rise (or fall) to restore the balance between how much consumers are willing and able to buy and producers are willing and able to sell.

Mastery of the supply and demand model depends on clear understanding of the definitions of demand and supply, and the key distinctions between "demand" and "quantity demanded" and between "supply" and "quantity supplied." Practice with the graphical model of demand and supply will greatly help clarify these concepts.

Sometimes governments implement price controls to keep the price higher or lower than the equilibrium price that would result from market forces. Price ceilings create shortages, and price floors create surpluses, and in both cases there is a rationing problem. Price controls also create a host of unintended side effects, including black market transactions, as disappointed or frustrated market participants try to get around the intended effects of the price controls.

Chapter Outline

3.1 Markets

◇ What is a market?

• A market is any institution or mechanism that brings together the buyers and sellers of a particular good or service.

• In this chapter we assume that markets are highly competitive, meaning that there are many buyers and sellers of a standardized product.

➲ This chapter is the most important one in the book. Be sure to spend extra time on it, and to return to it to review the fundamentals if you run into difficulties in later chapters.

Quick Quiz

1. The markets examined in this chapter:
  (a) sell nonstandard or differentiated products
  (b) have buyers cooperating to determine prices
  (c) are controlled by a single producer
  (d) are highly competitive

3.2 Demand

◇ What is demand?
  o What is the law of demand?
  o What does a demand curve show?
  o How is the market demand found?

• Demand is the relationship between the price of a product and the amount of the product that the consumer is willing and able to purchase in a specific time period. The relationship can be expressed in a table, graph, or equation.

• The law of demand states that, other things being equal, as price falls, the quantity demanded rises. That is, there is an inverse relationship between price and quantity demanded.

• Along with plenty of strong evidence for the law of demand are three analytical reasons:
  o If consumers experience diminishing marginal utility then they will be willing

to buy additional units of a good only if price is reduced.

- o   When price falls there is an income effect: the consumer's overall buying power increases so the consumer buys more of the good.
- o   When price falls there is a substitution effect: the consumer is motivated to buy more of the good that is now relatively less expensive instead of other goods for which it is a substitute.

- The demand curve is a graphic representation of the law of demand.
  - o   The graph has price on the vertical axis, and quantity demanded on the horizontal axis.
  - o   A change in price leads to a movement along the demand curve. This is called a change in quantity demanded.

- The market demand is derived by "adding up" the individual consumer demands at each possible price. The law of demand applies to both individual and market demand curves.

➷ Perhaps more than any other chapter, this chapter requires active practice. Pick up your pencil and draw graphs. Begin by plotting demand and supply schedules onto graphs. Study carefully the examples in the text and study guide to learn the appropriate labels for such graphs. Once you are confident of working with graphs with concrete numbers, go to the next step of drawing abstract graphs where numbers are implied on the axes, but not explicitly given.

✎ What are the determinants of demand, and how do they influence demand?

✎ What is the difference between a change in demand and a change in quantity demanded?

- The price determines the quantity demanded of a good, but factors other than price determine the location of the whole demand curve. These factors are known as the demand determinants:
  - o   tastes (or preferences) of buyers;
  - o   number of buyers in the market;
  - o   incomes of consumers;
  - o   prices of related goods (substitutes and complements);
  - o   expectations.

- A change in a demand determinant will shift demand to the left (a decrease) or the right (an increase), creating an entirely new demand curve. This is called a change in demand.
  - o   If tastes shift in favour of a good, its demand will increase.
  - o   If the number of buyers of a good increases, its demand will increase.
  - o   If consumer incomes increase, demand will increase if the good is normal, and demand will decrease if the good is inferior.
  - o   If an increase in the price of one good causes the demand for another good to decrease, the two goods are complements; if the price increase causes demand for the other good to increase, the two goods are substitutes.
  - o   If consumers expect prices or incomes to rise in the future they may increase their demand now.

- A change in demand and a change in the quantity demanded are not the same thing. This is obvious on the graph where a change in the price of the good causes a change in the quantity demanded, or movement along the curve, whereas a change in demand shifts the entire curve to a new location.

Quick Quiz

2.   A schedule which shows the various amounts of a product consumers are willing and able to purchase at each price in a series of possible prices during a specified period of time is called:
- (a)   supply
- (b)   demand
- (c)   quantity supplied
- (d)   quantity demanded

3.   The reason for the law of demand is best explained in terms of:
- (a)   complementary goods
- (b)   substitutable goods
- (c)   law of increasing costs
- (d)   diminishing marginal utility

4.   Which factor will decrease the demand for a product?
- (a)   a favourable change in consumer tastes
- (b)   an increase in the price of a substitute good
- (c)   a decrease in the price of a complementary good
- (d)   a decrease in the number of buyers

3.3 Supply

◈ What is supply?
- o What is the law of supply?
- o What does a supply curve show?
- o How is the market supply found?

• Supply is the relationship between the price of a product and the amount of the product that suppliers will offer to sell in a specific time period.

• The law of supply states that, other things being equal, as price rises, the quantity supplied rises. That is, there is a positive relationship between price and quantity supplied. The quantity supplied rises with price because the supplier can profitably produce more output at a higher price.

• The supply curve is a graphic representation of supply and the law of supply.
- o The graph has price on the vertical axis, and quantity supplied on the horizontal.
- o A change in price leads to a movement along the supply curve. This is called a change in quantity supplied.

◈ What are the determinants of supply, and how do they influence demand?

◈ What is the difference between a change in supply and a change in quantity supplied?

• The determinants of supply are:
- o factor prices;
- o technology;
- o taxes and subsidies;
- o prices of other goods;
- o price expectations;
- o number of sellers in the market.

• A change in any of the determinants will shift supply to the left (a decrease) or the right (an increase), creating an entirely new supply curve. This is called a change in supply.
- o If prices of factors (production resources) fall, supply will increase.
- o A technological change will improve the efficiency of production and increase the supply.
- o A new tax will raise the producer's costs and reduce the supply; a new subsidy will increase the supply.
- o Producers may reallocate their resources if the price of a related good changes. Depending on the case, supply could increase or decrease.
- o It is also difficult to generalize about how

a change in expectations about the future price will change today's supply.
- o An increase in the number of sellers will increase the supply.

• A change in supply and a change in the quantity supplied are different things. The difference is most obvious on a graph. A change in the price of the good causes a change in the quantity supplied, which on the graph is a movement to a different point on the same supply curve, whereas a change in supply involves a shift to a whole new supply curve.

➲ You have not mastered the chapter until you can clearly distinguish between a change in demand and a change in quantity demanded; the same for supply vs. quantity supplied. You should be able to articulate the difference verbally, and graphically.

Quick Quiz

5. A decrease in the supply of a product would most likely be caused by:
- (a) an increase in business taxes
- (b) an increase in consumer incomes
- (c) a decrease in factor prices
- (d) a decrease in the price of a complementary good

6. Which of the following could not cause an increase in the supply of cotton?
- (a) an increase in the price of cotton
- (b) better technology for producing cotton
- (c) a decrease in the price of the machinery and tools employed in cotton production
- (d) a decrease in the price of corn

7. An "increase in supply" means:
- (a) a rightward shift of the supply curve
- (b) a leftward shift of the supply curve
- (c) a movement up along a given supply curve
- (d) a movement down along a given supply curve

3.4 Supply and Demand: Market Equilibrium

◈ What is a market equilibrium?
- o What happens when there is a shortage or a surplus?
- o What does a supply curve show?
- o How is equilibrium affected by a shift in demand or supply?

- The market-clearing or equilibrium price of a good is that price at which quantity demanded and quantity supplied are equal; the equilibrium quantity is equal to the quantity demanded and supplied at the equilibrium price.
  - o If price is above the equilibrium, quantity demanded is less than quantity supplied, so there is a surplus. This will cause price to fall.
  - o If price is below the equilibrium, quantity demanded is greater than quantity supplied, so there is a shortage. This will cause price to rise.
  - o The only sustainable price is the equilibrium price.
  - o The rationing function of price is to create consistency between the decisions of sellers and of buyers, so as to eliminate any shortages or surpluses.
- Any change in a determinant of demand or supply will cause the curve to shift, and result in a new equilibrium price and quantity.
  - o Most changes shift only one of the two curves.
  - o When demand changes, and supply is unchanged, equilibrium price and quantity change in the same direction as demand.
  - o When supply changes, and demand is unchanged, quantity moves in the same direction as supply, but equilibrium price moves in the opposite direction.
  - o In complex cases where both supply and demand change, both curves will shift; either the direction of price change or quantity change will be predictable, the other will be indeterminate.

➲ The first step in analyzing how an event affects the market equilibrium is to determine which curve is directly affected by the event: supply or demand. The second step is to decide whether that curve increases or decreases. From there it is a simple matter to decide the direction of change for the equilibrium price and quantity.

➲ If algebraic work with demand and supply is relevant in the economics course you are studying, please look at the Appendix to Chapter 3.

Quick Quiz
8. If the quantity supplied of a product is greater than the quantity demanded for a prod-

uct, then:
- (a) there is a shortage of the product
- (b) there is a surplus of the product
- (c) the product is a normal good
- (d) the product is an inferior good

9. What would be the effect on the market for houses in a city that experiences a rise in population?
- (a) demand would increase, raising the equilibrium price and quantity of houses
- (b) supply would decrease, raising the equilibrium price and quantity of houses
- (c) demand would decrease, lowering the equilibrium price and quantity of houses
- (d) supply would increase, lowering the equilibrium price and quantity of houses

10. If the demand for tuna increases at the same time that the supply of tuna decreases:
- (a) the equilibrium price of tuna will rise, but the change in the equilibrium quantity of tuna cannot be predicted
- (b) the equilibrium quantity of tuna will fall, but the change in the equilibrium price of tuna cannot be predicted
- (c) the equilibrium price and quantity of tuna will both rise
- (d) the equilibrium price and quantity of tuna will both fall

3.5 Application: Government-set Prices
◈ What are government-set prices and how do they affect market equilibrium?
- o What are price ceilings?
- o What are price floors?
- Sometimes governments impose price ceilings when prices seem unfairly high to buyers, or impose price floors when prices seem unfairly low to sellers. Such controls prevent market forces from performing the rationing function.
- A price ceiling is a maximum legal price. It results in a shortage of the commodity; may bring about formal rationing by the government and a black market; and causes a misallocation of resources.
- A price floor is a minimum legal price. It results in a surplus of the commodity which may induce government to take measures to restrict the supply, increase demand, or purchase the surplus; and causes a misallocation of resources.
- Examples of price ceilings are: rent controls

on apartments, proposed controls on gasoline prices, and proposed credit card interest rate ceilings. Examples of price floors are agricultural price supports and minimum wage laws.

• Price controls always involve controversial tradeoffs because any benefits provided by the controls entail costs for some people, and create various unintended and undesirable side effects.

Quick Quiz

11. A price ceiling is intended to:
(a)   create a surplus
(b)   create a shortage
(c)   lower price for consumers
(d)   raises price for producers

12. Which is an example of a price floor?
(a)   rent controls on apartments
(b)   a minimum wage law
(c)   a maximum on university tuition rates
(d)   limits on interest rates charged by credit card companies

Terms and Concepts

market	supply
demand	law of supply
law of demand	supply curve
marginal utility	determinants of
income effect	supply
substitution effect	change in supply
demand curve	change in quantity
determinants of	supplied
demand	surplus
normal good	shortage
inferior good	equilibrium price
substitute goods	equilibrium quantity
complementary goods	rationing function of
change in demand	prices
change in quantity	price ceiling
demanded	price floors

Fill-In Questions

1. A market is the institution or mechanism that brings together the _____ and the _____ of a particular good or service.

2. The Latin phrase meaning "all other things being equal" is _____.

3. The graph of the demand schedule is called the demand _____ and according to the law of demand is _____ sloping.

4. A change in price causes a change in (demand, quantity demanded) _____, and results in a (movement along, shift in) _____ the demand curve. A change in consumer incomes causes a change in (demand, quantity demanded) _____, and results in a (movement along, shift in) _____ the demand curve.

5. Marianne tends to buy more books when the price of books falls because:
(a) her purchasing power is increased, so she can afford to buy more books and other goods; this is called the _____ effect.
(b) books become less expensive relative to magazines, so Marianne tends to buy more books and fewer magazines; and this is called the _____ effect.

6. Jean enjoys fashion magazines. She is willing to pay less for each additional subscription because she is successively less likely to actually read each extra one she buys. This is an example of the principle known as diminishing _____.

7. A change in price causes a change in (supply, quantity supplied) _____, and results in a (movement along, shift in) _____ the supply curve. A change in resource costs causes a change in (supply, quantity supplied) _____, and results in a (movement along, shift in) _____ the supply curve.

True-False

Circle T if the statement is true, F if it is false.

1. The classified ads section of a student newspaper could be considered a market.   **T F**

2. The law of demand states that as price increases, the demand for the product decreases, *ceteris paribus*.   **T F**

The next three questions are based on the accompanying graph.

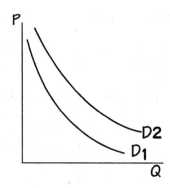

3. If the demand curve changes from D_1 to D_2 demand has increased. **T F**

4. The shift of the demand curve from D_1 to D_2 could be caused by a decrease in the price of complements. **T F**

5. The shift of the demand curve from D_1 to D_2 could be caused by a decrease in supply. **T F**

6. If two goods are complements, an increase in the price of one will cause the demand for the other to decrease. **T F**

7. A fall in the price of cable internet access will cause the demand for telephone internet access to decrease. **T F**

8. Since the amount purchased must equal the amount sold, demand and supply must always equal each other. **T F**

9. A decrease in quantity supplied can be caused by an increase in production costs. **T F**

10. If the supply curve for lipstick shifts to the right, the supply of lipstick has decreased. **T F**

11. When quantity supplied exceeds quantity demanded, the market price will tend to fall. **T F**

12. The equilibrium price is also referred to as the market-clearing price. **T F**

13. The rationing function of prices is the elimination of shortages and surpluses. **T F**

14. If government sets a price floor that is above the equilibrium price, this will raise the price and quantity in the market. **T F**

15. A government-set ceiling on credit card inter-

est rates would lead to actions by the issuers to reduce their costs or increase service charges.
T F

Multiple-Choice

Circle the letter that corresponds to the best answer.

1. An increase in the quantity demanded of oranges can be caused by:
(a)   a shift to the left of the supply curve of oranges
(b)   a shift to the right of the supply curve of oranges
(c)   a decline in the demand for orange juice
(d)   a rise in the demand for orange juice

2. A decrease in the quantity demanded:
(a)   shifts the demand curve to the left
(b)   shifts the demand curve to the right
(c)   is a movement down along the demand curve
(d)   is a movement up along the demand curve

3. If skiing at Banff and skiing at Whistler are substitutes, an increase in the price of skiing at Banff will:
(a)   decrease demand for skiing at Whistler
(b)   increase demand for skiing at Whistler
(c)   decrease quantity demanded of skiing at Whistler
(d)   increase quantity demanded of skiing at Whistler

4. Which pair of goods would most consumers regard as complementary goods?
(a)   coffee and tea
(b)   hockey sticks and skates
(c)   hamburger meat and bus rides
(d)   books and televisions

5. Which of the following is **not** among the determinants of demand?
(a)   consumer incomes
(b)   consumer expectations of future prices
(c)   prices of substitute goods
(d)   cost of resources

6. If an increase in income causes the demand for gumboots to decrease, then gumboots are:

(a) normal
(b) inferior
(c) substitute goods
(d) complementary goods

7. According to the law of supply:
(a) equilibrium quantity will increase when equilibrium price increases
(b) equilibrium quantity will decrease when equilibrium price increases
(c) the supply curve has a negative slope
(d) if other things remain the same, the quantity supplied increases whenever price increases

8. A supply curve indicates:
(a) the profit-maximizing quantities sellers place on the market at alternative prices
(b) the minimum quantities sellers place on the market at alternative prices
(c) the maximum quantities sellers will place on the market at different prices for inputs
(d) the quantities sellers place on the market in order to meet consumer demand at that price

9. The supply curve of the firm slopes upward in the short run because:
(a) the increased production requires the use of inferior inputs
(b) hiring more inputs for the extra production requires the payment of higher input prices
(c) the increased technology to produce more output is expensive
(d) productive efficiency declines because certain productive resources cannot be expanded quickly

10. A movement along a supply curve for a good would be caused by:
(a) improvements in production technology
(b) an increase in the price of the good
(c) an increase in the number of suppliers of the good
(d) a change in expectations

11. Which of the following would increase the supply of books?
(a) an increase in the demand for books
(b) an increase in the price of books
(c) an increase in the cost of paper

(d) a decrease in the wages paid to printers

12. Which of the following events would likely cause a furniture manufacturer to increase his supply of oak tables:
(a) an increase in the price of oak tables
(b) an increase in the cost of oak lumber
(c) a decrease in the demand for pine tables
(d) an increase in wages paid to staff

The next four questions are based on the following diagram.

13. Given the original demand and supply curves are D and S:
(a) the equilibrium price and quantity were P and Q1
(b) the equilibrium price and quantity were P and P1
(c) the equilibrium price and quantity were P1 and Q1
(d) the equilibrium price and quantity were P and Q3

14. The shift of the supply curve from S to S_1 is termed:
(a) an increase in supply
(b) an increase in quantity supplied
(c) a decrease in supply
(d) a decrease in quantity supplied

15. The shift in the supply curve from S to S_1 could be caused by:
(a) an increase in the price of the good
(b) a technological improvement in the production of the good
(c) a decrease in demand
(d) an increase in the cost of the resources used in the production of the good

16. If the price were prevented from adjusting when the supply shifted from S to S_1 the result

would be:
- (a)   a surplus of Q3 - Q1
- (b)   a shortage of Q2 - Q1
- (c)   a shortage of Q3 - Q1
- (d)   a surplus of Q3 - Q2

17. A market is in equilibrium when:
- (a)   inventories of the good are not rising
- (b)   suppliers can sell all of the good they decide to produce at the prevailing price
- (c)   quantity demanded equals quantity supplied
- (d)   demanders can purchase all of the good they want at the prevailing price

18. An increase in supply and an increase in demand will:
- (a)   increase price and increase the quantity exchanged
- (b)   decrease price and increase the quantity exchanged
- (c)   affect price in an indeterminate way and decrease the quantity exchanged
- (d)   affect price in an indeterminate way and increase the quantity exchanged

19. If scalping NHL playoff game tickets is profitable, this is a sign that the initial price at which the tickets were issued was:
- (a)   below the equilibrium price
- (b)   equal to the equilibrium price
- (c)   above the equilibrium price
- (d)   unreasonably high

20. A shortage of paper would cause the price of paper to rise. This would alleviate the shortage by:
- (a)   giving buyers incentives to use less paper
- (b)   giving producers incentives to find ways to supply more paper
- (c)   increasing the amount of paper being recycled
- (d)   all of the above

21. In 2001 fewer tents were sold, and the price of tents was higher, as compared to 2000. Which event alone might have caused the change?
- (a)   demand for tents was greater in 2001
- (b)   demand for tents was less in 2001
- (c)   supply of tents was greater in 2001
- (d)   supply of tents was less in 2001

22. Which of the following could raise the price of movie rentals in Saskatoon?

- (a)   a drop in the number of movie stores
- (b)   an increase in the price of VCRs
- (c)   a decrease in the population of Saskatoon
- (d)   a decrease in the price of admission to movie theatres

23. If new reserves of natural gas were discovered and brought into production, and population were to fall at the same time:
- (a)   the price of natural gas would rise
- (b)   the price of natural gas would fall
- (c)   the price of natural gas would not change
- (d)   the price of natural gas might rise or fall

This graph is used for the next two questions.

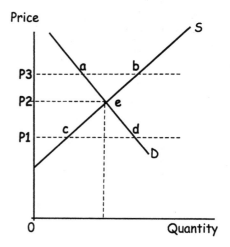

24. The distance **cd** measures:
- (a)   the shortage at a price ceiling of P1
- (b)   the surplus at a price ceiling of P1
- (c)   the shortage at a price floor of P1
- (d)   the surplus at a price floor of P1

25. A price floor set at which price would create a surplus?
- (a)   P1
- (b)   P2
- (c)   P3
- (d)   none of the above prices

26. An effective minimum wage law can be expected to:
- (a)   raise incomes for all workers who previously earned below the minimum wage
- (b)   have no effect on teenage unemployment
- (c)   create more jobs for teenagers
- [d]   reduce employment among teenagers

27. If the government fixes apartment rents below their equilibrium level, the effects in the long run

will include:
  (a)   an increased supply of apartments
  (b)   a decrease in the demand for apartments
  (c)   conversion of condos into rental units
  (d)   a reduction in the construction of new apartment units

Problems and Projects

1. Market Demand for Hockey Sticks

(a) Three individuals' demand schedules for hockey sticks are shown below. Assuming these are the only buyers, fill in the market demand schedule for sticks.

(b) If the market supply of sticks is fixed at 48 per year, what will be the equilibrium price and number of sticks bought by each consumer?

Price = $_____ per stick

Quantity = Elmer: _____ sticks; Toe: _____ sticks; Maurice: _____ sticks

Price (per stick)	Quantity Demanded (sticks per year)			
	Elmer	Toe	Maurice	Total
$5	10	6	8	_____
4	12	8	10	_____
3	15	11	12	_____
2	19	15	14	_____
1	24	18	16	_____

2. Demand and Supply Graphing

(a) Plot the demand and supply schedules below on the graph provided. Indicate the equilibrium price and quantity by drawing lines from the intersection of the demand and supply curves to the axes, labelling the values P* and Q*.

(b) At equilibrium, P* = _____, and Q* = _____.

(c) Fill in the last column of the table showing the amount of shortage or surplus that would exist at each price shown.

Price per Unit	Quantity Demanded	Quantity Supplied	Shortage (-) or Surplus (+)
$13	18	54	_____
12	21	48	_____
11	24	42	_____
10	27	36	_____
9	30	30	_____
8	33	24	_____
7	36	18	_____
6	39	12	_____

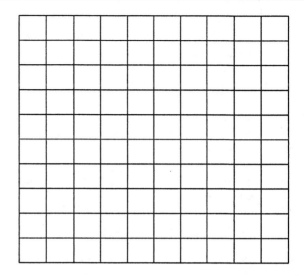

3. Determinants of Demand and Supply of Wine

Below are some events that affect the market for wine. In each space, indicate whether the event shifts demand (D) or supply (S), and whether it is an increase (+) or decrease (-) in the curve.

(a) Increase in the price of grapes   _____
(b) Increase in population of consumers   _____
(c) Increase in the price of cheese   _____
(d) Improvement in production technology   _____
(e) New subsidies for wine production   _____
(f)   Increase in the price of beer   _____
(g) Consumers expect a new tax on wine   _____

4. Supply and Demand for Beef

Consider the demand and supply model for the market for beef produced in Canada. For each of the following events, sketch a demand and supply graph showing the effect on the equilibrium price and quantity of Canadian beef.

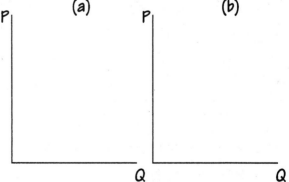

(a) A popular singer remarks that red meat in the diet may be a contributing factor in heart and circulatory diseases.

(b) The East Coast cod fishery is closed due to depleted fish stocks.

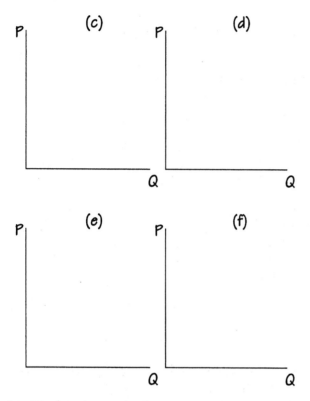

(c) Hoof and mouth disease in Europe leads to destruction of much of the supply of beef produced in that country.

(d) The price of livestock feed grains rises sharply due to a record harvest.

(e) Agriculture Canada discovers a new growth hormone that will increase the weight of beef cattle by 20% with the same feed intake.

(f) Many burger shops close down because of sharp increases in the minimum wage rate.

5. Shifts in Demand and Supply

The following table shows a number of different cases of a change in demand and/or supply. In the blank columns fill in the direction of which in equilibrium price and quantity: increase (+), decrease (-), or indeterminate (?).

Case	Demand	Supply	Price change	Quantity change
a	increases	constant	_____	_____
b	constant	increases	_____	_____
c	decreases	constant	_____	_____
d	constant	decreases	_____	_____
e	increases	increases	_____	_____
f	increases	decreases	_____	_____
g	decreases	decreases	_____	_____
h	decreases	increases	_____	_____

6. Golf and the Law of Demand

In the 1990s, most golf courses raised their prices but also had more golfers coming to play at their courses. This case (is, is not) _____ a violation of the law of demand. Three possible reasons for the observed behaviour are:

(a)_____

(b) _____

(c) _____

7. Market Demand and Supply for Firewood

The table below shows the demand and supply schedules for firewood in two small towns, Eastwick and Westwood. At first each town is a separate market because there is no passage across the river separating the towns.

Price	Eastwick Qd	Eastwick Qs	Westwood Qd	Westwood Qs	Total Qd	Total Qs
$225	80	100	45	105	____	____
200	90	90	55	95	____	____
175	100	80	65	85	____	____
150	110	70	75	75	____	____
125	120	60	85	65	____	____

(a) In Eastwick the equilibrium price is ____ per cord, and the equilibrium quantity is ____ cords per year.

(b) In Westwood the equilibrium price is ____ per cord, and the equilibrium quantity is ____ cords per year.

Now a bridge is built across the river, turning Eastwick and Westwood into one combined market.

(c) Fill in the market demand and supply schedules in the blank columns.

(d) The new equilibrium price is ____ per cord. This represents an increase in (Westwood, Eastwick) _____ and a decrease in _____.

(e) In Westwood quantity demanded is now ____ cords per year, and quantity supplied is now ____ cords per year. In Eastwick quantity demanded is now ____ cords per year, and quantity supplied is now ____ cords per year. Therefore, the town of _____ must import ____ cords per year from the town of _____.

8. Substitutes and Complements

How would a lengthy strike by transit drivers in

Winnipeg affect the market for gasoline in Winnipeg? Work this out by considering the relationships between buses and cars, and between cars and gasoline.

9. Price Controls and Taxes on Parking Spots

The graph below shows the demand and supply for daily parking spots in the downtown core of a Canadian city.

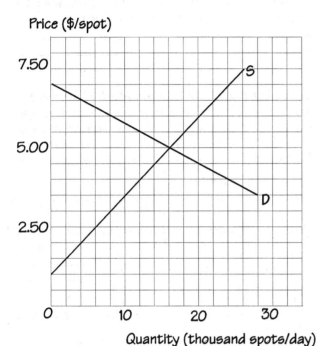

Price ($/spot)

Quantity (thousand spots/day)

(a) The current equilibrium price is _____ per spot, and _____ spots are rented each day.

(b) Citizen complaints about the cost of parking prompt the city council to impose a price ceiling of $4.00 per spot. The result will be a (shortage, surplus) _____ of ____ spots/day.

(c) Suppose that city council levies a new tax on parking lot operators in order to raise revenue to pay for a rapid transit system. The tax is set at $1.50 per spot. If the consumer pays $6.00, the supplier keeps $6.00-$1.50=$4.50. If the consumer pays $5.00, the supplier keeps _____.

(d) Show the new supply curve reflecting the tax. (The supply curve will shift upward by the amount of the tax because suppliers require this much extra in order to be willing to maintain the same supply as before.)

(e) The new equilibrium price is _____ per spot, and _____ spots are rented each day. Accordingly, the price consumers pay for one spot has (fallen, risen) _____ by $____, and the price that suppliers keep has _____ by $____. There-fore, the consumers' burden of the tax is _____ percent, and the suppliers' burden is _____ percent.

Discussion Questions

1. What is a market? For what kinds of goods does a laundromat bulletin board, or classified pages in a student newspaper, often serve as a market?

2. Carefully state the law of demand and explain the three reasons presented in this chapter to justify downward sloping demand curves.

3. The last time OPEC succeeded in sharply increasing the price of oil, drivers reacted by significantly reducing their gasoline consumption. Explain this in terms of the income effect and substitution effect.

4. Explain the difference between an increase in demand and an increase in quantity demanded. What factors cause a change in demand?

5. Define supply and explain why supply curves are upward sloping.

6. Explain the difference between a change in supply and a change in quantity supplied. What factors cause a change in supply?

7. Neither demand nor supply remains constant for long. Economic circumstances are always changing so the actual prices we see are often not equilibrium prices. Why then do economists spend so much time trying to determine the equilibrium price and quantity if these magnitudes change so frequently?

8. How are normal, inferior, substitute, complementary, and independent goods defined? During a recession (when consumer incomes are falling), who would fare better, firms that sell normal goods, or firms that sell inferior goods?

9. Analyze the following quotation and explain the fallacies contained in it. "An increase in demand will cause price to rise; with a rise in price, supply will increase and the increase in supply will push price down. Therefore, an increase in demand may or may not result in a price increase."

10. To reduce emissions of greenhouse gases, Canada wants to reduce the burning of fossil fuels. Explain why a new tax on automobiles or a subsidy for bicycles would help?

11. From the supply and demand perspective, what would you say has happened in the market for cell phones in the last decade? Are the falling prices and increased numbers of cell phones in use consistent with our economic theory?

12. Ticket agencies have usually set prices at a level where the best seats for concerts sell instantly and are then scalped (or resold for higher prices). In 2003 Ticketmaster announced plans to hold on-line auctions to sell the premium seats to some events. Why did the traditional pricing practice amount to a price control? Who stands to benefit and who stands to lose from the new auction scheme?

Answers

Quick Quiz
1. (d) p. 48
2. (b) p. 48
3. (d) p. 48
4. (d) p. 52
5. (a) p. 58
6. (a) p. 58
7. (a) p. 56
8. (b) p. 61
9. (a) p. 63
10. (a) p. 64
11. (c) p. 65
12. (b) p. 67

Fill-in Questions
1. buyers, sellers (either order)
2. ceteris paribus
3. curve, downward (negative)
4. quantity demanded, movement along; demand, shift in
5. (a) income; (b) substitution
6. marginal utility
7. quantity supplied, movement along; supply, shift in

True-False
1. T   It brings together buyers and sellers

2. F   The change is in quantity demanded, not demand
3. T
4. T
5. F   A supply shift has no bearing on the position of the demand curve
6. T
7. T   The two forms of internet service are substitutes
8. F   The two curves are not equal, though at equilibrium the two curves intersect, sharing a point where Qd equals Qs.
9. F   The decrease is in supply, not quantity supplied
10. F   The supply has increased
11. T   This is a surplus situation
12. T
13. T   Thus determining who gets the available output
14. T   Though quantity produced will exceed quantity demanded
15. T

Multiple-Choice
1. (b) There is a movement along the demand curve when the supply shifts, changing the equilibrium price
2. (d) This is caused by a rise in price
3. (b) Some skiers choose Whistler instead of Banff
4. (b) Complementary goods are used together
5. (d) Cost of resources affects supply, not demand
6. (b) Likely because consumers can substitute higher quality but more expensive footwear
7. (d) This law states a positive relationship between quantity supplied and price
8. (a) Sellers try to maximize profits
9. (d) For example, a restaurant cannot quickly expand its kitchen facilities
10. (b) All of the others shift the supply curve
11. (d) Lower wages means lower production costs and an increase in supply
12. (c) The supply of oak tables could shift right if producers move their resources away from making pine tables to make more oak tables
13. (d) Where S and D intersect
14. (c) Less is supplied at every possible price
15. (d) Increased costs for resources decreases supply
16. (c) If price cannot change, Qd is still at Q3, but Qs is now at Q1
17. (c) All of the other options are only partially correct

18. (d) Depending on which shifts more, demand or supply, price could rise or fall
19. (a) Scalpers profit from the shortage existing at the price at which tickets are first issued
20. (d) These are all aspects of the rationing function of prices
21. (d) Of the possibilities given, only the supply decrease affects both price and quantity as specified
22. (a) Fewer stores would mean a decrease in supply
23. (b) The supply shifts right, while demand shifts left, so both events contribute to a drop in the price
24. (c) $Qd - Qs = cd$. If P1 was a price floor the price would simply rise to equilibrium at P2
25. (c) A surplus of ab. None of the other prices would be an effective floor price.
26. (d) The higher wage increases the Qs (number willing to work) but reduces the Qd (number of workers demanded), causing some layoffs
27. (d) Developers will be deterred from supplying more apartment buildings

Problems and Projects
1. (a) 24, 30, 38, 48, 58; (b) $2 (where $Qd = Qs$). Elmer: 19; Toe: 15; Maurice: 14.
2. (a)

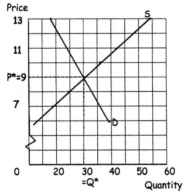

(b) $9, 30; (c) from top to bottom: +36, +27, +18, +9, 0, -9, -18, -27
3. (a) S-; (b) D+; (c) D- (complements for consumers); (d) S+; (e) S+; (f) D+ (substitutes for consumers); (g) D+ (buy more now before price rises).
4. (a) D shifts left: P -, Q -; (b) Fish and beef are substitutes for consumers, so as fish prices rise, then in the beef market D shifts right: P +, Q +; (c) Some buyers switch to Canadian beef, so D shifts right: P +, Q +; (d) Resource prices rise, so S shifts left: P +, Q -; (e) Improved production technology causes S to shift right; P -, Q +; (f) Less buyers of beef, so D shifts left: P -, Q -.

5. (a) +, +; (b) -,+; (c) -,-; (d) +,-; (e) ?,+; (f) +,?; (g) ?,-; (h) -,?
6. is not; (a) population growth, (b) increased incomes, (c) increased preferences for golf, or increased prices for substitute recreation activities, etc.
7. (a) $200, 90; (b) $150, 75; (c) Qd = 125, 145, 165, 185, 205; Qs = 205, 185, 165, 145, 125; (d) $175, Westwood, Eastwick; (e) 65, 85; 100, 80; Eastwick, 20, Westwood.
8. Cars and buses are substitutes, so when buses are out of service more people will drive cars. Cars and gasoline are complements, so more gasoline will be used. The demand for gasoline shifts to right. Equilibrium price and quantity both increase.
9. (a) $5.00, 16,000; (b) Shortage of $Qd - Qs$ = 24,000 - 12,000 = 12,000; (c) $3.50; (d) the new S curve is parallel to the original and $1.50 above it; (e) about 5.50, 12,000, risen, 0.50, fallen, 1.00; 33, 67.

Appendix to Chapter ③ The Mathematics of Market Equilibrium

Overview

This appendix shows how the demand and supply model can be represented mathematically. The demand curve and the supply curve can be expressed in equation form as functions of price. Only at the equilibrium price do both functions generate the same value for quantity. Therefore, given the equations for demand and supply, we can set the two equal to solve for equilibrium price and quantity.

This appendix deals with only straight-line demand and supply curves, so their equations can be represented as simple linear equations. Demand is given by $P = a - bQd$, and supply is given by $P = c + dQs$. Each parameter in the equations has an economic meaning. If the price reaches a or higher, the amount demanded will be zero. If the price reaches c or lower, the amount supplied will be zero. The value b indicates the amount by which price would have to rise to reduce quantity demanded by one unit. The value d indicates the amount by which price would have to increase to increase quantity supplied by one unit.

Normally the values for a, b, c, and d are known. With these parameters known, P and Qd are unknown in the demand equation, and P and Qs are unknown in the supply equation. There appear to be three unknowns (P, Qd, and Qs), but at the equilibrium price, Qd and Qs are equal. Therefore the only unknowns are equilibrium price and quantity, which can be represented as Q^* and P^*.

Appendix Outline

◇ How is equilibrium found in a mathematical model of demand and supply?

• A market equilibrium can be expressed as the price-quantity pair (Q^*, P^*) where quantity demanded equals quantity supplied ($Qd = Qs$).

• The market equilibrium results from the negotiating process that brings together the sellers' behaviour and the buyers' behaviour.
• The buyers' behaviour is represented in the equation: $P = a - bQd$. Buyers will buy only at prices below a, and b reflects how quantity demanded and price are related.
• The sellers' behaviour is represented in the equation: $P = c + dQs$. Sellers will sell only at prices above c, and d reflects how quantity supplied and price are related.
• The equilibrium values are solved from the parameter values as follows:
$$P^* = (ad + bc)/(a + d)$$
$$Q^* = (a-c)/(b + d)$$

⮕ Solving for the equilibrium price at which the demand and supply equations are equal is the mathematical equivalent of locating the intersection on a demand and supply graph to find the equilibrium price. There is only one value for price at which the two equations, or the two curves, have the same value for quantity.

⮕ If price is not at the equilibrium value there will be a shortage or a surplus, which can also be determined from the equations by substituting the given price into both equations and then comparing the resulting values for quantity demanded and quantity supplied.

Quick Quiz
1. For the demand equation $P = 20 - 5Qd$:
   (a) the price axis intercept is 20
   (b) the price axis intercept is 5
   (c) the price axis intercept is 4
   (d) the price axis intercept cannot be solved

2. Consider a demand equation of the general form $P = a - bQd$. If $b = 6$ and $a = 40$, then at what price will quantity demanded be 5?
   (a) the price axis intercept is 20
   (b) the price axis intercept is 5
   (c) the price axis intercept is 4

(d)   the price axis intercept cannot be solved

3. If the demand equation is $P = 20 - 5Qd$, and the supply equation is $P = 4 + 3Qs$, the equilibrium quantity is:
(a)   2
(b)   3
(c)   4
(d)   5

4. If the demand equation is $P = 20 - 5Qd$, and the supply equation is $P = 4 + 3Qs$, the equilibrium price is:
(a)   4
(b)   5
(c)   10
(d)   20

Fill-In Questions

1. The maximum price that buyers are willing to pay for a product is given by the (slope, intercept) _____ term in the (demand, supply) _____ equation.

2. The extent to which the producers are willing to supply more when price increases is reflected in the (slope, intercept) _____ term in the (demand, supply) _____ equation.

3. If demand is given by $P = a - bQd$, an increase in the value of parameter a indicates that the demand curve shifts to the (left, right) _____, and equilibrium price will (decrease, increase) _____.

4. If supply is given by $P = c + dQs$, a decrease in the value of parameter c indicates that the supply curve shifts to the (left, right) _____, and equilibrium price will (decrease, increase) _____.

True-False

Circle T if the statement is true, F if it is false.

1. If the demand curve is given by $P = 12 - 2Qd$, then quantity demanded is 3 if price is 6.   **T F**

2. If the supply curve is given by $P = 5 + 4Qs$, then price will be 7 if quantity supplied is 2.   **T F**

3. A change in either of the parameters in the demand equation will change the market equilibrium price.   **T F**

4. A change in either of the parameters in the supply equation will change the market equilibrium price.   **T F**

5. A change in either of the parameters in the demand equation will change the parameters in the supply equation.   **T F**

Multiple-Choice

Circle the letter that corresponds to the best answer.

Answer questions 1 through 6 on the basis of the following demand and supply equations:
$P = 100 - 2Qd$
$P = 40 + 4Qs$

1. The equilibrium price, P^*, will be:
(a)   50
(b)   60
(c)   70
(d)   80

2. The equilibrium quantity, Q^*, will be:
(a)   10
(b)   20
(c)   30
(d)   40

3. The lowest price at which producers are willing to begin selling output is:
(a)   10
(b)   20
(c)   30
(d)   40

4. Quantity demanded would become zero if the price rises above what level?
(a)   70
(b)   80
(c)   90
(d)   100

5. If price were 60, what would the situation be in this market?
- (a)   a surplus of 15
- (b)   a shortage of 15
- (c)   a surplus of 20
- (d)   a shortage of 20

6. The demand equation given could also be rewritten as:
- (a) $Qd = 100 - 2P$
- (b) $P = 50 - Qd$
- (c) $Qd = 100 - 0.5 Qd$
- (d) $Qd = 50 - 0.5 P$

Problems and Projects

1. Demand and Supply in the Shoe Market
The demand and supply in the market for shoes are given by the following equations:
$P = 100 - 0.1 Qd$ $P = 50 + 0.4 Qs$
(a) Rewrite the demand equation as a function of Qd: _____
(b) Rewrite the supply equation as a function of Qs: _____
(c) Using these new equations, fill in the table.
(d) Solve for the equilibrium price: _____

Price ($/pair)	Qd (pairs/yr)	Qs (pairs/yr)
100	_____	_____
90	_____	_____
80	_____	_____
70	_____	_____
60	_____	_____
50	_____	_____

2. The Market for Lemons
Suppose that the market for lemons can be characterized by the following equations:
$P = 4 - 0.01 Qd$
$P = 1 + 0.02 Qs$
(a) Solve for the equilibrium quantity: _____
(b) Solve for the equilibrium price: _____
(c) If price was fixed by government policy at $P = 2$, would there be a shortage or a surplus, and what would the amount be?
(d) If price was fixed by government policy at $P = 3.5$, would there be a shortage or a surplus, and in what amount?

3. The Market for Computer Printers
The data below represents the market for computer printers.

Price ($/printer)	Qd (printers/yr)	Qs (printers/yr)
100	4000	0
200	3000	0
300	2000	1000
400	1000	2000
500	0	3000

(a) Based on the demand schedule, what is the demand equation? _____
(b) Based on the supply schedule, what is the supply equation? _____
(c) Use the supply and demand equations to solve for equilibrium: $P^* =$ _____, $Q^* =$ _____

Discussion Questions

1. What aspect of a demand equation shows that the equation is consistent with the law of demand? What aspect of the supply equation ensures that there is a positive relation between price and quantity supplied?

2. Sketch a hypothetical straight-line demand curve. How would the position of this curve change if there were an increase in the parameter a? What if there were an increase in b?

3. Sketch a hypothetical straight-line supply curve. How would the position of this curve change if there were an increase in the parameter c? What if there were an increase in d?

Answers

Quick Quiz
1. (a) p. 73
2. (d) p. 73
3. (a) p. 74
4. (c) pp. 74-75

Fill-in Questions
1. intercept, demand
2. slope, supply
3. right, increase
4. right, decrease

True-False

1. T   Substitute in 6 for P and solve for Qd
2. F   Substitute in 2 for Qs and $P = 13$
3. T   If a or b changes the demand curve will shift
4. T   If c or d changes the supply curve will shift
5. F   The two equations are independent of each other

Multiple-Choice

1. (d) Set $Qd = Qs$ and solve for P^*
2. (a) Substitute $P^* = 80$ into either the Qd or the Qs equation
3. (d) Set $Qs = 0$
4. (d) Set $Qd = 0$
5. (b) Find that $Qd = 20$ and $Qs = 5$ at this P
6. (d) Rearrange the equation to solve for Qd

Problems and Projects

1. (a) $Qd = 1000 - 10 P$; (b) $Qs = -125 + 2.5 P$: (c) from top to bottom: Qd: 0, 100, 200, 300, 400, 500; Qs: 375, 350, 325, 300, 275, 250: (d) by setting the two equations equal, or by reading the table, we see that $P^* = 90$, where $Qd = Qs = 100$.
2. (a) 100; (b) 3; (c) $Qd = 200$, $Qs = 50$, so a shortage of 150; (d) surplus of 75
3. (a) $P = 500 - 0.1 Qd$; (b) $P = 200 + 0.1 Qs$; (c) $P^* = 350$, $Q^* = 1500$

Chapter 4

The Market System and International Trade

Overview

Chapter 3 explained how prices and quantities are determined in individual markets. This chapter widens the focus to consider the nature of the market system as a whole, with emphasis on describing the Canadian economy.

The market system or capitalism has six defining characteristics: private property rights; freedom of choice for consumers and freedom of enterprise for suppliers; the pursuit of self-interest; competition among economic units; coordination through markets and prices; and an active, but limited, role for government. The many demand and supply decisions made by households and firms determine market prices which in turn provide incentives and signals to these decision-makers, thereby coordinating the allocation of society's resources.

In a competitive market setting, with consumers and producers following their self-interest, their choices will coincide with the interests of society — as though individuals are guided by an "invisible hand" to serve the public interest. Accordingly, the role of government is quite limited.

Modern industrial economies have three other characteristics that increase dramatically the amount of goods and services that can be produced: (1) extensive use of advanced technology and capital goods; (2) specialization in production; and (3) use of money.

The challenge for any market economy can be summarized in four fundamental questions: (1) what goods and services will be produced; (2) how will the goods and services be produced; (3) who will get the goods and services; and (4) how will the system accommodate change?

The market system features three key virtues: efficiency, incentives, and freedom. However, where there are spillover costs or benefits, or public goods, the market fails to produce an efficient allocation of resources. Therefore there is a role for government to correct the inefficiencies.

The final section describes how globalization links the Canadian economy with the rest of the world. The theory of comparative advantage explains how all nations can gain if they specialize in production of goods in which they have lower opportunity costs, and then trade some of their output for goods produced by other nations.

Chapter Outline

4.1 Characteristics of the Market System

◈ What are the six defining characteristics of the market system?

• The market system, or capitalism, is an economic system is defined by: private property, freedom of enterprise and choice, self-interest, competition, self-regulating markets, and an active, but limited role for government.

o Resources are the private property of households and firms who are free to obtain, control, employ, and dispose of their property as they see fit.

o Freedom of enterprise means that firms are free to make business decisions about what to produce, where to sell, etc. Freedom of choice means that consumers can spend their incomes on whatever goods they want, and resource owners can supply their land, labour, etc. as they see fit.

o Self-interest is the motivating force behind decisions: consumers try to maximize their satisfaction, and entrepreneurs try to maximize their profits.

o A market is competitive if it has many independent buyers and sellers, each free to enter or exit the market, so that no individual buyer or seller has much power.

o Signals and incentives are conveyed through prices. Because buyers and sellers respond spontaneously to price changes, resource allocation is coordinated in a decentralized and spontaneous fashion, as if by an "invisible hand."

o Markets create a sufficiently self-regulating, self-adjusting, and efficient allocation of resources that the government's role is limited. Due to certain shortcomings of the market (discussed later in the chapter) government's role is nevertheless important.

• All modern industrial economies have three other main characteristics:

o There is extensive use of advanced technologies and roundabout production. By producing complex capital goods (e.g., machinery or computers) we raise the efficiency in producing final goods for consumers (e.g. food).

o Specialization prevails at all levels. Division of labour among workers means that each person produces only a very narrow range of goods and relies on the existence of markets and prices to trade for goods that others have produced. The same is true of regions and nations. Specialization creates efficiencies by making use of ability differences, by allowing learning by doing, and by saving time.

o To overcome the inconvenience and transactions costs of bartering, some system of money is inevitable. It is impossible to sustain a highly specialized economy without some form of money to facilitate exchanges. Anything that is generally accepted by sellers in exchange for goods and services is considered money.

Quick Quiz
1. Which is one of the main features of pure capitalism?
(a) central economic planning
(b) limits on freedom of choice
(c) the right to own private property
(d) an expanded role for government in the economy

2. In pure capitalism, freedom of enterprise means that:
(a) businesses are free to produce products that consumers want
(b) consumers are free to buy goods and services that they want

(c) resources are distributed freely to businesses that want them
(d) government is free to direct the actions of businesses

3. In pure capitalism, the role of government is best described as:
(a) nonexistent
(b) active but limited
(c) significant
(d) extensive

4.2 The Market System at Work

◈ What are the four fundamental questions that every economy must answer?

• The competitive market system functions with two groups of decision makers: households (consumers) and firms (businesses). Households are the ultimate suppliers of resources, and firms are the suppliers of goods purchased by consumers with the incomes from their resources. The market system communicates the decisions of millions of individual households and firms, and coordinates these decisions in a coherent allocation of resources.

• Faced with scarcity, every economy must find answers for the Four Fundamental Questions:
o What goods and services will be produced?
o How will the goods and services be produced?
o Who will get the goods and services?
o How will the system accommodate change?

• The market system, or price mechanism, is a communication and coordination system that provides answers to the Four Fundamental Questions.
o Consumers' "dollar votes" for the products they want, and firms' desires for profits determine the types and amounts of goods to be produced, and at what price.
o The profit motive drives businesses to use production methods that economize on resources, especially those resources that are relatively expensive.
o Goods are distributed to those consumers willing and able to pay the current market price. Consumers' incomes are determined by the quantities and prices of the labour, property, and other resources

they supply in resource markets. The market system does not guarantee an equitable distribution of income and consumer goods.

o   Changes in consumer tastes, technology, and resource supplies are signalled by price changes that give households and firms incentives to adjust their choices. Thus price changes guide the reallocation of resources to accommodate change.

• Competition in the economy compels firms and households acting in their own self-interest to promote (as though led by an "invisible hand") the interests of society as a whole, though this is not their intention. Adam Smith first noted this concept in his 1776 book, The Wealth of Nations.

➲ The crux of the market system is the dual role played by prices: to provide both signals and incentives. An increase in the price of a product signals that for some reason scarcity of this product has increased. The price increase gives consumers the incentive to reduce their consumption (as they ration their limited incomes) and gives producers the incentive to produce more (in order to maximize profits).

• The market system has several merits. The two economic arguments for the system are the efficient allocation of resources and the incentives for using resources productively. The personal freedom allowed in a market economy is its major non-economic virtue.

➲ Consider how amazing it is that a market system works at all! How can millions of independent decisions by consumers and producers possibly add up to a coherent allocation of resources that virtually guarantees that your neighbourhood store will have milk and bread every time you come to buy them? Nobody is in control of the whole economy; nobody has the responsibility to coordinate the allocation of resources. Yet, as if guided by an "invisible hand," the economy is coordinated in a manner that is spontaneous and decentralized.

Quick Quiz

4. The maximization of profit tends to be the driving force in the economic decision making of:
  (a)   entrepreneurs
  (b)   workers
  (c)   consumers

  (d)   legislators

5. To decide how to use its scarce resources to satisfy human wants pure capitalism relies on
  (a)   central planning
  (b)   roundabout production
  (c)   markets and prices
  (d)   barter

6. Which of the following would necessarily result, sooner or later, from a decrease in consumer demand for a product?
  (a)   a decrease in the profits of firms in the industry
  (b)   an increase in the output of the industry
  (c)   an increase in the supply of the product
  (d)   an increase in the prices of resources employed by the firms in the industry

4.3 Market Failure

◈ Why does market failure occur?
  o   What are spillover costs?
  o   What are spillover benefits?
  o   What are public goods?

◈ How can government correct market failure?

• Market failure occurs when the competitive market system results in the "wrong" production level for some goods, or fails to produce any of certain goods.

  o   Spillover costs exist when production or consumption of a good inflicts costs on a third party without compensation. Environmental pollution is an example. Such goods tend to be overproduced. Government can correct the overproduction by legislation or by specific taxes.

  o   Spillover benefits exist when production or consumption of a good creates benefits for third parties. Not enough is produced of such goods. Government can correct the allocation problem by subsidizing producers or consumers or by directly providing the good.

  o   Public goods are neither rivalrous nor excludable. Because everybody can use them simultaneously free of cost, they are subject to the free-rider problem and will tend to be underproduced. Government will tend to directly provide public goods.

• Government can be added to the circular flow model. Government buys goods and services from the product market, employs labour, capital, etc.

from resource markets, and finances its expenditures from net tax revenues collected from businesses and households.

Quick Quiz

7. Which economic situation would result in overallocation of resources to the production of a good?

  (a)   spillover benefits
  (b)   spillover costs
  (c)   a free-rider program
  (d)   inflation

8. How does government correct for spillover benefits?

  (a)   by taxing consumers
  (b)   by taxing producers
  (c)   by subsidizing producers
  (d)   by separating ownership from control

9. Which of the following is included in the circular flow diagram?

  (a)   businesses
  (b)   households
  (c)   government
  (d)   all of the above

4.4 Canada and International Trade

◇ How is Canada's economy connected to the rest of the world?

◇ According to the principle of comparative advantage how do nations gain from specializing and trading with each other?

• Canada is linked to other nations through flows of: goods and services, capital and labour, information and technology, and financial instruments. Through the process of globalization such links are becoming stronger and more numerous, and the economy is becoming more competitive.

• Specialization and trade among economic units (individuals, firms, provinces, regions, or nations) are based on the principle of comparative advantage. Specialization and trade increase productivity and output. Adam Smith wrote about this in 1776, and the idea was fully explained by David Ricardo in the early 1800s.

• The principle of comparative advantage is shown with an example of two individuals able to do two jobs, or with an example of two nations producing two goods.

  o A chartered accountant (CA) needing her house painted can paint it herself or hire a house painter. The CA will try to minimize her opportunity cost. By comparative advantage, even if the CA can do the job in less time than the painter can, if the CA incurs a lower opportunity cost by hiring the painter, the CA will specialize in accounting. Likewise, the painter will specialize in painting, and hire a CA to prepare his tax return, if this minimizes his opportunity costs.

  o Mexico and Canada both can produce corn and soybeans. Assuming each nation has a constant opportunity cost ratio, each nation has the lower opportunity cost — and therefore comparative advantage — in producing one of the two goods. By specializing in producing one good, each nation can trade for the other nation's good. The terms of trade, or ratio at which one good is traded for another, lies between the cost ratios for the two nations.

➲ If the data on production possibilities reflect constant costs, opportunity costs can be found easily by dividing a producer's maximum outputs of each of the two goods. For example, suppose Norway's maximum outputs are 100 fish or 20 tables. What is the cost of 1 table? Divide the number of tables into the number of fish: 100 fish/20 tables = 5 fish per table. What is the cost of 1 fish? Divide the number of fish into the number of tables: 20 tables/100 fish = 1/5 table per fish.

• When two nations specialize and trade according to their comparative advantage, both nations can consume more of both goods than their domestic production possibilities curves would permit. This reduces the scarcity problem.

• The circular flow model can be adapted to include a government sector and "rest of the world" sector.

Quick Quiz

10. Why do nations specialize and engage in trade?

  (a)   to protect multinational corporations
  (b)   to increase output and income
  (c)   to improve communications
  (d)   to control other nations

11. Bolivia sacrifices production of 2 blankets to produce 10 potatoes. Chile sacrifices 1 blanket to produce 8 potatoes. Which country has a comparative advantage?

(a)   Bolivia in blankets
(b)   Bolivia in potatoes
(c)   Chile in blankets
(d)   Bolivia in both blankets and potatoes

Terms and Concepts

private property	dollar votes
freedom of enterprise	derived demand
freedom of choice	guiding function of
self-interest	prices
competition	creative destruction
roundabout	"invisible hand"
production	market failure
specialization	spillover costs
division of labour	spillover benefits
medium of exchange	exclusion principle
barter	public good
money	free-rider problem
household	quasi-public goods
firm	absolute advantage
Four Fundamental	comparative advantage
Questions	terms of trade
consumer sovereignty	

Fill-In Questions

1. The ownership of resources by private individuals and organizations is the institution of _____.

2. In a market system private businesses have freedom of _____ and consumers have freedom of _____.

3. List the six characteristics of the market system.

(a)   _____
(b)   _____
(c)   _____
(d)   _____
(e)   _____
(f)   _____

4. If Robinson Crusoe spends time building a canoe to help him to catch more fish, he is engaging in _____ production.

5. Adam Smith believed that economic units seeking to further their own self-interest and operating within the capitalistic system will simultaneously, as though directed by an _____, promote the _____ interest.

6. List the Four Fundamental Questions to which every society must respond.

(a)   _____
(b)   _____
(c)   _____
(d)   _____

7. Three ways in which division of labour enhances a society's output are:

(a)   _____
(b)   _____
(c)   _____

8. Exchange by barter requires a _____ of wants.

9. Government frequently reallocates resources when it finds instances of _____ failure. The two major cases of such failure of the competitive market involve _____ effects and _____ goods.

10. Spillovers occur when benefits or costs associated with the production or consumption of a good are incurred by a _____ party. Spillovers are also called _____.

11. Governments can resolve the problem of spillover benefits through _____ paid to the _____ or the _____ of the good.

12. Public goods are not subject to the _____ principle. Once a public good is produced, the benefits from the good cannot be confined to the purchaser. This results in a _____ effect.

13. In the circular flow model, imports and exports are added as flows to the _____ market. Canadian expenditures pay for (exports, imports) _____, and foreign expenditures pay for _____.

14. If Nigeria can produce 10 kg of coffee at a cost of 1 barrel of oil, and Kenya can produce 25 kg of coffee at a cost of 1 barrel of oil, then _____ has the lower cost for producing oil, and _____ has the lower cost of producing coffee. The comparative advantage for oil lies with _____ and for coffee lies with _____.

15. The amount of one product that a nation must export in order to import one unit of another product is the _____.

True-False

Circle T if the statement is true, F if it is false.

1. Self-interest means the same as selfishness.
T F

2. In a competitive market every seller has significant influence over the market price. **T F**

3. In the market system most prices are set by a government agency. **T F**

4. If property rights did not exist for intellectual property, individuals would have less incentive to create music, books, and computer software.
T F

5. In the market system prices serve as signals for the allocation of resources. **T F**

6. Because the market system is efficient in resource use, every person is better off under this form of economic organization than any alternative. **T F**

7. In capitalism the distribution of output depends upon the distribution of resources. **T F**

8. The market system ensures that all households will receive an equitable share of the economy's output of goods and services. **T F**

9. The "invisible hand" refers to government intervention in the market. **T F**

10. Pollution is a cause of market failure because the price of the polluting product does not reflect all the resource costs used in its production. **T F**

11. A spillover or externality is a cost or benefit that is imposed upon an individual or group external to the market transaction. **T F**

12. A public good is any good or service that is provided free by the government. **T F**

13. A free-rider problem occurs when people can receive benefits of a good without contributing to the cost of providing it. **T F**

14. The first economists to explain the principle of comparative advantage were Adam Smith and David Ricardo. **T F**

15. The principle of comparative advantage applies just as well to individuals or regions as it does to nations. **T F**

16. If two nations produce only coal and lumber, one of the nations could have the comparative advantage over the other in both coal and lumber. **T F**

Multiple-Choice

Circle the letter that corresponds to the best answer.

1. Which of the following is not one of the six characteristics of the market system?
(a) competition
(b) freedom of enterprise and choice
(c) self-interest
(d) central economic planning

2. The "invisible hand" is used to explain how in the market system:
(a) property rights are defined
(b) taxes and subsidies are determined
(c) the self-interest of individuals is harnessed for the benefit of society
(d) spillover effects occur

3. In the market system a decrease in the demand for a good should result in all but:
(a) an increase in the price of the resources producing the good
(b) a decrease in the profitability of producing the good
(c) a movement of resources out of the production of the good
(d) a decrease in the price of the good

4. Roundabout production refers to:
(a) the use of resources by government

(b)   the use of resources to produce consumer goods directly

(c)   the use of resources to produce services

(d)   the use of resources to produce capital goods that in turn are used to produce other goods

5. Which of the following is **not** an example of a capital good?

(a)   money

(b)   a warehouse

(c)   a forklift

(d)   a computer

6. Which of the following is **not** a condition for a market to be highly competitive:

(a)   the presence of a large number of buyers

(b)   the freedom to enter or leave a particular market

(c)   the presence of a large number of sellers

(d)   a fair price determined by a public agency

7. Which of the following is a reason that specialization in production increases efficiency?

(a)   trade is rendered unnecessary

(b)   barter transactions are rendered unnecessary

(c)   individuals usually possess very similar resources and talents

(d)   experience or "learning-by-doing" results in increased output

8. Barter:

(a)   is the main method of trading in a market economy

(b)   is the action of haggling over the price of a good

(c)   is the exchange of a good for money

(d)   is the exchange of a good for a good

9. Which of the following is **not** a necessary consequence of specialization?

(a)   people will barter

(b)   people will engage in trade

(c)   people will be dependent upon each other

(d)   people will produce more of one thing than they would produce in the absence of specialization

10. Which of the following is **not** a virtue of the market system?

(a)   allocative efficiency

(b)   productive efficiency

(c)   equitable distribution of income

[d]   ability to adapt to changes in tastes, technologies, and resource supplies

11. The term "division of labour" means the same as:

(a)   specialization

(b)   barter

(c)   economies of scale

(d)   coincidence of wants

12. All modern economies have the following characteristics except for:

(a)   specialization

(b)   limited government interference

(c)   use of money

(d)   roundabout means of production

13. The economist who first wrote about the "invisible hand" was:

(a)   John Maynard Keynes

(b)   Karl Marx

(c)   David Ricardo

(d)   Adam Smith

14. If external benefits accompany the production of a good:

(a)   too much of the good will be produced by a competitive market

(b)   too little of the good will be produced in a competitive market

(c)   a tax on the production of the good will result in the optimum production of the good

(d)   the good is exported to foreign countries

15. In the case where producing a good creates spillover costs, government could promote the optimal output by:

(a)   banning production of the good

(b)   taxing the producers of the good

(c)   subsidizing consumers of the good

(d)   subsidizing producers of the good

16. Which of the following is a good example of a good or service providing spillover benefits?

(a)   a cup of hot tea

(b)   a new muffler on a car

(c)   a sofa

(d)   a pair of skis

17. Suppose that in order to relieve traffic congestion, user charges are imposed on drivers using

urban expressways. This would be a response to what economic problem?
(a)   spillover benefits
(b)   spillover costs
(c)   the free-rider problem
(d)   inequitable income distribution

18. Public goods differ from private goods in that public goods are:
(a)   divisible
(b)   subject to the exclusion principle
(c)   not subject to the free-rider problem
(d)   nonrivalrous and not subject to the exclusion principle

19. Quasi-public goods are goods and services:
(a)   to which the exclusion principle could be applied
(b)   that have large spillover benefits
(c)   that private producers would overproduce
(d)   that have large spillover benefits, and to which the exclusion principle could be applied

20. If the market system tends to overallocate resources to the production of good X:
(a)   good X could be a public good
(b)   good X could involve spillover benefits
(c)   good X could involve spillover costs
(d)   good X could be prone to the free-rider problem

21. Government expenditures, taxes, and transfer payments in the circular flow affect:
(a)   the distribution of income
(b)   the allocation of resources
(c)   the level of economic activity
(d)   all of the above

22. If Canada can produce 1 bottle of syrup at a cost of 2 cigars, and Cuba can produce 1 bottle of syrup at a cost of 6 cigars, what would be a mutually beneficial term of trade:
(a)   2 cigars per 1 syrup
(b)   3 cigars per 1 syrup
(c)   6 cigars per 1 syrup
(d)   8 cigars per 1 syrup

The next four questions are based on the data in the table that shows maximum production levels for the regions of Heath and Cliff, both of which have constant costs of production, and are able to trade with one another.

Heath		Cliff	
Wool	Peat	Wool	Peat
100	20	120	40

23. In Heath, the domestic opportunity cost of:
(a)   1 wool is 5 peat
(b)   1 wool is 1/5 peat
(c)   1 peat is 1.2 wool
(d)   1 peat is 1/5 wool

24. In Cliff, the domestic opportunity cost of:
(a)   1 peat is 3 wool
(b)   1 peat is 2 peat
(c)   1 wool is 3 peat
(d)   1 peat is 1/3 wool

25. Which of the following statements is **false**?
(a)   Heath has the comparative advantage in wool
(b)   Cliff should specialize in peat
(c)   Heath and Cliff could both gain from trading with one another
(d)   Heath has the comparative advantage in both wool and peat

26. The terms of trade will be:
(a)   more than 3 wool for 1 peat
(b)   fewer than 5 wool for 1 peat
(c)   between 3 and 5 wool for 1 peat
(d)   not between 3 and 5 wool for 1 peat

27. Countries A and B will be unable to mutually gain from trade and specialization if:
(a)   A has more resources than B
(b)   A's resources are more productive in both goods than B's
(c)   A and B have identical opportunity cost ratios between the two goods
(d)   none of the above

Problems and Projects

1. Rationing of Parking Spots
Consider a college with fewer parking spots than students who want to drive to school. At present the college offers free parking on a first-come-first-served basis. They are considering charging for parking, setting the fee high enough that there would always be a few spots open.
(a) Why would the system of charging for parking change the allocation of parking spots?

(b) Why would some students be in favour of the change while others would not?

(c) What socially beneficial incentives would be created by the proposed parking fee?

2.   Cost Minimization

A firm can produce 100 units of product X by combining labour, land, capital, and entrepreneurial ability in three different ways as shown in the table below. It can hire labour at $2 per unit, land at $3 per unit, capital at $5 per unit, and entrepreneurial ability at $10 per unit.

Resource	Method		
	A	B	C
Labour	8	13	10
Land	4	3	3
Capital	4	2	4
Entrepreneurial ability	1	1	1

(a) Which is the least cost method of producing 100 units of X? _____

(b) If the wage for labour rises from $2 to $3 per unit, which is the least cost method to produce 100 units of X? _____

(c) If the firm produces 100 X, the increase in the wage rate gives the firm the incentive to (increase, decrease) its use of labour from _____ units to _____ units.

3.   Electricity and the Price Mechanism

In 2001 electric power prices increased sharply in Alberta.

(a) What did the price increase signal?

(b) What incentives for power consumers and producers were created by the price increase?

(c) If households and firms responded to these incentives, how would this be socially beneficial?

(d) What is the primary motivation for consumers and producers to make choices that are socially beneficial?

4.   Circular Flow Diagram

The circular flow diagram below includes business firms, households, and government (the public sector). Product and resource markets are also shown.

(a) Identify the sector that corresponds to each box:

a. _____

b. _____

c. _____

d. _____

e. _____

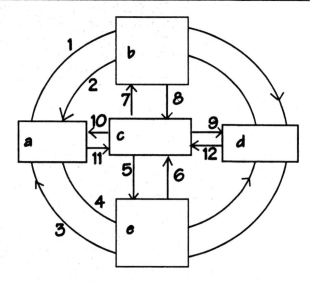

(b) Supply a label or an explanation for each of the twelve flows in the model:

1: _____

2: _____

3: _____

4: _____

5. _____

6: _____

7: _____

8: _____

9: _____

10: _____

11: _____

12: _____

(c) If government wished to increase the production of public goods and decrease the production of private goods in the economy, which flows could it increase? _____, _____, _____.

5.   Property Rights in Grades

The grade that you earn in your economics course this term will be the product of your work, and you probably consider this grade your private property.

(a) How would your incentives to study change if you did not have the right to communicate your grade to potential employers or other colleges or universities?

(b) How would your incentives change if you had to share your "output" on exams with your classmates (i.e., everybody is awarded the class average grade)?

(c) Are there any reasons for restricting your property rights in your grade? For example, should you be able to sell or give your grade to another student?

6. Types of Market Failure

Match each example on the right with the type of situation on the left:

(a) spillover cost   (1) a radio broadcast
(b) spillover benefit (2) a noisy house party
(c) public good   (3) vaccinations

7. Comparative Advantage in Tailoring

Julius and Murray are tailors. Their production possibilities tables for trousers and jackets are given below. Initially they work independently, with Julius choosing production alternative D, and Murray choosing E from his alternatives.

JULIUS: Production Possibilities Table

Product	Production Alternative					
	A	B	C	D	E	F
Trousers	75	60	45	30	15	0
Jackets	0	10	20	30	40	50

MURRAY: Production Possibilities Table

Product	Production Alternative						
	A	B	C	D	E	F	G
Trousers	60	50	40	30	20	10	0
Jackets	0	5	10	15	20	25	30

(a) For Julius 1 pair of trousers costs _____ jackets, and 1 jacket costs _____ pairs of trousers.
(b) For Murray 1 pair of trousers costs _____ jackets, and 1 jacket costs _____ pairs of trousers.
(c) The comparative advantage in making trousers lies with _____ because his opportunity cost is (lower, higher) _____. The comparative advantage in making jackets lies with ___-_____ because his opportunity cost is (lower, higher) _____.
(d) If Julius and Murray form a partnership, Julius should specialize in making _____, and Murray should specialize in _____.
(e) Working independently Julius and Murray would produce a total of 50 pairs of trousers and 50 jackets. If each specializes fully, their combined output will be _____ pairs of trousers, and _____ jackets. Thus, the gain from specialization is _____ pairs of trousers and _____ jackets.

8. Comparative Advantage in Fruit

Venezuela and Costa Rica have the production possibilities tables shown below.

(a) Find the opportunity costs:
Venezuela: 1 apple costs _____
      1 banana costs _____
Costa Rica: 1 apple costs _____
      1 banana costs _____
(b) Determine which country has the comparative advantage in each good:
Apples: _____   Bananas: _____

VENEZUELA: Production Possibilities Table

Product	Production Alternative					
	A	B	C	D	E	F
Apples	40	32	24	16	8	0
Bananas	0	4	8	12	16	20

COSTA RICA: Production Possibilities Table

Product	Production Alternative					
	A	B	C	D	E	F
Apples	75	60	45	30	15	0
Bananas	0	5	10	15	20	25

(c) From the information given we cannot determine specifically what the terms of trade will be. However, the terms of trade must be greater than _____ apples per banana, and less than _____ apples per banana.
(d) Suppose that each nation would choose production alternative C if specialization and trade were impossible. The combined production in the two countries would be _____ apples and _____ bananas.
(e) If each nation specializes completely according to comparative advantage, their combined production will be _____ apples and _____ bananas.
(f) Their combined gains from specialization will be _____ apples and _____ bananas.
(g) Suppose that the nations specialize and then agree to trade 25 apples for 10 bananas. This trade will leave Venezuela consuming _____ apples and _____ bananas. Costa Rica will consume _____ apples and _____ bananas.
(h) Compared to production alternative C, this leaves Venezuela with a gain of _____ apples and _____ bananas. Compared to production alternative C, this leaves Costa Rica with a gain of _____ apples and _____ bananas.

Discussion Questions

1.   List the Four Fundamental Questions that all economies must answer. Which of these

questions does the market system answer, and how so?

2. What property rights does the owner of a motor vehicle have? What restrictions or limits are there on those rights, and why do these restrictions exist? Do these restrictions increase or decrease the value of owning a vehicle?

3. How does the pursuit of self-interest by all economic units in the market system model ultimately benefit society? Give an example of a choice you make that is in your self-interest, but not selfish.

4. At one time the world price of oil was expected to hit $100 a barrel by the 1990s. If so, the Canadian economy would presumably have allocated more resources to oil production. How would market forces have produced such a result? How would market forces have changed the gasoline consumption habits of Canadian households?

5. What are the advantages of "indirect" or "roundabout" production? If you were stranded on a tiny island in the Pacific, what roundabout production might you undertake?

6. In order for a market to be competitive, why must there be many buyers and many sellers? What might be some consequences if there are few buyers or few sellers?

7. How does an economy benefit from specialization and division of labour?

8. What are the disadvantages of barter, and how does money overcome these disadvantages?

9. What is "market failure" and what are the two major kinds of such failures?

10. If the person living down the hall from you plays her music very loudly, is there a spillover cost or spillover benefit? If a homeowner builds an extra high fence between his house and his neighbours', is there a spillover cost or spillover benefit?

11. Based on ideas from this chapter, what is the case for government supporting needle exchange programs for intravenous drug users?

12. Discuss how the concepts of spillover effects and public goods might apply to the Internet?

13. How are private goods different from public goods? Why does there tend to be underallocation of resources to public goods in the absence of government intervention?

14. What basic method does government employ in Canada to reallocate resources away from the production of private goods and toward the production of public goods?

15. Sketch how the international trade component can be built into the circular flow model.

16. Explain how comparative costs determine which producer has the comparative advantage. What determines the terms of trade? What is the gain that results from specialization and trade according to comparative advantage?

17. Suppose that Dr. Ocula is an outstanding eye surgeon with good enough hand-eye coordination that he keyboards faster than anyone else in town. Use the principle of comparative advantage to explain why he hires someone else to do the word-processing in his office, even though he could do it faster himself.

Answers

Quick Quiz
1. (c) p. 77
2. (a) pp. 77-78
3. (b) pp. 79
4. (a) p. 82
5. (c) pp. 83-84
6. (a) p. 84
7. (b) pp. 86-87
8. (c) pp. 87-88
9. (d) p. 91
10. (b) p. 96
11. (a) p. 95

Fill-in Questions
1. private property
2. enterprise, choice
3. private property; freedom of enterprise and choice; self-interest; markets and prices; competition; limited, but active government
4. roundabout

5. "invisible hand," social (or public)
6. what goods and services will be produced?; how will the goods and services be produced?; who will get the goods and service?; how will the system accommodate change?
7. making use of differences in ability, fostering learning by doing, saving time
8. coincidence
9. market; spillover, public
10. third; externalities
11. subsidies, consumers, producers
12. exclusion; free-rider
13. product; imports, exports
14. Nigeria, Kenya; Nigeria, Kenya
15. terms of trade

True-False
1. F   You might consider it in your self-interest to help other people, or donate to charities
2. F   No seller has significant influence
3. F   Most prices are set mainly by market forces
4. T   The prospect of earning royalties is an incentive to produce
5. T
6. F   Some individuals fare poorly under a market system, particularly those who have few resources
7. T   Those with more resources can earn higher incomes and have more spending power
8. F   The market offers no guarantees of equitability
9. F   The "invisible hand" refers to market forces
10. T
11. T
12. F   Many goods provided by government free of charge are not public goods
13. T   Because the exclusion principle does not apply
14. T
15. T
16. F   If one nation has the comparative advantage in coal the other nation has the comparative advantage in lumber

Multiple-Choice
1. (d) Central planning is characteristic of the command system
2. (c) Socially beneficial results stem from self-interested behaviour, without any central control
3. (a) Less demand for the good means less demand and lower price for resources used in producing the good

4. (d) Making a better axe allows us to cut more firewood later
5. (a) All of the others are human-made resources designed to help produce other things
6. (d) There is no assumption that government or any public agency would be involved
7. (d) As we gain experience we become more efficient at those tasks in which we specialize
8. (d) Price haggling is "bargaining"
9. (a) When we specialize we must trade, but it need not be by the inefficient barter system
10. (c) The market system often produces extreme discrepancies in incomes that do not seem equitable
11. (a)
12. (b) Many modern economies have a great deal of government interference
13. (d) In his book *The Wealth of Nations*
14. (b) Too little is produced because the producer will not take into account all of the benefits of the good
15. (b) Banning the product would reduce output to zero, which is not typically the optimal amount
16. (b) Cutting sound pollution for neighbours
17. (b) Each driver adds to the highway congestion, thereby imposing added time costs on other drivers
18. (d) They can be consumed simultaneously by many people, and those who do not pay cannot be excluded from using them
19. (d) Both aspects of this description are necessary
20. (c) All of the others are prone to underproduction
21. (d) Check the circular flow diagram
22. (b) Anything more than 2 and less than 6 cigars per syrup
23. (b) 20 peat / 100 wool = 1/5 peat / wool
24. (a) 120 wool / 40 peat = 3 wool/peat
25. (d) The comparative advantage in peat lies with Cliff
26. (c) The terms of trade must be between the two producers' opportunity cost ratios
27. (c) There is no reason to trade in this case

Problems and Projects
1. (a) Some students who are willing and able to arrive early or to spend time hunting for a spot may be unwilling to pay for a spot, whereas others may be willing and able to pay; (b) differences in availability of money and time; (c) students who place a low value on parking would have

incentive to walk, bus, carpool, thus leaving spots for those who value them more; firms seeking profit would have more incentive to provide near campus parking for a fee.

2. (a) B at $55; (b) A at $66; (c) decrease, 13, 8.

3. (a) increased scarcity of electricity; (b) to consume less by economizing on energy or switching to alternate sources; and to produce more; (c) there would be electric power available, and the available amount would be allocated to highest valued uses, thus minimizing the effects of increased scarcity.

4. (a) a: business firms, b: resource markets, c: government, d: households, e: product markets; (b) 1: businesses pay costs for resources that become money income for households, 2: households provide resources to businesses, 3: household expenditures become receipts for businesses, 4: businesses provide goods and services to households, 5: government spends money in product market, 6: government receives goods and services from product market, 7: government spends money in resource market, 8: government receives resources from resource market, 9: government provides goods and services to households, 10: government provides goods and services to businesses, 11: businesses pay net taxes to government, 12: households pay net taxes to government; (c) 9, 10, 11.

5. (a) If you could not use a good grade to help you get jobs, scholarships, etc. you may have less incentive to study; (b) If you get a better mark on an exam, your share of that improved mark would be very small, so you would have less incentive to study; (c) Restricted property rights in grades are probably justified because if students could sell their grades to other people then good grades would no longer indicate what they are supposed to, and would therefore no longer be meaningful or valuable.

6. (a) 2: neighbours suffer cost; (b) 3: one person being vaccinated reduces the risk of disease for other people, too; (c) 1: everybody can listen to a radio broadcast.

7. (a) 2/3, 1 1/2; (b) 1/2, 2; (c) Murray, lower, Julius, lower; (d) jackets, trousers; (e) 60, 50; 10, 0

8. (a) 1/2 banana, 2 apples, 1/3 banana, 3 apples; (b) Costa Rica, Venezuela; (c) 2, 3; (d) 69, 18; (e) 75, 20; (f) 6, 2; (g) 25, 10, 50, 10; (h) 1, 2, 5, 0

Chapter 5

Supply and Demand: Elasticity and Applications

Overview

This chapter extends some of the basic tools of demand and supply from Chapter 3, and applies the tools to the analysis of some important real world situations.

The law of demand states that when price rises, quantity demanded will fall, ceteris paribus, but it does not tell us how much the quantity responds to the price change. Price elasticity of demand is a numerical measure of the responsiveness of quantity demanded to price changes. The first two sections of the chapter cover: (1) the meaning of this elasticity; (2) how the price elasticity formula works; (3) how to interpret elasticity coefficient values; (4) how total revenue varies according to elasticity; (5) the determinants of this elasticity; and (6) how to apply the concept to economic questions.

The next two sections deal with other elasticities. Price elasticity of supply measures responsiveness of quantity supplied to price changes. Income elasticity measures the responsiveness of quantity demanded to changes in income is termed income elasticity of demand. Finally, the responsiveness of quantity demanded to a change in the price of another good is called cross elasticity of demand.

The remainder of the chapter is dedicated to applications of the supply and demand model and elasticity concepts to illuminate the effects of various public issues and government policy choices in the areas of taxation, rent control, agricultural price supports, and health care.

Chapter Outline

5.1 Price Elasticity of Demand

◈ What is price elasticity of demand and how is it calculated?

◈ What is the difference between elastic and inelastic?

• Price elasticity of demand is a measure of the responsiveness, or sensitivity, of the quantity demanded to changes in the price of the product. Elasticity is a number that can be computed from data on two points on the same demand curve (or schedule).

• The formula for the price elasticity of demand coefficient is:

$$E_d = \frac{\% \text{ change in quantity demanded of X}}{\% \text{ change in price of X}}$$

• To calculate the percentage changes in quantity and price between two price-quantity combinations, use the average of the two quantities and the average of the two prices as the reference points. This approach eliminates the annoying ambiguity in the exact value of the elasticity coefficient. Thus:

$$E_d = \frac{\Delta Q}{(Q_0 + Q_1)/2} \div \frac{\Delta P}{(P_0 + P_1)/2}.$$

• Say the elasticity coefficient is 3. Then at this particular point on the demand curve a 1 percent change in price will cause a 3 percent change in quantity demanded. Because price and quantity demanded are inversely related, the price and quantity will change in opposite directions.

• From the law of demand, price and quantity demanded are inversely related, so the price elasticity of demand coefficient is technically a negative number. For convenience, we ignore the minus sign and refer simply to the absolute value of the coefficient.

• Because elasticity is a ratio of two percentages, the coefficient is a pure number, and it is not affected by the choice of units used to measure price and quantity. Use of percentages also facilitates comparisons between different goods.

• The elasticity coefficient can range in (absolute) value from 0 to infinity. A perfectly inelastic demand has a coefficient of 0, while a perfectly elastic demand has a coefficient of infinity. Demand is termed elastic (inelastic, unit elastic) when the elasticity coefficient is greater than (less than, equal to) 1.

➲ The slope of a demand curve is not a reliable indicator of its elasticity. Except for horizontal and vertical demand curves, a constant-slope demand curve has a different elasticity at each point. It is also useful to know that on a straight line demand curve the price elasticity equals one at the midpoint.

Quick Quiz

1. If price goes up by 5% and quantity demanded falls by 2%, demand is:
(a)   elastic
(b)   inelastic
(c)   unit elastic
(d)   perfectly elastic

2. When the price of CDs falls from $17 to $13, the number sold rises from 9 million to 11 million. The price elasticity of demand coefficient is:
(a)   2.00
(b)   1.33
(c)   0.75
(d)   0.50

3. Compared to the lower-right portion, the upper-left portion of a straight line demand curve is:
(a)   more elastic
(b)   more inelastic
(c)   equally elastic
(d)   equally inelastic

5.2 The Total-revenue Test

◈ What is total revenue?

◈ How does price elasticity of demand affect the change in total revenue when price changes?
•   Suppliers' total revenue is the price per unit multiplied by the number of units sold.
•   Whether total revenue rises or falls when price changes depends on the product's price elasticity of demand.
o   When demand is elastic (inelastic), the change in price and the change in total revenue go in opposite (the same) directions.
o   When elasticity is one, total revenue is maximized. A small price change will lead to no change in revenue because quantity demanded changes by the same percentage as price. The price and quantity

changes have exactly offsetting effects on total revenue.

➲ Master the total-revenue test for assessing price elasticity of demand. If you need only determine whether demand is elastic or inelastic, determining the direction of total revenue change can be easier than computing price elasticity. Also be aware that if you know whether elasticity is greater or less than one that you can infer the direction of change in total revenue for a given price change.

◈ What factors determine the elasticity of demand for a particular good?
•   There are four key determinants of price elasticity of demand. Demand for a good is more price elastic:
o   the more good substitutes the product has
o   the greater the proportion of income that is spent on the good
o   if the good is a luxury rather than a necessity, and
o   (usually) the longer the period under consideration.
•   The relationship between price elasticity of demand and total revenue has great practical importance for public policy choices and business decisions.
o   Because demand for farm products is inelastic, large crops lead to huge price decreases and lower total revenues for producers.
o   Governments seeking revenue increases through sales taxes will tend to tax commodities with inelastic demands.
o   The effects of decriminalizing drugs would depend on the elasticity of demand for heroin and crack cocaine, for example. If demand is inelastic, then lower prices caused by legalization will lead to little extra drug use, and likely a drop in crime, as addicts need less money to purchase drugs. On the other hand, if demand is elastic then there will be much more drug use and associated crime.
o   A minimum wage law increases wage rates, but also reduces the number of workers demanded, particularly teenage workers. However, research suggests that the demand for teenage workers is inelastic, so the total income earned by

teenagers will rise because the gain in the hourly wage will be proportionally larger than the loss in jobs or hours worked.

Quick Quiz

4. If you were the sales manager for a pizza company, and you learned that the price elasticity of demand for your pizza is 1.5, then to increase total revenues, you should:
(a)   raise the price of the pizza
(b)   cut the price of the pizza
(c)   not change the price of the pizza
(d)   decrease demand for the pizza

5. The demand for Honda Civics is more elastic than demand for all cars as a whole group. Why?
(a)   Honda Civics are luxury cars
(b)   Hondas Civics are the best made cars
(c)   there are more complements for Honda Civics than for cars as a whole
(d)   there are more substitutes for Honda Civics than for cars as a whole

6. Which is a true statement?
(a)   increasing the sales tax on an elastic product will increase the government's tax revenue
(b)   a minimum wage law will do more harm to workers if the demand for their labour is elastic
(c)   cutting the supply of heroin does limited good because the demand is very elastic
(d)   farmers necessarily earn less income when bad weather reduces the amount of crop they can harvest

5.3 Price Elasticity of Supply

◈ What is price elasticity of supply and how is it calculated?

◈ What is the role of time in determining the price elasticity of supply?

•   Price elasticity of supply measures the sensitivity of quantity supplied to changes in the price of the product:

$E_S = \dfrac{\text{\% change in quantity supplied of good X}}{\text{\% change in price of good X}}$

•   The elasticity of supply is greater the more time sellers have to adjust to a price change. Therefore we distinguish between elasticities in the market period, short run, and long run.
  o   The market period is the time immediately after a price change during which

producers don't have time to adjust quantity supplied. If such a time exists for a particular seller, then elasticity of supply is zero.
  o   The short run is a period over which the plant capacity of individual producers and the industry is fixed. Because there is time to adjust the production by adjusting some resources, the supply curve has some elasticity.
  o   The long run is a period where producers have enough time to make all desired resource adjustments and for the number of producers to change. The elasticity of supply is greatest in the long run.

➲ Most of the chapter deals with price elasticity of demand. Once you are fully comfortable with this elasticity you will have little trouble understanding the others because every elasticity is a measure of responsiveness of some dependent variable to changes in an independent variable. The percentage change in the dependent variable is the numerator, and the percentage change in the independent variable is the denominator.

Quick Quiz

7. If a 5% fall in the price of tomato sauce causes the quantity supplied to decrease by 7%, the supply of tomato sauce is:
(a)   inelastic
(b)   elastic
(c)   unit elastic
(d)   perfectly inelastic

8. The chief determinant of price elasticity of supply of a product is:
(a)   whether consumers can easily substitute for the product
(b)   whether the good is a luxury or a necessity
(c)   how much time producers have to respond to a price change
(d)   whether the product is a durable or a nondurable good

5.4 Cross Elasticity and Income Elasticity of Demand

◈ What is cross elasticity of demand and how is it measured?

◇ What is income elasticity of demand and how is it measured?

• Cross elasticity of demand measures the sensitivity of quantity demanded for one product to changes in the price of another product. It is measured as:

$$E_{XY} = \frac{\% \text{ change in quantity demanded for good } X}{\% \text{ change in price of good } Y}$$

• The sign of the cross elasticity determines how goods X and Y are related: if positive, X and Y are substitute goods; if negative, X and Y are complementary goods; if zero, X and Y are independent.

• Income elasticity of demand measures the sensitivity of quantity demanded to changes in income:

$$E_i = \frac{\% \text{ change in quantity demanded}}{\% \text{ change in income}}$$

• A positive income elasticity designates a normal good; a negative income elasticity designates an inferior good.

• When incomes are growing across the economy, industries that produce normal goods with high income elasticities will tend to be growing faster than other industries.

Quick Quiz

9. If a rise in the price of good X causes the consumers to buy more of good Y, the cross-price elasticity between X and Y is:

(a) negative, so X and Y are substitutes
(b) negative, so X and Y are complements
(c) positive, so X and Y are substitutes
(d) positive, so X and Y are complements

10. If generic jam is an inferior good:

(a) people will buy more generic jam if their incomes fall
(b) people will buy more generic jam if the price rises
(c) people will stop buying generic jam if they become aware of a higher quality substitute
(d) people will only buy generic jam if it is advertised heavily

5.5 Elasticity and Real-world Applications

◇ How does elasticity affect the answers to the following questions?

　o How is the burden of a per unit tax divided between producers and consumers?

　o How do the long-run effects of rent control differ from the short-run effects?

　o Why have prices of antiques risen so much, and why are gold prices so volatile?

• A per unit sales tax levied on the producer shifts the supply curve up by the amount of the tax, creating a new equilibrium at a higher price. The price increase is the consumer's tax burden. The after-tax price received by the producers is lower than the pre-tax price. The drop is the producer's burden.

　o Given the supply, the more inelastic the demand, the larger the portion of the tax shifted to consumers.

　o Given the demand, the more inelastic the supply, the larger the portion of the tax borne by producers.

• Rent controls cause shortages of apartments. Because the price elasticity of supply of apartments is greater in the long run, these shortages become more severe over time, leading to increasing problems such as black markets and discrimination against some apartment-seekers.

• Because the supply of antiques is inherently highly inelastic, growing demand has produced large price increases.

• The price of gold fluctuates due to wide demand fluctuations together with a highly inelastic supply, meaning that even when demand is particularly high or low the suppliers will continue to supply nearly the same amount.

Quick Quiz

11. Suppose coffee outlets are hit with a new sales tax of $0.10 on every cup of coffee sold. If the tax pushes the new price (including tax) up by only $0.02, then:

(a) the demand is relatively more inelastic than the supply
(b) the supply is relatively more elastic than the demand
(c) the demand is relatively more elastic than the supply
(d) neither supply nor demand is elastic

12. Which is among the potential effects of a rent control on apartments?

(a) surpluses of apartments
(b) increased construction of new apartment buildings
(c) increased quality of apartments
(d) discrimination against tenants who are

members of minority groups

5.6 The Economics of Agricultural Price Supports

◇ How does each supply management program below work to improve farm incomes?
- o Offers to purchase
- o Deficiency payments
- o Supply restrictions
- • Canada's federal and provincial governments have a number of programs designed to improve farmers' incomes.
- • The Net Income Stabilization Account (NISA) and crop insurance programs serve as risk management tools by allowing farmers to access funds when incomes are abnormally low.
- • The marketing of several important agricultural products is coordinated through supply management programs. There are three basic methods by which such programs support prices:
  - o Using an "offers to purchase" plan the government stands ready to purchase whatever quantity producers wish to sell at an established floor price. Such a program results in a gain to farmers, higher prices for consumers, and surplus output that must be bought by the government (and paid for by taxpayers). There is also inefficiency because too many resources are allocated to agricultural production.
  - o Under a "deficiency payments" approach the government guarantees to pay farmers the difference between the market price and the government's promised price floor. How the benefit from this subsidy is divided between farmers and consumers depends on the elasticities of demand and supply. Once again, there is a cost to taxpayers, and an inefficiently large amount of resources is allocated to farming.
  - o Under "crop restriction" the government sets a quota, or maximum allowable output for each farmer. Price is supported by restricting supply, yet the government is not required to buy a large surplus or pay large deficiency payments.

Quick Quiz

13. Under which price support program will the government end up purchasing surplus farm output?

- (a) offers to purchase
- (b) deficiency payments
- (c) supply restrictions
- (d) price ceiling

14. What is a typical consequence of price support programs in agriculture?
- (a) surplus output
- (b) higher incomes for producers
- (c) overallocation of resources to farm production
- (d) all of the above

5.7 The Economics of Health Care

◇ What peculiarities of the health care market contribute to shortages in the Canadian health care system?
- • Ethical and equity considerations lead most of us to believe that everybody is entitled to basic health care, regardless of ability to pay.
- • Asymmetric information may create incentive problems. Physicians (health care suppliers) are more knowledgeable than patients (the health care demanders) concerning what services should be consumed. Therefore, unnecessary services may be provided.
- • Given that the insurance company pays, people may demand more health care services. They may even be less careful about lifestyle choice that affect their health, and therefore require more health care, because they are insured. This is the problem of moral hazard.
- • If health insurance is voluntary, those most likely to need health care services are more likely to buy insurance. This so-called adverse selection problem tends to leave some people without insurance.
- • Consumption of some health care services creates positive externalities (or spillover benefits), meaning that the efficient amount of health care services exceeds the amount people would buy for themselves.
- • Proposed solutions to the shortages include imposing user fees, diverting more tax revenues to the supply of health care.
- • Canada's system of health care consumes 10% of our GDP compared with the American system which consumes 14% of US GDP.

Quick Quiz

15. Which of the following factors tends to increase the amount of health care demanded?

(a)   health care insurance
(b)   asymmetric information
(c)   moral hazard
(d)   all of the above

16. If people with a family history of heart disease are more likely to choose to buy health insurance, this is an example of:
(a)   positive externality
(b)   asymmetric information
(c)   moral hazard
(d)   adverse selection

Terms and Concepts

price elasticity of
   demand
elastic demand
inelastic demand
unit elasticity
perfectly inelastic
   demand
perfectly elastic
   demand
total revenue (TR)
total-revenue test
price elasticity of
   supply
market period
short run

long run
cross elasticity of de-
   mand
income elasticity of
   demand
price supports
deficiency payments
crop restriction
quota
asymmetric informa-
   tion
moral hazard problem
adverse selection
   problem

Fill-In Questions

1. Elasticity of demand is a measure of the _____ of quantity demanded to changes in the price of the good and can be computed from the formula: Ed = percentage change in _____ / percentage change in _____.

2. Suppose that when Duffers' Paradise Golf Club raises their green fees from $23 to $27 that the number of golfers falls from 105 per day to 95 per day. The change in quantity demanded is ____ golfers. The average of the two quantities is _____ golfers. Therefore the percentage change in quantity is (____/____) x 100% = ____%. The change in price is $____. The average of the two prices is $____. Therefore the percentage change in price is (____/____) x 100% = ____%. The elasticity coefficient is (____%/____%) = ____.

3. If a relatively large rise in price results in a relatively small drop in quantity demanded, demand is _____; if a relatively small rise in price results in a relatively large drop in quantity demanded, demand is _____.

4. If a change in price causes no change in quantity demanded, demand is perfectly (elastic, inelastic) _____ and the demand curve is (horizontal, vertical) _____. The elasticity coefficient at any point on this demand curve is _____. If an extremely small change in price results in an extremely large change in quantity demanded, demand is perfectly _____ and the demand curve is nearly _____. The elasticity coefficient at any point on this demand curve is nearly _____.

5. If the price of a commodity drops:
(a) when demand is inelastic, the loss of revenue due to the lower price is (greater than, less than, equal to) _____ the gain in revenue due to the greater quantity demanded;
(b) when demand is elastic, the loss of revenue due to the lower price is _____ the gain in revenue due to the greater quantity demanded;
(c) when demand is of unitary elasticity, the loss of revenue due to the lower price is _____ the gain in revenue due to the greater quantity demanded.

6. List four determinants of price elasticity of demand.
(a) _____
(b) _____
(c) _____
(d) _____

7. If the supply curve is vertical then supply is infinitely _____. In this case a change in price causes _____ change in the quantity supplied.

8. The main factor affecting the price elasticity of supply is _____. In the _____ period producers are unable to adjust to demand changes. This is reflected in a _____ supply curve. In the _____ run firms have enough time to use existing plants more intensively. This is reflected in an _____ supply curve. In the _____ run there is time for existing firms to _____ their plant capacities, and for the number of firms to _____. This is reflected in a supply curve that is _____ elastic than the short run supply curve.

9. Because cigarettes have few good substitutes, their demand is _____. If government increases the tax on cigarettes by $1.00 per package, the _____ curve will shift _____ by the amount of the tax. If the equilibrium price increases by $0.75, the producers' burden is _____% of the tax, and the consumers' burden is _____% of the tax.

10. The market for health care has some unusual characteristics.
(a) People with a genetic disposition towards heart disease are more likely to choose to carry optional health insurance. This is an example of (moral hazard, asymmetric information, adverse selection) _____.
(b) People with health insurance may be less likely to maintain a healthy diet. This is an example of _____.
(c) People tend to depend on the advice of their physician to decide whether or not they need medical tests and treatments. This is an example of _____.

True-False

Circle T if the statement is true, F if it is false.

1. If the relative change in price is greater than the relative change in quantity demanded, the price elasticity coefficient is greater than one. **T F**

2. Along a downward sloping linear demand curve, demand tends to be elastic at higher prices and inelastic at lower prices. **T F**

3. If demand for wheat is inelastic, an increase in the harvest will reduce farm incomes from wheat sales. **T F**

4. If the quantity demanded of a product increases from 100 to 150 units when the price decreases from $14 to $10, demand is elastic in this price range. **T F**

5. If the price elasticity of demand coefficient is 3, this means that a one dollar decrease in price will

lead to a three unit increase in quantity demanded. **T F**

6. The demand for "necessities" tends to be inelastic, for "luxuries" elastic. **T F**

7. The price elasticity of demand will tend to be greater the fewer substitutes there are for the good. **T F**

8. Other things being equal, the larger the portion of one's income spent on a good the greater the elasticity of demand for that good. **T F**

9. The demand for a product tends to be more inelastic the longer the time period under consideration. **T F**

10. If supply is perfectly inelastic, an increase in demand will not change the equilibrium price. **T F**

11. The supply of a product tends to be more elastic the longer the time period under consideration. **T F**

12. A zero or near-zero coefficient for cross elasticity suggests that the two goods are unrelated or independent goods. **T F**

13. If the bottle depot is willing to pay $2 per dozen bottles, and will buy whatever quantity people bring in, then the depot's demand curve for bottles is perfectly elastic. **T F**

14. Given the supply, the more inelastic is the demand, the greater is the producer's burden of a new excise tax. **T F**

15. Deficiency payments and offers to purchase both result in excessive production of agricultural products. **T F**

16. Health insurance reduces the patient's price of receiving medical services and therefore increases the quantity demanded of some medical services. **T F**

17. Once an artist is deceased the supply of her paintings becomes totally elastic, tending to increase their prices. **T F**

Multiple-Choice

Circle the letter that corresponds to the best answer.

1. The price elasticity of demand measures:
   (a) the percentage change in quantity demanded as a result of a 1 percent change in supply
   (b) the change in quantity demanded as the result of a 1 percent change in price
   (c) the percentage change in quantity demanded as a result of a 1 percent change in price
   (d) the slope of the demand curve

2. If when the price of slushees rises from $1.50 to $2.00 the quantity of slushees demanded falls from 1,000 to 900, the price elasticity of demand coefficient is:
   (a) 3.00
   (b) 2.71
   (c) .37
   (d) .33

3. If a 1 percent fall in the price of a commodity causes the quantity demanded of the commodity to increase 2 percent, demand is:
   (a) inelastic
   (b) elastic
   (c) unit elastic
   (d) perfectly elastic

4. If the price elasticity of demand for restaurant meals were 2.0, what would be the effect of a 5% increase in restaurant prices?
   (a) quantity demanded will fall by 2.5%
   (b) quantity demanded will fall by 2.8%
   (c) quantity demanded will fall by 3.0%
   (d) quantity demanded will fall by 10.0%

5. Moving down a straight-line demand curve that has a slope of -2:
   (a) the elasticity of demand coefficient is a constant equal to 2
   (b) the elasticity of demand coefficient always equals 1
   (c) the elasticity of demand coefficient declines as the price is lowered
   (d) the elasticity is largest at the intercept value on the quantity axis

6. If sellers' total revenues are the same before and after a price decrease, then demand is:
   (a) unit elastic
   (b) inelastic
   (c) elastic
   (d) perfectly inelastic

7. Suppose the only beer store in town increased the price of a litre of beer from $2.75 to $3.25. If the number of litres of beer sold decreased by 22 percent, then the elasticity of demand for beer is about:
   (a) .67
   (b) .90
   (c) 1.0
   (d) 1.32

8. Since bacon and eggs are complementary goods, the cross elasticity of demand between them would be:
   (a) greater than 1
   (b) negative
   (c) 1
   (d) vary between -1 and +1

9. A legislature that wants to maximize its revenue from sales taxes would be wise to tax:
   (a) goods that have no substitutes
   (b) goods that have no complements
   (c) inferior goods
   (d) luxury goods

10. An increase in supply will lead to an increase in total expenditure on a good if:
   (a) demand is elastic
   (b) demand is unit elastic
   (c) demand is inelastic
   (d) none of the above

11. If demand is perfectly inelastic, a decrease in supply will result in:
   (a) a decrease in the equilibrium price
   (b) an increase in the equilibrium quantity
   (c) a decrease in equilibrium quantity
   (d) no change in equilibrium quantity

12. A perfectly elastic demand curve is:
   (a) parallel to the quantity axis
   (b) downward sloping with a slope of -1
   (c) parallel to the price axis
   (d) a "long-run" demand curve

13. If the income elasticity of demand for turnips is -0.2, what is the effect of an 8% decrease in incomes?
- (a)   quantity demanded will fall by 1.6%
- (b)   quantity demanded will rise by 1.6%
- (c)   quantity demanded will fall by 4%
- (d)   quantity demanded will rise by 4%

14. Which of the following data would be evidence that CDs are a normal good?
- (a)   price elasticity of demand is 0.3
- (b)   cross price elasticity with cassette players is –0.8
- (c)   income elasticity is 0.2
- (d)   price elasticity of supply is 0.9

15. Which of the following is not characteristic of a good for which the demand is price inelastic?
- (a)   the good has many good substitutes
- (b)   the buyer spends a small percentage of his/her total income on the good
- (c)   the good is regarded by consumers as a necessity
- (d)   the period of time for which demand is given is very short

16. Which of the following lists correctly ranks the products in descending order of price elasticity of demand (i.e., from most elastic to least elastic)?
- (a)   soft drinks, colas, Pepsi
- (b)   colas, soft drinks, Pepsi
- (c)   colas, Pepsi, soft drinks
- (d)   Pepsi, colas, soft drinks

17. Generally in the long run the supply curve:
- (a)   is less elastic than in the short run
- (b)   is more elastic than in the short run
- (c)   has the same elasticity as in the short run
- (d)   is perfectly elastic

18. Suppose the quantity available of a good is fixed. The elasticity of supply would:
- (a)   be fixed at some positive value
- (b)   be fixed at some negative value
- (c)   be zero
- (d)   change along the supply curve from a small value to a large value

19. If supply is perfectly elastic, an increase in demand will result in:
- (a)   an increase in the equilibrium price
- (b)   a decrease in the equilibrium price
- (c)   a decrease in the equilibrium quantity
- (d)   an increase in the equilibrium quantity

20. Which of the following pairs of goods would be most likely to have a positive cross price elasticity of demand?
- (a)   sport sandals and running shoes
- (b)   skis and ski boots
- (c)   tea cups and hard-hats
- (d)   mechanical pencils and lead refills

21. Which of the following pairs of goods would be most likely to have a negative cross price elasticity of demand?
- (a)   tea and coffee
- (b)   fire extinguishers and blue jeans
- (c)   camp stoves and tents
- (d)   steak and hamburger

Questions 22 through 24 refer to the following graph of the market for cabbages.

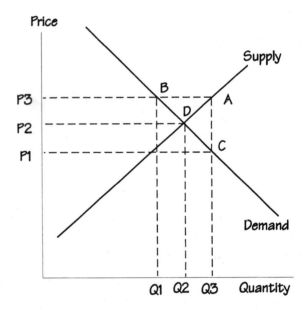

22. If the government announces a price ceiling at P_3, what is the effect?
- (a)   a surplus of AB
- (b)   a shortage of AB
- (c)   a shortage of BD
- (d)   there is no effect on the market

23. If the government sets a price floor of P_3 and enforces this with an "offers to purchase" approach, then the government will be forced to spend:
- (a)   P3 for all units between Q1 and Q2

(b)   P2 for all units between Q1 and Q3
(c)   P3 for all units between Q1 and Q3
(d)   P2 for all units between Q1 and Q2

24. If a price floor of P₃ is imposed and the government uses a "deficiency payments" approach, the government will have to spend an amount shown by the area:
(a)   0P3AQ3
(b)   Q1Q3AB
(c)   P1CAP3
(d)   0Q1BP3

25. Agricultural supply management boards often impose quotas as a strategy to:
(a)   increase the supply of the product
(b)   prevent surpluses from arising when the price is supported
(c)   prevent the price from rising too high for consumers
(d)   none of the above

26. Which of the following statements about the market for health care is true?
(a)   due to asymmetric information, physicians may seek to increase their income by prescribing medical procedures of questionable value
(b)   user fees would have no effect on the amount of health care services demanded
(c)   the American health care system provides service more equitably and efficiently than the Canadian health care system
(d)   people who have health insurance are more likely to exercise regularly

Problems and Projects

1. Price Elasticity and the Market for Skis
Northern Ski puts one brand of skis on sale. By cutting their price 25% they find that their sales of this brand increase by 40%.
(a) What is the price elasticity of demand coefficient, and is the demand for this brand elastic or inelastic?
(b) If Northern Ski put all brands of skis on sale for 25% off, should they expect to sell 40% more skis in total?

2. Interpreting Price Elasticities
For each case below determine whether the demand is elastic, inelastic, or unit elastic.

(a) When the Flin Flon Flyers cut prices by 10%, they sold 20% more tickets to their roller hockey games.
(b) When an airline increased their fares by 5%, their total revenues climbed by 3%.
(c) Momma's Deli finds that no matter whether they charge a little more or a little less for their bagels, their total revenue from bagels remains the same.

3. Price Elasticity and Changes in Total Revenue
Complete the summary table that follows.

If demand Is:	The elasticity coefficient is	If P rises, TR will	If P falls, TR will
Elastic	_____	_____	_____
Inelastic	_____	_____	_____
Unit elastic	_____	_____	_____

4. Total Revenue and Price Elasticity
Fill in the next table by computing total revenue at the each price level, the price elasticity coefficients between these prices, and indicating whether the demand is elastic, inelastic, or unit elasticity between each pair of prices. (Each elasticity coefficient is entered between two prices because it is an "average" over that price interval.)

P	Qd	Total Revenue	Elasticity coefficient	Character of demand
10	300	_____		
			_____	_____
9	400	_____		
			_____	_____
8	500	_____		
			_____	_____
7	600	_____		
			_____	_____
6	700	_____		
			_____	_____
5	800	_____		
			_____	_____
4	900	_____		
			_____	_____
3	1000	_____		

5. Graphing Demand and Total Revenue
This question uses the data in the previous question.

(a) On the first graph, plot the demand curve (price vs. quantity demanded). Using the same horizontal scale, on the second graph plot the total revenue curve (total revenue vs. quantity demanded).

(b) Based on your answers in the previous question, the demand curve is price elastic between the prices _____ and _____. In this range, as quantity increases, the total revenue curve is (increasing, decreasing, flat) _____. The demand curve has unitary elasticity between the prices _____ and _____. In this area the total revenue curve is _____. The demand curve is inelastic between the prices _____ and _____. Here the total revenue curve is _____. These results illustrate that along a straight-line demand curve, price elasticity _____ as price increases, and that total revenue is _____ at the point of unit elasticity.

6. Supply Elasticity

On the following graph are three different supply curves (S1, S2, S3) for a product bought and sold in a competitive market.

(a) Match the supply curves to the period:
    market period S2
    short run   S3
    long run   S1

(b) No matter what the period of time under consideration, if the demand for the product were D1, the equilibrium price of the product would be _____ and the equilibrium quantity would be _____.

(c) If demand increases from D1 to D2: (1) in the market period, the equilibrium price would increase to _____ and the equilibrium quantity would be _____; (2) in the short run, the price of the product would increase to _____ and the quantity would increase to _____; (3) in the long run, the price of the product would be _____ and the quantity would be _____.

(d) The longer the period of time allowed for sellers to adjust their outputs, the (more, less) _____ elastic is the supply of their product.

(e) When demand increases, the more elastic the supply of a product, the (greater, less) _____ is the effect on equilibrium price, and the _____ is the effect on equilibrium quantity.

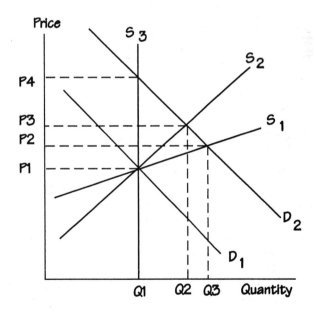

7. Rising Tuition: Effects on Enrolment in the Short Run and the Long Run

Suppose that your college or university sets a target of increasing annual tuition revenue by

4%. To achieve this, they raise the tuition fee per student by 8%. At the end of the first term after the increase, the president of the school reports to the board of governors that the "tuition fee increases have proven to be even more successful than we had hoped — total tuition revenue is up 5% compared to last semester."
(a) Assuming that the ceteris paribus condition holds, is the school's demand elastic or inelastic in the short run?
(b) Why might the elasticity be greater over time?
(c) If the demand is much more elastic in the long run, what is the significance of that?

8. Elasticity and the Incidence of a Tax
The graph below shows a supply curve and two hypothetical demand curves. Note that regardless of whether demand is initially given by D1 or by D2 the equilibrium price and quantity are the same.

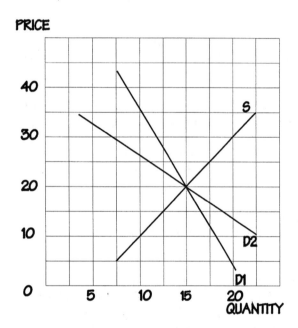

(a) Show the effect of a $10 per unit tax.
(b) If demand was initially D1 the imposition of the tax raises price to _____. The equilibrium quantity falls to _____. The tax burden is a price increase of _____ for consumers, and a price decrease of _____ for producers.
(c) If demand was initially D2 the imposition of the tax raises price to _____. The equilibrium quantity falls to _____. The tax burden is a price increase of _____ for consumers, and a price decrease of _____ for producers.
(d) The difference between the results in (b) and (c) illustrates that, in general, a tax will impose a

greater burden on consumers, and a lesser burden on producers, the more (elastic, inelastic) _____ is the demand curve.

9. Identifying and Interpreting Elasticities
In each case below, identify:
   (1) which good is the central focus,
   (2) which of the four types of elasticity studied in the chapter is relevant,
   (3) whether the speaker expects the elasticity to be negative (-) or positive (+), and
   (4) whether the speaker is hoping for a large (L) or a small (S) elasticity.
(a) "Our company publishes crossword puzzle magazines. We expect that the falling household incomes that we're seeing in this recession will actually help our sales." (1) _____ (2) _____ (3) _____ (4) _____
(b) "We've been having trouble attracting qualified machinists to work at this factory. Now we're going to try offering a higher wage rate." (1) ____ (2) _____ (3) _____ (4) _____
(c) "The frosts in the California orange groves have killed a big portion of their crop. Those of us growing apples in the Okanagan Valley should really benefit." (1) _____ (2) _____ (3) _____ (4) _____
(d) "The city really needs more revenue to fund social programs like the food bank. That's why we need a new tax on hotel rooms." (1) ___ (2) _____ (3) ____ (4) _____

10. Algebra of Price Controls
This problem uses algebra to express demand and supply. Demand is represented by the equation $Qd = 100 - 3P$ and supply by the equation $Qs = 10 + 7P$. Price in $ is expressed by P, and quantity is represented by Q.
(a) Equilibrium is found where quantity demanded equals quantity supplied. Therefore, P* = _____, and Q* = _____.
(b) If government institutes a price floor of $11, Qd = _____, Qs = _____. Therefore, there is a (shortage, surplus) _____ of _____ units. To maintain the floor price government may be required to (buy, sell) _____ a quantity of _____ units.

11. Price Support for Apples
The next graph shows the market for apples.
(a) In the absence of any government intervention the equilibrium price of apples will be $___

per kg, and the equilibrium quantity will be ____ kg/yr.

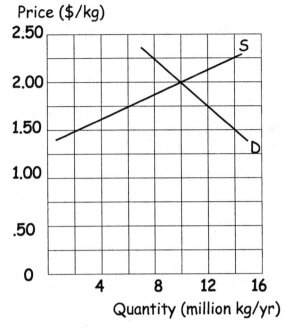

Price ($/kg)

Quantity (million kg/yr)

Now government adopts a price floor of $2.25/kg.
(b) If this price support is implemented by an offers-to-purchase program, consumers will buy _____ kg/yr, apple growers will produce _____ kg/yr, and the government will be required to purchase the (shortage, surplus) _____ of _____ kg/yr at a cost of $____ per year.
(c) If the same level of price support is implemented by a deficiency payment program, growers will produce _____ kg/yr, consumers will buy _____ kg/yr, and the government will be required to pay $____ per kg for _____ kg/yr, for a total cost of $____ per year.
(d) Which of the following groups would prefer one method of price support of the others: consumers, producers, taxpayers?

Discussion Questions

1. Explain the price elasticity of demand concept in terms of: (a) the relative sensitivity of quantity demanded to changes in price; (b) the behaviour of total revenue when price changes; (c) the elasticity coefficient; (d) the relationship between the relative (percentage) change in quantity demanded and the relative (percentage) change in price.

2. What is meant by perfectly elastic demand? And what is meant by perfectly inelastic demand? What does the demand curve look like in each case?

3. In computing your price elasticity of demand for pizzas between two prices, say $10 and $12, it makes a considerable difference whether the higher price or the lower price is used as the initial reference point. (The same is true of quantities.) How do we eliminate the confusion that would arise if the elasticity coefficient varied and depended upon whether a price rise ($10 to $12) or price fall ($12 to $10) were being considered?

4. It is common to see many vacant seats at movie theatres. Presumably this is no surprise to the theatre owners. Why don't theatre owners drop their prices far enough to fill all seats? Give an explanation based on the concept of price elasticity of demand.

5. What is the relationship, if any, between the elasticity of demand and the slope of the demand curve?

6. What factors determine the price elasticity of demand for a product?

7. Of what practical importance is the price elasticity of demand? Cite examples of its importance to business firms, workers, farmers, and governments.

8. Explain what determines the elasticity of supply of a product.

9. Imagine that your annual income increases by 20%. Estimate the percentage by which your demand for the following goods would change: concerts, toothpaste, clothing. Accordingly, what is your income elasticity for each good?

10. Name a few types of businesses whose sales would slump dramatically if a recession were to pull average incomes down. Name a few whose sales would rise under the same circumstances. Which of these businesses sell normal goods, and which sell inferior goods?

11. What are some of the unintended consequences that normally result when a price ceiling is implemented? When a price floor is implemented?

12. Ticket-scalping at NHL hockey games and some rock concerts is quite similar to the consequences of government-set price ceilings. Why does ticket scalping occur, and what are its effects? In your opinion, is it a good thing or a bad thing? How would you defend your opinion?

13. Suppose that a college in financial difficulty has more students applying than they have spaces for, but is prevented by a government policy from raising tuition fees to a market clearing level. Based on the theory of price ceilings, what specific predictions can you make about how the college might respond?

Answers

Quick Quiz
1. (b) pp. 106-107
2. (c) p. 107
3. (a) p. 108
4. (b) p. 110
5. (d) p. 112
6. (b) p. 114
7. (b) p. 115
8. (c) pp. 115-116
9. (c) p. 117
10. (a) p. 118
11. (c) pp. 119-120
12. (d) pp. 121-122
13. (a) p. 124
14. (d) pp. 124-126
15. (d) pp. 127-128
16. (d) p. 127

Fill-in Questions
1. sensitivity, quantity, price
2. 10; 100; 10, 100, 10; 4; 25; 4, 25, 16; 10, 16, 0.63.
3. inelastic, elastic
4. inelastic, vertical; zero; elastic, horizontal; infinity
5. (a) greater than, (b) less than, (c) equal to
6. number of substitutes; proportion of income spent on the good; necessity or luxury; time period under consideration
7. inelastic; no
8. time; market; vertical; short; up-sloping; long, expand, increase; more
9. inelastic; supply, upward, 25, 75.

10. (a) adverse selection; (b) moral hazard; (c) asymmetric information

True-False
1. F   in this case elasticity would be less than
2. T   unlike the slope – which is constant – elasticity is different at different points on the curve
3. T   because price falls by bigger percentage than quantity increases
4. T   (50/125)/(4/12) = 1.20
5. F   a 1% rise in P leads to 3% drop in Qd
6. T   even if P rises a great deal, necessities are still purchased; luxuries may not be
7. F   opposite is true
8. T   a given P increase affects consumer more if for a product that uses up a big share of consumer's income
9. F   more elastic as substituting becomes easier over time
10. F   equilibrium P will rise; equilibrium Q is unchanged
11. T   more time for firms to expand capacity and new firms to enter
12. T   P change for one has no effect on Qd of other
13. T   their demand for bottles is horizontal
14. F   the more is the consumer's tax burden
15. T   because they raise the effective price for producers
16. T
17. F   supply becomes totally inelastic

Multiple-Choice
1. (c)
2. (c)   (100/950)/(0.50/1.75) = .37
3. (b)   2.0 is greater than 1
4. (d)   x% / 5% = 2, therefore x = 10
5. (c)
6. (a)   the effect of P change exactly offsets effect of Qd change, because they are the same percentage
7. (d)   (.50/3.00) x 100% = 16.7%; 22%/16.7% = 1.32
8. (b)   if P of eggs rises, Qd for bacon will fall
9. (a)   there would be little drop in Qd as tax raises P
10. (a)   Qd increases by bigger proportion than P falls
11. (d)   demand is vertical so Qd cannot change
12. (a)   demand is horizontal
13. (b)   8% x –0.2 = -1.6%

14. (c) a normal good has a positive income elasticity
15. (a)
16. (d) Pepsi is most easily substituted
17. (b) as existing firms have time to expand, and new firms have time to enter the industry
18. (c) percentage change in Qs is zero
19. (d) there is no price change
20. (a) substitutes
21. (c) complements
22. (d) the equilibrium price is below the maximum allowed, so the equilibrium price is maintained
23. (c) they must buy up the whole surplus
24. (c)
23. (a) Qs exceeds Qd
25. (b)
26. (a) a case of the principal agent problem

Problems and Projects

1. (a) 40/25 = 1.6, which is elastic (because > 1.0); (b) overall sales of skis will probably increase by less 40% because the demand for all skis as a whole group is less elastic than the demand for a particular brand. It easier to substitute between individual brands than between skis and some other product.
2. (a) elastic, (b) inelastic, (c) unit elastic
3. Elastic: greater than 1, decrease, increase; Inelastic: less than 1, increase, decrease; Unit elastic: equal to 1, remain constant, remain constant
4. Total revenue: 3000, 3600, 4000, 4200, 4200, 4000, 3600, 3000; Elasticity coefficient: 2.71, 1.89, 1.36, 1.00, 0.73, 0.53, 0.37; Character of demand; elastic, elastic, elastic, unit elastic, inelastic, inelastic, inelastic
5. (a) see graph below; (b) 7, 10; increasing; 6, 7; flat; 3, 6; decreasing; increases, maximized
6. (a) market period = S_3; short run = S_2; long run = S_1; (b) P_1, Q_1 (c)(1) P_4, Q_1; (2) P_3, Q_2, (3) P_2, Q_3; (d) more (e) less, greater
7. (a) inelastic; (b) current students may be unlikely to transfer schools or quit school, but in the long run the school will attract less new students; (c) the 5% increase in total tuition revenue may eventually turn into a decrease
8. (a) the supply shifts vertically parallel by $10; (b) $26; 13; $6, $4; c) $24; 12; $4, $6; d) inelastic

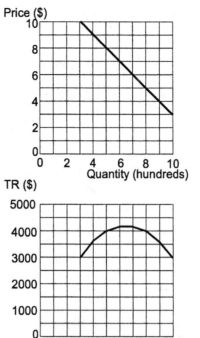

9. (a) crossword puzzle magazines, income elasticity, -, L; (b) machinists, elasticity of supply, +, L; (c) apples, cross price elasticity, +, L; (d) hotel rooms, price elasticity of demand, -, S
10. (a) 9, 73; (b) 67, 87; surplus, 20; buy, 20
11. (a) 2.00, 10 million; (b) 8 million, 14 million, surplus, 6 million, area *ebfg* = 13.5 million; (c) 14 million, 14 million, area *abcd* = 10.5 million. (d) consumers prefer the deficiency payment approach because the price of apples to consumers is lower; producers are equally happy under either approach because the final price they receive is the same; taxpayers prefer deficiency payment plan because it costs less (in this example).

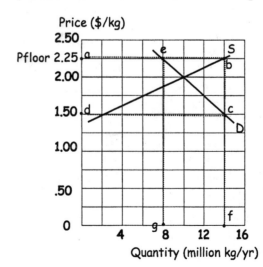

Chapter 6

The Theory of Consumer Choice

Overview

This chapter takes a closer look at how consumers make their spending decisions, and offers two complementary explanations for why consumers behave according to the law of demand.

The first explanation, already touched on in Chapter 3, is based on income and substitution effects. If the price of a product increases, the consumer will buy less because: (1) the consumer now has less real income (or buying power) and (2) the product's opportunity cost has increased in terms of other products the consumer could buy. The second explanation is based on the law of diminishing marginal utility. According to this theory, consumers get less additional utility (or benefit) from each additional unit that they consume of any product. Therefore, the price that the consumer is willing to pay for each additional unit also decreases.

Diminishing marginal utility also provides a theory of how a consumer makes his/her spending decisions in order to maximize his/her utility. This model takes four dimensions of the consumer's situation as given: (1) the consumer is rational, (2) the consumer has clear-cut preferences; (3) the consumer has a budget constraint (or fixed, limited income); and (4) the prices of goods are not affected by the consumer. To maximize total utility, the consumer allocates his/her income between products such that the last dollar spent on each product yields the same marginal utility. The numerical example used to illustrate this principle also shows that each point on a consumer's demand curve for a particular good corresponds to a utility maximizing allocation of the consumer's income.

The consumer choice theory explains many real-world phenomena including: the growth of the market for DVDs, the diamond-water paradox, the value of time in consumption, and the relative efficiency of cash and non-cash gifts.

When consumers receive more value or satisfaction from a purchase than the price they paid, they are said to enjoy a consumer surplus. This measure of net value gain is used in later chapters to compare economic efficiency in different situations.

Chapter Outline

6.1 A Closer Look at the Law of Demand

◇ Why is the demand curve downward sloping?

- o How is this explained using income and substitution effects?
- o How is this explained using concepts of marginal utility?

• Both the income effect and the substitution effect can explain the law of demand.

- o If the price of a good falls, the consumer's income can purchase more. In the case of a normal good, this income effect leads to increased purchases.
- o If the price of a good falls, its relative price (or opportunity cost) measured in other goods falls. This leads the consumer to substitute in favour of buying more of this good.

• The utility of a good or service is the satisfaction that a consumer gets from consuming it.

- o Utility does not imply usefulness.
- o Utility is a subjective notion, because it varies widely from person to person.
- o Utility is difficult to quantify, but we assume that consumers can measure utility in units called "utils."

➲ Utility is a useful abstraction for explaining consumer behaviour. Do not be distracted by the fact that utility is not measurable. It is true that in advanced economics little use is made of this model precisely because of this problem; nevertheless the model is instructive because we can think of consumers making choices "as if" they are applying the utility-maximizing rule, whether or not utility is observable.

• Total utility is the total amount of satisfaction a person receives from consuming a specific number of units of a good. Marginal utility is the extra satisfaction a person receives from consuming one extra unit of a good. Marginal utility is also the change in total utility from consuming one extra unit.

➲ Master the difference between marginal and total utility. Think of consumers as allocating their incomes one dollar at a time; the next dollar always being allocated to the good that produces the highest marginal utility from one more dollar spent.

• The principle that the marginal utility will decline as the consumer gets additional units of a product is known as the law of diminishing marginal utility. For example, the extra utility from consuming the fifth unit of a good is less than the marginal utility from the fourth unit.

• Diminishing marginal utility provides an explanation for the law of demand: consumers will only wish to purchase more units of a good as long as the marginal utility is higher than the price.

• The more sharply a consumer's marginal utility for a good falls as more is consumed, the more inelastic is the consumer's demand for that good.

Quick Quiz

1. The substitution effect encourages a consumer to buy more of a good when its price falls because:

(a) the real income of the consumer has increased

(b) the real income of the consumer has decreased

(c) the product is now relatively less expensive than it was

(d) other products are now relatively less expensive than they were

2. In which case will the income effect created by a price change tend to increase the quantity demanded for a commodity

(a) when the price of a normal good rises

(b) when the price of a normal good falls

(c) when the price of a normal good rises or falls

(d) when the price of an inferior good falls

3. Alison's total utility from going to folk festivals is shown below. She begins to experience diminishing marginal utility after how many festivals?

Festivals	0	1	2	3	4	5	6
Total Utility	0	15	33	43	50	55	54

(a) after the 6th festival

(b) after the 5th festival

(c) after the 3rd festival

(d) after the 2nd

6.2 Theory of Consumer Choice

◇ How does the consumer choose which goods to buy?

• Diminishing marginal utility provides an explanation for consumer choices. This theory relies on four assumptions about the consumer:

o rational behaviour based on attempting to maximize his or her total utility;

o clear-cut preferences between various goods and services;

o budget constraint (a fixed, limited income);

o prices of goods and services are given and fixed.

• The consumer spends his/her income so as to maximize the satisfaction received from consuming the goods. If there are just two goods, A and B, the consumer is maximizing utility when the last dollar spent on either good yields the same amount of extra utility. This is the utility-maximizing rule, and it can also be summarized as (MUA/PA) = (MUB/PB).

➲ Economists do not claim that consumers actually perform such mental gymnastics at the grocery store. However, to the extent that consumers behave "as if" they make such calculations, this model will permit us to make correct predictions about how consumer choices respond to price changes or income changes.

Quick Quiz

4. When Kate is spending all of her income on paint and brushes, she finds that 1 tube of paint costs $10 and produces MU = 20 utils, and that 1 brush costs $12 and produces MU = 30 utils. Kate should:

(a)   buy more paint and more brushes because the MU of each is positive
(b)   buy more brushes and fewer tubes of paint since MU/P is higher for brushes
(c)   buy more paint and fewer brushes because paint is less expensive
(d)   buy fewer brushes and fewer tubes of paint.

5. Niels spends his income on guitar strings and plaid shirts. A rise in the price of plaid shirts will cause Niels to alter his consumption of strings and shirts so that the MU of the last package of strings purchased is:
(a)   increased
(b)   decreased
(c)   unchanged
(d)   equal to the MU of the last shirt purchased

6.3 Utility Maximization and the Demand Curve

◇ How is the demand curve derived using the utility-maximizing rule?

•   Suppose the consumer is presently consuming amounts of A and B such that the utility-maximizing rule is met. Then let the price of A falls while income, tastes, and the price of B remain constant. At the initial amounts of A and B the utility-maximizing rule is no longer met. The consumer will purchase more of A until the utility-maximizing condition is again fulfilled.

•   This yields two different prices of A and the two different utility-maximizing quantities of A the consumer will purchase, given that the price of B, income, and preferences are all fixed. Thus, two points on the demand curve for A have been found. Other points can be derived by taking other prices for A and finding new utility-maximizing quantities of A and B.

Quick Quiz
6. Which is a true statement about a demand curve?
(a)   all points on the demand curve represent the same amount of total utility for the consumer
(b)   all points on the demand curve represent the same amount of marginal utility for the consumer
(c)   at all points on the demand curve the utility-maximizing rule is met

(d)   both (b) and (c) are true

6.4 Applications and Extensions

◇ How can marginal utility theory be applied to real-world situations?

•   DVDs and DVD players are dominating the market for movies because with their high quality and low prices, they offer a higher marginal-utility-to-price ratio than video cassettes and VCRs they are replacing.

•   Diamonds are expensive, but of limited usefulness, while water is inexpensive, but essential for life. This paradox is resolved by explaining the distinction between marginal and total utility. Water is so abundant that its price is very low, so we consume it up to the point that its marginal utility becomes nearly zero. Diamonds are so rare that they are very expensive, and so their marginal utility is still very high at our utility-maximizing consumption level of diamonds.

•   Marginal utility theory recognizes the fact that consumption takes time, and time is a scarce resource. The full price of any consumer good or service is its market price plus the value of the time taken to consume it (i.e., the income that the consumer could have earned had that time been used for work).

•   For recipients, non-cash gifts are less efficient than cash gifts. A cash gift allows the recipient to choose whatever goods he or she prefers, whereas with a non-cash gift there is no choice.

Quick Quiz
7. The price of water is far below the price of diamonds because:
(a)   the MU of a diamond is far below the MU of a jug of water
(b)   the MU of a diamond is far above the MU of a jug of water
(c)   the total utility of diamonds is far above the total utility of water
(d)   the total utility of water is far above the total utility of diamonds

8. Eddie can get to work at his law office in downtown Toronto by taking a cab ride for $50, or a bus ride for $2. The bus ride takes half an hour longer. The full price of the trip is the same by both modes of transportation if Eddie earns how much per hour?
(a) $48

(b) $96
(c) $25
(d)   the full price of the cab is higher no matter what

9. If you want to spend $50 on a gift for a classmate, and maximize the economic efficiency of the gift in the sense discussed in the text, which would likely be the worst choice?
(a) $50 in cash
(b) $50 gift certificate for the grocery store where your friend regularly shops
(c) $50 voucher redeemable at your school's bookstore
(d)   a non-returnable item of clothing costing $50

6.5 Consumer Surplus

◈ What is consumer surplus and how is it measured?

•   The difference between the maximum a consumer is willing to pay for a good and its actual market price is consumer surplus.

•   Diminishing marginal utility implies diminishing willingness to pay for additional units. Therefore the consumer enjoys more consumer surplus on the first units and ceases to buy more units at the point where the last unit purchased yields no additional consumer surplus.

•   Consumer surplus is represented graphically as the area underneath the demand curve and above the market price.

➲ Consumer surplus can be a puzzling concept because in real life we rarely stop to determine the amount we are "willing to pay." Next time you are on a desperate run to the convenience store for some item you might ask yourself, what would be the highest hypothetical price at which you'd be willing to buy that item in that situation.

Quick Quiz

10. Pat goes to an auction intending to pay up to $300 (but not a single dollar more!) for a nice table that she looked at in the display window of the auction house. If she makes a winning bid of $195, then her consumer surplus is:
(a) $495
(b) $195
(c) $105
(d)   more than $105

11. If Svend buys 6 pairs of socks at $5 a pair, the amount of consumer surplus he will get on the 6th pair, as compared to the consumer surplus on the 5th pair, is:
(a)   higher because it is better to have more socks
(b)   lower because the MU of the 6th is lower than the MU of the 5th pair
(c)   higher because he might get a discount by buying more
(d)   the same because the price per pair is constant at $5

Terms and Concepts

income effect
substitution effect
total utility
marginal utility
law of diminishing
marginal utility

rational behaviour
budget constraint
utility-maximizing rule
consumer surplus

Fill-In Questions

1. The law of demand (which states that demand curves are downward sloping) can be explained in terms of the _____ and _____ effects.

2. A fall in the price of a product tends to (increase, decrease) _____ the purchasing power of a consumer. This causes the _____ effect. A fall in price makes the product (more, less) _____ expensive relative to other goods. This causes the _____ effect.

3. The extra satisfaction obtained from consuming one more unit of a good is called (marginal, total) _____ utility. The satisfaction obtained from some number of units of a product is called _____ utility. One can calculate _____ utility by summing the _____ figures.

4. The marginal utility theory of consumer behaviour assumes that:
(a)   the consumer is _____
(b)   the consumer has clear-cut _____ for various goods.
(c)   the consumer has a limited and fixed _____.

(d)   the consumer faces fixed _____ for various goods.

5. It is the (marginal, total) _____ utility and not _____ utility that is relevant to the price people are willing to pay for a good. This point explains the _____ paradox.

True-False

Circle T if the statement is true, F if it is false.

1. Utility is a measure of the satisfaction received from the consumption of goods and services.   **T F**

2. Marginal utility is the extra utility derived from consuming an extra unit of a good or service.   **T F**

3. Decreasing marginal utility means that total utility falls when another unit of the good is consumed.   **T F**

4. When a consumer is maximizing total utility, the marginal utilities of the last unit of every product bought are identical.   **T F**

5. When utility is maximized, the consumer allocates money income so that the last dollar spent on each product purchased yields the same amount of extra utility.   **T F**

6. If a good were offered free, consumption would be extended to the point where the marginal utility of the last unit equals zero.   **T F**

7. The price of water is low because the marginal utility received from water is low.   **T F**

8. High labour productivity gives time a high market value.   **T F**

9. The rise of the "fast food" industry is partly due to the increased value of time.   **T F**

10. One reason for the growth in demand for DVDs has been the reduction in price of DVD players that are complements to DVDs.   **T F**

11. For a high-priced criminal lawyer, home-grown vegetables might have a higher full price than vegetables purchased in the most expensive market in Toronto.   **T F**

12. If Kristi's grandmother gives her $20 instead of giving her a scarf that cost $30, Kristi and her grandmother might both be better off.   **T F**

Multiple-Choice

Circle the letter that corresponds to the best answer.

1. Which of the following best expresses the law of diminishing marginal utility?
(a)   the more a person consumes of a product, the smaller becomes the utility received from its consumption
(b)   the more a person consumes of a product, the smaller becomes the extra utility received as a result of consuming an additional unit
(c)   the less a person consumes of a product, the smaller becomes the utility received from its consumption
(d)   the less a person consumes of a product, the smaller becomes the extra utility received as a result of consuming an additional unit of the product

2. The substitution effect deals with the change in consumption of a good due to:
(a)   the change in the consumer's preferences
(b)   the change in the consumer's actual money income
(c)   the change in the real buying power of the consumer's money income
(d)   the change in the price of the good relative to others

3. Sabina Azula buys only two goods: food and clothing. Both are normal goods for Sabina. If the price of food decreases, Sabina's consumption of clothing will:
(a)   increase due to the income effect
(b)   increase due to the substitution effect
(c)   decrease due to the substitution effect
(d)   both (a) and (c)

The next two questions use the table below showing total utility data for a consumer of chocolate bars.

Chocolate bars consumed	Total utility
0	0
1	9
2	19
3	27
4	35
5	42
6	42
7	40

4. This consumer begins experiencing diminishing marginal utility after he consumes the:
(a)   first chocolate bar
(b)   second chocolate bar
(c)   sixth chocolate bar
(d)   seventh chocolate bar

5. If this consumer can eat chocolate bars free of charge, how many will he eat?
(a)   six or seven
(b)   five or six
(c)   two
(d)   as many as possible

6. An individual consumes two products, A and B, with prices P_A, P_B. Utility is maximized when, if all income is spent, the following condition is met:
(a)   MUA = MUB
(b)   MUA<MUB
(c)   MUA/PA = MUB/PB
(d)   MUA/PB = MUB/PA

7. Suppose the price of A is $3, and the price of B is $2; that Diego is spending his entire income and buying 4 units of A and 6 units of B; and the marginal utility of both the 4th unit of A and the 6th unit of B is 6. It can be concluded that:
(a)   Diego is maximizing utility and should not adjust his purchases
(b)   Diego should buy more of A and less of B
(c)   Diego should buy less of A and more of B
(d)   Diego should buy less of both A and B

8. Suppose that the price of A is $3 and the price of B is $6 and the consumer is maximizing utility. If MU_A = 7 at this point, it can be concluded that:
(a)   the utility received from good A must equal the utility received from good B

(b)   the consumer must be purchasing an equal number of units of good A and good B
(c)   the two goods are substitutes
(d) MU_B = 14

9. A decrease in the price of good X, other things remaining the same, will:
(a)   decrease the marginal utility for the last unit of X that will be purchased
(b)   increase the total utility from purchases of X
(c)   have no effect on total utility from purchases of X
(d)   both (a) and (b)

Answer the next three questions on the basis of the following table. The price of good A is $4 and the price of good B is $5, and income is $35. Suppose the utility received from good A is independent of the number of units of good B consumed. Total utility from consumption is obtained by adding the utility from A to the utility from B.

Units of A	Total Utility	MU of A	Units of B	Total Utility	MU of B
1	32	32	1	20	20
2	60	28	2	35	15
3	72	12	3	40	5
4	80	8	4	43	3
5	84	4	5	45	2
6	86	2	6	46	1

10. How many units of A and B will be purchased?
(a)   5 of A and 3 of B
(b)   5 of A and 4 of B
(c)   5 of A and 5 of B
(d)   4 of A and 4 of B

11. What is the total utility for the consumer when the utility-maximizing combination of A and B is purchased?
(a)   120
(b)   124
(c)   126
(d)   118

12. If the consumer's income were reduced to $22, the consumer would maximize satisfaction by consuming:
(a)   2 of A and 2 of B
(b)   3 of A and 3 of B

(c)   2 of A and 3 of B
(d)   3 of A and 2 of B

13. Other things being equal, demand is likely to be inelastic if the marginal utility of the product:
(a)   decreases rapidly as additional units are consumed
(b)   decreases slowly as additional units are consumed
(c)   increases rapidly as additional units are consumed
(d)   increases slowly as additional units are consumed

14. The full price of a product to a consumer is:
(a)   its market price
(b)   its market price plus the value of its consumption time
(c)   its market price less the value of its consumption time
(d)   the value of its consumption time less its market price

15. If the opportunity cost of the time spent in consumption is added to the market price of a good when making a purchase decision, we can expect:
(a)   the same combination of goods will be purchased as when time is ignored
(b)   more of the time-intensive good will be purchased
(c)   the consumer's demand curve for the good to be upward sloping
(d)   none of the above

16. Compared to cash gifts, non-cash gifs are:
(a)   of greater total utility but of less marginal utility
(b)   of less total utility but of greater marginal utility
(c)   more efficient because they do not waste resources
(d)   less efficient because they do not generally match recipients' preferences

17. Gene is willing to pay $10 to go to one movie, $8 to go to second movie, and $6 to go to a third movie. If the price of movies is $7, how many movies will Gene choose to see, and how much consumer surplus will he enjoy in total?
(a)   2 movies and $4
(b)   3 movies and $3
(c)   2 movies and $2

(d)   3 movies and $2

18. If the market price of a product falls, what are the consequences for consumers?
(a)   they buy more units and they obtain more consumer surplus
(b)   they buy fewer units and they obtain more consumer surplus
(c)   they buy more units and they obtain less consumer surplus
(d)   they buy fewer units and they obtain more consumer surplus

Use this graph for the two questions that follow.

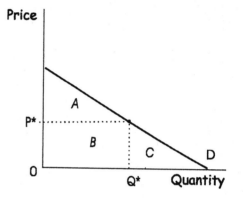

19. Given the demand curve in the graph, if the market price is P*, the total amount the consumer is willing to pay for Q* units is area:
(a)   A
(b)   B
(c)   A + B
(d)   A + B + C

20. Given the demand curve in the graph, if the market price is P*, the total amount of consumer surplus received is area:
(a)   A
(b)   B
(c)   A + B
(d)   A + B + C

Problems and Projects

1.   Utility Maximization Rule
Suppose that a consumer's utility levels from consuming goods A, B, and C are given in the table that follows. The utility of the consumer is calculated by adding together the utility obtained from each good. "U" denotes total utility and "MU" denotes marginal utility. Assume the consumer's

income equals $17 and the three goods' prices are given by Pa = $1, Pb = $2, and Pc = $4.

Good A				Good B				Good C			
Qa	Ua	MUa	MUa/ Pa	Qb	Ub	MUb	MUb/ Pb	Qc	Uc	MUc	MUc/ Pc
1	6	6	___	1	36	___	___	1	22	___	___
2	11	5	___	2	64	___	___	2	38	___	___
3	15	___	___	3	72	___	___	3	50	___	___
4	18	___	___	4	76	___	___	4	54	___	___
5	20	___	___	5	79	___	___	5	56	___	___

(a) Fill in the blanks for the marginal utility and marginal utility per dollar spent.

(b) Consider the first unit purchased. The individual would choose good B because the marginal utility per dollar spent for the first unit of good B is _____ as compared to _____ for good A and _____ for good C.

(c) After the consumer has purchased that first unit, the consumer now has $_____ left to spend.

(d) For the next purchase the consumer would take good _____ since the marginal utility per dollar spent on that unit of good _____ is _____ as compared to _____ for good _____ and _____ for good _____.

(e) After the second purchase, the consumer now has $_____ left to spend.

(f) The third item purchased would be good _____ and the marginal utility per dollar spent to get that unit is _____.

(g) To maximize utility the consumer will buy _____ units of good A, _____ units of B, and _____ units of C. Total utility will be _____.

(h) The marginal utility of the last dollar spent on each good will be _____.

(i) The consumer could have purchased 2 units of C, 2 units of B, and 5 units of A, but did not. Why? _____

2. Utility and Demand Curves

Ms. Thompson's weekly budget is $36. The only two goods she wants to purchase are D and E. The marginal utility schedules for these two goods are shown in the next table. The price of E is fixed at $4. The marginal utility per dollar from good E at this price is also shown in the table. For good D you are given the marginal utility per dollar spent on D when the price of D is $6, $4, $3, and $2.

Complete the demand schedule in the table that follows to show how much of good D Ms. Thomp-

son will buy each week at each of these four possible prices of D.

	Good D					Good E	
Q	MU	MU/$6	MU/$4	MU/$3	MU/$2	MU	MU/$4
1	45	7.5	11.25	15	22.5	40	10
2	30	5	7.5	10	15	36	9
3	20	3.33	5	6.67	10	32	8
4	15	2.5	3.75	5	7.5	28	7
5	12	2	3	4	6	24	6
6	10	1.67	2.5	3.33	5	20	5
7	9	1.5	2.25	3	4.5	16	4
8	7.5	1.25	1.88	2.5	3.75	12	3

Price of D	Quantity of D demanded
$6	_____
$4	_____
$3	_____
$2	_____

3. The Full Price of Consuming Time-Intensive Goods

Assume that the only two goods a consumer can purchase are R (recreation) and M (material goods). The market price of R is $2 and the market price of M is $1. The consumer spends all her income in such a way that the marginal utility of the last unit of R bought is 12 and the marginal utility of the last unit of M bought is 6.

(a) If we ignore the time it takes to consume R and M, is the consumer maximizing the total utility she gets from R and M? _____

(b) Suppose that it takes 4 hours to consume each unit of R and 1 hour to consume each unit of M; and the consumer can earn $2 an hour by working.

1) The full price per unit of R is $_____.
2) The full price per unit of M is $_____.

(c) If we can take into account the full price of each of the commodities, is the consumer maximizing total utility? _____
How do you know this? _____

(d) If the consumer is not maximizing utility, should she consume more of R or of M? _____
Why should she do this? _____
Will she then use more or less time on R? _____

4. Consumer Surplus and a Community Swimming Pool

The town of Summerland is considering building a swimming pool for public use. Their economist estimates that the demand curve for swimming is as shown in the graph.

(a) If the town charges $2.00 to swim, the amount of consumer surplus to swimmers is $_____ per year. [Hint: the area of a triangle is computed as ½ x base x height]

(b) If the town allows people to swim free of charge all of the benefit they receive will be in consumer surplus. This would amount to $_____ per year.

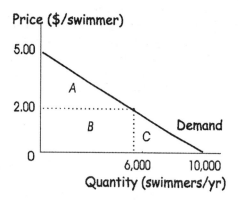

Discussion Questions

1. Is it possible to compare the marginal utility received by John and Joe when each consumes a third lobster? How does the subjective nature of utility limit the practical usefulness of the marginal utility theory of consumer behaviour?

2. "The marginal utility of money is diminishing. Therefore society's total utility will be increased by taking money from the rich and giving it to the poor." What is wrong with this argument?

3. What essential assumptions are made about consumers in developing the marginal utility theory of consumer behaviour? What is meant by the "budget constraint"?

4. Mr. Ritz says, "I don't clip cents-off coupons out of the paper — it's not worth it to me." Mr. Brown, who reads the same newspaper, shops at the same store, and buys the same goods, says "I save lots of money by using the coupons from the paper." What concept discussed in this chapter might explain the difference in their behaviours?

5. Suppose you take two hours off work to see the dentist. The dentist charges you $360. What is your full price for this dental service?

6. My doctor always schedules patients 15 minutes apart, even though he knows that it takes more than 15 minutes of his time for most patients. The result is a crowded waiting room and long delays. Why doesn't the doctor schedule patients 20 or 30 minutes apart?

7. If you won a charity golf tournament and could choose between a $1000 cash prize and a new set of golf clubs with a retail value of $1000, which would you prefer? Why? What concept from the chapter is relevant?

8. The Gap advertises a leather jacket for $349. You love the jacket, and after thinking long and hard about whether or not to buy it, the decision comes down to a coin-flip which determines you should buy the jacket. When you arrive at the store you find the sales clerk changing the price tag to "final markdown - $299." What was the maximum you were willing to pay for the coat, and how much consumer surplus do you get by buying this coat?

Answers

Quick Quiz
1. (c) p. 135
2. (b) p. 135
3. (d) pp. 135-136
4. (b) pp. 139-140
5. (b) pp. 140-141
6. (c) pp. 143-144
7. (b) pp. 145-146
8. (b) p. 146
9. (d) pp. 146-147
10. (c) p. 147
11. (b) p. 147

Fill-in Questions
1. income, substitution
2. increase; income; less; substitution
3. marginal; total; total; marginal
4. (a) rational; (b) preferences (tastes); (c) income; (d) prices
5. marginal, total; diamond-water

True-False
1. T
2. T
3. F   total utility may still be rising, but at a decreasing rate
4. F   MU/P is equal for all goods, but not MU

5. T   in other words, MU/P is equal for all goods

6. T

7. T

8. T   high productivity leads to high hourly wage rates

9. T   to avoid the opportunity cost of time for food preparation, people are willing to pay to have food prepared for them

10. T

11. T   full price includes the monetary value of time which may be several hundred dollars per hour

12. T   if Kristi values the scarf less than $20 in cash

Multiple-Choice

1. (b)

2. (d)

3. (d) the lower price for food raises her real income, so she consumes more clothing due to the income effect; and the higher relative price for clothing causes a substitution effect that reduces her clothing purchases

4. (b) MU is 9, 10, 8, 8, 7, 0, -2

5. (b) MU of the sixth = 0, and MU of the seventh = -2

6. (c)

7. (c) MUA/PA =2, MUB/PB = 3, so buy more B as it is creating more utility per dollar spent at the margin

8. (d) MUB/PB must equal MUA/PA

9. (d) both statements because more X is bought

10. (a) for each purchase choose the good with higher MU/P until $35 is fully spent

11. (b) 84 + 40

12. (d) repeat decision process until $22 is spent

13. (a) when MU drops off sharply, it takes large price cuts to induce more consumption

14. (b)

15. (d) the law of demand still holds, but consumption patterns would be different

16. (d) if given cash, the recipient might spend the price of the gift on something different that would provide more utility

17. (a) (10-7)+(8-7)

18. (a)

19. (c) the area under the demand curve for quantity Q*

20. (a) the value received for quantity Q* in excess of the price paid

Problems and Projects

1. (a) Blank values, from top to bottom: MUA: 4, 3, 2; (MUA/PA): 6, 5, 4, 3, 2; MUB: 36, 28, 8, 4, 3; (MUB/PB): 18, 14, 4, 2, 1.5; MUC: 22, 16, 12, 4, 2; (MUC /PC): 5.5, 4, 3, 1, 0.5; (b) 18, 6, 5.5; (c) $15; (d) B, B, 14, 6, A, 5.5, C; (e) $13; (f) A; 6 (g) 3, 3, 2; 125 (h) 4 (i) utility would equal 122, which is less than the 125 that can be obtained; or, MU/P would not be equal for all three goods

2. 2, 3, 4, 6

3. (a) yes, because MUr/Pr = MUm/Pm; (b) (1)$10, (2)$3; (c) No; The marginal utility to price ratio is not the same for the two goods: 12/$10 < 6/$3; (d) M; because its MU/P ratio is greater; less

4. (a) Area A =(0.5)(5-2)(6,000) = $9,000/yr; (b) Areas A +B+C =(0.5)(5)(10,000) = $25,000/yr

Appendix to Chapter 6 — Indifference Curve Analysis

Overview

This appendix outlines a more advanced approach to the theory of consumer choice. The model uses the concepts of budget lines (representing what the consumer can buy) and indifference curves (representing what the consumer would prefer to buy).

A consumer's ability to buy goods A and B is limited by his or her fixed income, and by the prices of A and B. These "objective" variables define the budget line, or set of all attainable combinations of goods A and B.

Information about the consumer's subjective preferences for A and B is shown by indifference curves. Each indifference curve shows all combinations of A and B yielding one particular level of total utility for the consumer. A complete set of such curves – known as the indifference map – gives a full picture of how the consumer ranks all possible combinations of A and B. Unlike the marginal utility theory, for this approach it is not necessary to be able to quantify how many "utils" of satisfaction the consumer gets from A or B.

By overlaying the consumer's indifference map on the budget line, we find the equilibrium point where the budget line is tangent to the highest attainable indifference curve. At this tangency the slope of the budget line (which is the opportunity cost of A in terms of B) equals the marginal rate of substitution (which is the rate at which the consumer is willing to trade A for B while maintaining the same utility). If the price of a good changes, the budget line shifts, and a new equilibrium is found on a different indifference curve. A demand curve, say for A, can be derived by finding a series of such tangency points as the price of A is varied.

Appendix Outline

◇ How can consumer choices be explained using budget lines and indifference curves?

• A budget line graphs the different combinations of two goods that a consumer can purchase at given prices, with a given money income. Because all the income is spent, the consumer can only buy more of one good by giving up some of the other. Therefore the budget line is negatively sloped.

o An increase (decrease) in money income will cause a parallel shift of the budget line to the right (left).

o A change in one of the prices will change the slope of the budget line. The intercept will increase (decrease) on the axis showing the good whose price has decreased (increased). The intercept will remain unchanged for the good whose price has not changed.

o If the two goods are X and Y, with X on the horizontal axis and Y on the vertical axis, the absolute value of the slope of the budget line is written as P_X/P_Y.

• An indifference curve graphs the various combinations of two goods that give the consumer the same total utility.

o An indifference curve is downward sloping: since both goods generate utility, if utility is to remain constant when the quantity of one good increases, the quantity of the other good must decrease.

o We assume indifference curves are convex to the origin: the more a consumer has of one good, the smaller is the quantity of the second good that he or she is willing to give up to obtain an additional unit of the first good.

o The consumer has an indifference curve for every level of total utility; indifference curves farther to the right on the graph show higher levels of total utility.

o The slope of the indifference curve measures the marginal rate of substitution, which is the rate at which the consumer is willing to substitute one good for the other while maintaining a constant utility level.

➲ Because each consumer has different preferences, one consumer's indifference curve map looks somewhat different from another consumer's. Nevertheless, their maps will share the common properties discussed in this appendix.

• At the point of maximum satisfaction the budget line is tangent to an indifference curve.
  o This condition also implies that the relative price ratio between the two goods is equal to the consumer's marginal rate of substitution between the two goods.
  o This condition is identical to the utility-maximizing rule in the marginal utility approach.

➲ When a consumer moves from one indifference curve to another, this indicates a change in the level of utility achieved, *not* a change in preferences. If the consumer's preferences change, all indifference curves in the consumer's map would change shape or position.

• The budget line and indifference curve approach to explaining consumer choices depends on weaker assumptions than does the marginal utility approach presented in Chapter 6. The approach presented here depends on the consumer being able to rank and choose between combinations of goods. Unlike the marginal utility approach, it does not depend on measurable utility whereby one can tell by *how much* one combination is preferred over another.
• To find a demand curve for good X, vary the price of X and note the different quantities of X at which the new budget lines are tangent to an indifference curve.

Quick Quiz
1. Sheila spends her $300 monthly budget on books costing $50 each and coffees costing $2 each. What are the intercepts of her budget line?
  (a) 6 books and 150 coffees
  (b) 4 books and 50 coffees
  (c) 2 books and 100 coffees
  (d) 5 books and 25 coffees

2. Suppose that a consumer has an income of $8, the price of R is $1, and the price of S is $0.50. Which combination is on the consumer's budget line?
  (a) 8R and 1S
  (b) 7R and 1S

  (c) 6R and 6S
  (d) 5R and 6S

The following two questions are based on these budget line diagrams. Each one shows a change in one of the parameters that determine the location of the budget line.

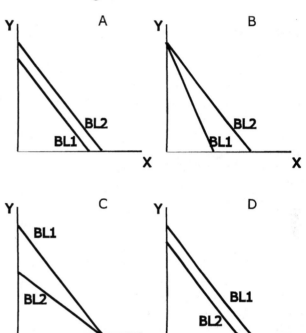

3. Which diagram shows a decrease in money income?
  (a) A
  (b) B
  (c) C
  (d) D

4. Which diagram shows a decrease in the price of good X?
  (a) A
  (b) B
  (c) C
  (d) D

5. A student has 6 pens and 3 binders. This combination could be on the same indifference curve as which of the following combinations?
  (a) 7 pens and 5 binders
  (b) 3 pens and 6 binders
  (c) 9 pens and 2 binders
  (d) both (b) and (c)

6. The consumer's optimum between consumption of goods X and Y is found where:

(a)   equal amounts of X and Y are purchased
(b)   the budget line and indifference curve intersect
(c)   the relative price ratio between X and Y equals the consumer's MRTS
(d)   none of the above

Terms and Concepts

budget line
indifference curve
marginal rate of substitution (MRS)

indifference map
equilibrium position

Fill-In Questions

1. A budget line shows all combinations of two products that can be purchased with a given _____, holding constant the _____ of the two goods.

2. When the quantities of X are measured on the horizontal axis, and the quantities of Y on the vertical, the budget line has a slope equal to the ratio of the _____ to the _____.

3. If the quantity of X is measured horizontally and the quantity of Y is measured vertically, an increase in the price of X will fan the budget line (inward, outward) _____ around a fixed point on the _____ axis. The budget line becomes (steeper, flatter) _____.

4. An indifference curve slopes (downward, upward) _____; and the slope of an indifference curve measures the marginal _____ of _____. The indifference curve is (concave, convex) _____ to the origin.

5. At the consumer's utility maximizing combination of goods, the budget line is _____ to the indifference curve. At this point, the _____ of the budget line and the _____ of the indifference curve are _____.

6. The marginal utility approach to consumer behaviour requires that we assume utility (is, is not) _____ numerically measurable. The indifference curve approach (does, does not) _____ require that assumption.

True-False

Circle T if the statement is true, F if it is false.

1. The slope of the budget line when good X is on the horizontal and Y is on the vertical is: (price of Y/price of X).   **T F**

2. If good Y is on the vertical axis and good X on the horizontal, an increase in the price of Y, *ceteris paribus*, makes the budget line steeper. **T F**

3. An indifference curve gives the various combinations of two goods that give the consumer the same level of total utility.   **T F**

4. Indifference curves slope downward because in order to keep utility constant, increases in the consumption of one good must be offset by decreases in the consumption of the second good.
T F

5. The following combinations of goods X and Y could not lie on the same indifference curve: (3X and 5Y) and (6X and 7Y).   **T F**

6. An indifference curve exists only for those combinations of goods the consumer can afford.
T F

7. A change in tastes can change the slope of an indifference curve.   **T F**

8. If a number of indifference curves are placed on the same graph, the resulting figure is called an indifference map.   **T F**

9. To find a demand curve, change the consumer's income and note the combinations of goods where the budget line and indifference curves are tangent.   **T F**

10. If the price of cheese is $4 and the price of steak is $8, at Philly's equilibrium his marginal rate of substitution is 2 cheese per 1 steak. **T F**

Multiple-Choice

Circle the letter that corresponds to the best answer.

1. Along a consumer's budget line:
  (a)   utility is constant
  (b)   income is constant
  (c)   prices of the two goods are changing
  (d)   marginal rate of substitution is constant

2. A decrease in income will:
  (a)   shift the budget line inward and increase its slope
  (b)   shift the budget line outward and increase its slope
  (c)   shift the budget line outward and have no effect on its slope
  (d)   shift the budget line inward and have no effect on its slope

3. If good Y is on the vertical axis and good X is on the horizontal axis, a lower price for X will, *ceteris paribus*:
  (a)   rotate the budget line outward, leaving fixed the Y axis intercept
  (b)   rotate the budget line inward, leaving fixed the X axis intercept
  (c)   shift the budget line outward in a parallel fashion
  (d)   shift the budget line inward in a parallel fashion

4. If the consumer's income is $200, the prices are $10 for good X and $20 for good Y, the budget line can be found by joining the intercept terms, which are:
  (a)   10 on the X axis and 5 on the Y axis
  (b)   20 on the X axis and 10 on the Y axis
  (c)   20 on the X axis and 20 on the Y axis
  (d)   10 on the X axis and 20 on the Y axis

5. When the income of the consumer is $20, the price of T is $5, the price of Z is $2, and the quantity of T is measured horizontally, the slope of the budget line is:
  (a)   2/5
  (b)   2.5
  (c)   4.0
  (d)   0.4

6. An indifference curve shows the different combinations of two goods that:

  (a)   give the consumer equal marginal utilities
  (b)   cost the same
  (c)   give a consumer equal total utility
  (d)   can be purchased with a given income

7. The amount of one good the consumer is willing to give up to get an additional unit of another good is called:
  (a)   slope of the budget line
  (b)   the income constraint
  (c)   marginal rate of substitution
  (d)   relative price ratio

Use the next diagram to answer the next four questions.

8. Which combination is currently unattainable for this consumer?
  (a)   A
  (b)   B
  (c)   C
  (d)   D

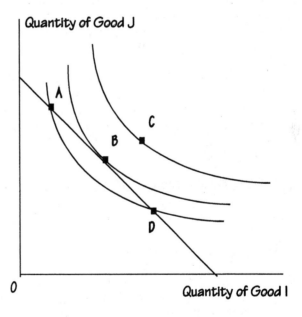

9. For this consumer it can be said that:
  (a)   combination A is preferred to combination D
  (b)   combination A is preferred to combination C
  (c)   combination B is preferred to combination C
  (d)   combination B is preferred to combination A

10. Given the preferences and budget line depicted, the consumer will purchase combination:
(a) A
(b) B
(c) C
(d) D

11. Which of the following may allow the consumer to purchase combination *C*?
(a) a decrease in income
(b) an increase in the price of good I
(c) an increase in the price of good J
(d) a decrease in the price of good I

12. To derive the demand for good I, the price of I is varied. Held constant is:
(a) money income of the consumer
(b) price of good J
(c) consumer's tastes
(d) all of the above

13. The fact that the marginal rate of substitution diminishes along an indifference curve is reflected in:
(a) the convexity of the indifference curve
(b) the negative slope of the indifference curve
(c) the fact that many indifference curves exist
(d) the negative slope of the budget line

Use the next diagram to answer the next two questions.

14. If the budget line shifts from BL1 to BL2, it could be because:

(a) the price of K has increased
(b) the price of K has decreased
(c) the price of L has increased
(d) the price of L has decreased

15. The diagram shows that when the budget line shifts from BL1 to BL2, this consumer will:
(a) buy more of both K and L
(b) buy less of K and more of L
(c) buy less of both K and L
(d) buy more of K and less of L

16. Mike loves his car, and spends all his income on gas and car washes. At his equilibrium, Mike's marginal rate of substitution is 6 car washes per tank of gas. If it costs him $7 to wash his car, what does a tank of gas cost him?
(a) $42
(b) $36
(c) $35
(d) we don't have enough data to know

17. Jamila is consuming at a point on her budget line where her marginal rate of substitution is 3 apples per 1 cappuccino. The market prices are $0.50 for apples, and $2 for cappuccino. Therefore:
(a) Jamila is in a utility-maximizing equilibrium
(b) Jamila can increase utility by purchasing more apples and fewer cappuccinos
(c) Jamila can increase utility by purchasing fewer apples and more cappuccinos
(d) Jamila can increase utility by purchasing more apples and more cappuccinos

18. If at his current consumption levels Kris's marginal utility from hats is 50 utils per hat, and his marginal utility from CDs is 10 utils per CD, then his marginal rate of substitution is:
(a) 5 hats per CD
(b) 40 hats per CD
(c) 5 CDs per hat
(d) 1/5 CD per hat

Problems and Projects

1. Consumer's Budget Line
Michelle spends all of her income of $200 on gasoline (G) and sandwiches (S). The prices per unit are: PG = $0.50 and PS = $2.

(a) The maximum amount of gasoline that Michelle can consume is _____.
(b) The maximum number of sandwiches that Michelle can consume is _____.
(c) Therefore the intercepts of Michelle's budget line are _____ G and _____ S.
(d) Graph Michelle's budget line on the following graph, showing G on the vertical axis and S on the horizontal.
(e) Michelle (can, cannot) _____ afford to buy a combination of 200 G and 60 S because this combination of goods is located (outside, inside, on) _____ her budget line.
(f) The slope of this budget line is _____.
(g) The opportunity cost of one sandwich is ___ gasoline.
(h) If Michelle's income drops to $160, the new intercepts of her budget line are _____ G and _____ S.

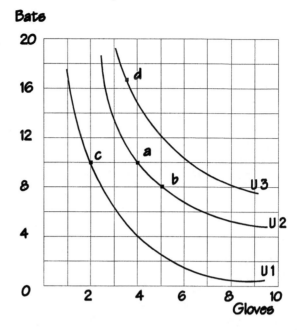

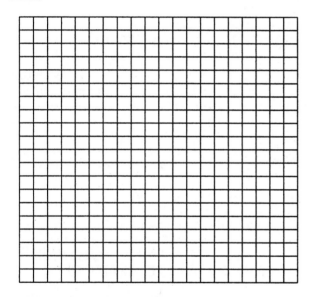

2. Consumer's Preferences

Sammy's preferences between bats and gloves are represented by the three indifference curves pictured in the next graph (U1, U2, U3). Several combinations of goods are labelled (a, b, c, d). Answer the next few questions based on this graph.
(a) Which of the four labelled combinations of goods would Sammy prefer? _____
(b) Which two of the four combinations of goods is Sammy indifferent between? _____ and _____.
(c) Sammy's marginal rate of substitution is the rate at which he is willing to trade bats for gloves to remain equally satisfied. The MRS calculated between points a and b is _____ bats per 1 glove.

3. Consumer's Optimum and Demand Curve

This problem uses Sammy's indifference curves from the previous problem to derive points on Sammy's demand for gloves. Assume that Sammy's income is fixed at $1000, and that the price of a bat is $50.
(a) Draw in Sammy's budget line if the price of a glove is $125, and label it BL₁. (Hint: use the same technique used in problem 1 to find Michelle's budget line.)
(b) Where is Sammy's utility-maximizing equilibrium for this budget line? (Hint: the budget line is tangent to one of the given U curves, and at one of the points already labelled.) _____
(c) Draw in Sammy's new budget line if the price of a glove goes up to $250, ceteris paribus, and label it BL₂.
(d) Where is Sammy's utility-maximizing equilibrium for BL₂? _____
(e) Use your results above to fill in values for Sammy's demand schedule for gloves:

Price per Glove	Quantity Demanded of Gloves
$125	_____
250	_____

Discussion Questions

1. Explain why the slope of the budget line is negative.

2. Explain why the slope of the indifference curve is negative, and why the curve is convex.

3. Explain why the budget line can be called "objective" whereas the indifference curve is "subjective."

4. Explain how the consumer's indifference map and budget lines are used to derive the consumer's demand for one of the products. In deriving demand what is varied and what is held constant?

5. Sketch an indifference curve-budget line diagram that shows the case of a person buying a combination of goods where the indifference curve cuts down through the budget line. Is the individual getting the maximum possible utility from his or her income? Draw in a new budget line to show that the individual could obtain the same level of utility now being enjoyed with a smaller income.

6. As consumers we don't actually use indifference curves and budget lines to decide what to buy at the grocery store; so how can this theory be useful in explaining consumer behaviour?

7. What is the "important difference between the marginal utility theory and the indifference curve theory of consumer demand"?

Answers

Quick Quiz
1. (a) pp. 153-154
2. (d) pp. 153-154
3. (d) p. 154
4. (b) p. 154
5. (d) pp. 154-155
6. (c) pp. 156-157

Fill-in Questions
1. income, prices
2. price of X, price of Y
3. inward, vertical (Y); steeper
4. downward, rate, substitution; convex
5. tangent; slope, slope, equal
6. is; does not

True-False
1. F   it's the reciprocal of this

2. F   because the Y intercept decreases, the budget line becomes flatter
3. T
4. T
5. T   the second basket would be preferred because it has more of both X and Y
6. F   indifference curves exist for all combinations, attainable or unattainable
7. T   if it changes the consumer's willingness to give up one good for more of the other
8. T
9. F   change the price of the good in question, not income
10. T   because the slope of the budget line must equal the MRS

Multiple-Choice
1. (b)
2. (d)   a parallel inward shift
3. (a)   only the X intercept changes because only the price of X changed
4. (b) $200/$10 = 20 and $200/$20 = 10
5. (b)   intercepts are 4T and 10Z, 10/4 = 2.5 Z per T
6. (c)
7. (c)
8. (c)   point C lies outside the budget line
9. (d)   B lies on a higher indifference curve than A
10. (b)   B lies on the highest attainable indifference curve, and the budget line and indifference curve are tangent at this point
11. (d)   this is the only option given that expands the budget line; the other options shrink the budget line
12. (d)   these are among the ceteris paribus conditions when we move along a demand curve
13. (a)
14. (b)
15. (a)   the tangency point on BL2 has more L and more K than the tangency point on BL1
16. (a)   MRS = price ratio; X/$7 = 6/1
17. (b)   MRS = 3 A/C and this is lower than relative price ratio = 4 A/C.
18. (c)   5 CDs add as much to his total utility as 1 hat

Problems and Projects
1. (a) 400; (b) 100; (c) 400, 100; (d) see BL1 on graph; (e) cannot, outside (see point *e* on graph); (f) 4G/1S; (g) 4; (h) 320, 80 (see BL2 on graph)
2. (a) d because it's on the highest indifference curve; (b) a, b because they are on the same indifference curve; (c) 2 because he is willing to

move from 10 to 8 bats in order to have 5 instead of 4 gloves

3.   (a)   see BL1 on graph; (b) a; (c) see BL2 (d) c; (e) 4, 2 because these are the number of gloves purchased at the equilibrium at each of these two prices

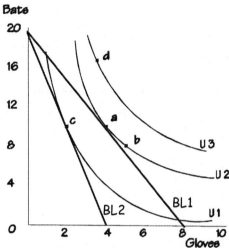

Chapter 7 — The Organization and Costs of Production

Overview

This important chapter is the first of several that dig into the story behind the supply curve. We begin with a description of the general nature and organization of business firms and then discuss production and costs. In future chapters we will see how these factors influence a firm's choices in various market structure setting.

We assume that all firms attempt to maximize profits, but firms differ drastically in form and size. The three major legal forms are the sole proprietorship, the partnership, and the corporation. Each form has its advantages and disadvantages. A key point is that a corporation offers its owners limited liability.

A main focus of the chapter is the nature of production costs. Unlike accountants, economists count all opportunity costs, both explicit and implicit. Consequently, economic profits differ from accounting profits.

We must distinguish clearly between the short run and long run because different adjustment options are open to the firm within each timeframe. In the short run the firm's plant is fixed, so output can be increased or decreased only by changing the amount of variable resources employed (usually labour). If the firm continues to add labour, their production sooner or later becomes less and less efficient as the plant becomes overcrowded with more and more workers (who must share the existing space and equipment). This is the idea behind the law of diminishing returns, a concept which also affects the shapes of short-run cost curves.

In the long run firms have time to change plant size, and to enter or leave the industry. The key cost curve in the long run is the average cost curve. The shape of this curve depends on the disadvantages and advantages of expanding output. If the advantages dominate, then the firm experiences economies of scale, and the long-run average total cost curve is declining.

Chapter Outline

7.1 The Firm and the Business Sector

◈ What different forms can a business organization take and what are the advantages of each?

- We can distinguish between a plant, a firm, and an industry:
    o A plant is a physical establishment where production takes place (e.g., a factory, store, or mine).
    o A firm is a business organization that owns one or more plants where it produces its output.
    o An industry is a group of firms that produce the same or similar products.
- Multiplant firms can be organized in various ways:
    o A horizontally integrated firm owns multiple plants performing much the same function.
    o A vertically integrated firm owns plants that operate at different stages of the production process.
    o A conglomerate owns plants producing goods across a number of markets or industries.
- The entrepreneur has three choices of legal forms under which to operate a business firm:
    o A sole proprietorship is owned and operated by one person, so has the advantages of ease of organization, maximum freedom, and strong individual incentive to operate efficiently. Its drawbacks are lack of financial resources, the burden for a single person to perform all management functions, and unlimited liability for the owner.
    o A partnership is owned by two or more owners who pool their resources in order to mobilize more financial resources and take advantage of greater specialization than the sole proprietorship can provide. Partnerships can be hampered by dis-

agreements in management, lack of continuity, and unlimited liability for each owner — even for the consequences of decisions made by their partners.

o   A corporation is a legal entity distinct and separate from its owners (or stockholders). Limited liability for investors enables corporations to attract large amounts of financial capital, allowing for the use of mass-production technologies. Disadvantages include bureaucracy and expense in organization, and double taxation of income. From a social viewpoint, corporations can shelter business operators from legal consequences of unscrupulous actions.

•   Two main sources of financing for corporations are the sales of stocks and bonds.

o   A stockholder is a part owner of the firm, and is entitled to share in any profits.

o   A bondholder is a lender to the firm, and is entitled to specified regular interest payments, and when the bond reaches maturity, the return of the original investment.

•   Very large corporations often face the principal-agent problem. The corporation is owned by many, many stockholders (principals) who each have only a small stake, and are not involved in managing the corporation. For this they hire managers (agents). Unfortunately, the agents' goals may be in conflict with the principals' goals of maximizing profits.

Quick Quiz

1. Which statement is false?
(a)   limited liability means that shareholders are not personally responsible for the corporation's debts
(b)   a restaurant chain that owns meat packing plants is vertically integrated
(c)   a main advantage of the partnership is that disputes between owners are rare
(d)   the principal-agent problem is common in large corporations that are run by executives

2.   Compared to a sole proprietorship, a partnership has the advantage of providing:
(a)   limited liability for all partners
(b)   greater continuity
(c)   simpler decision-making
(d)   more access to capital

3.   The owners of a corporation are called:
(a)   shareholders
(b)   bondholders
(c)   executives
(d)   all of the above

7.2 Economic Costs

✧ What are economic costs?

o   How do economic costs differ from accounting costs?

o   How is economic profit defined?

•   The economic cost (or opportunity cost) of resources used in production is measured as their value in their next best use, and is therefore the amount needed to attract these resources to their current use and hold them there.

•   Economic costs may be explicit or implicit.

o   An explicit cost is a direct monetary outlay from a firm to a resource supplier (e.g. wages, payments to suppliers of raw materials).

o   An implicit cost is the opportunity cost of using a self-owned, self-employed resource. A key type of implicit cost is "normal profit." Unless the entrepreneur earns a return equal to what his/her skills could command in a different business, he/she will leave to seek the higher return available elsewhere.

o   Economic profit (or pure profit) is total revenue received in excess of all economic costs (explicit and implicit). In contrast, accounting profit is equal to total revenue less accounting (explicit) costs.

✧ What is the difference between the short run and the long run?

•   The specific relationship between costs and output depends upon whether the firm is able to make short-run or long-run changes in the amount of resources it employs.

o   In the short run the firm's plant is a fixed resource, so the level of output can be changed only by changing the usage of labour and other variable factors.

o   In the long run all resources can be altered, so even plant size is variable.

Quick Quiz

4.   William runs an antiquarian bookstore out of his house. He ships books to customers who

place orders by telephone or email. Which of the following would be among William's implicit costs of doing business?
- (a) the rent he pays for his house
- (b) the wage he could earn by working for a salary in a different bookstore
- (c) the postage he pays to ship books to customers
- (d) the long distance phone charges he pays for calling his customers in other cities

5. The owner of a business would be willing to continue in the business if earning any amount of:
- (a) accounting profit
- (b) economic profit
- (c) normal profit
- (d) none of the above

6. Suppose that a physiotherapy clinic uses space and labour. The owners of the clinic would be facing a short run situation during a period of time in which:
- (a) they can adjust the size of their labour force and adjust the amount of space the clinic has
- (b) they can adjust the size of their labour force but the clinic space is fixed
- (c) they cannot change either the number of workers or the size of their space
- (d) they can change their price but not either their space or their labour

7.3 Short-run Production Relationships

⌘ How are inputs and outputs related in the short run?

⌘ What is the law of diminishing returns?

• Short-run production relationships show how output varies with labour when the plant size is fixed.
- o Total product (TP) shows total output at each level of labour input.
- o Marginal product (MP) shows the extra output from adding an extra unit of labour.
- o Average product (AP) (or labour productivity), shows total output per unit of labour.
• The law of diminishing returns states that as successive units of a variable resource (say, labour) are added to a fixed resource (say, capital),

beyond some point the marginal product will decline.

➲ This section and the ones that follow are difficult and important for much of the material in the next few chapters. Therefore this chapter requires and deserves more of your time than most chapters.

➲ Many different concepts of productivity and cost are described in this chapter. Be sure that you understand their definitions, that you also know them by their abbreviations, and that you know and can apply their formulas – forwards and backwards.

➲ The difference between marginal and average relationships is crucial. Marginal always refers to something incremental (i.e. for one unit more). Average is always a per unit measure found by dividing a total measure by a number of units.

Quick Quiz
7. Which formula is incorrect:
- (a) $AP = Q/L$
- (b) MP = change in L / change in Q
- (c) $Q = AP \times L$
- (d) all of these are correct

8. The law of diminishing returns pertains to:
- (a) marginal product in the short run
- (b) marginal product in the long run
- (c) average product in the short run
- (d) average product in the long run

9. A factory employing 100 workers produces 4,000 units of output. The marginal product of one additional worker would be 20 units of output. Therefore, if this worker is added:
- (a) average product will rise
- (b) marginal product will rise
- (c) total product will rise
- (d) none of the above

7.4 Short-run Production Costs

⌘ How are outputs and costs related in the short run?

• In the short run, a firm's total costs are the sum of fixed and variable costs. As output increases:
- o total fixed costs (TFC) do not change;

o total variable costs (TVC) increase, at first increase at a decreasing rate and then at an increasing rate; and
o total costs (TC) at first increase at a decreasing and then at an increasing rate.
- Average fixed, average variable, and average total cost are equal, respectively, to the firm's fixed, variable, and total cost divided by the output of the firm. As output increases:
  o average fixed cost (AFC) decreases;
  o average variable cost (AVC) at first decreases and then increases; and
  o average total cost (ATC) at first decreases and then increases.
- Marginal cost (MC) is the extra cost incurred in producing one additional unit of output.
  o Because the marginal product of the variable resources increases and then decreases (by the law of diminishing returns), MC decreases and then increases as output increases.
  o At the minimum point on AVC, AVC and MC are equal; and at the minimum point on ATC, ATC and MC are equal.
  o Given fixed input prices, the MC and AVC curves are mirror images of the MP and AP curves, respectively.
- Changes in resource prices or technology will cause the cost curves to shift.

➲ In graphs and tables, marginal product and marginal cost are always treated as "in between." For example, the marginal cost value calculated from data at output levels of 10 units and 20 units should be graphed at 15 units.

Quick Quiz

10. The additional cost to produce one more unit of output is:
   (a) MP
   (b) MC
   (c) AVC
   (d) ATC

11. That cost which does not vary with the amount produced is:
   (a) TFC
   (b) AFC
   (c) TC
   (d) MC

12. When MP and AP are both falling:
   (a) MC and AVC are both falling

   (b) MC and ATC are both rising
   (c) MC and AVC are both rising
   (d) ATC and AVC are both rising

13. A factory producing 4,000 units of output has total fixed costs of $10,000 per day, and average variable cost of $5.00 per unit of output. Which of the following is incorrect?
   (a) ATC = $9.00 per unit
   (b) AFC = $2.50 per unit
   (c) TVC = $20,000 per day
   (d) TC = $30,000 per day

7.5 Long-run Production Costs

✧ How do the firm's costs in the long run depend on the firm's size?
- In the long run all resources employed by the firm are variable resources; therefore all costs are variable costs. The chapter focuses on the long-run average total cost derived from the set of ATC curves for all possible plant sizes.
- The long-run ATC curve shows the lowest per-unit cost that can be achieved at each output level, given that the firm has had time to change to a plant of the most appropriate size.
  o If the firm expands its output by expanding its plant, long-run ATC tends to fall at first because of the economies of large-scale production, but if this expansion continues far enough, long-run ATC will begin to rise because of the diseconomies of large-scale production.
  o A firm that has constant returns to scale has a flat long-run ATC curve.
- Economies of scale result from the greater possibilities in larger plants for specialization of labour and management, and the ability to employ more efficient capital equipment. Diseconomies of scale are caused by managerial problems of coordination and control encountered in large firms.
- Economies or diseconomies of scale are an important determinant of an industry's structure. Minimum efficient scale (MES) is the lowest level of output at which a firm can minimize long-run average costs.
  o In an industry with constant returns to scale over a wide output range, large and small firms could both be viable.
  o In an industry where the long-run average-cost curve declines over a wide range of output, there may be insufficient con-

sumer demand to allow for efficient production by more than a small number of large firms.

o   When economies of scale extend beyond the market size, the conditions exist for a natural monopoly, meaning that per-unit costs are minimized only if the product is made by only a single firm.

➲ You have not mastered the various concepts until you can correctly sketch from memory: (1) the productivity curves, (2) the short-run total cost curves, (3) the short-run average and marginal cost curves, and (4) the long-run average cost curve. You should also be able to explain the relationship between the curves in each set that you draw.

Quick Quiz

14. The long-run average cost curve is constructed from a set of:
   (a)   short-run average total cost curves
   (b)   short-run average variable cost curves
   (c)   long-run average variable cost curves
   (d)   long-run marginal cost curves

15. A down-sloping long-run average cost curve indicates:
   (a)   diminishing returns
   (b)   constant returns to scale
   (c)   diseconomies of scale
   (d)   economies of scale

Terms and Concepts

plant	marginal product (MP)
firm	average product (AP)
industry	law of diminishing
sole proprietorship	returns
partnership	fixed costs
corporation	variable costs
stocks	total cost
bonds	average fixed cost
limited liability	(AFC)
double taxation	average variable cost
principal-agent prob-	(AVC)
lem	average total cost (ATC)
economic	marginal cost (MC)
(opportunity) cost	economies of scale
explicit costs	diseconomies of scale
implicit costs	constant returns to
normal profit	scale

economic profit	minimum efficient
short run	scale
long run	natural monopoly
total product (TP)	

Fill-In Questions

1. McDonald's is an example of a(n) (plant, firm, industry) _____. The McDonald's restaurant in Salmon Arm is an example of a(n) _____. McDonald's and all other fast food restaurants together represent a(n) _____.

2. A multi-plant firm would be a (vertical, horizontal) _____ combination of plants if each plant is at the same stage in the production process, and a _____ combination if each plant is at a different stage in the production process. A firm that owns plants that operate across different markets and industries is termed a _____.

3. The main legal forms of business enterprise are: _____, _____, and _____.

4. A purchaser of a corporate (stock, bond) _____ owns a portion of the corporation, whereas a purchaser of a corporate _____ is simply lending to the corporation.

5. The separation of ownership and control that is typical in (large, small) _____ corporations with (many, few) _____ stockholders may create a _____ problem. In this situation the (managers, stockholders) _____ are the principals, and the _____ are their agents.

6. Costs exist because resources are _____ and have _____ uses. The economic cost of a resource is also known as its _____ cost, measuring its value in its next best use.

7. A monetary payment a firm makes to outside suppliers is called an (explicit, implicit) _____ cost. An _____ cost is the opportunity cost of self-owned, self-employed resources.

8. Accounting profit equals total revenues minus _____ costs. Economic profit is defined as accounting profit minus _____ costs.

9. The law of diminishing returns is that as successive units of a (fixed, variable) _____ resource are added to a _____ resource, eventually the (total, marginal) _____ product of the (fixed, variable) _____ resource will decrease. Marginal product ultimately diminishes because too much of the _____ resource is being used relative to the _____ resource.

10. When the total product:
(a) increases at an increasing rate, the marginal product is (rising, falling) _____;
(b) increases at a decreasing rate, the marginal product is (positive, negative, zero) _____, but (rising, falling) _____;
(c) is at a maximum, the marginal product is (positive, negative, zero) _____;
(d) decreases, the marginal product is (positive, negative, zero) _____.

Questions 11 to 15 are based on the table below:

Units of Labour	Units of Capital	Total Product	Total Cost of Labour	Total Cost of Capital	Total Cost of Production
1	1	10	$15	$30	$45
2	1	27	30	30	60
3	1	40	45	30	75
4	1	50	60	30	90
5	1	56	75	30	105
6	1	58	90	30	120

11. The variable input is (labour, capital) _____ and the fixed input is _____. When production is 56 units of output, total variable cost is $____ and total fixed cost is $____.

12. The marginal product of the 4th unit of variable input is _____; the marginal product of the 6th unit of variable input is _____.

13. The law of diminishing returns (does, does not) _____ hold in this case because with one (fixed, variable) _____ input, the (average, marginal, total) _____ product of the _____ input (increases, decreases) _____.

14. In the table, as output goes from 10 to 27 units, total costs increase from $____ to $____. Therefore marginal cost will be ____/____ = ____.

15. In the table:
(a) the average variable cost of 50 units of output is $____
(b) the average fixed cost of 50 units of output is $____
(c) the average total cost of 50 units of output is $____

16. Suppose that the average weight of players on the Argonauts football team was 120 kg. If a new player weighing 140 kg is signed to the team without anyone being dropped, the average weight will (increase, decrease) _____. This example indicates that when the marginal value is (greater, less) _____ than the average value, the average value will (increase, decrease) _____.

17. When marginal cost is less than average variable cost, average variable cost is (rising, falling, constant) _____.

18. Economies of scale explain the _____ -sloping part of the (long-run, short-run) _____ ATC curve. Diseconomies of scale explain the _____ -sloping part of the same curve. If the curve is flat the firm is experiencing _____ returns to scale.

19. The smallest level of output at which a firm can minimize long-run average cost is termed _____. Relatively large and small firms could both be viable an the same industry if there is an extended range of _____ returns to scale. The conditions for a _____ exist when unit costs are minimized if a single firm produces all output for the market.

True-False

Circle T if the statement is true, F if it is false.

1. Best Western Hotels would be considered a conglomerate because it owns plants in a number of different provinces. **T F**

2. Imperial Oil Ltd. would be considered a horizontal combination since it owns some plants that refine crude oil and other plants that sell the refined product. **T F**

3. The partnership form of business organization allows for greater specialization in management than the sole proprietorship form.   **T F**

4. The return paid to stockholders by the corporation is called a dividend.   **T F**

5. A shareholder is liable for the unpaid debts of the corporation he/she owns.   **T F**

6. The economic costs of a firm are whatever payments it must make to resource owners to attract their resources from alternative employments.   **T F**

7. The separation of ownership and control in a corporation means that managers and executives may make decisions contrary to the stockholders' goal of profit-maximization.   **T F**

8. Economic profit is a return over and above the alternative cost of all inputs.   **T F**

9. Normal profit is an implicit cost.   **T F**

10. It is possible for a firm to have an accounting profit but to suffer an economic loss at the same time.   **T F**

11. If marginal product is negative, total output decreases when an extra unit of the variable input is utilized in production.   **T F**

12. In the short run marginal cost can be calculated from either the change in total cost or the change in total variable cost.   **T F**

13. One explanation of why the long-run average cost curve of a firm rises after some level of output has been reached is the law of diminishing returns.   **T F**

14. A firm that is experiencing constant returns to scale can double output by doubling its employment of all inputs.   **T F**

15. Diseconomies of scale are caused by problems of coordination and communication that arise in large firms.   **T F**

Multiple-Choice

Circle the letter that corresponds to the best answer.

1. A single firm owns and operates three plants: a farm growing wheat, a flour-milling plant, and a bakery. This group of plants is an example of a:
(a)   horizontal combination
(b)   vertical combination
(c)   conglomerate combination
(d)   corporation

2. Which of the following is **not** one of the advantages of a sole proprietorship?
(a)   ease of organization
(b)   ease of decision-making
(c)   strong incentive for the owner
(d)   easy access to capital

3. Which of the following is a disadvantage of a partnership compared to a proprietorship?
(a)   greater access to capital
(b)   greater access to specialized management
(c)   unlimited liability for another partner's decisions
(d)   all of the above

4. Limited liability is associated with:
(a)   sole proprietorships
(b)   partnerships
(c)   corporations
(d)   both proprietorships and partnerships

5. Which form of business organization is most effective in raising financial capital?
(a)   corporation
(b)   partnership
(c)   proprietorship
(d)   vertical combination

6. Which form of business organization is treated as a legal entity, distinct and separate from its owners?
(a)   corporation
(b)   partnership
(c)   proprietorship
(d)   all of the above

7. Double taxation of corporate profits arises because:
(a)   personal income tax must be paid on dividends but not on interest earned

(b) both the federal government and the provinces in Canada levy a corporation profits tax

(c) American-owned corporations in Canada are taxed by both Canadian and American governments

(d) a corporation pays a corporate profits tax and a shareholder also pays a personal income tax on any dividends received from the corporation

8. The separation of ownership and control in corporations raises questions concerning:
(a) accountability of corporate managers to corporate stockholders
(b) dividend policy
(c) managerial benefits
(d) all of the above

9. Normal profit is defined as the cost of obtaining the services of:
(a) management
(b) entrepreneurs
(c) capital
(d) land

10. The revenues of a firm less its explicit costs are defined as the firm's:
(a) normal profit
(b) accounting profit
(c) economic profit
(d) economic rent

The next three questions refer to the following table that shows a firm's short-run production relationship between the variable factor (labour) and output. Assume that plant capacity is fixed.

Amount of Labour	Amount of Output
1	3
2	8
3	12
4	15
5	17
6	18
7	17

11. The marginal product of the fourth unit of labour is:
(a) 2 units of output
(b) 3 units of output
(c) 4 units of output
(d) 5 units of output

12. When the firm hires four units of labour, the average product of labour is:
(a) 3 units of output
(b) 3.75 units of output
(c) 4 units of output
(d) 15 units of output

13. Diminishing returns becomes operative when:
(a) the second unit of labour is employed
(b) the third unit of labour is employed
(c) the fifth unit of labour is employed
(d) the seventh unit of labour is employed

14. Because the average product of a variable resource at first increases, and later decreases as a firm increases its output:
(a) AVC at first decreases then increases
(b) AFC decreases as the output of the firm expands
(c) TVC at first increases by increasing amounts and then increases by decreasing amounts
(d) MC at first increases then later decreases

15. Because the marginal product of a resource at first increases and then decreases as the output of the firm increases:
(a) AFC declines as the firm's output increases
(b) AVC at first increases and then decreases
(c) TVC at first increases by increasing amounts and then increases by decreasing amounts
(d) MC at first decreases and then increases

16. Marginal cost and average variable cost are equal at the output at which:
(a) marginal cost is a minimum
(b) marginal product is a maximum
(c) average variable cost is a minimum
(d) average variable cost is a maximum

The table below refers to a firm with a fixed cost of $500, and variable costs as indicated in the table. Use the data for the three questions that follow.

Output	Total Variable Cost
1	$ 200
2	360
3	500
4	700
5	1,000
6	1,800

17. The average variable cost when the firm produces 4 units of output is:
- (a) $175
- (b) $200
- (c) $300
- (d) $700

18. The average total cost of 4 units of output is:
- (a) $175
- (b) $200
- (c) $300
- (d) $700

19. The marginal cost of the sixth unit of output is:
- (a) $200
- (b) $300
- (c) $700
- (d) $800

Questions 20 through 27 are based on the next diagram that shows a firm's short-run cost curves.

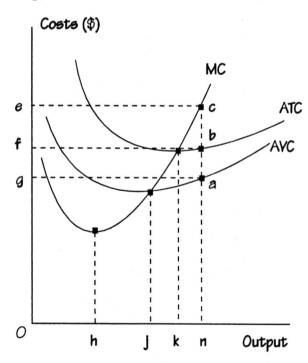

20. The marginal cost of the *n*th unit of output is distance:
- (a)   0e
- (b)   0f
- (c)   0g
- (d)   0h

21. The average fixed cost at output 0*n* is distance:
- (a)   0e
- (b)   0f
- (c)   gf
- (d)   0g

22. Total fixed cost for 0*n* units of output is area:
- (a)   ecfb
- (b)   0fbn
- (c)   0gan
- (d)   fgab

23. Total variable cost of 0*n* units of output is area:
- (a)   0nag
- (b)   0nfb
- (c)   0nec
- (d)   fbec

24. Total cost of 0*n* units of output is area:
- (a)   0nag
- (b)   0nbf
- (c)   0nce
- (d)   fbce

25. Average total cost is at a minimum at output:
- (a)   0h
- (b)   0j
- (c)   0k
- (d)   0n

26. The point of diminishing returns for this firm comes at output:
- (a)   0h
- (b)   0j
- (c)   0k
- (d)   0n

27. This firm's average product of labour is maximized at output:
- (a)   0h
- (b)   0j
- (c)   0k
- (d)   0n

28. Identify the incorrect formula:
- (a)   ATC = AFC + AVC
- (b)   AVC = TVC / Q
- (c)   MC = ATC - AVC
- (d)   TFC = AFC x Q

29. If a firm has ATC = $5 when output is 100 units, and ATC = $6 when output is 110 units, what is the MC between these two output levels?
(a) $0.10
(b) $1.00
(c) $5.50
(d) $16.00

30. If a firm has TFC = $1000, and TC = $3000 when output is 100 units, how much is the AVC at 100 units of output?
(a) $2.00
(b) $20.00
(c) $30.00
(d) $2000.00

31. If a firm's MC is $12 between output of 3 units and 4 units, and TVC is $100 when output is 3 units, what is AVC when output is 4 units?
(a) $12.00
(b) $25.00
(c) $28.00
(d) $112.00

32. Based on the following table that shows short-run cost schedules for plants of three different sizes, what is the long-run average cost of producing 30 units of output, assuming that the firm can eventually build any one of these plants?
(a) $7
(b) $8
(c) $9
(d) $10

Plant 1		Plant 2		Plant 3	
Output	ATC	Output	ATC	Output	ATC
10	$10	10	$12	10	$14
20	9	20	10	20	11
30	8	30	9	30	9
40	9	40	8	40	7
50	10	50	9	50	9

33. Using the table above, at what output is long-run average cost at a minimum?
(a) 20
(b) 30
(c) 40
(d) 50

34. The minimum efficient scale of plant is:
(a) the size of plant where average fixed cost is a minimum

(b) the size of plant where average variable cost is falling
(c) the smallest level of output at which a firm can minimize long-run total costs
(d) the smallest level of output at which a firm can minimize long-run average cost

35. The long-run average costs of producing a particular product is one of the factors that determines:
(a) the competition among firms producing the product
(b) the number of firms in the industry producing the product
(c) the size of each of the firms in the industry producing the product
(d) all of the above

36. In the short run, which of the following curves will not shift as a result of an increase in the price of labour?
(a) average fixed cost
(b) average variable cost
(c) average total cost
(d) marginal cost

37. In the short run, which of the following curves will shift when total fixed cost increases?
(a) average fixed cost
(b) average variable cost
(c) marginal cost
(d) none of these will shift

38. A sunk cost:
(a) affects decisions in the short run
(b) affects decisions in the long run
(c) affects decisions in the short run and in the long run
(d) is irrelevant for decisions

39. Increasing plant size can lead to lower average costs of production due to:
(a) specialization of labour
(b) specialization of management
(c) use of more efficient capital
(d) all of the above

Problems and Projects

1. Forms of Business Organization
Indicate whether each business characteristic below is associated with the sole proprietorship

(PROP), partnership (PART), corporation (CORP), two of these, or all three of these legal forms.

(a) Much red tape and legal expense in beginning the firm _____

(b) Unlimited liability _____

(c) No specialized management _____

(d) Has life independent of its owner(s) _____

(e) Its owners are called stockholders _____

(f) Greatest ability to acquire funds for the expansion of the firm _____

(g) Permits some but not a great degree of specialized management _____

(h) Possibility of unresolved disagreement among owners over courses of action _____

(i) Business owner can avoid responsibility for business losses _____

(j) Issues common shares with voting rights _____

2. Economic Costs and Profits in the Jewelry Business

The Jack of Diamonds Jewelers reports the following results for 2001:

Total sales revenue	$2,000,000
Cost of diamonds	1,500,000
Staff wages and benefits	300,000
Rent	100,000
Forgone wages for owner	45,000
Forgone interest	5,000
Forgone entrepreneurial income	10,000

(a) The total explicit cost = $____.

(b) The accounting profit = $____.

(c) The total implicit cost = $____.

(d) The normal profit = $____.

(e) The economic profit = $____.

3. Production Function for Jeans

The following table shows the daily production at Texas Style Textiles, a firm that manufactures jeans using labour, capital, and materials. Capital is held constant in the short run.

(a) In the parentheses at the head of each column, indicate the units of measurement.

(b) Fill in the values for average product of labour (AP).

(c) Fill in the values for marginal product of labour (MP).

(d) There are increasing returns to labour from the first to the _____ unit of labour, and diminishing returns from the _____ to the eighth unit of labour.

(e) When total production (TP) is increasing, MP is (positive, negative) _____, and when TP is decreasing, MP is _____.

(f) When the MP is greater than AP, AP (increases, decreases) _____.

Labour	Total Production	Average Product of Labour	Marginal Product of Labour
(workers/day)	(jeans/day)	( )	( )
0	0	—	
1	80	_____	_____
2	200	_____	_____
3	330	_____	_____
4	400	_____	_____
5	450	_____	_____
6	480	_____	_____
7	490	_____	_____
8	480	_____	_____

4. Cost Formula Matching

Match each cost concept from the list on the left with the correct formula on the right.

(a) TC   (i)   AVC x Q

(b) AVC   (ii)   TFC + TVC

(c) MC   (iii) TVC / Q

(d) ATC   (iv)   change in TC / change in Q

(e) TVC   (v)   TFC / Q

(f) AFC   (vi)   AFC + AVC

5. Production and Costs in the Tax Preparation Industry

Centurion Tax Services has a fixed amount of capital (office space and computer equipment). It varies its output of tax returns by varying the number of clerks it employs. The table below shows the relationships between the amount of labour employed, output, marginal product of labour, and average product of labour.

(a) Assume there is a fixed cost of $200 for capital resources. Fill in the TFC column.

(b) Assume each unit of labour costs $50. Compute the cost of labour, or TVC, for each quantity

of labour that Centurion might employ, and enter these figures in the table.
(c) Fill in the AVC column.
(d) Fill in the MC column.

Labour	Output	Marginal Product of Labour	Avg Product of Labour	Total Variable Cost	Marginal Cost	Avg Variable Cost	Total Fixed Cost	Avg Fixed Cost	Total Cost	Avg Total Cost
clerks	returns	returns/clerk	returns/clerk	$	$/return	$/return	$	$/return	$	$/return
0	0									
		5			—					
1	5		5	—		—	—	—	—	—
		6			—					
2	11		5.5	—		—	—	—	—	—
		7			—					
3	18		6	—		—	—	—	—	—
		6			—					
4	24		6	—		—	—	—	—	—
		5			—					
5	29		5.8	—		—	—	—	—	—
		4			—					
6	33		5.5	—		—	—	—	—	—
		3			—					
7	36		5.1	—		—	—	—	—	—
		2			—					
8	38		4.8	—		—	—	—	—	—

(e) When MP increases, the MC (increases, decreases) _____, and when MP decreases, the MC _____.

(f) When AP increases, the AVC (increases, decreases) _____, and when AP decreases, the AVC _____.

(g) Fill in the AFC column.

(h) Fill in the ATC column.

(i) In this example, ATC falls and then rises. At the output level closest to the lowest value of ATC, the AFC is (falling, rising) _____ and AVC is _____.

(j) MC has approximately the same value as AVC and ATC in the vicinity of the _____ values for each.

6. Graphing Costs

Using the two graphs that follow, plot the data from question 5 as follows:
(a) On the first graph plot TFC, TVC, and TC.
(b) On the other graph plot AFC, AVC, ATC and MC.

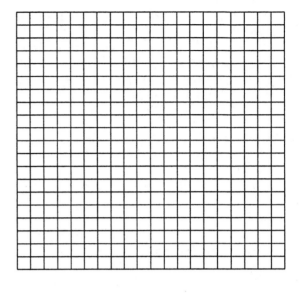

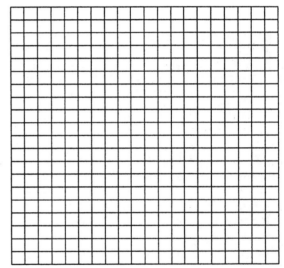

7. Sleuthing Coal Mine Costs

An economic historian has recovered the following table of costs from a 19th century coal mine. The document is crumbling with age, so many of the entries are illegible (marked as blanks). Use your knowledge of cost relationships to fill in the blank values.

	Q = 1	Q = 2	Q = 3	Q = 4	Q = 5
TFC	____	____		____	____
TVC	____	____	9.00	____	____
TC	____	25.00	____	____	4.00
AFC	____	____	____	____	4.00
AVC	3.00	____	____	____	4.00
ATC	____	____	____	8.50	____

8. Short-Run and Long-Run Average-Total-Cost Curves

The diagram below shows the short-run average-total-cost schedules for three different plant sizes. Assume that these are the only possible plant sizes that a firm might build.

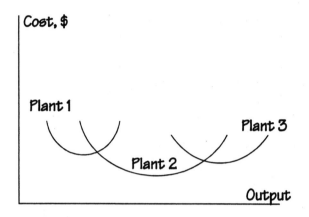

(a) Draw the firm's long-run average cost curve in this diagram.

(b) On the output axis, indicate the range of production levels for which Plant 1 is most efficient, the range for which Plant 2 is most efficient, and the range for which Plant 3 is the most efficient.

9. Self Employed Textbook Dealer

Suppose last year you went into business buying and selling used textbooks. It cost you $10,000 to buy used books from students at the end of the term. The purchase was financed by a bank loan that has been repaid with an interest cost of $665. Part-time help cost $7,000 for the year. You operated the business out of your garage and paid utility expenses of $500 for the year. You bought a cash register, shelves, etc. with $1,200 from your savings account. Your part-time helper happened to be an accounting student who told you that you should make an allowance of $200/year for the wear and tear on the equipment you bought.

You estimate that you worked 500 hours in your store but did not take any wage payment. The previous year you had worked in the campus bookstore and earned $5 per hour. Previously, you had rented your garage to a neighbour for $20 per month. Your savings were earning 10% interest.

(a) List the explicit and the implicit costs.

(b) Suppose you sold all the purchased books for $21,600. (1) Did you make an accounting profit? (yes, no) _____; how much? _____; (2) an economic profit? (yes, no); _____; how much? _____.

(c) Should you stay in this business given the results?

Discussion Questions

1. What is the difference between a plant and a firm? Between a firm and an industry? Which of these three concepts is the most difficult to apply in practice? Why? Distinguish between a horizontal, a vertical, and a conglomerate combination.

2. What are the principal advantages and disadvantages of each of the three legal forms of business organization? Which of the disadvantages of the proprietorship and partnership explain why most big businesses use the corporate form?

3. Explain what "separation of ownership and control" of the modern corporation means. What problems does this separation create for stockholders and the economy? How does it relate to the "principal-agent problem"?

4. Suppose you start up a courier business, and use your own vehicle. What explicit and implicit costs would you incur? How would you determine what amount to assign to the implicit costs?

5. What is the difference between normal and economic profit? Why is the former an economic cost? How do you define accounting profit?

6. What type of adjustments can a firm make in the long run that it cannot make in the short run? What adjustments can it make in the short run? How long is the short run?

7. State precisely the law of diminishing returns. Is this a short run or a long run phenomenon? Why?

8. Distinguish between a fixed cost and a variable cost. Why are short-run total costs partly fixed and partly variable, and why are long-run costs entirely variable?

9. Suppose that you are in a garage band that decides to issue a CD. What might be some of the fixed costs associated with producing and selling the CD, and what might be some of the variable costs?

10. Given that the price of inputs is fixed, what is the connection between marginal product and marginal cost?

11. What happens to the average total cost, average variable cost, average fixed cost, and marginal cost curves when the price of a variable input increases or decreases? Describe what other factor can cause short-run cost curves to shift.

12. What does the long-run average-cost curve of a firm show? What relationship is there between long-run average-cost and the short-run average-total-cost schedules of the different-sized plants a firm might build?

13. Why is the long-run average-cost curve of a firm U-shaped? What is meant by and what are some causes of economies of large scale? What is meant by and what causes diseconomies of large scale?

14. How do the economies and diseconomies of scale influence the size and number of firms in an industry?

Answers

Quick Quiz
1. (b) p. 162
2. (d) p. 162
3. (a) pp. 162-163
4. (b) p. 165
5. (b) pp. 165-166
6. (b) pp. 166-167
7. (d) p. 167
8. (a) p. 168
9. (c) pp. 169-170
10. (b) p. 175
11. (a) p. 170
12. (b) p. 177
13. (a) pp. 174-177
14. (a) pp. 180-181
15. (d) p. 182

Fill-in Questions
1. firm; plant; industry
2. horizontal; vertical; conglomerate
3. sole proprietorship, partnership, corporation
4. stock, bond
5. large, many, principal-agent; stockholders, managers
6. scarce, alternative; opportunity
7. explicit; implicit
8. explicit; implicit and explicit
9. variable, fixed, marginal, variable; variable, fixed
10. (a) rising, (b) positive, falling (c) zero, (d) negative
11. labour, capital; 75, 30
12. 10; 2
13. does, fixed, marginal, variable, decreases
14. 45, 60; $15/17, $0.88
15. (a) 1.20, (b) 0.60, (c) 1.80
16. increase; greater, increase
17. falling
18. down, long-run; up, constant
19. minimum efficient scale; constant; natural monopoly

True-False
1. F   it would be a conglomerate if it owns plants producing different products
2. F   this describes a vertical combination
3. T
4. T
5. F   the shareholder can lose his/her investment, but is not personally liable to any extent for the firm's debts
6. T   opportunity costs, in other words
7. T   if managers and executive follow self-interest
8. T   over and above explicit and implicit costs
9. T   because entrepreneurial ability has an opportunity cost
10. T   if implicit costs exceed accounting profit
11. T
12. T   since TFC is fixed, TVC and TC vary at exactly the same rate
13. F   diminishing returns is relevant only in the short run, because it deals with one fixed input
14. T   and therefore ATC is constant
15. T

Multiple-Choice
1. (b)   three different stages of production
2. (d)   difficult to raise capital beyond proprietor's own savings or personal credit
3. (c)   the others are advantages
4. (c)   others have unlimited liability

5. (a) able to sell shares to large numbers of investors many of whom wish to invest only small amounts with limited liability

6. (a)

7. (d)

8. (d) all are issues due to the principal-agent problem

9. (b)

10. (b) because accountants do not calculate implicit costs

11. (b) (15-12)/(4-3) = 3

12. (b) 15/4 = 3.75

13. (b) MP of third L is 4, MP of second L is 5

14. (a) AVC and AP shapes are inversely related

15. (d) MC and MP shapes are linked

16. (c)

17. (a) 700/4 = 175

18. (c) (500+700)/4 = 300

19. (d) (1800-1000)/(6-5) = 800

20. (a)

21. (c) AFC = ATC - AVC

22. (d) TFC = AFC x Q

23. (a) TVC = AVC x Q

24. (b) TC = ATC x Q

25. (c)

26. (a) maximum MP occurs at same output as minimum MC

27. (b) maximum AP occurs at same output as minimum AVC

28. (c) MC = change in TC / change in Q

29. (d) ((6 x 110) - (5 x 100))/(110-100)

30. (b) TVC = TC – TFC; AVC = TVC/Q

31. (c) TVC at Q = 4 is 100 +12; AVC = 112/4 = 28

32. (b) this cost can be reached by building Plant 1

33. (c) a cost of $7 per unit can be reached by building Plant 3 and producing 40

34. (d)

35. (d) MES is the key concept

36. (a) assuming labour is the variable input

37. (a) AFC = TFC/Q

38. (d) it exists regardless of how much is produced and whether or not the firm shuts down

39. (d)

Problems and Projects

1. (a) CORP; (b) PROP and PART; (c) PROP; (d) CORP; (e) CORP; (f) CORP; (g) PART; (h) PART; (i) CORP; (j) CORP

2. (a) 1,900,000, (b) 100,000, (c) 60,000, (d) 10,000, (e) 40,000

3. (a) jeans/worker; jeans/worker; (b) AP = 80, 100, 110, 100, 90, 80, 70, 60; (c) MP = 80, 120, 130, 70, 50, 30, 10, -10; (d) third, fourth; (e) positive, negative; (f) increases

4. (a)-(ii); (b)-(iii); (c)-(iv); (d)-(vi); (e)-(i); (f)-(v)

5. (a) TFC = 200 at all output levels; (b) TVC = 50, 100, 150, 200, 250, 300, 350, 400; (c) AVC = 10.00, 9.09, 8.33, 8.33, 8.62, 9.09, 9.72, 10.53; (d) MC = 10.00, 8.33, 7.15, 8.33, 10.00, 12.50, 16.67, 25.00; (e) decreases, increases; (f) decreases, increases; (g) AFC = 40.00, 18.18, 11.11, 8.33, 6.90, 6.06, 5.55, 5.26; (h) ATC = 50.00, 27.27, 19.44, 16.66, 15.52, 15.15, 15.27, 15.79; (i) falling, rising; (j) minimum

6. See textbook Figure 7.3 (p. 173) and Figure 7.5 (p. 176) for the shapes your curves should exhibit.

7. Values (including those already given) from left to right in the table: TFC = 20, 20, 20, 20, 20; TVC = 3, 5, 9, 14, 20; TC = 23, 25, 29, 34, 40; AFC = 20.00, 10.00, 6.67, 5.00, 4.00; AVC = 3.00, 2.50, 3.00, 3.50, 4.00; ATC = 23.00, 12.50, 9.67, 8.50, 8.00.

8. (a) The curve is made up of segments of the short-run curves, choosing at each output the lowest cost point; (b) Plant 1 is most efficient for all levels of output below where the curve for Plant 1 intersects the curve for Plant 2; Plant 2 is most efficient from that level of output up to the output where the Plant 2 curve intersects the Plant 3 curve; beyond that point, Plant 3 is most efficient.

9. (a) Explicit costs: book purchase $10,000, interest payment $665, wages for part-time help $7000, utilities $500 = total of $18,165. Implicit costs: forgone own wages $3500, forgone garage rent $240, forgone saving account interest $120, depreciation $200 = total of $4,060; (b) (1) yes; Accounting profit = total revenue – explicit costs (including depreciation) = $21,600 – ($18,165 + $200) = $3,235; (2) no; Economic profit = total revenue – explicit costs – implicit costs = $21,600 - $18,165 - $4,060 = -$625; (c) No. Since economic profit is less than zero, you are not earning enough to cover the opportunity costs of all of your resources (even without allowing any compensation for entrepreneurial services).

Chapter 8 Pure Competition

Overview

This chapter is the first of three that analyze the behaviour of firms in various market structures. The goal of any firm is to maximize profit — the difference between revenues and costs. The theory of costs developed in Chapter 7 applies to all firms, but the revenue or demand side of the profit equation depends on the type of market in which the firm operates. Therefore, the firm's choices about production levels and pricing depend on such factors as the number of competitors, conditions of entry, and the nature of the product. Chapter 8 studies the firm's choices under the market structure called pure competition. Chapters 9 and 10 analyse firms in pure monopoly, oligopoly and monopolistic competition.

A purely competitive market has a very large number of firms, all selling a standardized product for a price over which they have no control. It is very easy for firms to enter or exit the market, and non-price competition does not exist. Under these conditions, how does an individual firm behave, and how does the entire industry respond to changing market conditions? The key questions that we address are:
(1) How much output should the firm produce to maximize profits?
(2) What will be the market price of the product?
(3) How much output will the industry produce?
(4) Under what conditions will the firm decide to shut down production?
(5) Under what conditions will firms enter or leave the industry?
(6) How efficient is the allocation of resources in a purely competitive market?

Chapter Outline

8.1 Four Market Structures

◈ What are the four basic market structures?
• The defining characteristics of market structure include number of firms in the industry, type of product (differentiated or standardized), degree of control over price, and ease of entry.
• The four basic market structures discussed in this text are:
  o pure competition
  o pure monopoly
  o monopolistic competition
  o oligopoly

➲ The purely competitive model is the standard against which other market models — pure monopoly, monopolistic competition, and oligopoly — are compared for economic efficiency. Therefore a thorough understanding of this chapter will really help you to understand the next two chapters.

Quick Quiz
1. Suppose air travel between Vancouver and Calgary is provided by only two airlines that compete directly on price and service. What kind of market structure is this?
  (a)   pure competition
  (b)   pure monopoly
  (c)   monopolistic competition
  (d)   oligopoly

8.2 Characteristics of Pure Competition and the Firm's Demand Curve

◈ What conditions characterize a purely competitive market?

• A purely competitive market has a large number of independent firms selling a standardized product. No firm is able to control the market price. Firms are free to enter or leave the market in the long run.
• Although pure competition is rare in practice, this market model is highly relevant because some industries closely approximate this market structure model, and because this model provides an efficiency standard against which to evaluate other market structures.

- A purely competitive firm is called a "price taker" because it sells only a minute part of the industry output of a standardized good, and the firm cannot influence the market price.
  - o The market demand curve is down-sloping, but the individual firm's demand is horizontal (perfectly elastic).
  - o Total revenue increases at a constant rate as the firm increases its output. On a graph TR will be a straight line rising from the origin, with a slope dependent on the price.
  - o Price, average revenue, and marginal revenue are equal and constant at the market price. On a graph all three are the identical horizontal line when plotted against output.

Quick Quiz

2. In pure competition the firm's demand curve is also the firm's:
  - (a)   price
  - (b)   marginal revenue
  - (c)   average revenue
  - (d)   all of the above

3. We study pure competition because:
  - (a)   many real world markets are purely competitive
  - (b)   pure competition is a standard for evaluating efficiency
  - (c)   many real world markets closely approximate pure competition
  - (d)   both (b) and (c)

8.3 Profit Maximization in the Short Run

◈ How does the purely competitive firm choose its output level?

◈ Under what condition will the firm not to produce any output?

- There are two complementary ways to analyze the purely competitive firm's choice of output level in the short run.
- In the total-revenue and total-cost approach, the firm will choose to produce the output at which total economic profit is the greatest or total loss is the least, provided that the total revenue is greater than or equal to total variable cost. If not, the firm will minimize its losses by closing down and producing no output.

- In the marginal-revenue and marginal-cost approach, the firm will produce the output at which MR = MC (or, equivalently, P = MC), provided price is greater than average variable cost. If price is below average variable cost, the firm's loss is greater than its fixed costs, so the firm will minimize losses by closing down.

⮕ Results are derived using both graphical and numerical examples. Make sure that you can handle problems of either style.

⮕ Perhaps students' most common error in this chapter is to believe that the firm in the short run will shut down if its revenue does not cover its total fixed costs. Fixed costs are assumed to be unavoidable in the short run, so they are irrelevant to the decision of whether or not to operate. The firm should operate only if it earns enough revenue to cover its total variable costs (in other words, if $P \geq AVC$). If not, it will minimize losses by shutting down and limiting its loss to the total fixed cost.

Quick Quiz

4. Where MR = MC:
  - (a)   TR less TC is maximized
  - (b)   TR equals TC
  - (c)   TR less TC is minimized
  - (d)   any of the above could be true

5. In the short run the firm should cease production immediately if price falls below:
  - (a)   MC
  - (b)   AFC
  - (c)   AVC
  - (d)   ATC

8.4 Marginal Cost and Short-run Supply

◈ What determines the short-run supply curve for the purely competitive firm, and for the whole industry?

- Based on the rules for determining output, the short-run supply curve of the individual firm is that part of its short-run MC curve that is above average variable cost. At any price below this shutdown point the firm produces no output.
- The supply curve is upward sloping because the law of diminishing returns causes the marginal cost to begin rising after some point.

- The firm's break-even point is the point on the supply curve where price equals average total cost.
- The short-run supply curve of the industry is found by adding horizontally the supply curves of all individual firms.
- The short-run supply curve of the industry and the market demand determine the short-run equilibrium price and output of the industry. At this equilibrium firms may have either economic profits or losses.

Quick Quiz

6. The firm's short-run supply curve is its:
 (a)   MC curve
 (b)   MC curve above AFC
 (c)   MC curve above AVC
 (d)   MC curve above ATC

7. What would cause the firm's supply curve to shift to the left?
 (a)   an increase in the price of variable resources
 (b)   an increase in fixed costs
 (c)   the exit of some firms from the industry
 (d)   all of the above

8. The short-run equilibrium price in pure competition is determined at the intersection of:
 (a)   market demand and firm supply
 (b)   firm demand and market supply
 (c)   firm demand and firm supply
 (d)   market demand and market supply

8.5 Profit Maximization in the Long Run

✍ How do long-run adjustments affect price and output determination in the firm and the industry?

- The existence of economic profits or losses in the short-run equilibrium will trigger long-run adjustments. The analysis makes three simplifying assumptions about the industry:
  - o   The only long-run adjustment is in the entry or exit of firms.
  - o   All firms have identical costs.
  - o   The industry has constant costs, meaning that exit or entry of firms has no effect on resource prices (this assumption is relaxed later in the section).
- If economic profits exist, new firms will enter in the long run, increasing the total industry supply, and reducing the equilibrium price until

it equals the minimum average total cost at which firms can supply the product. The adjustments continue until the firms in the industry make only normal profits (zero economic profits).

- If losses occur, some firms will leave the industry in the long run, reducing total industry supply, and raising equilibrium price until it equals the minimum average total cost. The adjustments continue until remaining firms earn enough revenue to cover their opportunity costs, making normal profits (zero economic profits). At this point price and minimum average total cost are equal.
- When firms enter (leave) the industry, the demands for the resources used in the industry increase (decrease). How these demand shifts change resource prices will define whether the industry is one of increasing costs, decreasing costs, or constant costs. This will also dictate the slope of the industry's long-run supply curve.
  - o   In a constant-cost industry, entry or exit has no effect on resource input prices, so firms' ATC curves are unchanged. Therefore, there is no change in the minimum price at which firms can cover their opportunity costs. Because the long-run equilibrium price is unchanged, and the industry can supply larger quantities at a constant price, the long-run supply curve is horizontal at the price level equal to the minimum average total cost.
  - o   In an increasing-cost industry, entry of new firms pushes resource prices upwards, raising firms' ATC curves. The minimum price at which firms can cover their costs is increased. Therefore, an increase in demand will raise the long-run equilibrium price, so the industry can supply larger quantities only at higher prices. The long-run industry supply curve is upward sloping.
  - o   In a decreasing-cost industry, entry of firms pushes resource prices downwards, lowering firms' ATC curves. Firms can now cover their costs at lower prices, so the long-run equilibrium price will fall and the industry will supply more output at lower prices. The long-run supply curve will be downward sloping.

➲ The essential idea for understanding long-run equilibrium in pure competition is that economic profit must be zero. Though firms hope to make profits, they are forced by competition to sell at a price at which zero economic profit is the very best they can achieve. At this point price equals minimum average total cost.

Quick Quiz

9. If economic profits in a purely competitive industry are above zero in the short run, then in the long run:
(a)   firms will enter and price will fall
(b)   firms will enter and price will rise
(c)   firms will exit and price will fall
(d)   firms will exit and price will rise

10. In the long run the price in a purely competitive industry will be equal to:
(a)   minimum AVC
(b)   minimum ATC
(c)   where AVC equals MC
(d)   both (a) and (c)

11. If expansion in the number of construction firms operating in a particular city leads to an increase in wage rates for carpenters, electricians, etc., this is a sign that the construction industry is:
(a)   a purely competitive industry
(b)   an increasing cost industry
(c)   a decreasing cost industry
(d)   a constant cost industry

8.6 Pure Competition and Efficiency

◈   Does the market structure of pure competition lead to efficient results?

• Productive efficiency requires production in the least costly way. This is achieved when the average total cost of producing goods is at its minimum. This is achieved in the long run when the purely competitive firm produces where P = MC = ATC minimum.

• Allocative efficiency is achieved when society's resources are used to produce the combination of goods most wanted by consumers. This result can be occurs at a quantity level where three different conditions are met:
  ○   The marginal benefit to consumers equals marginal cost of production: MB = MC.
  ○   The consumer's maximum willingness to pay for the last unit of output equals the minimum acceptable price to the seller for selling that last unit.

  ○   Combined consumer surplus and producer surplus are maximized.

Quick Quiz

12. A purely competitive industry will achieve productive efficiency in the long run because it will produce the output level where:
(a)   P = MC
(b)   ATC is at its minimum
(c)   MB = MC
(d)   MC is at its minimum

13. If an industry is producing where MB > MC, this means that the industry is:
(a)   producing too much to achieve productive efficiency
(b)   producing too little to achieve productive efficiency
(c)   producing too much to achieve allocative efficiency
(d)   producing too little to achieve allocative efficiency

14. A purely competitive industry that is achieving allocative efficiency will maximize:
(a)   consumer surplus
(b)   producer surplus
(c)   consumer surplus plus producer surplus
(d)   output

Terms and Concepts

pure competition	MR = MC rule
pure monopoly	short-run supply curve
monopolistic competi-	long-run supply curve
tion	constant-cost industry
oligopoly	increasing-cost
imperfect competition	industry
price-taker	decreasing-cost
average revenue	industry
total revenue	productive efficiency
marginal revenue	allocative efficiency
break-even point	producer surplus

Fill-In Questions

1. The four distinct characteristics of pure competition are: (a) a _____ number of independent firms; (b) each firm has (no, some) _____ control over the market price; (c) the product is _____; (d) there are (no, some) _____ barriers to entry of new firms.

2. In pure competition the industry demand curve is _____-sloping, but the demand curve for the individual firm is perfectly (elastic, inelastic) _____, so that the firm's marginal revenue is constant and (less than, greater than, equal to) _____ the price of the product.

3. Economic profit is calculated as _____ minus _____. The firm's maximum profit is found at the output level where (marginal, total) _____ revenue minus _____ cost is the greatest. Equivalently, the firm's maximum profit is found at the output level where _____ revenue is equal to _____ cost.

4. A firm should produce in the short run only if it can obtain a _____ or suffer a loss no greater than its _____. Provided that it produces any output at all, it will produce that output at which its profit is a (maximum, minimum) _____ or its loss is a _____.

5. In the short run the firm is suffering a loss if price is below _____, but should continue to produce if price is higher than _____.

6. The short-run supply curve of the firm is that part of the _____ curve that is above its _____ curve. The short-run market supply curve is the _____ of the individual firms' supply curves.

7. If firms in an industry are obtaining economic profits, firms will (enter, leave) _____ the industry, the industry will employ (more, fewer) _____ resources and produce (more, less) _____ output, the price of the industry's product will (rise, fall) _____, and the industry's economic profits will (increase, decrease) _____ until they are equal to _____.

8. If the entry of new firms into an industry tends to raise the costs of all firms in the industry, the industry is a(n) (constant-, increasing-, decreasing-) _____ cost industry; and its long-run supply curve is (horizontal, down-sloping, up-sloping) _____.

9. The supply curve in a decreasing-cost industry has a (positive, negative, zero) _____ slope because an increase in industry output causes the prices of industry inputs to (increase, decrease, stay the same) _____.

10. The purely competitive industry achieves allocative efficiency where price and _____ are equal. It will achieve productive efficiency where price and _____ are equal and the latter is at a (minimum, maximum) _____.

True-False

Circle T if the statement is true, F if it is false.

1. There are no barriers to entry or exit in a purely competitive market.　　**T F**

2. If there are many firms in an industry, then the industry is purely competitive.　　**T F**

3. The demand curve for the individual purely competitive firm is horizontal at the market price.　　**T F**

4. In the short run a purely competitive firm maximizes profits by producing where price equals average total cost.　　**T F**

5. The competitive firm will shut down in the short run if fixed costs cannot be met at all possible output levels.　　**T F**

6. The break-even point is found in the short run where the firm's total revenue equals total costs.　　**T F**

7. A firm that is suffering losses may be wise to continue to produce in the short run even if they never expect to earn economic profits.　　**T F**

8. When a purely competitive firm is in a long-run equilibrium, product price will be exactly equal to the firm's minimum average total cost.　　**T F**

9. Given sufficient time for entry or exit, the economic profits in a purely competitive industry will tend to disappear.　　**T F**

10. The long-run supply curve for an industry could be downward-sloping.　　**T F**

11. In a constant-cost industry the long-run supply curve is infinitely elastic.　　**T F**

12. Consumer surplus equals the total utility value received less the total expenditures on the product. **T F**

13. If the industry is producing at a quantity where MB < MC, there is underproduction **T F**

Multiple-Choice

Circle the letter that corresponds to the best answer.

1. The four market structure models differ in their assumptions concerning:
(a) the number of firms in the industry
(b) the ease or difficulty for new firms in entering the industry
(c) whether the product is standardized or differentiated
(d) all of the above

2. Which of the following is not one of the four market models?
(a) pure competition
(b) monopoly
(c) monopolistic competition
(d) imperfect competition

3. In which of the following market models is the seller of a product a "price taker"?
(a) pure competition
(b) monopoly
(c) monopolistic competition
(d) oligopoly

4. Entry is blocked in:
(a) pure competition
(b) monopoly
(c) monopolistic competition
(d) oligopoly

5. The market model in which there is considerable interdependence among firms is:
(a) pure competition
(b) monopoly
(c) monopolistic competition
(d) oligopoly

6. Which of the following is not characteristic of pure competition?
(a) large number of sellers
(b) advertising by individual sellers
(c) easy entry
(d) standardized products

7. The demand schedule or curve confronted by the individual purely competitive firm is:
(a) perfectly inelastic
(b) inelastic but not perfectly inelastic
(c) perfectly elastic
(d) unit elastic

8. For the purely competitive firm, price equals:
(a) marginal revenue
(b) average revenue
(c) both marginal revenue and average revenue
(d) none of the above

9. Using the total-revenue and total-cost approach the competitive firm should produce, given total variable costs are covered, the level of output where:
(a) total revenue is a maximum
(b) total revenue equals total cost
(c) a normal profit is realized
(d) the positive difference between total revenue and total cost is maximized

10. Using the marginal-revenue and marginal-cost approach the competitive firm should produce, given average variable cost is covered, the level of output where:
(a) average cost equals price
(b) average variable cost equals price
(c) marginal cost equals price
(d) marginal cost equals average variable cost

11. A firm would be earning an economic profit in the short run if it is producing the quantity where marginal cost equals price and:
(a) average fixed cost is less than price
(b) average variable cost is greater than price
(c) average total cost is greater than price
(d) average total cost is less than price

12. A firm will be willing to operate at a loss in the short run if:
(a) the loss is no greater than its average fixed costs
(b) the loss is no greater than its total fixed costs
(c) the loss is no greater than its total variable costs

(d)   the loss is no greater than its average variable costs

13. Which of the following is an incorrect formula for calculating economic profit?
(a)   TR - TC
(b)   TR - ATC
(c)   (P – ATC) x Q
(d)   both (a) and (c)

14. Suppose that at the present rate of output a competitive firm finds that marginal cost is less than price. To maximize profits this firm should:
(a)   close down
(b)   reduce output
(c)   increase output
(d)   reduce the price

Questions 15 through 21 are based on the following cost data for a firm that sells in a purely competitive market.

Output	AFC	AVC	ATC	MC
1	$300	$100	$400	$100
2	150	75	225	50
3	100	70	170	60
4	75	73	148	80
5	60	80	140	110
6	50	90	140	140
7	43	103	146	180
8	38	119	157	230

15. The total fixed costs for this firm are:
(a) $100
(b) $200
(c) $300
(d) $400

16. If the market price for the product is $140, this firm will produce:
(a)   0 units
(b)   6 units
(c)   7 units
(d)   8 units

17. If the market price for the firm's product is $180, the firm's maximum profit in the short run will be:
(a)   an economic profit of $238
(b)   an economic profit of $592
(c)   an economic profit of $1,071
(d)   an economic profit of $0

18. If the market price is $60, this firm will:
(a)   produce 3 units and lose $330
(b)   produce 3 units and lose $300
(c)   close down and break even
(d)   close down and lose $300

19. If the market price is $110, this competitive firm will:
(a)   close down
(b)   produce 5 units at a loss of $150
(c)   produce 5 units at a profit of $150
(d)   produce 7 units and break even

20. This firm's shut-down price is:
(a) $38
(b) $40
(c) $70
(d) $140

21. This firm's break-even price is:
(a) $38
(b) $40
(c) $70
(d) $140

22. An increase in a firm's fixed cost would:
(a)   lower the firm's shutdown price in the short run
(b)   raise the firm's shutdown price in the short run
(c)   have no effect on the firm's shutdown price
(d)   force the firm to immediately cease production

23. An increase in the wage rate that a firm must pay its variable factor (labour) would:
(a)   lower the firm's shutdown price in the short run
(b)   raise the firm's shutdown price in the short run
(c)   have no effect on the firm's shutdown price
(d)   force the firm to immediately cease production

Questions 24 through 30 are based on the next diagram showing the short-run costs of a purely competitive firm.

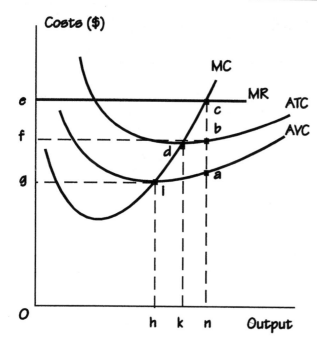

24. Given that the price is $0e$ the profit-maximizing competitive firm should produce:
- (a) ci units
- (b) $0n$ units
- (c) $0k$ units
- (d) $0h$ units

25. The marginal cost at the profit-maximizing rate of output is:
- (a) an dollars
- (b) nb dollars
- (c) $0f$ dollars
- (d) $0e$ dollars

26. Total revenue at the profit-maximizing rate of output is given by the area
- (a) $0nbf$
- (b) $0ecn$
- (c) $0gan$
- (d) $efab$

27. Total cost at the profit-maximizing rate of output is given by the area:
- (a) $ecn0$
- (b) $0gan$
- (c) $fbag$
- (d) $0fbn$

28. Economic profit is given by the area:
- (a) $ecbf$
- (b) $fbag$
- (c) $ecag$
- (d) $ecdf$

29. The firm's short-run supply curve is represented by:
- (a)   the ATC curve above point d
- (b)   the AVC curve above point i
- (c)   the MC curve above i
- (d)   the MR curve

30. The lowest price at which this firm will continue to produce output in the short run is:
- (a) $0e$
- (b) $0f$
- (c) $0g$
- (d)   the firm will produce at any price

31. In a competitive firm, technological progress that increases the productivity of labour would:
- (a)   shift the MC curve downward
- (b)   shift the MC curve upward
- (c)   shift the AFC curve downward
- (d)   reduce the profit-maximizing output level

The next two questions are based on this diagram showing cost curves in the long run for a representative single firm (on the left) and the supply and demand in its purely competitive constant-cost industry (on the right).

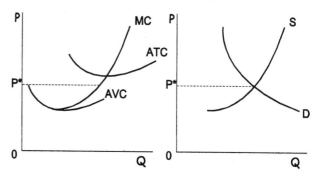

32. P* (the current price) is:
- (a)   the long run equilibrium price
- (b)   above the long run equilibrium price
- (c)   below the long run equilibrium price
- (d)   a zero profit equilibrium price

33. Given the current equilibrium at P*, the number of firms in the industry will:
- (a)   eventually increase
- (b)   eventually decrease
- (c)   not change from its current level
- (d)   will decrease to zero

34. If each firm in a purely competitive market is enjoying economic profits, then in the long run we can expect:
(a)   the market supply curve to increase
(b)   the demand curve to increase
(c)   the market supply curve to decrease
(d)   the demand curve to decrease

35. The long-run supply curve under pure competition is upward sloping when increased product demand leads to:
(a)   more firms entering the market
(b)   firms building bigger plants
(c)   input price increases
(d)   economies of scale

36. In a decreasing-cost industry, if the number of firms shrinks, then:
(a)   resource prices and the industry price will rise
(b)   resource prices and the industry price will fall
(c)   resource prices will rise and the industry price will fall
(d)   resource prices will fall and the industry price will rise

37. Productive efficiency is achieved in the long run in a competitive industry because competition forces each firm to produce where:
(a)   marginal cost equals price
(b)   fixed cost is zero
(c)   economic profits are positive
(d)   long-run average total cost is minimized

38. An economy is producing the goods most wanted by society when for each and every good:
(a)   price and average cost are equal
(b)   price and marginal cost are equal
(c)   economic profit is positive
(d)   the amount sold equals the amount produced

39. Which statement is false for a purely competitive industry?
(a)   where P = MC allocative efficiency is achieved
(b)   where P = ATC at its minimum, productive efficiency is achieved
(c)   where P = AVC at its minimum point is the firm's shutdown point in the short run
(d)   none of these statements is false

Problems and Projects

1.   Market Structure Characteristics
Slot the following into the appropriate spaces in the table below. (Hint: some answers are used more than once.)

one	considerable
few	very easy
many	blocked
a very large number	fairly easy
standardized	fairly difficult
differentiated	none
some	unique

	Market Structure Model			
Market characteristics	Pure Competition	Monopoly	Monopolistic Competition	Oligopoly
Number of firms	_____	_____	_____	_____
Type of product	_____	_____	_____	_____
Control over price	_____	_____	_____	_____
Conditions of entry	_____	_____	_____	_____
Non-price competition	_____	_____	_____	_____

2.   TR and TC Approach to Profit Maximization
The following table shows data for Blue Lite, a match maker, who sells their product in a purely competitive market.

Output (boxes/yr)	Total Cost ($/yr)	Total Revenue ($/yr)	Profit ($/yr)
0	200	_____	_____
1000	250	_____	_____
2000	275	_____	_____
3000	325	_____	_____
4000	400	_____	_____
5000	500	_____	_____
6000	625	_____	_____
7000	775	_____	_____
8000	950	_____	_____

(a) Assume that the market price for matches is $0.16 per box. Fill in the total revenue column.
(b) Fill in the profit column.
(c) What level of output maximizes profits for Blue Lite? _____
(d) In the next table, in the TR1 and Profit 1 columns, recompute the results for Blue Lite assuming that the price of matches is now $0.09 per box.

Output	TC	TR 1	Profit 1	TR 2	Profit 2
0	$200	$___	$___	$___	$___
1000	250	___	___	___	___
2000	275	___	___	___	___
3000	325	___	___	___	___
4000	400	___	___	___	___
5000	500	___	___	___	___
6000	625	___	___	___	___
7000	775	___	___	___	___
8000	950	___	___	___	___

(e) If Blue Lite chooses to produce at this price, they would produce _____ boxes/year. Their loss at this output is $_____ per year. Because Blue Lite's total fixed cost is $_____ per year, they (should, should not) _____ continue in the short run to produce matches at a price of $0.09. Their loss by continuing to produce is $_____ per year (less than, more than) _____ their loss if they close down and incur only their total fixed cost.

(f) Recompute the results in the TR2 and Profit 2 columns assuming that the price of matches is now $0.03 per box.

(g) If Blue Lite does produce at this price, they would produce _____ boxes/year. Blue Lite (should, should not) _____ continue in the short run to produce matches at this price. Their loss by producing at this price is $_____ per year, compared to a total fixed cost of $_____ per year.

3. MC and MR Approach to Profit Maximization

A purely competitive firm faces the following demand schedule and marginal cost schedule.

(a) Compute the average revenue (AR) and marginal revenue (MR) schedules from the demand schedule data.

Q d	P	AR	MR	MC
1	$10	$___	$___	$4
2	10	___	___	3
3	10	___	___	4
4	10	___	___	6
5	10	___	___	9
6	10	___	___	13
7	10	___	___	18

(b) If the P, AR, and MR schedules were graphed as a function of Qd, all three would be the same horizontal line at price = $_____.

(c) Given the MC and MR data, the profit-maximizing quantity is _____. The last unit produced adds $_____ to revenues and adds $_____ to costs. Therefore, it adds $_____ to profits. If one more unit would be produced it would add $_____ to revenues, and $_____ to costs, therefore reducing profits by $_____. Therefore, at the optimum, every unit has been produced that can contribute anything to profit.

4. Graphical Approach to Profit Maximization

The firm whose cost curves are shown in the next graph sells vitamins in a purely competitive market. Output is measured in bottles per day, and costs are in $ per bottle. The AVC curve includes costs for labour and ingredients. The firm also pays fixed costs for their production facility and machinery.

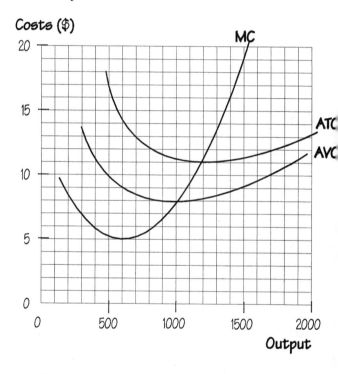

(a) If the market price of vitamins is $19 per bottle, how many bottles will this firm wish to sell? _____

(b) On the graph show the rectangle of profit earned at $19 per bottle.

(c) What is the firm's break-even price? _____

(d) Find the short-run shutdown price. _____

Treat the remaining questions as separate cases.

(e) If there is an unexpected increase in the demand for vitamins, which of the results (a) through (d) would change, and why?

(f) If there is an increase in the rent on the production facility, which of the results (a) through (d) would change, and why?

(g) If there is an increase in the price of ingredients, which of the results (a) through (d) would change, and why?

5. The Firm and the Industry in the Short Run

The pumpkin industry is purely competitive, and consists of 100 identical firms, each with costs as shown in the schedule below.

Output	ATC	MC
20	$7.00	
		$2.00
40	4.50	
		3.00
60	4.00	
		4.00
80	4.00	
		5.00
100	4.20	
		6.00
120	4.50	

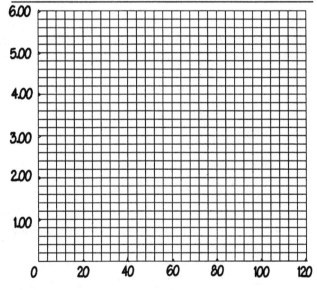

(a) Plot the average total costs and marginal costs for a typical firm on the left-hand panel of the graphs provided. Remember to plot MC at the midpoints of the output ranges. (For example, plot $3 at quantity = 50.)

(b) Suppose that the minimum AVC for this firm is $2.50. If so, the firm's supply curve is its _____ curve above $_____.

(c) The right-hand panel shows the market demand for pumpkins. Derive and plot the short-run market supply (Hint: the industry consists of 100 firms with supply curves identical to the one shown in your left-hand graph).

(d) From the short-run equilibrium now shown in the industry graph, the market price is $_____, and the market quantity is _____.

(e) Based on the market price from the industry graph, and the individual firm's supply curve, the firm will maximize profits (or minimize losses) by producing an output of _____.

(f) The industry result and the firm result are consistent because multiplying the firm's output by the number of firms gives _____ (which should equal the industry output).

(g) On the diagram show the area that represents the firm's short-run profit (or loss) at this equilibrium.

6. The Firm and the Industry in the Long Run

This question uses the pumpkin market graphs in the previous question. Assume that the short-run average total cost and marginal cost data also represent long-run ATC and MC. Also assume this is a constant-cost industry.

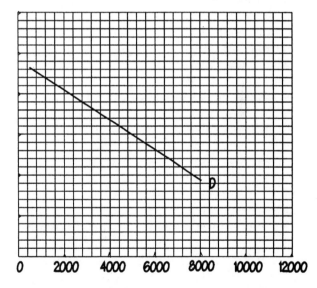

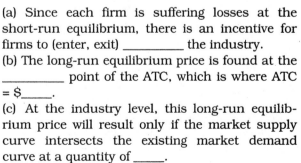

(a) Since each firm is suffering losses at the short-run equilibrium, there is an incentive for firms to (enter, exit) _____ the industry.

(b) The long-run equilibrium price is found at the _____ point of the ATC, which is where ATC = $_____.

(c) At the industry level, this long-run equilibrium price will result only if the market supply curve intersects the existing market demand curve at a quantity of _____.

(d) At this long-run equilibrium price, each firm will wish to produce a quantity of _____ (by the P = MC rule).

(e) Given the equilibrium quantity for the industry, and the optimum quantity for the firm, the long-run equilibrium number of firms is approximately _____ (divide the two). Therefore, about _____ firms must leave the industry.

(f) Draw in the new short-run industry supply curve after the number of firms has changed.

(g) Because this is a constant-cost industry, the long-run industry supply is a _____ line, which is located at a price equal to the individual firm's minimum ATC. Draw in this supply curve.

7.   The Shutdown Decision

Skeena Mills and Stikine Forest Products are hypothetical firms in a purely competitive lumber market. They have different cost structures. At normal price ranges for lumber they produce the same quantity of lumber, but Stikine makes a larger short-run profit than Skeena does. However, when lumber prices fall temporarily, Stikine closes down temporarily, while Skeena continues producing. Sketch a pair of diagrams showing ATC, AVC and MC for each firm consistent with the facts presented.

8. Consumer Surplus, Producer Surplus and Allocative Efficiency

Five individuals (A through E) wish to rent houses in Vancouver for a short time during the 2010 Olympics. Their maximum willingness to pay is shown below:

    A $28,000
    B $22,000
    C $19,000
    D $14,000
    E $11,000

Five Vancouver residents (F through J) are willing to rent out their homes during the Olympics. The minimum acceptable price for each is:

    F $8,000
    G $9,000
    H $10,000
    I $12,000
    J $16,000

Assume that there is a website that brings together the homeowners and the renters, with the rental prices being set through a competitive auction procedure.

(a)   How many of the five homes should be rented to reach the point of allocative efficiency?

(b) What is the total amount of consumer surplus plus producer surplus at the point of allocative efficiency?

Discussion Questions

1.   Explain why all firms in a purely competitive market must charge exactly the same price.

2.   If pure competition is so rare in the real world, why is it covered in this course?

3.   Suppose the market for rice is purely competitive. Since consumers' demand for rice is surely down-sloping, how can it be that the individual producer faces a horizontal or perfectly elastic demand curve?

4.   Why is the firm willing to produce at a loss in the short run if the loss is no greater than fixed costs? At what point does a firm drop out of the industry?

5.   Suppose a firm has determined that they should leave the industry in the long run. How does the firm decide when, practically speaking, they should wind up their business? If all firms were experiencing losses, would they all drop out of the industry at the same time?

6.   What factors determine the short-run supply for an individual purely competitive firm, and for its industry?

7.   What determines the equilibrium price and output of a purely competitive industry in the short run?

8.   Why must economic profits be zero in long-run equilibrium for a purely competitive industry? What forces the purely competitive firm into this position?

9.   If economic profits end up at zero in long-run equilibrium, why should entrepreneurs bother starting up businesses in purely competitive industries? Consider the difference between normal profits and economic profits.

10. What is a constant-cost industry? What is an increasing-cost industry? Under what economic conditions is each likely to be found? What will be the nature of the long-run supply curve in each of these industries?

11. Why would a restaurant industry in a large city likely be a constant-cost industry? Why would a hotel industry on a very small island likely be an increasing-cost industry?

12. What two kinds of efficiency are necessary if the economy is to make the best use of its resources?

13. What are the three conditions that describe the situation of allocative efficiency?

Answers

Quick Quiz
1. (d) p. 192
2. (d) pp. 193-194
3. (d) p. 193
4. (a) pp. 196-198
5. (c) pp. 200-201
6. (c) p. 204
7. (a) p. 205
8. (d) p. 205
9. (a) p. 209
10. (b) p. 208
11. (b) pp. 210-211
12. (b) p. 214
13. (d) p. 214
14. (c) p. 217

Fill-in Questions
1. (a) large; (b) no; (c) standardized; (d) no
2. downward, elastic, equal to
3. total revenue, total cost; total, total; marginal, marginal
4. profit, total fixed cost; maximum, minimum
5. ATC; AVC
6. MC, AVC, horizontal sum
7. enter, more, more, fall, decrease, zero
8. increasing, up-sloping
9. negative, decrease
10. MC; ATC, minimum

True-False
1. T
2. F   not necessarily; it could also be monopolistic competition
3. T   therefore the individual firm is a "price taker"
4. F   profit-maximization occurs where P = MC

5. F   it is variable costs that must be met in order for the firm to continue operating
6. T
7. T   losses may be minimized in this way
8. T
9. T   as more firms enter, the industry supply increases, and price falls
10. T   in the case of a decreasing-cost industry
11. T   horizontal, in other words
12. T
13. F   since MB is falling and MC is rising, this must describe a case of overproduction

Multiple-Choice
1. (d)
2. (d)   imperfect competition refers to more than one market structure model
3. (a)   only pure competition does the firm have no control whatsoever over price
4. (b)
5. (d)
6. (b)   no individual seller would have any incentive to advertise since the product is identical to any other sellers' products
7. (c)   demand is horizontal for the firm
8. (c)   price-taking behaviour
9. (d)   economic profit is this difference
10. (c)
11. (d)   profit = (P – ATC) x Q
12. (b)   since the total fixed cost would become the loss if the firm chooses to shutdown rather than produce
13. (b)
14. (c)   since MC is rising as output rises, increase output until MC rises enough to equal P
15. (c)   TFC = AFC x Q
16. (b)   set Q where P = MC
17. (a)   set Q at 7 where P = MC; (P – ATC) x Q = (180-146) x 7
18. (d)   close down because P is below AVC, and lose TFC = 300
19. (b)   set Q = 5 where P = MC; (P – ATC) x Q = (110-140) x 5
20. (c)   the minimum value for AVC
21. (d)   the minimum value for ATC
22. (c)   fixed costs have no effect on decisions in the short run
23. (b)   the AVC curve (and MC and ATC) would shift upwards
24. (b)   where P = MC
25. (d)   P = MC
26. (b)   P x Q
27. (d)   ATC x Q

28. (a) (P – ATC) x Q
29. (c) MC above AVC
30. (c) minimum AVC is the shutdown price
31. (a) lower production costs at all output levels
32. (c) in the long run price = minimum long run ATC
33. (b) when profits are below zero, firms begin to exit at the end of the short run
34. (a) as some firms enter
35. (c) increasing-cost industry
36. (a) in this type of industry resource costs are lower when the industry is larger
37. (d)
38. (b)
39. (d)

Problems and Projects

1. Number of firms: very large number, one, many, few; Type of product: standardized, unique, differentiated, standardized or differentiated; Control over price: none, considerable, some, considerable; Conditions of entry: very easy, blocked, fairly easy, fairly difficult; Non-price competition: none, considerable, considerable, considerable.

2. (a) 0, 160, 320, 480, 640, 800, 960, 1120, 1280; (b) -200, -90, 45, 155, 240, 300, 335, 345, 330; (c) 7000; (d) TR1 = 0, 90, 180, 270, 360, 450, 540, 630, 720; Profit 1 = -200, -160, -95, -55, -40, -50, -85, -145, -230; (e) 4000, 40, 200; should, 160, less than; (f) TR2 = 0, 30, 60, 90, 120, 150, 180, 210, 240; Profit 2 = -200, -220, -215, -235, -280, -350, -445, -565, -710; (g) 2000; should not; 215, 200

3. (a) AR and MR both $10 at all Q values; (b) 10; (c) 5; 10, 9; 1; 10, 13, 3

4. (a) 1500; (b) Rectangle shows (P - ATC) x Q = (19-11.5) x 1500; (c) minimum ATC = $11; (d) minimum AVC = $8; (e) Q* increases because P = MC at higher Q, Profit rectangle becomes larger because Q increases and (P-ATC) increases; (f) Profit rectangle becomes smaller because ATC shifts up, so (P-ATC) decreases; the break-even point increases because ATC shifts up; (g) MC, ATC, AVC all shift up, so Q* falls, profit decreases, break-even price and shutdown price both rise.

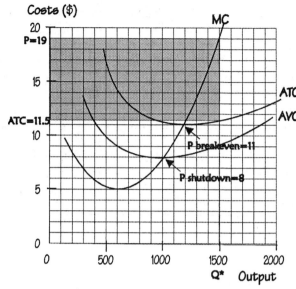

5. (b) MC, $2.50; (d) about $3, about 5000; (e) 50; (f) 5000; (g) rectangle: (P - ATC) x Q

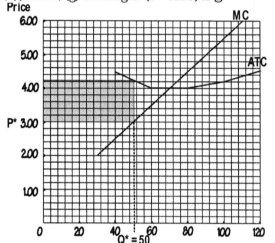

6. (a) exit; (b) minimum, $4.00; (c) about 2000; (d) 70; (e) 29; 71; (g) horizontal (see S_{LR}).

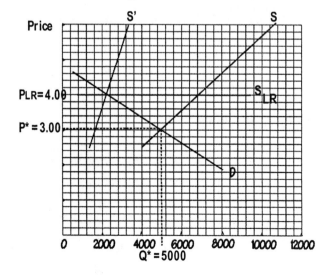

7. Skeena's ATC is higher than Stikine's, but Stikine's AVC is higher than Skeena's, so Stikine's short-run shutdown price is higher.

8. (a) For the first 4 homes marginal willingness to pay exceeds the minimum acceptable price, so these should be rented (i.e., for 4th home 14,000 > 12,000, but for 5th home 11,000 < 16,000, so the 5th should not be rented). (b) Total willingness to pay = 28,000 + 22,000 + 19,000 + 14, 000 = 83,000, while the total minimum acceptable to sellers = 8,000 + 9,000 + 12,000 + 16,000 = 45,000. Total CS + PS = 83,000 − 45,000 = $38,000.

Chapter 9 Pure Monopoly

Overview

This chapter, on pure monopoly, is the second of three chapters dealing with specific market structure models. Pure monopoly exists when there is only one seller of a product for which there are no close substitutes, and where other potential sellers are blocked from entering the market. Under these conditions the seller is a "price maker." We study pure monopoly because there are some important examples in the Canadian economy (especially in local markets), and because some characteristics of monopoly will help us to understand the market models of monopolistic competition and oligopoly (discussed in Chapter 10).

Sooner or later, the monopoly firm will lose its exclusive position in the market unless there are obstacles preventing the entry of other firms. Barriers to entry can stem from economies of scale, legal protection (patents and licenses), ownership or control of essential resources, or pricing and other strategic behaviour. None of these barriers are likely to be impenetrable in the long run, except perhaps barriers sanctioned by government.

The pure monopoly market structure is compared to that of pure competition. Key results include:

1. In both market structures firms maximize profits by setting output where marginal cost equals marginal revenue.

2. Unlike the price-taking firms in pure competition, the monopoly firm faces a down-sloping demand which is not perfectly elastic, so marginal revenue is below price, and both fall as output rises. Therefore the monopolist must choose both quantity and price.

3. The monopolist has no supply curve.

4. In pure monopoly barriers to entry can protect economic profits indefinitely.

5. Unlike pure competition, pure monopoly achieves neither productive nor allocative efficiency.

Most comparisons between pure competition and pure monopoly are based on the assumption that costs are identical. However, costs could be either higher or lower under pure monopoly, in which case some of the conclusions from such comparisons change. Another factor is whether technological progress is more likely under pure monopoly. However, monopoly is believed to be inefficient overall, and governments have several policy options for controlling the behaviour of monopolies.

Chapter Outline

9.1 Characteristics of Pure Monopoly

⟡ Under what conditions will pure monopoly arise?

• The market structure of pure monopoly has these characteristics:
  o There is only a single firm in the market.
  o The firm's product has no close substitutes.
  o The firm is a "price-maker."
  o The firm has no immediate competitors because entry to the market is totally blocked.

• While pure monopoly is not very common, some important examples exist: public utilities, professional sports teams, and even gas stations in small, remote towns. The study of pure monopoly also helps us to understand firms that are "almost" monopolies.

➲ How narrowly or broadly a market is defined will affect the degree of monopoly power a firm has in its market. The Vancouver Canucks are the only supplier of live NHL-level hockey in British Columbia, which sounds like a monopoly!

But for a consumer who is willing to substitute televised NHL hockey, or live junior A games, etc., the Canucks have less monopoly power.

• Pure monopoly can exist in the long run only as long as barriers to entry keep potential competitors out of the market. There are several types of barriers:

o Economies of scale can bar entry and produce the conditions for "natural monopoly" if the firm's long-run average-cost curve declines over a wide output range.

o Governments create legal barriers by awarding firms patents and licenses.

o Ownership or control of a specific resource critical to the production of a good can bar competitors.

o Strategic price-cutting or advertising specifically aimed at making new competitors unprofitable may also deter entry.

• The analysis of pure monopoly behaviour makes three assumptions: (1) patents, economies of scale, or resource ownership secure the firm's monopoly position; (2) government does not regulate the firm; and (3) the firm charges a single price for all units, to all consumers.

• The monopolist is the entire industry, so its demand curve is the down-sloping industry demand curve. Therefore:

o More output can be sold only by reducing price. Therefore, marginal revenue is below price for every level of output except for the first unit.

o The monopolist chooses some price-quantity point along the industry demand curve and is, therefore, a "price maker."

o The monopolist sets price in the elastic part of the demand curve, because marginal revenue is negative in the inelastic portion.

⮑ In monopoly, the demand and marginal revenue curves are distinct. The MR curve is twice as steep as the demand, so the MR curve lies, at all points, halfway between the demand and the price axis. So, when sketching this graph draw the demand curve first, and then sketch in the MR curve accordingly.

Quick Quiz

1. Which is not an essential part of the definition of pure monopoly?

(a) single seller in a market

(b) product has no close substitutes

(c) other firms are barred from entering the market

(d) the firm's exclusive position in the market is protected by the government

2. An example of a legal barrier to entry is:

(a) any barrier that is not prohibited by law

(b) economies of scale

(c) a patent or a trademark

(d) ownership of a special resource

3. In pure monopoly marginal revenue is:

(a) equal to price

(b) above price

(c) below price

(d) any of the above

9.2 Output and Price Determination in a Monopoly

◇ How are price and output determined in a pure monopoly?

• We assume that a monopolist hires inputs in a purely competitive market and utilizes the same technology as a competitive firm, as described in the previous chapter.

• The monopolist chooses the output level at which the marginal cost and marginal revenue are equal, and charges the price corresponding to this output on the demand curve.

⮑ When displaying the monopolist's data in a table (e.g., Table 9-1), it is customary to show MR and MC "between the lines" because MR and MC are calculated going from one quantity to another. To follow the same principle when graphing, be sure to plot each point on MR and MC at the quantity right in the middle between the two quantities from which the calculation was made.

⮑ The monopolist's price is on the demand curve. First locate the monopolist's profit-maximizing output where MR = MC. Then go up to the demand curve to find the maximum price consumers are willing to pay for this quantity.

• The monopolist has no supply curve because no unique relationship exists between price and quantity supplied. Different demand conditions can bring about different prices at the same output level.

- Three common misconceptions about monopolists are that they charge as high a price as possible, that they seek the maximum profit **per unit** of output, and that monopoly status is a guarantee of profitability.

Quick Quiz

4. If the monopolist's demand curve shifts to the right, its MR curve will:
- (a)   shift twice as far to the right
- (b)   shift half as far to the right
- (c)   shift to the left
- (d)   not shift at all

5. At the profit-maximizing point for the monopolist:
- (a) $P = MR$
- (b) $P > MR$
- (c) $P < MR$
- (d)   any of the above, depending on the situation

6. In pure monopoly:
- (a)   the goal is to maximize profit per unit of output
- (b)   a rise in MC will shift the supply curve
- (c)   a price can always be found which guarantees economic profits
- (d)   the firm is a price maker but is constrained by the demand curve

9.3 Economic Effects of Monopoly

◇ From a social perspective, how efficient is pure monopoly compared to pure competition?

◇ In the efficiency comparison, what difference does it make if costs are not the same for a monopoly as for a purely competitive industry?

- Because output is set below the level at which $P = MC$, monopoly does not achieve allocative efficiency.
- Because it fails to produce at the point of minimum ATC, monopoly does not achieve productive efficiency.
- On both counts pure monopoly fails to measure up to the standard of pure competition.
- As compared to a purely competitive market, monopoly transfers income from consumers to the owners of the firm, tending to increase inequality of incomes.

- Contrary to what has been assumed so far, a pure monopoly may face higher or lower costs of production as compared to purely competitive firms.
  - o   If there are economies of scale in production, output can be produced at a lower long-run average cost by a monopolist than by many small firms. Simultaneous consumption and network effects create extensive economies of scale for firms in some information technology industries.
  - o   Lack of competition makes the monopolist more susceptible to X-inefficiency (operation at greater than lowest cost for a particular level of output).
  - o   Firms may incur rent-seeking expenditures (such as lobbying fees, and public relations expenditures), to gain or preserve monopoly position. These expenditures increase costs but add nothing to society's output.
  - o   Cost-saving technological advances more be more common under monopoly than pure competition. A monopoly, however, does not have a strong incentive to innovate, except perhaps to reinforce barriers to entry.
- The various types of inefficiency that are possible under pure monopoly cause society to consider what action government might take in the public interest. Three general policy options are available: prosecute monopoly power gained through anticompetitive actions, regulate natural monopolies, or simply allow monopoly to exist (especially in cases where the monopoly power seems unsustainable in the long run).

Quick Quiz

7. As compared to pure competition, pure monopoly usually falls short of the efficiency standard in terms of:
- (a)   allocative efficiency
- (b)   productive efficiency
- (c)   both (a) and (b)
- (d)   neither (a) nor (b)

8. Pure monopoly may not be less efficient than pure competition in cases where:
- (a)   economies of scale are significant
- (b)   technological advances occur more quickly under monopoly
- (c)   both (a) and (b)
- (d)   neither (a) nor (b)

9.4 Price Discrimination and Monopoly

◈ Under what circumstances will a monopolist charge more than one price?

• To increase profits, a pure monopolist may engage in price discrimination by selling the same product at different prices (where the price differences are not justified by cost differences). This practice is common in Canada.

• To price discriminate, the seller must have some monopoly power, be able to segregate buyers into groups having different elasticities of demand, and be able to prevent the resale of the product.

• The seller charges a higher price to the group with the more inelastic demand.

• Perfect price discrimination increases the monopoly profits. Surprisingly, it also reduces allocative inefficiency of monopoly because it results in increased output.

Quick Quiz

9. In terms of preventing resale, which of the following firms would be in the weakest position to price discriminate?
  (a)   airline
  (b)   house painter
  (c)   lawyer
  (d)   bookstore

10. Which is likely an example of price discrimination?
  (a)   hotels charging more for extra people in a room
  (b)   restaurants giving discounts to people who present coupons
  (c)   stores charging higher prices for larger sizes of clothing items
  (d)   none of these are price discrimination

9.5 Regulated Monopoly

◈ What principles do governments use when they subject monopolies to rate regulation, and what are the consequences for efficiency?

• Natural monopolies have often been subject to rate (price) regulation as governments try to improve the efficiency of resource allocation.

• A natural monopoly exists when economies of scale are so extensive that one firm can supply the entire market at lower average cost than could a number of competing firms.

• In Canada industries traditionally covered by such regulations include public utilities (such as retail distributors of natural gas, electricity, and local phone service). Many of these industries have been at least partially deregulated in recent year.

• To achieve the socially optimal price, where P = MC, the regulatory agency could set a ceiling price at the level where the demand curve is cut by the marginal cost. This would achieve allocative efficiency.

• Because the monopoly may suffer a loss at the socially optimal price, government may set the ceiling at a level where the average total cost and demand intersect, thus allowing the monopolist a "fair return" where opportunity costs are recouped, but no economic profit is gained.

• The dilemma of regulation is that the optimal social price may cause losses for the monopolist, while a fair-return price results in a less efficient resource allocation. While not perfect, fair-return price regulation nevertheless reduces the allocative inefficiency that would exist under unregulated monopoly.

Quick Quiz

11. If a regulated monopoly is allowed to charge a "fair return" price, this likely means that price will be set equal to:
  (a)   average variable cost
  (b)   average total cost
  (c)   marginal cost
  (d)   average total cost plus a reasonable margin for profit

12. The basic dilemma facing the regulator of monopoly is that if price is set at the level required to achieve allocative efficiency, then:
  (a)   price will be below average total cost
  (b)   price will equal marginal cost
  (c)   the monopoly will make economic profit
  (d)   none of the above

9.6 Monopoly and Deadweight Loss

◈ How can the inefficiency of monopoly be represented using the concepts of consumer surplus and producer surplus?

• At the output level chosen by a single-price monopolist, P > MC. Therefore, the marginal benefit to consumers exceeds the marginal cost of production, and the monopolist is not producing as much output at consumers would like.

• The resulting loss of consumer surplus and producer surplus and is called the deadweight loss of monopoly.

Quick Quiz

13. Deadweight loss refers to:

(a)   excess production costs due to X-inefficiency

(b)   inefficiency or resource loss because monopolists produce too much output

(c)   net loss of consumer surplus and producer surplus due to monopoly

(d)   transfer from consumer surplus to producer surplus due to monopoly pricing

Terms and Concepts

pure monopoly	rent-seeking
barriers to entry	behaviour
simultaneous con-	price discrimination
sumption	socially optimal price
network effects	fair-return price
X-inefficiency	deadweight loss

Fill-In Questions

1. Pure monopoly is a market structure in which a single firm is the sole seller of a product for which there are no _____ and into which entry in the long run is _____.

2. The demand schedule confronting the pure monopolist is _____ sloping; this means that marginal revenue is (greater, less) _____ than price and that both marginal revenue and price (increase, decrease) _____ as output increases.

3. Suppose a car dealer can sell 5 cars at $20,000 each, or 6 cars at $19,000 each. The revenue from the sale of the sixth car would be $_____, but to sell the sixth car the dealer would have to cut the price and lose a total of $_____ on the _____ cars that he could otherwise have sold at the higher price. Therefore, the marginal revenue from the sixth car is the gain of $_____ minus the loss of $_____, for an overall change in total revenue of $_____.

4. The profit-maximizing monopolist will always want to choose a price-quantity combination somewhere in the (elastic, inelastic) _____

segment of its demand curve. The monopolist will avoid the _____ segment, because there the (total, marginal) _____ revenue is (negative, positive) _____ .

5. Given the same costs, the monopolist will find it profitable to sell (more, less) _____ output and to charge a (higher, lower) _____ price than would a purely competitive firm.

6. A monopoly that spends money lobbying the government to impose tariffs that would keep foreign competitors out of the Canadian market is said to be engaging in _____ behaviour.

7. There is price discrimination whenever a product is sold at different _____ and these differences are not justified by differences in the _____ of supplying the product.

8. Price discrimination is possible only when the following three conditions are found:

(a)   _____

(b)   _____

(c)   _____

9. The misallocation of resources resulting from monopoly can be eliminated if a ceiling price is set equal to _____. However, since such a price is often _____ than average total cost, the regulation will cause the monopolist to suffer a loss.

True-False

Circle T if the statement is true, F if it is false.

1. In the monopoly model the firm and the industry are one and the same.   **T F**

2. A natural monopoly is defined as a firm that holds a government-granted franchise.   **T F**

3. A purely competitive firm is a price-taker, but a monopolist is a price-maker.   **T F**

4. On a graph the marginal revenue curve is half as steep as the demand curve.   **T F**

5. Marginal revenue is less than price for down-sloping demand curves because in order to sell an extra unit the firm must lower the price of all previous units sold. **T F**

6. A monopoly may attempt to establish an entry barrier through a policy of dramatic price-cutting whenever it appears another firm might enter the market. **T F**

7. At the profit-maximizing monopoly output, price is greater than marginal cost. **T F**

8. When a monopolist is maximizing its total profit, it is also maximizing its per unit (or average) profit. **T F**

9. When there are substantial economies of scale in production, the monopolist may charge a price that is lower than the price that would prevail if the product were produced by a purely competitive industry. **T F**

10. Rent-seeking behaviour adds to the inefficiency of monopoly. **T F**

11. If a movie theatre sells tickets to students at 25% below the regular adult price, then this is an example of price discrimination, assuming students and adults are equally costly to serve. **T F**

12. The price that achieves allocative efficiency is called the socially optimal price. **T F**

13. A "fair-return" price for a regulated utility would set price equal to average cost. **T F**

Multiple-Choice

Circle the letter that corresponds to the best answer.

1. Which of the following is the best example of a pure monopoly?
- (a) a neighbourhood grocer in Saskatoon
- (b) the only gas station in a remote town
- (c) the manufacturer of Crest toothpaste
- (d) a bank in downtown Winnipeg

2. For the monopolist:
- (a) price equals marginal revenue
- (b) price is greater than marginal revenue
- (c) price is less than marginal revenue

- (d) price and marginal revenue are unrelated

3. In order to maximize profits the monopolist should set output at the level where:
- (a) price equals marginal cost
- (b) price equals average cost
- (c) marginal revenue equals marginal cost
- (d) marginal revenue equals average cost

4. Reasons for the existence of monopoly include all but:
- (a) patents
- (b) declining long-run average costs over a large range of output relative to industry demand
- (c) control of a raw material
- (d) inelastic demand for the product

5. Which of the following is the key characteristic of a natural monopoly?
- (a) economies of scale throughout the range of market demand
- (b) it is a public utility
- (c) it has low fixed costs
- (d) its has large economic profits

6. Because the monopolist is the sole producer in the industry:
- (a) the demand curve for the monopolist is the industry demand curve
- (b) the monopolist's demand curve will be inelastic
- (c) the monopolist will not lose sales when price is raised
- (d) the marginal revenue will be greater than price at all levels of output

7. At its present output a monopolist determines that its marginal cost is $18 and its marginal revenue is $21. The monopolist will maximize profits or minimize losses by:
- (a) increasing price while keeping output constant
- (b) decreasing price and increasing output
- (c) decreasing both price and output
- (d) increasing both price and output

8. If a monopolist's MC curve shifts up, how will the monopolist respond?
- (a) increase price and increase output
- (b) decrease price and increase output
- (c) decrease price and decrease output

(d)   increase price and decrease output

The next three questions refer to the following demand and cost data for a monopolist.

Output	Price	Total Cost
0	$80	$50
1	70	60
2	60	72
3	50	86
4	40	102
5	30	120

9.   The marginal revenue of the third unit of output is:
(a) $10
(b) $20
(c) $30
(d) $40

10. The profit-maximizing monopolist produces:
(a)   1 unit
(b)   2 units
(c)   3 units
(d)   4 units

11. The profit-maximizing monopolist sets price at:
(a) $20
(b) $30
(c) $40
(d) $50

12. At the output which maximizes profits, the monopoly may not be productively efficient because:
(a)   the average total cost of producing is not a minimum
(b)   the marginal cost of producing the last unit is less than its price
(c)   marginal cost may not be at its minimum value
(d)   average revenue exceeds the cost of producing an extra unit of output

Use the next diagram for the next three questions.

13. The profit-maximizing monopolist would produce:
(a)   *0k* units
(b)   *0l* units
(c)   *0m* units

(d)   zero units

14. The profit-maximizing monopolist would set a price of:
(a)   *0a*
(b)   *0b*
(c)   *0f*
(d)   *0i*

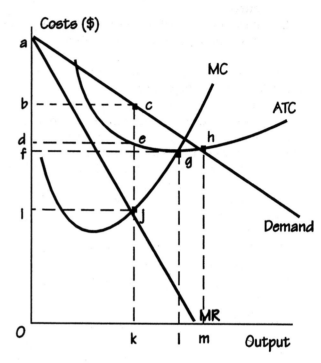

15. The profit-maximizing monopolist would earn an economic profit of:
(a)   *deji*
(b)   *bck0*
(c)   *abc*
(d)   *bced*

16. The concept of "simultaneous consumption" would be most applicable for which firm's product?
(a)   a newspaper
(b)   a dentist
(c)   a tanning salon
(d)   an apple grower

17. Kim would have more fun with her hockey cards if more of her friends also enjoyed collecting and trading cards. This is an example of which economic concept?
(a)   economies of scale
(b)   network effects
(c)   barriers to entry

(d)   X-inefficiency

18. Which of the following is true:
(a)   having a monopoly does not guarantee that the firm will earn economic profits
(b)   monopolists generally have lower ATC curves than pure competitors
(c)   a monopolist's supply curve is its MC curve
(d)   barriers to entry permanently protect most monopolies from competition

19. Which of the following is probably not an example of price discrimination?
(a)   a plumber charging a higher hourly rate for customers who live in bigger houses
(b)   a taxicab charging more for longer trips
(c)   a university charging higher tuition for executive MBA students than for other students in the same courses
(d)   a ski hill charging different lift fees for local residents than for tourists

20. Which is not one of the conditions for successful price discrimination?
(a)   the buyer must be unable to resell the product
(b)   the product must be a service
(c)   the seller must have some monopoly power
(d)   the seller must be able to segment the market

21. As compared to a competitive industry with the same costs, a monopolized industry will have:
(a)   more output and a higher price
(b)   more output and a lower price
(c)   less output and a lower price
(d)   less output and a higher price

The next five questions are based on the next graph.

22. The monopoly depicted in the graph is:
(a)   a natural monopoly because the demand curve is downward sloping
(b)   a natural monopoly because ATC is still falling where it intersects demand
(c)   a natural monopoly because MR and MC intersect at an output level below the social optimum
(d)   not a natural monopoly

23. If unregulated, which price and output combination would this monopolist choose?
(a)   Pa and Qa
(b)   Pd and Qa
(c)   Pb and Qb
(d)   Pc and Qc

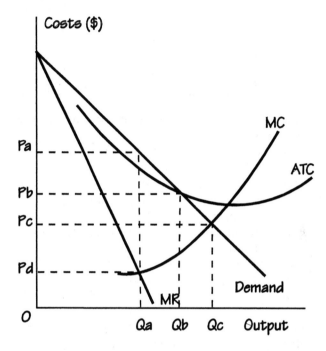

24. If the government regulates this monopolist so as to avoid allocative inefficiency, the price and output combination should be:
(a)   Pa and Qa
(b)   Pd and Qa
(c)   Pb and Qb
(d)   Pc and Qc

25. The problem with the regulated solution found in the previous question is that:
(a)   the monopolist incurs a loss
(b)   the monopolist still earns excessive profits
(c)   the monopolist produces too little output
(d)   the monopolist produces too much output

26. A regulatory compromise is to charge a price that allows the monopolist a "fair return" but also results in an output level close to the social optimum. Such a price and output combination is:
(a)   Pa and Qa
(b)   Pd and Qa
(c)   Pb and Qb
(d)   Pc and Qc

27. A firm experiencing X-inefficiency would likely:
(a) pay managers salaries above the going market rate
(b) produce more output than is optimal
(c) earn unusually high profits
(d) experience economies of scale

28. The DeBeers company enforced their diamond monopoly for many years by:
(a) convincing independent producers to market through one central agency
(b) cutting prices to discipline producers who sold outside the cartel
(c) buying and stockpiling diamonds produced by independent mines
(d) all of the above

29. The inefficiency of monopoly compared to pure competition may be at least somewhat offset by:
(a) a higher rate of technological progress in monopoly
(b) economies of scale in monopoly
(c) fair return regulation
(d) all of the above

Use this graph for the three questions that follow.

Price

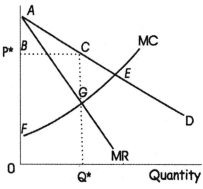

30. The area of consumer surplus under pure monopoly is:
(a) ABC
(b) ACGF
(c) CGE
(d) BCGF

31. The area of producer surplus under pure monopoly is:
(a) ABC
(b) ACGF
(c) CGE
(d) BCGF

32. The area of deadweight loss under pure monopoly is:
(a) ABC
(b) ACGF
(c) CGE
(d) BCGF

Problems and Projects

1. Hot Dog Vending Monopoly

Billy Bob is a pure monopolist selling hot dogs outside a bar at closing time. His demand schedule and total cost schedule are given in the table that follows.

(a) Compute the following values to fill the table: total revenue, marginal revenue, average total cost, and marginal cost.

(b) Why would Billy Bob never sell more than 5 hot dogs no matter what the level of costs?

Qd	P	TR	MR	TC	ATC	MC
0	$10	$___	--	$4.00	--	--
1	9	___	$9	4.25	___	$0.25
2	8	___	___	5.00	___	___
3	7	___	___	6.25	___	___
4	6	___	___	8.00	___	___
5	5	___	___	10.25	___	___
6	4	___	___	13.00	___	___
7	3	___	___	16.25	___	___

Price, Cost

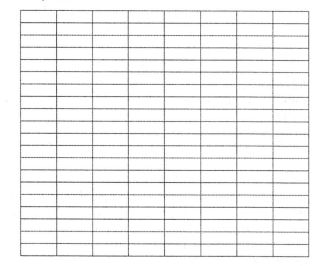

Output

(c) Use the marginal-revenue and marginal-cost approach to find the profit-maximizing output.

(In numerical examples it can happen that there is no output level where marginal revenue and marginal cost are equal. In that case the extra unit should be produced as long as marginal revenue is greater than marginal cost.)

(d) What price will Billy Bob charge for a hot dog?

(e) How much economic profit will he make?

(f) Plot price, marginal revenue, marginal cost, and average cost in the graph below. (Remember to plot MR and MC at the "midpoints" of the quantity ranges over which they are calculated.)

(g) Indicate on the graph the monopoly output, price and total profit.

2. Price Discrimination in Hot Dogs

Assume that Billy Bob (from the previous question) is able to engage in perfect price discrimination (selling each hot dog at the maximum price that a buyer is willing to pay).

(a) Complete the following table by computing total revenue at each quantity and the marginal revenue this discriminating monopolist obtains for each additional unit sold. [The total and marginal revenue will not be the same as in the table in the previous question.]

Qd	P	TR	MR
0	$10	$___	- -
1	9	___	$9
2	8	___	___
3	7	___	___
4	6	___	___
5	5	___	___
6	4	___	___
7	3	___	___

(b) The table shows that Billy Bob's marginal revenue as a discriminating monopolist is equal to the _____.

(c) Assuming the costs are as given in the previous question, as a discriminating monopolist Billy Bob would produce _____ hot dogs, charge the buyer of the last one produced a price of $_____, and make total economic profit of $_____.

(d) Compared to the situation where he charges each buyer the same price, perfect price discrimination (increases, decreases) _____ profits, and _____ output.

(e) In the situation described, do you think that Billy Bob would be successful in price discriminating? Why?

3. A Regulated Ferry Monopoly

Trogg is thinking about building a raft to carry passengers from his island to the mainland. It would cost him 60 clams to build, and the raft would last for one season. Marginal costs are zero. The demand for raft trips for the season is given by the following table:

Qd (trips)	P (clams/trip)	TR (clams)	Profit (clams)
0	8	___	___
5	7	___	___
10	6	___	___
15	5	___	___
20	4	___	___
25	3	___	___
30	2	___	___
35	1	___	___
40	0	___	___

(a) Trogg (should, should not) _____ build the raft because the best he can do is a (profit, loss) _____ of _____ clams. At this optimum he charges _____ clams per trip and sells _____ trips.

(b) The optimal social price for raft rides is _____ clams, because at this price the condition for allocative efficiency is met: _____ = _____.

(c) The problem with the optimal social price is that Trogg would lose _____ clams.

(d) If the Cave Clan Council regulates Trogg in order to allow the whole society to benefit as much as possible from the raft service without driving Trogg out of business, then a fair-return price would be _____ clams.

4. A Saloon Monopoly

One-Eyed Jack's is the only saloon in Dry Gulch. The demand for Jack's whiskey is given by: Q = 100 - P where Q is the number of shots sold per day, and P is the price in cents per shot. Jack's only variable costs are for the whiskey itself: a constant 20 cents per shot. (Therefore the MC and AVC curves are horizontal at 20 cents.) Jack's fixed costs are $12 per day for building rental and wages for himself, the barmaid and the piano player. There are no other costs.

(a) To maximize profits, how much whiskey should One-Eyed Jack's sell per day? (Hint: graph the demand curve, the MR curve, and MC curve.)

(b) What price will be charged?

(c) What is the total daily profit?

(d) Why is Jack's a natural monopoly?

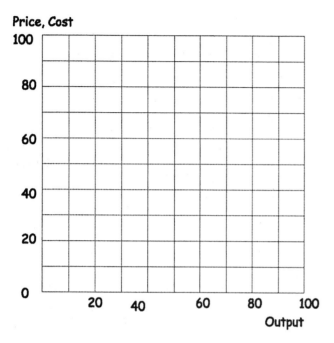

Price, Cost

Output

5. The Monopoly Graph

Use the next graph that shows a profit-maximizing pure monopolist to fill in these blanks:

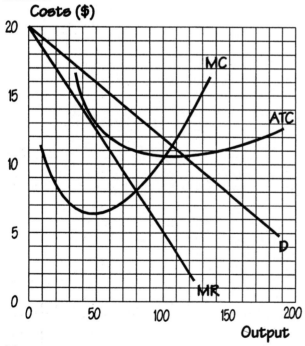

Costs ($)

Output

(a) output _____

(b) marginal revenue at this output _____

(c) marginal cost at this output _____

(d) price at this output _____

(e) total revenue at this output _____

(f) average cost at this output _____

(g) total cost of this output _____

(h) profit per unit of output _____

(i) total profit _____

Discussion Questions

1. Explain the price elasticity of demand concept in terms of: (a) the relative sensitivity of quantity demanded to changes in price; (b) the behaviour of total revenue when price changes; (c) the elasticity coefficient; (d) the relationship between the relative (percentage) change in quantity demanded and the relative (percentage) change in price.

2. Describe the characteristics of the purely monopolistic market structure. Why is it included in the text if it is fairly rare in practice?

3. What is meant by a barrier to entry? What are the different kinds of barriers to entry? How important are they in pure competition, pure monopoly, monopolistic competition, and oligopoly?

4. For each type of barrier to entry, give an example of a firm in your community that has some monopoly power by virtue of this type of barrier.

5. Why are most natural monopolies also public utilities? What does government hope to achieve by granting exclusive franchises to and regulating such natural monopolies?

6. If you owned a National Hockey League franchise in Charlottetown, you would have more of a monopoly than if you owned the New York Rangers NHL franchise. Why? Would you have a natural monopoly in Charlottetown? Would you be able to make a profit?

7. The lone movie theatre in Jasper, Alberta, presumably has some monopoly power. What factors limit this monopoly power?

8. How do patent laws contribute to monopoly power? How can patents be justified considering that monopoly leads to allocative and productive inefficiency?

9. Compare the pure monopolist and the individual pure competitor with respect to:
(a) the demand schedule
(b) the marginal-revenue schedule
(c) the relationship between marginal revenue and the price
(d) the condition that must be met at the profit-maximizing output
(e) the ability to set price
(f) long-run economic profits
(g) long-run efficiency

10. Explain why marginal revenue is always less than price when the demand is down-sloping.

11. Suppose you are a pure monopolist and discover you are producing and selling an output at a point on the inelastic part of the demand curve. Explain why a decrease in output accompanied by a price increase must improve your profits.

12. For what reasons might a monopolist have lower or higher average costs than purely competitive firms?

13. What are some symptoms of X-inefficiency?

14. What is meant by price discrimination and what conditions must be realized before it is workable? In what ways might price discrimination be considered socially harmful or beneficial?

15. How do public utility regulatory agencies attempt to eliminate the misallocation of resources that results from monopoly? Explain the dilemma that almost invariably confronts the agency in this endeavour; and explain why a fair-return price only reduces but does not eliminate misallocation.

Answers

Quick Quiz
1. (d) p. 224
2. (c) p. 226
3. (c) p. 228
4. (b) pp. 227-228
5. (b) pp. 230-232
6. (d) p. 233
7. (c) pp. 234-235
8. (c) pp. 235-237
9. (d) p. 239
10. (b) p. 239

11. (b) p. 242
12. (a) p. 243
13. (c) pp. 243-244

Fill-in Questions
1. close substitutes, blocked
2. downward, less, decrease
3. 19,000, 5,000; 19,000, 5,000, 14,000
4. elastic; inelastic, marginal, negative
5. less, higher
6. rent-seeking
7. prices, cost
8. (a) monopoly power; (b) market segregation; (c) no resales
9. marginal cost; higher

True-False
1. T
2. F   key is economies of scale
3. T
4. F   twice as steep
5. T
6. T
7. T
8. F   objective of maximum total profit doesn't usually match where per unit profit is maximum
9. T   so monopoly can be more efficient than pure competition
10. T   resources are wasted on lobbying, etc.
11. T
12. T
13. T   when P = ATC, economic profit = 0, but normal profit still exists

Multiple-Choice
1. (b) competition or substitutes seem to exist in the other cases
2. (b)   P is on demand curve; MC = MR below demand curve
3. (c)   this is the same rule as for pure competition
4. (d)
5. (a) a firm with significant economies of scale, often with high fixed costs
6. (a)
7. (b) expand output until MC = MR; to sell more output, price must decrease
8. (d) new MC will intersect MR at lower output; this will correspond to a higher price on the demand curve
9. (c)   150 – 120 = 30\
10. (c) for third unit, MR = 30, MC = 14; for fourth unit MR = 10, MC = 16, so profit would fall by 6 if 4 units are produced rather than 3

11. (d) P = 50 corresponds to Qd = 3 in the demand schedule
12. (a) ATC is not usually minimum where MC = MR
13. (a) MC = MR
14. (b) up to the D curve from where MC = MR
15. (d) (P – ATC) x Q
16. (a) once the newspaper is written, laid out and typeset, the MC to print additional copies is very low
17. (b) the consumer's benefits or value for the good depends on how many others consume the same good
18. (a)
19. (b) longer trips entail more cost
20. (b) price discrimination can be used for either goods or services
21. (d) hence allocative inefficiency
22. (b)
23. (a)
24. (d) where P = MC
25. (a) at Qc, ATC is above P
26. (c) P = ATC, so economic profit = 0
27. (a) they have insufficient incentive to minimize costs
28. (d) see the Last Word
29. (d)
30. (a) the area below the demand curve and above P*, up to Q*
31. (d) the are below P* and above MC, up to Q*
32. (c) the area below demand and above MC between Q* and where demand and MC intersect

Problems and Projects

1. (a) Total revenue: $0, 9, 16, 21, 24, 25, 24, 21; Marginal revenue: $9, 7, 5, 3, 1, -1, -3; Average total cost: $4.25, 2.50, 2.08, 2.00, 2.05, 2.17, 2.32; Marginal cost: $.25, .75, 1.25, 1.75, 2.25, 2.75, 3.25; (b) Total revenue falls after 5 hot dogs

so it would never pay to sell 6 or more; (c) 4 hot dogs (MR > MC up this point, and MR < MC thereafter); (d) $6; (e) $16; (f) see graph (shaded area is profit).
2. (a) Total revenue: $0, 9, 17, 24, 30, 35, 39, 42; Marginal revenue: $9, 8, 7, 6, 5, 4, 3. (b) price; (c) 6, $4, $26; (d) increases, increases; (e) probably not; segregating groups of buyers and preventing resale would be nearly impossible
3. (a) should; profit; 20; 4; 20; (b) 0; P = MC; (c) 60; (d) 2, because then Trogg's TR = TC = $60
4. (a) 40 (b) $0.60 (c) $4 (d) his ATC is continually falling (since AVC is fixed, the ever decreasing AFC keeps pulling down his ATC if he can sell more drinks)

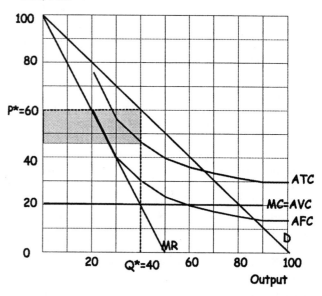

Price, Cost

5. (a) 80 (b) $8.00 (c) $8.00 (d) $13.50 (e) $1080 (f) $11.00 (g) $880 (h) $2.50 (i) $200

Price, Cost

Chapter **10**

Monopolistic Competition and Oligopoly

Overview

This final chapter on models of market structures deals with monopolistic competition and oligopoly. Both market structures are between the extremes of pure competition and pure monopoly, and are the most prevalent market structures in Canada.

As its name suggests, monopolistic competition is a blend of pure competition and pure monopoly. The number of firms and the entry and exit conditions are similar to pure competition, but because each firm offers a version of the product that is differentiated from other sellers' versions, each firm has some monopoly power, or control over price. The firm's demand curve is down-sloping, but quite elastic. Advertising, product differentiation, and other forms of nonprice competition are the outstanding features of monopolistic competition. Control over price is quite limited because close substitutes are sold by many other sellers. To maximize profits, the monopolistic competitor juggles three factors: price, product, and advertising. Given the product quality and level of advertising, the price-output analysis of the monopolistic competitor in the short run is identical to that outlined in Chapter 9 for the pure monopolist. The monopolistic competitor may earn an economic profit (or incur a loss) in the short run, but in the long run firms will enter or leave the industry until only normal profits remain.

Though monopolistic competitors achieve neither productive efficiency nor allocative efficiency in long-run equilibrium, an evaluation of the welfare effects of this market structure is complicated because monopolistic competition also produces both socially beneficial and detrimental effects related to product differentiation, development, and advertising.

Oligopoly is closer to pure monopoly than to pure competition. An oligopoly is a market dominated by a few large sellers, and difficult for new sellers to enter. Because each of the dominant firms in an oligopoly has a significant market share, each firm's pricing and sales strategies will have a noticeable impact on their rivals' sales. Oligopolists are then "price makers" who are also mutually interdependent; if one firm sells more by cutting price, advertising more, or developing new products, rivals will suffer a noticeable loss in sales, and might respond with competitive strategies of their own. A firm contemplating a competitive action is well aware of this, and chooses its action with such reactions in mind. Economists have a variety of models of oligopoly behaviour that incorporate this mutual interdependence, including the simple game theory model that succinctly illustrates the key point that oligopolists have both an incentive to collude, and an incentive to cheat on collusive agreements!

Three other oligopoly models are also presented: the kinked demand curve model, the collusion (or cartel) model, and the price leadership model. Each is based on a distinct set of assumptions meant to represent some typical real world oligopolies. The differences in assumptions lead to some different conclusions about pricing, output, etc.

Most economists agree that allocative and productive inefficiency are usual in oligopolistic industries. They tend to disagree over the degree to which oligopolists collude and exploit their monopoly power. Oligopoly may be the market structure most conducive to technological advances that can make society better off. Chapter 11 looks at these issues.

Chapter Outline

10.1 Characteristics of Monopolistic Competition

◈ What are the conditions under which monopolistic competition will arise?

• A monopolistically competitive industry has a relatively large number of independent firms, differentiated products, and easy entry and exit in the long run. Many Canadian industries are monopolistically competitive.

• Product differentiation is the hallmark of monopolistic competition. The main elements on which firms compete are: product attributes, service, location, brand names and packaging, advertising, and pricing.

• Product differentiation gives each firm some control over price because some consumers will have some degree of preference for particular brands, or versions of the product.

Quick Quiz

1. Which is not a characteristic of monopolistic competition?
(a) freedom of entry
(b) homogeneous products
(c) large number of firms
(d) some degree of brand loyalty by consumers

2. Products can be differentiated by:
(a) distinctive packaging
(b) creating brand image through advertising
(c) offering a unique warranty
(d) any of the above

3. In Canada, which industry is a good example of monopolistic competition?
(a) dairy farming
(b) airlines
(c) cablevision
(d) restaurants

10.2   Price and Output in Monopolistic Competition

◇ How are price and output set under monopolistic competition?

• Assume that each firm is selling a product of given quality and characteristics, and is engaged in a given amount of advertising.

• The demand curve facing each firm is highly, but not perfectly, elastic. Because each firm sells a unique product, the firm has price-making power, but not very much, because many rivals offer closely substitutable products. The firm's demand is less elastic than a pure competitor's, but more elastic than a pure monopolist's.

• In the short run, the individual firm will produce the output at which marginal cost and marginal revenue are equal and charge the price at which that much output can be sold. In the short run the firm may realize profits or incur losses.

• If short-run profits exist, entry of new firms in the long run will tend to decrease the demand curve for the product of the individual firm until economic profits are eliminated (price and average cost end up equal to each other). If short-run losses exist, some firms will exit, tending to increase the demand curves of surviving firms until economic profits are once again zero.

• In monopolistic competition firms end up with excess capacity and neither allocative nor productive efficiency is reached. Because the price is at least slightly above marginal cost, the monopolistic competitor will produce too little output to achieve allocative efficiency. Excess capacity exists because there are too many firms for each firm to sell enough to reach its minimum-ATC output.

• In an effort to exceed the normal profit that they will tend to earn in long-run equilibrium, monopolistic competitors continually try to make their products more appealing, develop new varieties, and improve their advertising. If these strategies are successful, the demand curve shifts to the right and becomes more inelastic. To the extent that such non-price competition leads to new product innovations and quality improvements that consumers value, the wastes of monopolistic competition may be offset.

➲ If you have trouble seeing why monopolistic competition **must** result in excess capacity in the long-run equilibrium, try to sketch a diagram that shows all of the following: 1) a downward sloping demand, 2) output set where MC = MR, 3) this output also at the minimum of ATC, and 4) losses being incurred at every other possible output level. Such a diagram is impossible to draw.

Quick Quiz

4. The demand curve for the individual firm in monopolistic competition is:
(a) perfectly elastic
(b) quite elastic
(c) quite inelastic
(d) perfectly inelastic

5. If firms in a monopolistically competitive market are making economic profits in the short run, then in the long run:
(a) some firms will exit
(b) economic profits will increase
(c) individual firms' demand curves will become more inelastic

(d) individual firms' demand curves will shrink due to entry of new firms

6. In terms of efficiency, the individual firm in monopolistic competition achieves:
(a) allocative efficiency
(b) productive efficiency
(c) both productive and allocative efficiency
(d) neither productive nor allocative efficiency

10.3 The Characteristics of Oligopoly

◇ What are the conditions under which oligopoly will arise?

• An oligopoly is a market dominated by a few large producers of a homogeneous or differentiated product. Firms are "price makers" but are also mutually interdependent. Oligopoly is a common industry structure in Canada.

• An oligopoly is usually the result of economies of scale, other barriers to entry, or a merger of two or more rivals.

• The degree of market domination by large firms can be measured by a concentration ratio or the Herfindahl index. One standard for defining oligopoly is a 40% four-firm concentration ratio (that is, 40% of the market is held by the largest four firms). Any numerical measure of industry concentration is subject to criticism because the relevant market can be very difficult to define. Markets can be localized, national, or international.

Quick Quiz

7. An oligopoly is a market that is dominated by how many firms?
(a) one
(b) a few
(c) quite a few
(d) many

8. A market consists of three firms each with annual sales of $10 million, four firms each with sales of $5 million, and five each with sales of $4 million. The four-firm concentration ratio is:
(a) 30%
(b) 40%
(c) 45%
(d) 50%

9. Which of the following does not contribute to the existence of oligopoly?

(a) the economies of large-scale production
(b) the gains in profits that result from mergers
(c) high barriers to entry
(d) the profits that result from cheating on a cartel agreement

10.4 Oligopoly Pricing Behaviour: A Game Theory Overview

◇ How can game theory help explain strategic behaviour by oligopolists?

• A simple game theory model illustrates the strategic problem every oligopolist faces because each firm's profits depend on its own actions and those of its rivals.

• In a game theory model, the players (participants) operate within rules (constraints) which govern the strategies (alternative courses of action) that they can follow. Players seek the highest payoffs (final outcomes) for themselves.

• Games may be cooperative (where players can make binding agreements) or non-cooperative (where agreements between players are impossible).

• In game theory there is not necessarily a unique equilibrium, but often a game will have a dominant strategy equilibrium where each player has a best strategy, regardless of what strategy other players will follow. This is a variant of the Nash equilibrium where no player has an incentive to change strategy given the strategies chosen by other players.

• The prisoner's dilemma is a famous game theory model in which whatever the other player does, each player is better off not cooperating.

• An example of a two-firm oligopoly (or duopoly) with each rival deciding whether to set price high or low, leads to three conclusions:
  o An oligopoly has few enough firms that one firm's actions affect a rival's profits enough that the rival is likely to react. The initial action should be based on the anticipated reaction. This is known as mutual interdependence.
  o Mutual interdependence creates an incentive to collude rather than to compete, because competition simply erodes potential profits for all firms in the industry.
  o If a collusive agreement is made, each firm has an incentive to cheat on the agreement.

Quick Quiz
10. A game theory model generally includes all of the following components except which one?
  (a)   rules
  (b)   payoffs
  (c)   strategies
  (d)   regulations

11. The prisoner's dilemma model illustrates that:
  (a)   oligopolists may benefit from collusion
  (b)   oligopolists have an incentive to cheat on collusive agreements
  (c)   both (a) and (b)
  (d)   none of the above

10.5   Three Oligopoly Strategies

⍟ How do these three oligopoly pricing strategies work?
  o   Kinked-demand curve model
  o   Collusive pricing model
  o   Price leadership model
• Oligopolies vary so much that no single model can adequately explain behaviour in all oligopolies. Even so, most models fit with the observation that oligopolies generally have inflexible prices, and that when prices do change, firms tend to change their prices together. This is a feature of all three oligopoly models presented in this section of the chapter.

➲ There is no standard model of oligopoly. Be sure to know the different assumptions that give rise to each of the four models presented in this chapter (the three in this section plus the game theory model).

• In the kinked-demand curve model, which is a non-collusive model, each firm believes that when it lowers its price rivals will lower their prices, and when it increases its price rivals will not increase their prices. Therefore the firm is reluctant to change its price. Even if its variable costs change, it may not change price unless the cost shift is large. This model provides a theory for price inflexibility, but does not explain how prices are set initially.
• In the collusive pricing model, firms jointly set their price and their combined output at the same level that a pure monopolist would select. Firms may reach this equilibrium through overt collusion in a formal cartel, through a covert collusive conspiracy, or through a tacit understanding.
• Numerous obstacles make collusive agreements difficult to maintain (even the highly successful OPEC cartel has been vulnerable to many of these problems):
  o   demand and cost differences
  o   entry of new firms and growth of firms that are outside the agreement
  o   cheating on the agreement
  o   recession
  o   legal prohibitions
• In the price leadership model the dominant firm in the industry (usually the biggest or most efficient) initiates all price changes, and other firms follow. The outcome is similar to collusion, but price leadership does not depend on formal agreements. Price changes, which are often publicly signaled by the leader, are infrequent and occur only in response to significant changes in cost or demand conditions. In some cases the leader chooses a price designed to maximize long-run profits by deterring entry, rather than maximize short-run profits (this is known as limit pricing).
• Oligopoly is like pure monopoly in failing to generate either allocative or productive efficiency. Evidence of sustained profits in many oligopolies supports this view. On the brighter side, three mitigating factors work to limit the extent of the inefficiency:
  o   Recently, more oligopolies are facing competition from foreign producers.
  o   Through "limit pricing," some oligopolies hold prices down somewhat to deter entry.
  o   Sustained profits may give oligopolists more incentive and ability to invest in research and development than firms in other market structures.

Quick Quiz
12. The oligopolist's demand curve has a kink at the going price if the oligopolist believes that:
  (a)   competitors will match both price cuts and price increases
  (b)   competitors will match neither price cuts nor price increases
  (c)   competitors will not notice either price cuts or price increases
  (d)   competitors will match price cuts but not price increases

13. Which is definitely a non-collusive oligopoly model?
- (a) kinked-demand curve model
- (b) cartel model
- (c) price leadership model
- (d) none of the above

14. A cartel tends to be most successful when:
- (a) there are numerous producers
- (b) entry is easy
- (c) the product is standardized
- (d) producers have very different cost conditions

10.6   Oligopoly and Advertising

◈ How does advertising affect consumers and firms in oligopoly?

• Oligopolists tend to compete through product development and advertising. Such forms of competition are preferred to price cutting because: 1) price cuts are easily duplicated by rivals and can spark price wars, and; 2) oligopolists usually have enough resources to engage in advertising and product development.
• Advertising has both positive and negative effects for the economy:
  - o Where advertising provides information, it reduces search costs, promotes competition by enabling new products and brands to gain market share, and therefore helps firms to obtain economies of scale.
  - o Where advertising is mainly persuasive, it promotes brand loyalty and monopoly power, acting as a barrier to entry. If advertising is self-cancelling, it is inefficient.

➲ After reading this chapter, make sure to review Table 8-1 on the four basic market structure models. Everything in that table should be clear to you by now. It should also help you to avoid the common but disastrous mistake of confusing pure monopoly with monopolistic competition. These are two distinct market structures!

Quick Quiz
15. Advertising is more likely to be efficiency-enhancing when it:
- (a) strengthens brand loyalty
- (b) provides information about new firms and products
- (c) creates economies of scale

- (d) is self-cancelling

Terms and Concepts

monopolistic competition	import competition
product differentiation	Herfindahl Index
non-price competition	game theory model
excess capacity	dominant strategy equilibrium
oligopoly	Nash equilibrium
homogeneous oligopoly	prisoner's dilemma
differentiated oligopoly	collusion
mutual interdependence	kinked-demand curve
concentration ratio	price war
interindustry competition	cartel
	tacit understandings
	price leadership

Fill-In Questions

1. In a monopolistically competitive market, a (few, relatively large number of) _____ producers sell (standardized, differentiated) _____ products; these producers behave (independently, collusively) _____; and in the long run, entry into the market is (difficult, easy) _____.

2. The demand curve faced by a monopolistic competitor will be (more, less) _____ elastic than the demand facing a monopolist and (more, less) _____ elastic than the demand facing a pure competitor. The elasticity of the monopolistic competitor's demand curve will depend upon the number of _____ and the degree of _____.

3. In the long run, the entry of new firms into a monopolistically competitive industry will (expand, reduce) _____ the demand for the product produced by each firm in the industry and (increase, decrease) _____ the elasticity of that demand.

4. In the long run, the price charged by the individual firm in monopolistic competition will tend to equal _____, its economic profits will tend to equal _____, and its average cost will be (below, equal to, above) _____ the minimum average total cost.

5. In monopolistic competition, allocative efficiency is not achieved because _____ is (less than, equal to, greater than) _____ marginal cost. Productive efficiency is not achieved because production does not take place at the minimum point of the _____ curve.

6. A four-firm concentration ratio is calculated by dividing the sales of the _____ firms in the industry by the sales of the _____. An industry is usually considered an oligopoly when this concentration ratio is at least ____%.

7. The basics of strategic behaviour by oligopolists can be understood from a _____ theory perspective. A payoff matrix for two oligopolists indicates the _____ generated when the two firms charge various _____. The payoff matrix calls attention to three key characteristics of oligopoly: (1) mutual _____, (2) _____ tendencies, and (3) the incentive to _____.

8. The kinked-demand model reflects the assumption that if the oligopolist raises its price, its rivals (will, will not) _____ raise their prices, and if it lowers its price its rivals _____ lower their prices. Thus, the individual oligopolist sees a demand curve that is relatively (elastic, inelastic) _____ at prices above the current price, and relatively _____ at prices below the current price.

9. When oligopolists collude, the price they set and their combined output tend to be the same as would be set in a _____ industry.

10. A cartel is a formal agreement among _____ to fix the _____ of the product, _____ up the market, or otherwise restrict _____ among them. A cartel is an example of a (collusive, non-collusive) _____ oligopoly.

11. A successful cartel, or _____ agreement, is more likely to be successful when: (a) firms have (similar, different) _____ costs and demand curves; (b) there are (many, few) _____ firms in the industry, (c) cheating is (easy, difficult) _____ to detect; (d) the level of demand is (shrinking, growing) _____; (e) it is (easy, difficult) _____ to enter the industry; and (f) price-fixing collusion is (illegal, legal) _____.

12. A strategy of setting price at a level that will discourage new entry is called _____ pricing.

13. The ability of advertising to provide consumers with _____ about new products, increases the ability of new firms to enter markets, thereby (increasing, decreasing) _____ the price-making power of established firms. On the other hand, advertising by established firms (raises, lowers) _____ the ATC curve for new entrants, thereby _____ the price-making power of established firms.

True-False

Circle T if the statement is true, F if it is false.

1. In monopolistic competition each firm determines its policies after considering the possible reactions of rival firms.   **T F**

2. The fewer the firms in an industry and the greater the extent of product differentiation, the greater will be the elasticity of the individual seller's demand curve.   **T F**

3. In the short run, a monopolistic competitor may earn economic profits or losses.   **T F**

4. Productive efficiency is achieved in the long run in a monopolistically competitive industry since economic profits tend to be zero for the firm.   **T F**

5. Monopolistically competitive industries tend to be overcrowded with firms, with each firm producing below its capacity output.   **T F**

6. Economists agree that from a social perspective the positive effects of advertising outweigh the negative effects.   **T F**

7. Advertising by established firms can contribute to monopoly power by making entry more difficult and expensive for new firms.   **T F**

8. Differences between individual firms' products have economic significance whether the differences are real or merely imagined by consumers.   **T F**

9. Oligopolistic firms may produce either homogeneous or differentiated products. **T F**

10. The larger the Herfindahl index the greater the degree of market power in the industry. **T F**

11. Two industries can have the same concentration ratio yet have different Herfindahl index values. **T F**

12. Mergers increase market concentration. **T F**

13. Oligopoly prices tend to be inflexible. **T F**

14. Canada has laws against collusive price-fixing. **T F**

15. Price leadership is almost always based on a formal written or oral agreement. **T F**

Multiple-Choice

Circle the letter that corresponds to the best answer.

1. Which of the following is not characteristic of monopolistic competition?
  (a)   product differentiation
  (b)   a relatively large number of firms
  (c)   collusive agreements among firms
  (d)   relatively easy industry entry in the long run

2. A similarity between a pure monopoly firm and a monopolistically competitive firm is that both:
  (a)   earn economic profits in the long run
  (b)   operate where P = MC in the short run
  (c)   operate at the minimum point of their long-run average cost in the long run
  (d)   face downward sloping demand curves

3. Which of the following is not an example of product differentiation and other non-price competition under monopolistic competition?
  (a)   an economics textbook publisher offering a free website to supplement the text
  (b)   a sporting goods store in Toronto brings Wayne Gretzky in to sign autographs
  (c)   a hotel in Vancouver begins offering free airport limousine service
  (d)   all of the above

Questions 4 through 7 are based on the following graph showing a monopolistically competitive firm in short-run equilibrium.

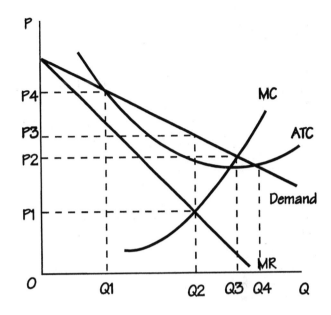

4. The equilibrium output for this firm will be:
  (a)   Q1
  (b)   Q2
  (c)   Q3
  (d)   Q4

5. The firm's profit-maximizing price will be:
  (a)   P1
  (b)   P2
  (c)   P3
  (d)   P4

6. At this equilibrium the firm will:
  (a)   realize an economic profit
  (b)   suffer an economic loss and eventually exit
  (c)   suffer an economic loss and remain in business
  (d)   break even and eventually exit

7. If this is an increasing cost industry, and firms enter this industry in the long run:
  (a)   the ATC curve will shift up and demand will decrease
  (b)   the ATC curve will shift up and demand will increase
  (c)   the MR curve will shift up and demand will decrease
  (d)   the MR curve will shift up and demand will increase

Questions 8 to 12 are based on this graph of a monopolistic competitor in long-run equilibrium.

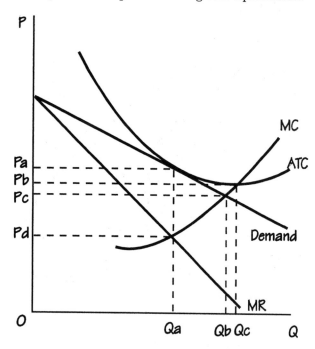

8. Long-run equilibrium output will be:
(a) Qa
(b) Qb
(c) Qc
(d) 0

9. Long-run equilibrium price will be:
(a) Pa
(b) Pb
(c) Pc
(d) Pd

10. This firm is:
(a) earning an economic profit
(b) covering explicit costs but not implicit costs
(c) earning a normal profit
(d) operating at the minimum average total cost of production

11. In order to meet the productive efficiency criterion this firm would have to produce an output of:
(a) Qa
(b) Qb
(c) Qc
(d) above Qc

12. The amount of excess capacity in this firm is:
(a) Qb-Qa

(b) Qc-Qb
(c) Qc-Qa
(d) there is no excess capacity

13. Even though prices may be higher under monopolistic competition than pure competition, consumers benefit from:
(a) lower prices than in the purely competitive model
(b) greater output than in the purely competitive model
(c) greater product variety than in the purely competitive model
(d) less advertising expenses than in the purely competitive model

14. Economic profits tend to be driven to zero in monopolistic competition. However, some firms may be able to sustain economic profits due to:
(a) especially effective product differentiation
(b) an exceptionally well-known brand name
(c) a one-of-a-kind superior location
(d) any of the above

15. How many firms are there in an oligopoly?
(a) one
(b) a few
(c) many
(d) very many

16. Concentration ratios take into account:
(a) interindustry competition
(b) import competition
(c) the existence of separate local markets
(d) none of the above

Questions 17 through 20 are based on the following payoff matrix for a two-firm oligopoly. The numbers in the matrix represent the profits for a high-price or low-price strategy.

		Firm A	
		High-price	Low-price
Firm B	High-price	A = 600 B = 600	A = 875 B = 200
	Low-price	A = 200 B = 875	A = 350 B = 350

17. If the firms collude to maximize joint profits, the total profits for the two firms will be:
(a) $700
(b) $1075
(c) $1200

(d) $1475

18. If Firm A always pursues a high-price strategy, the best strategy for Firm B is:
(a)   a low-price strategy for earnings of $875
(b)   a low-price strategy for earnings of $350
(c)   a high-price strategy for earnings of $600
(d)   a high-price strategy for earnings of $275

19. Suppose the firms collude and agree to keep prices high. If Firm B cheats, and cuts price, it will:
(a)   gain an extra $400
(b)   gain an extra $275
(c)   decrease its profit by $675
(d)   decrease its profit by $150

20. If both firms act independently and do not collude, what is the dominant strategy for each?
(a)   high-price for A and high-price for B
(b)   high-price for A and low-price for B
(c)   low-price for A and high-price for B
(d)   low-price for A and low-price for B

21. Mutual interdependence means that:
(a)   each firm sells a product similar but not identical to the products sold by its rivals
(b)   each firm sells a product identical to the products sold by its rivals
(c)   each firm must consider the reactions of its rivals when it determines its price policy
(d)   each firm faces a perfectly elastic demand for its product

22. In the kinked demand curve model, an individual oligopolist's demand curve is:
(a)   more inelastic above the going price than below the going price
(b)   more elastic above the going price than below the going price
(c)   elastic above the going price and inelastic below the going price
(d)   of unitary elasticity at the going price

23. In the oligopolistic market structure the kinked demand analysis provides an explanation of:
(a)   barriers to entry
(b)   "sticky" prices
(c)   price leadership
(d)   mergers

Use the next diagram for questions 24 and 25.

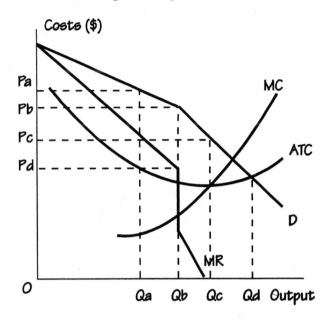

24. The profit-maximizing price and output for this oligopolistic firm is:
(a)   Pa and Qa
(b)   Pb and Qb
(c)   Pc and Qc
(d)   Pd and Qd

25. How would this firm respond to a small rise in their MC curve?
(a)   reduce output, raise price, and maintain profits
(b)   maintain output, maintain price, and have smaller profits
(c)   maintain output, raise price, and maintain profits
(d)   none of the above

26. A two-player game in which one player's gain must equal the other player's loss is an example of:
(a)   a zero sum game
(b)   a positive sum game
(c)   a prisoner's dilemma
(d)   a perfect cartel

27. Once a Nash equilibrium is reached:
(a)   allocative efficiency is achieved
(b)   both players are choosing the strategy that maximizes their joint payoffs
(c)   the players are colluding on their strategy
(d)   neither player has an incentive to change strategies

28. In a two player game with a dominant strategy equilibrium:
  (a)   both players choose the same strategy
  (b)   both players have a strategy that is best, no matter what their rival's strategy is
  (c)   each player chooses the strategy of trying to dominate their rival
  (d)   the players' joint profits are maximized

29. Which of the following is a shortcoming of the kinked-demand curve model?
  (a)   the model suggests that prices are relatively inflexible under oligopoly
  (b)   the model suggests that costs fluctuate unpredictably
  (c)   the model assumes product differentiation
  (d)   the model does not explain how price is determined in the first place

30. For collusion to be successful, oligopolists must be able to:
  (a)   keep prices and profits as low as possible
  (b)   block or restrict the entry of new producers
  (c)   engage in technological improvements of their products
  (d)   reduce legal obstacles that protect market power

31. When oligopolists collude, the results are generally:
  (a)   greater output and higher price
  (b)   greater output and lower price
  (c)   smaller output and lower price
  (d)   smaller output and higher price

32. Another name for a "gentlemen's agreement" as applied to oligopolists is:
  (a)   limit pricing
  (b)   joint-profit maximization
  (c)   tacit understanding
  (d)   illegal conspiracy

33. Which of the following is an obstacle to collusion among oligopolists?
  (a)   a general business recession
  (b)   a small number of firms in the industry
  (c)   a homogeneous product
  (d)   the patent laws

34. Prices in an industry characterized by price leadership tend to be:

  (a)   quite flexible and when firms change prices they are apt to change them at the same time
  (b)   quite inflexible and when firms change prices they are not apt to change them at the same time
  (c)   quite inflexible and when firms change prices they are apt to change them at the same time
  (d)   quite flexible and when firms change prices they are not apt to change them at the same time

35. The price leader in an oligopolistic industry:
  (a)   necessarily sets the price that maximizes industry profit
  (b)   determines production quotas for each firm
  (c)   is usually the largest or most efficient firm in the industry
  (d)   is assured that other firms will initiate similar price changes

36. Market shares in oligopolistic industries are usually determined on the basis of:
  (a)   tacit collusion
  (b)   non-price competition
  (c)   gentlemen's agreements
  (d)   joint profit maximization

37. According to the positive view of advertising, advertising does all of the following with the exception of:
  (a)   providing useful information to consumers
  (b)   promoting monopoly power
  (c)   diminishing monopoly power by calling attention to an array of substitute goods or services
  (d)   facilitating the introduction of new products and, hence, enabling technological progress

38. According to the negative view of advertising:
  (a)   advertising has no effect on costs or output
  (b)   advertising lowers both costs and output
  (c)   advertising raises costs and makes entry more difficult
  (d)   advertising raises costs but raises output substantially

Problems and Projects

1. Distinguishing Between Monopolistic Competition and Oligopoly

For each market situation described below, explain which market structure model seems to fit best: monopolistic competition or oligopoly.

(a) Grocery Stores: two food stores serve a town of 5,000 inhabitants. These stores feature many identical brands, and some different ones. They tend to have slightly different prices on specific items, but discount their prices at the same times.

(b) Tourist Accommodations: About one hundred hotels, motels, and lodges compete for tourists seeking accommodation in a resort town in the Rockies. Most of these firms advertise widely. All are required by local regulations to belong to the Tourist Bureau that does some collective advertising and promotional for all members. Each year there is some turnover in the group of firms operating in this market.

(c) Banking: A country has numerous financial institutions, big and small, but a few banks issue the vast majority of loans. These banks have nearly identical interest rates and services, and tend to change their interest rates within days of one another.

2. Pizza Restaurants in Monopolistic Competition

Roma Pizza is a restaurant operating as a monopolistic competitor near the campus of a major university. Their most popular pizza now sells for a price of $14, and is being produced with ATC = $12. If Roma could sell enough pizzas, they could reduce this cost to $10.

(a) Sketch Roma's short run situation on a graph like those used in this chapter.

(b) How and why is Roma's demand curve likely to change in the long run?

(c) What will be the effect of this demand change on Roma's profits if the restaurant continues to produce the same pizzas and engage in their current promotional activities?

(d) What happens to Roma's demand curve and average total cost curve if Roma introduces new varieties of pizzas, or higher quality pizzas, or if Roma increases advertising? Will these measures necessarily improve Roma's profits?

(e) Will Roma ever be able to sell enough pizzas to push average total cost down to $10?

3. Concentration in DVD Player Market

The following are hypothetical sales data for firms that manufacture DVD players in Canada:

Firm	1999 Sales million $	1999 Market Share	2002 Sales million $	2002 Market Share
Alpha	15	___	30	___
Beta	20	___	40	___
Delta	10	___	20	___
Poseidon	40	___	60	___
Gamma	60	___	90	___
Omicron	75	___	200	___
Omega	25	___	50	___
Epsilon	5	___	10	___

(a) Calculate the four-firm concentration ratio for 1999 and use the result to determine what type of market structure these firms operate in.

(b) Calculate the Herfindahl index for 1999.

(c) Give at least two reasons why the concentration ratio or Herfindahl index might overstate the amount of monopoly power held by these Canadian manufacturers of DVD players.

(d) Recalculate the concentration ratio and Herfindahl ratio using 2002 data. What shortcoming of the concentration ratio calculation does comparing the 1999 and 2002 results on these two indicators of market power reveal?

4. A Computer Chip Duopoly

Suppose that two manufacturers, Apogee and Bristol, control the whole market for a particular computer chip. There is no brand loyalty, so each firm's profit depends only on their pricing strategy, and that of their rival. Each firm can set a high or low price, and neither firm knows what strategy its rival will follow. If both charge a high price, the profits will be $25 million for Apogee and $18 million for Bristol. If both charge a low price, profits will be $6 million for Apogee and $5 million for Bristol. If Apogee charges a high price and Bristol a low price, Apogee's profits will be $2 million and Bristol's profits will be $30 million. If Apogee charges a low price and Bristol charges a high price, Apogee's profits will be $35 million and Bristol's will be $3 million.

(a) Set up a payoff matrix showing each firm's profits for the four possible pricing outcomes.

(b) If Bristol sets a high price, Apogee gets a higher profit by setting a (high, low) _____ price. If Bristol sets a low price, Apogee gets a higher profit by setting a _____ price. Therefore, if there is no collusion, Apogee will set a _____ price.

(c) If Apogee sets a high price, Bristol gets a higher profit by setting a (high, low) _____ price. If Apogee sets a low price, Bristol gets a higher profit by setting a _____ price. Therefore, without collusion, Bristol will set a _____ price.

(d) If the two firms do not collude, Apogee will get a profit of $_____ and Bristol will get a profit of $_____. Their combined profits will be $_____. These profits (are, are not) _____ the maximum possible.

(e) Given the result in (d), Apogee and Bristol (will, will not) _____ have an incentive to collude. If they collude they would choose a _____ price, resulting in a combined profit of $_____.

(f) If a collusive agreement is formed, Apogee (will, will not) _____ have an incentive to cheat on the agreement. If Apogee cheats — and Bristol does not — Apogee's profits would (increase, decrease) _____ by $_____. Similarly, if Bristol cheats — and Apogee does not — Bristol's profits would (increase, decrease) _____ by $_____. Therefore, it is quite likely that the collusive agreement, if formed, (would, would not) _____ last long.

5. Kinked-Demand Curve Model

Mammoth Enterprises competes in a homogeneous oligopoly in which all firms set price at $15. At this price Mammoth sells 10 units. Mammoth believes that if they raise their price their rivals will still charge $15. Mammoth also believes that if they cut their price their rivals will match the price cut. Accordingly, Mammoth expects to sell 2 units less for every $1 price increase above $15, 1 unit more for every $1 cut in price.

(a) Fill in the table showing Mammoth's demand schedule, total revenue, marginal revenue, and marginal cost.

(b) In the graph the follows, plot Mammoth's demand, marginal revenue, and marginal cost curves. Be sure to plot the marginal revenue and marginal cost curves at the midpoint of the two quantities involved in the calculation for each.

(c) Use the graph to confirm that Mammoth's profit-maximizing price is $15 and output is 10 under these assumptions about costs and demand.

(d) Use the graph to confirm that if Mammoth's marginal cost curve shifts up by $1 (parallel to original MC), that Mammoth will not change their output or their price.

(e) Use the graph to confirm that if Mammoth's marginal cost curve shifts up by $4 (parallel to original MC), that Mammoth will change their output and price.

Price	Qd	TR	MR	MC
$18	___	$___		
			$___	$6.00
17	___	___		
			___	7.00
16	___	___		
			___	8.00
15	___	___		
			___	8.50
14	___	___		
			___	9.00
13	___	___		
			___	9.50
12	___	___		
			___	10.00
11	___	___		

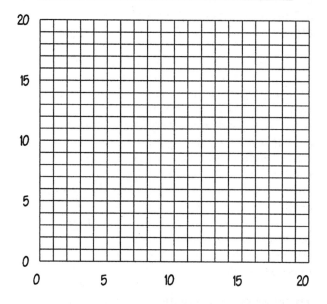

Discussion Questions

1. What are the three chief characteristics of monopolistic competition? In what sense is there competition and in what sense is there monopoly in such a market? Does product differentiation create competition or does it create monopoly?

2. What is meant by product differentiation? By what methods can products be differentiated? What methods are used in the markets for breakfast cereals, perfumes, rock music, and jeans?

3. What is the difference between the elasticity of the demand curve faced by the monopolistically competitive firm and the purely competitive firm? What two factors determine just how elastic that demand curve will be?

4. Why will the monopolistic competitor produce a long-run output smaller than the most "efficient" output? In answering, assume that the firm is producing a given product and selling it with a given amount of promotional activity.

5. Using a graph that includes the average total cost curve and the demand curve, show why it is impossible for a monopolistic competitor who is both maximizing profit and making zero economic profit to also be producing at the minimum point on the average total cost curve.

6. What strategies, besides price cutting, could a firm in monopolistic competition try in order to protect and boost its profits in the long run?

7. How do product differentiation and product development tend to offset the "wastes" associated with monopolistic competition?

8. Is advertising simply a waste of resources, or does it promote a more efficient use of resources? What arguments support the claim that it is wasteful and detrimental, and what arguments support the view that it is beneficial to the economy?

9. Why does it make sense for a monopolistic competitor to advertise, and why does it not make sense for a pure competitor?

10. What are the essential characteristics of an oligopoly? How does oligopoly differ from monopolistic competition? How is oligopoly like a chess game whereas monopolistic competition is not?

11. Explain how the concentration ratio and the Herfindahl Index in a particular industry are computed. How do these indicators measure monopoly power? What are the shortcomings of these indicators as measures of the extent of competition in an industry?

12. What are the underlying causes of oligopoly, and what is the essential "mutual interdependence" that drives the strategies of oligopolists?

13. Suppose your economics instructor announces that grades in the course will be determined purely on a curve (your grade is set strictly in relation to other students, regardless of how good or poor is the absolute performance of the students). If students care only about their grades, should they study? And will they study? How is this scenario like the prisoner's dilemma?

14. What assumptions give rise to the kinked demand curve? How can the kinked demand curve be used to explain why oligopoly prices are relatively inflexible? Under what conditions will an oligopolist who believes it faces a kinked demand choose to change price?

15. Why do producers find it advantageous to collude? What are the obstacles to collusion?

16. Why do oligopolists engage in little price competition and in extensive non-price competition?

Answers

Quick Quiz
1. (b) p. 250
2. (d) pp. 250-251
3. (d) p. 252
4. (b) pp. 252-254
5. (d) pp. 253-255
6. (a) p. 33
7. (b) p. 257
8. (d) p. 259
9. (d) p. 258
10. (d) p. 261
11. (c) pp. 261-262
12. (d) pp. 265-267
13. (a) pp. 264-272
14. (c) p. 270

Fill-in Questions
1. relatively large number of, differentiated; independently; easy

2. more, less; rival firms, product differentiation (or substitutability)

3. reduce, increase

4. average total cost, zero, above

5. price, greater than, average total cost

6. largest four, whole industry; 40

7. game; profits; prices; (1) interdependence, (2) collusive, (3) cheat

8. will not, will; elastic, inelastic

9. pure monopoly

10. sellers, price, divide, competition; collusive

11. collusive; (a) similar; (b) few; (c) easy; (d) growing; (e) difficult; (f) legal

12. limit

13. information, decreasing; raises, increasing

True-False

1. F   firms in this market model behave independently

2. F   the less will be the elasticity

3. T

4. F   productive efficiency is not achieved, because minimum ATC is not reached

5. T   this is a defining characteristic of long-run equilibrium

6. F   there is no such consensus

7. T   new firms may have no choice but to advertise extensively, raising their ATC prohibitively unless their output is large

8. T   if these differences are the basis for consumer choices of different brands

9. T

10. T   a pure monopoly has a value of 10,000 and a purely competitive industry has a value approaching 0

11. T   it depends on the relative market shares of the top four firms

12. T   by reducing the number of firms

13. T   fear of price wars, preference for non-price competition

14. T

15. F   more often tacit understanding

Multiple-Choice

1. (c) firms behave independently, not collusively

2. (d) because their products have no perfect substitutes

3. (d) all are potential competitive strategies by firms with numerous competitors

4. (b) where MC = MR

5. (c) on the demand curve at the Q where MC = MR

6. (a) P3 is above ATC

7. (a) ATC shifts up as competition for resources drives up their prices, and demand decreases as market share shrinks

8. (a) where ATC is tangent to demand, so economic profit is zero

9. (a)

10. (c) P = ATC implies zero economic profit, but a normal profit is included in ATC

11. (c) where ATC is minimized

12. (c) the difference between minimum efficient scale and actual output

13. (c)

14. (d) if new entrants cannot match these advantages

15. (b)

16. (d) therefore a concentration ratio can be a misleading indicator of monopoly power

17. (c)

18. (a) 875 > 600

19. (b)

20. (d) regardless of what the other firm may do, each firm earns a higher payoff if they choose the low-price strategy

21. (c) this is the essence of oligopoly

22. (b) if they raise price they believe competitors will not match their raise; if they cut price they believe competitors will match their cut

23. (b) cost changes, unless major, tend not to lead to price changes

24. (b) where MC = MR

25. (b) the MC still intersects MR at the same Q

26. (a)

27. (d) assuming that their rival does not change strategy

28. (b)

29. (d) the model does not predict the price at which the kink occurs

30. (b) otherwise, as the cartel raises prices, new competitors will offer lower prices and take market share

31. (d) as prices are increased Qd decreases

32. (c)

33. (a) cartel members would experience falling sales and excess capacity, tempting them to cut price

34. (c) basically automatically following leader

35. (c) and therefore has the credibility and power to lead

36. (b) collusion is not the norm, but neither is vigorous price competition

37. (b) promoting monopoly power would be negative

38. (c) by increasing the minimum output at which new firms can be viable

Problems and Projects

1. (a) Oligopoly: number of firms, clear mutual interdependence, timing of price changes; (b) Monopolistic competition: number of firms, product differentiation, entry and exit; (c) Oligopoly: few firms are dominant, pattern of price changes.

2. (a)

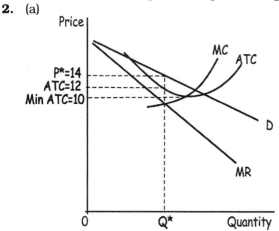

(b) Economic profits attract new firms, shifting Roma's D curve to the left as market share falls, and making it more elastic as the number of substitutes increases; (c) Roma's profits will tend towards zero; (d) If these non-price competition strategies are successful, Roma's D curve will decrease less than otherwise (or could even increase). Their D will not become as elastic as otherwise. Advertising costs raise ATC curve, so Roma's profits may not improve; (e) No; entry of competitors will prevent Roma from gaining market share, and in long-run equilibrium Roma's output will have excess capacity.

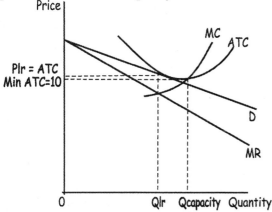

3. (a) 200/250 = 80%, oligopoly; (b) Convert each firm's sales into a percentage of whole mar-

ket (for Omega, 25/250 = 10%); square that number (10 x 10 = 100); add up these values for all firms: end result = 1952; (c) import competition is not reflected, competition from VCRs or other potentially substitutable products is not reflected; (d) 80%, 2288; The concentration ratio does not reflect distribution of market shares among firms. Total market share held by the largest firms was unchanged from 1999 to 2002, but Omicron grew relative to other large firms.

4. (a)

		APOGEE	
		High-price	Low-price
BRISTOL	High-price	A = 25	A = 35
		B = 18	B = 3
	Low-price	A = 2	A = 6
		B = 30	B = 5

(b) low, low, low; (c) low, low, low; (d) 6 million, 5 million; 11 million; are not; (e) will; high; 43 million; (f) will; increase, 10 million; increase, 12 million; would not.

5. (a) Quantity demanded: 4, 6, 8, 10, 11, 12, 13, 14; Total Revenue: $72, 102, 128, 150, 154, 156, 156, 154; Marginal Revenue: $15, 13, 11, 4, 2, 0, -2; (b) See the graph below (ignore for now MC_d and MC_e); (c) the MC = MR in the vertical break section where Q = 10; on demand curve, P_c = 15 at Q_c = 10; (d) MC is now $MC_d = MC+1$. It still = MR in the vertical break section, so $Q_d = Q_c$ = 10; (e) MC is now $MC_e = MC+4$. It = MR in the upper down-sloping section of MR, resulting in a higher price and smaller quantity: P_e = 16 and Q_e = 8.

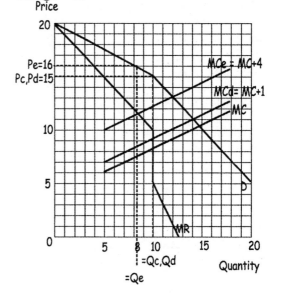

Chapter 11 · Technology, R&D, and Efficiency

Overview

Over the short run and the long run the firm is limited to operating with the same technology. This chapter discusses the very long run: a period long enough for technology to change and for firms to introduce entirely new products. We learn about the nature of technological advance, the firm's decision-making regarding research and development (R&D), the relationship of market structure to technological advance, and the connection between technological progress and efficiency.

Technological advance occurs in three steps (invention, innovation, and diffusion), with all three occurring in response to economic incentives, rather than happening randomly — or because of non-economic forces. Entrepreneurs and other innovators working within very small "startup" companies, large established firms, and within the non-profit sector combine resources in unique ways to produce new products.

Because the benefits of R&D are so uncertain, it is difficult to know exactly what the optimal level is, though the theory is straightforward: pursue R&D up to the point where the expected return from the marginal dollar spent on R&D equals the opportunity cost of the investment measured by the interest rate on the funds. Innovation can increase the firm's profits through adding revenue (via product innovation) or by reducing costs (via process innovation).

Since innovators are vulnerable to imitators, why not simply wait for other firms to innovate first? The many incentives to be first include the valuable property rights accruing to the innovator (patents, copyrights, trademarks) and as well as numerous marketing and strategic advantages.

Is there one particular market structure best suited to technological progress? Examining the incentives and opportunities for innovation in each of the four market structures studied in previous chapters leads to the inverted-U theory that indicates that R&D effort is highest in oligopolies.

Process innovation improves productive efficiency by lowering average total costs for the producer. Product innovation contributes to allocative efficiency by providing a more-preferred mix of goods and services. These conclusions are tempered by the fact that innovation can either create and entrench monopoly power, or destroy monopoly power (through a process that Schumpeter called "creative destruction"). Where innovation creates monopoly power the efficiency benefits of innovation are offset – perhaps entirely. Health care is an important sector of our economy where technological advances and their efficiency impacts are expected to be prominent for years to come.

Chapter Outline

11.1 Technological Advance: Invention, Innovation, and Diffusion

⟡ What is technological advance, and what are the three steps in the process?

- Technological advance consists of the provision of new and better goods and services and new and better ways of producing or distributing them. Technological advance is possible within the time period called the very long run.
- Technological advance is a three-step process:
    o Invention is the first discovery of a product or process through the use of imagination, ingenious thinking, and experimentation and the first proof that it will work.
    o Innovation, which draws on invention, is the first successful commercial introduction of a new product, the first use of a new method, or the creation of a new form of business enterprise. We distinguish between product innovation and process innovation.

o   Diffusion is the spread of an innovation through imitation or copying.

• Research and development (R&D) includes direct efforts at invention, innovation, and diffusion. Compared to other industrial nations, Canadian firms and governments spend a relatively small share of GDP on R&D.

• Technological advance was once seen as a process external to the economy: a random outside force. In the modern view, technological advance is an internal process driven by the market economy. Invention, innovation, and diffusion are not predictable in their specifics, but they occur in response to incentives in our economic system.

Quick Quiz

1. The correct sequence for the three-step process of technological advance is:
   (a)   invention, innovation, diffusion
   (b)   innovation, invention, diffusion
   (c)   diffusion, invention, innovation
   (d)   diffusion, innovation, invention

2. The widespread adoption of the "big box" retail store concept is an example of:
   (a)   invention
   (b)   innovation
   (c)   diffusion
   (d)   all of the above

11.2   Role of Entrepreneurs and Other Innovators

◇ What roles do entrepreneurs and others play in the process of technological advance?

• The role of entrepreneurs and other innovators is central to the process of technological advance.
   o   Entrepreneurs (or entrepreneurial teams) take on the role of initiator, innovator, and risk-bearer.
   o   Other innovators carry some of the same roles, but do not bear personal financial risk.
   o   Entrepreneurs often form startups: new firms trying to create and introduce new products or processes of production or distribution.
   o   Innovation also occurs within existing firms, large and small. Often the R&D is housed within a separate division of a corporation.

   o   Successful innovators have the ability to anticipate the future.
   o   Most nations, including Canada, rely on government and universities for much basic scientific research.

Quick Quiz

3. Identify the true statement:
   (a)   most R&D spending is on basic scientific research
   (b)   universities are becoming increasingly involved in the innovation process
   (c)   the vast majority of innovation takes place within "start-ups"
   (d)   all of the above

11.3   A Firm's Optimal Amount of R&D

◇ How does the firm choose its optimal amount of research and development activity?

• The firm chooses its optimal amount of expenditures on R&D by expanding the activity until its marginal benefit equals its marginal cost.

• R&D can be financed through bank loans, bonds, retained earnings, venture capital, or the personal savings of entrepreneurs.

• Whatever the source of the R&D financing, we assume that its opportunity cost can be represented in a constant interest rate. The horizontal interest-rate cost-of-funds curve thus captures the marginal cost of R&D.

• The marginal benefit from R&D is reflected in the firm's expected profit from the last dollar spent on R&D. Because the firm would first pursue those R&D projects with bigger pay-offs, this expected-rate-of-return curve slopes downward.

• A higher interest rate will reduce the optimal level of R&D expenditures; an overall increase in expected profitability will raise the optimal level of R&D expenditures.

• Two points deserve emphasis:
   o   the firm invests in the optimal amount of R&D, not the maximum amount of R&D that they could afford
   o   decisions are made on the basis of expected, not guaranteed, returns.

➲ No brand new technical tools are introduced in this chapter. The choice of optimal level of expenditures on R&D is merely another application of the already familiar "marginal benefit equals marginal cost" model.

- Innovation can increase a firm's profits by raising revenues or by lowering costs.
  - o Revenue increases can result from product innovation that allows consumers to increase their total utility.
  - o Cost reductions result from process innovation. The total product curve shifts up, enabling the firm to produce the same goods with fewer resources, and shift down the average total cost curve.
- Any innovator is subject to the problem of imitation by rivals. Some firms may rely on reverse engineering or a fast-second strategy instead of systematically investing in their own R&D. Given these options, what incentive is there to bear R&D expenses?
  - o Patents legally protect the inventor against imitation.
  - o Copyrights (for books, software, videos, etc.) and trademarks (for product names, logos, etc.) prevent direct copying.
  - o Brand-name recognition may give a major marketing advantage for many years.
  - o Some innovations involve trade secrets on unique processes or products. A head-start through innovation may yield cost advantages through learning by doing.
  - o Time lags before imitation can occur give a window of opportunity to make profits.
  - o An innovator may have the chance to be bought out at a profit by a larger rival.

Quick Quiz

4. The expected-rate-of-return curve for R&D is down-sloping because of:
(a)   increasing interest rates
(b)   increasing rates of imitation by other competitors
(c)   diminishing returns to R&D activity
(d)   diminishing market power over time as patents expire

5. An increase in the interest rate would:
(a)   cause a leftward shift in the expected-rate-of-return curve for R&D. and therefore a decrease in R&D
(b)   cause a movement upwards along the expected-rate-of-return curve for R&D, and therefore a decrease in R&D activity
(c)   a movement down along the expected-rate-of-return curve for R&D, and therefore an increase in R&D activity

(d)   a rightward shift in the expected-rate-of-return curve for R&D, and therefore an increase in R&D activity

11.4   Role of Market Structure

◈ Is there some market structure or firm size that generates the most technological advance?

- This question must be considered in any full evaluation of the efficiency of different market structures. Therefore, we survey the strengths and shortcomings of each market structure in relation to technological advance.
  - o Pure competitors appear to have strong reason and desire to innovate, but easy entry would quickly erode potential profits. Lack of resources to finance R&D is also an obstacle.
  - o Monopolistic competitors have a strong incentive to innovate in order to differentiate their products and gain market share. Impediments to R&D are similar to those found in pure competition.
  - o Oligopolists are often large enough to finance R&D, and barriers to entry can sustain profits long enough to pay off R&D investments. On the other hand, the market power and entry barriers may create some complacency among oligopoly firms.
  - o Pure monopolists rarely have much incentive to innovate, except as a defensive strategy. They have already gained control over their markets, so there seems little reason to take risks on R&D spending.
- Such comparison of market structures led to the inverted-U theory relating market structure and technological advance. This theory suggests that R&D activity is very weak in the least concentrated industries (pure competition) and in the most concentrated (pure monopoly), but strongest in "loose" oligopolies. In such markets, where concentration ratios are around 50%, firms typically have strong incentives for innovation and good access to financing.

Quick Quiz

6. The market structure that seems to be the most conducive to technological advance is:
(a)   pure competition
(b)   pure monopoly

(c)   monopolistic competition
(d)   oligopoly

7. Studies indicate that R&D expenditures as a percentage of industry sales are maximized in industries with four-firm concentration ratios of about:
(a)   30%
(b)   50%
(c)   70%
(d)   90%

11.5   Technological Advance and Efficiency

◈ How are productive and allocative efficiency in the economy affected by technological advance?

• Process innovations improve productive efficiency, thereby shifting upwards the firm's production function, and shifting downward the firm's average total cost curve.

• Product innovations improve allocative efficiency because they increase consumer utility by expanding the range of product choices. However, where a process or product innovation creates monopoly power, society may lose part of the benefit of the innovation because the monopolist restricts output to maximize profits.

• Technological advances provide many possibilities for alleviating the problems facing Canada's health care system; but at what resource cost?

• Joseph Schumpeter argued that innovation leads to "creative destruction" as a new product or process explodes the monopoly of one firm and replaces it with a new temporary monopoly. However, this process is neither automatic nor inevitable.

⮑ The potentially contradictory effects of innovation on efficiency are important. An innovation creates potential benefits for society, but if the innovation gives the firm monopoly power which it can exploit to restrict output, then economic efficiency may not increase.

Quick Quiz
8. The introduction of websites that enable filesharing of recorded music has cut into the profits of the recording industry. This is an example of:
(a)   creative destruction
(b)   fast-second strategy

(c)   brand-name recognition
(d)   profitable buyout

9. Which is an example of a technological advance that improves productive efficiency?
(a)   a box manufacturer learns to make equally strong boxes out of lighter weight, least expensive cardboard
(b)   an automobile manufacturer begins to build cars with anti-lock brakes
(c)   a computer manufacturer begins to make computers with ultra high resolution monitors
(d)   a fashion designer introduces a new style of pants

Terms and Concepts

technological advance	interest-cost-of-funds
very long run	curve
invention	expected-rate-of-return
patent	curve
innovation	optimal amount of
product innovation	R&D
process innovation	imitation problem
diffusion	fast-second strategy
start-ups	inverted-U theory of
venture capital	R&D
	creative destruction

Fill-In Questions

1. In the _____ run the firm must work with fixed plant, equipment, and technology. In the _____ run the firm can adjust its plant and equipment but must still work with the same technology. In the _____ run the firm has the opportunity to change also the technology.

2. When McDonald's discovered how to cook hamburgers so that they were ready when customers ordered them, this was an example of a _____ innovation. When Sony discovered how to make a small portable personal stereo, this was an example of a _____ innovation.

3. The three steps in technological advance are:
(a) _____; (b) _____; (c) _____

4. Small companies formed by entrepreneurs to introduce innovations are called _____.

5. The rate of spending on R&D will decrease if the interest rate (falls, rises) _____. The rate of R&D spending will also decrease if the expected-rate-of-return curve (falls, rises) _____.

6. Xerox, Kleenex, and Levis are such leaders in their product groups that they have historically enjoyed a huge _____ recognition advantage.

7. Innovators enhance society's _____ efficiency when they find new production processes that lower the _____ curve. Innovators enhance _____ efficiency when they introduce new products that expand choices for consumers. However, _____ efficiency can also be compromised if the innovation increases the amount of _____ power held in a market.

True-False

Circle T if the statement is true, F if it is false.

1. As a percentage of the nation's GDP, Canada spends less on R&D than do most industrial nations.   **T F**

2. It is optimal for a corporation to engage in as much R&D as they can afford.   **T F**

3. It is rational to invest in R&D only if the returns are guaranteed.   **T F**

4. New products can entice consumers to switch from existing products in order to increase their total utility.   **T F**

5. One incentive for a small firm to innovate is a potential buyout by a larger firm.   **T F**

6. A firm pursuing a fast-second strategy will be content to allow other firms to produce the innovations.   **T F**

7. The diffusion stage for ballpoint pens occurred when the first prototype ballpoint pen was manufactured.   **T F**

8. Typically, firms in both pure competition and monopolistic competition would have difficulty

raising enough capital to finance an R&D program.   **T F**

9. Most economists agree that monopoly is the market structure most conducive to stimulating technological advance.   **T F**

10. Lengthening periods of patent protection would give inventors greater incentive to create new products and processes.   **T F**

Multiple-Choice

Circle the letter that corresponds to the best answer.

1. Which one of the following is not considered one of the three steps in technological advance?
(a)   invention
(b)   innovation
(c)   diffusion
(d)   exclusion

2. An "innovator" is defined as an entrepreneur who:
(a)   makes basic policy decisions in a business
(b)   combines factors of production to produce a good or service
(c)   invents a brand new product or production process
(d)   introduces new products to the market or employs a new method of production

3. Which of the following sectors are important sources of technological advance in Canada?
(a)   business firms
(b)   universities
(c)   government
(d)   all of the above

4. Reverse engineering is:
(a)   a strategy used in imitation
(b)   a process used in getting a patent
(c)   the opposite of technological advance
(d)   the process of moving to labour intensive production

5. The modern view of technological advance is that:
(a)   technological advance happens randomly and unpredictably

(b) governments can directly control techno-logical advances

(c) technological advance occurs at a consistent and predictable pace

(d) technological advance occurs in response to economic incentives

6. The firm should increase spending on R&D if:

(a) MB > MC

(b) MC > MB

(c) MB = MC

(d) the firm has any more new ideas

7. An investor's purchase of shares in a new high-risk business is an example of what kind of financing?

(a) bank loans

(b) bonds

(c) retained earnings

(d) venture capital

8. For a company that has invented a new migraine drug, the expected-rate-of-return curve will shift up if:

(a) the cost of manufacturing the drug increases

(b) the population of migraine suffers grows

(c) other companies create similar drugs

(d) none of the above

9. If a firm becomes more efficient through experience, they are likely gaining from:

(a) learning by doing

(b) fast-second strategy

(c) brand-name recognition

(d) trade secrets

10. The inverted-U theory refers to the relationship between:

(a) the interest rate and the expected rate of return

(b) the amount of R&D expenditures and the expected rate of return

(c) the market concentration ratio and the amount of R&D expenditures

(d) the amount of R&D expenditures and the interest rate

11. Identify the true statement:

(a) purely competitive firms that innovate can enjoy the profits for a long time

(b) monopolistic competitors that innovate can differentiate their products more effectively

(c) oligopolists are generally too small to raise the financing needed to innovate

(d) monopolists generally have the strongest incentives to innovate

12. Process innovation will:

(a) shift the TP curve upward and the ATC curve downward

(b) shift the TP curve downward and the ATC curve upward

(c) shift the TP curve downward and the ATC curve downward

(d) shift the TP curve upward and the ATC curve upward

13. The idea that innovation may generate "creative destruction" is attributed to:

(a) Bill Gates

(b) Karl Marx

(c) Joseph Schumpeter

(d) Adam Smith

14. If a firm implements a process innovation:

(a) both consumer surplus and producer surplus will increase

(b) consumer surplus will increase and producer surplus will decrease

(c) consumer surplus will decrease and producer surplus will increase

(d) both consumer surplus and producer surplus will decrease

15. If a product innovation increases the demand for a product:

(a) both consumer surplus and producer surplus will increase

(b) consumer surplus will increase and producer surplus will decrease

(c) consumer surplus will decrease and producer surplus will increase

(d) both consumer surplus and producer surplus will decrease

Problems and Projects

1. Sorting Out Invention, Innovation and Diffusion

Sort the following events as either: invention (INV), innovation (INN), or diffusion (DIF).

(a) A pen manufacturer becomes the first to commercially manufacture rolling ball pens with replaceable cartridges. _____

(b) After a European automaker introduces a special shoulder harness, an "after market" manufacturer begins selling harnesses that can be installed in any car. _____

(c) A computer manufacturer patents a new computer hard disk drive the size of a box of matches. _____

(d) A mountain bike maker "reverse engineers" the new suspension design of a leading competitor. _____

(e) A retailer creates the first "big box store" concept. _____

2.   Optimal R&D Level

The Frozen North Sporting Goods Company has five different R&D projects for potential investment as listed below.

Project	R&D Cost, million $	Expected Rate of Return %
A. Graphite hockey sticks	3	8
B. Perma-sharp skates	16	9
C. Lightweight helmets	10	11
D. Clear-vue visors	7	7
E. Extra-flex gloves	8	5

(a) Use the list to fill in the expected-rate-of-return schedule below. Hint: at each level of rate of return, determine which projects (and how many dollars of R&D investment) will produce at least this rate of return. The correct results are already filled in at a 9% return.

Expected Rate of Return %	R&D Cost, million $	Projects Undertaken
5	_____	_____
6	_____	_____
7	_____	_____
8	_____	_____
9	26	C, B
10	_____	_____
11	_____	_____

(b) If Frozen North can acquire any amount of financing at a constant interest rate of 7.5%, which projects would they undertake, and what would be their optimal level of R&D spending?
Projects: _____; R&D Spending: _____

3.   Defending Against Imitation

Match the product on the left with the type of protection for innovation on the right.

(i)   instant camera
(ii) seven secret herbs and spices
(iii) famous product name
(iv) recorded music

(a) trademark
(b) copyright
(c) trade secret
(d) patent

Discussion Questions

1. What is meant by technological advance, and what are its three steps?

2. How are product innovations different from process innovations?

3. What is the firm's incentive to invest in technological advantage? What risks are there to such investment?

4. How is the firm's optimal level of R&D spending chosen? What can the government do to influence this optimal level?

5. Draw the graph showing the optimal level of R&D, explain each of the two curves, and explain how a shift up or down in either would shift the R&D level.

6. What are some key reasons why firms may choose to imitate rather than innovate? What defenses against imitation exist in our economy?

7. If you had a great idea for an innovation, but insufficient financing on your own, what would be the advantages and disadvantages of the different types of financing that you might arrange?

8. Analyze the incentives and opportunities for R&D and technological advance that exist under each of the four basic market structures.

9. What is the evidence on the relation between market structure and innovation?

10. Why does technological advance not necessarily improve the efficiency of our economy? Will technological advances in the health care sector improve efficiency?

11. Give a few examples of your own of creative destruction.

Answers

Quick Quiz
1. (a) p. 279
2. (c) p. 280
3. (b) p. 282
4. (c) p. 284
5. (b) pp. 284-286
6. (d) p. 293
7. (b) p. 293
8. (a) p. 295
9. (a) pp. 293-294

Fill-in Questions
1. short; long; very long
2. process; product
3. (a) invention; (b) innovation; (c) diffusion
4. startups
5. rises; falls.
6. brand-name
7. productive, ATC; allocative; allocative, monopoly

True-False
1. T   see Global Perspective 12-1
2. F   only up to where marginal benefit = marginal cost
3. F   by its nature, the benefits of R&D are almost always uncertain
4. T
5. T   the small firm may come up with an invention that it doesn't have the capital to exploit
6. T
7. F   a prototype is a basic working model at the invention stage
8. T
9. F   oligopoly, according to the inverted-U theory, and supporting evidence
10. T   they could enjoy the economic profits for a longer period of time

Multiple-Choice
1. (d)
2. (d)   an inventor and an innovator play different roles
3. (d)
4. (a)   imitation based on careful study of a rival's new product to learn how it is made
5. (d)

6. (a)   increase until MB has fallen, and MC risen, to the point that they are equal
7. (d)   venture capital because it is quite speculative, or risky
8. (b)   demand for the product would then rise
9. (a)
10. (c)
11. (b)   product differentiation is the main form of competition in monopolistic competition
12. (a)
13. (c)
14. (a)   equilibrium P will decrease, and Q will increase, and the CS and PS triangles will expand
15. (a)   equilibrium P and Q will both increase, and the CS and PS triangles will expand

Problems and Projects
1. (a) INN; (b) DIF; (c) INV; (d) DIF; (e) INV
2. (a) top to bottom: R&D cost: 44, 36, 36, 29, 26, 10, 10, Projects: C,B,A,D,E; C,B,A,D; C,B,A,D; C,B,A; C,B; C; C; (b) C,B,A; $29 million.
3. (i)-(d); (ii)-(c); (iii)-(a); (iv)-(b)

Chapter 12

Competition Policy and Regulation

Overview

This chapter deals with three areas of government policy toward business: anti-combines policy, industrial regulation, and social regulation.

Since the late 1800s the Canadian government has been concerned with adverse effects on consumers and competitors of firms exploiting their monopoly power. Monopoly power exists where there is industrial concentration: the situation of a single firm or a few firms selling most of the output in a market. Concentration implies the opportunity for firms to set output where MC = MR, and raise price above marginal cost, causing allocative inefficiency.

Since 1889 Canada has had so-called anti-combines laws to present the abuse of monopoly power and, in some cases, to prevent the formation of monopolies. We currently operate under the Competition Act of 1986. A significant change in the 1986 legislation was to shift jurisdiction from the criminal law to civil law, making it easier to prosecute monopolies and mergers harmful to the public interest. The Act also established a revised framework under the Competition Tribunal for adjudicating cases.

Current legislation recognizes certain trade-offs between competition and other goals such as international competitiveness or the rate of technological advance. Several high-profile merger cases (including the 1999 airline merger, and bank mergers proposed in 1998) have highlighted these concerns.

In an industry where monopoly is the only efficient market structure (natural monopoly) public ownership or industrial regulation may be necessary to ensure socially acceptable performance by the monopoly. The public interest theory of regulation holds that a natural monopoly should be subjected to price regulation that allows the monopoly to charge a price high enough to cover their opportunity costs, including a normal profit (or "fair return"). But regulation is itself prone to some serious problems. It may introduce inappropriate incentives. For example, when the allowable price is based on costs, the monopolist may be prone to X-inefficiency. Also, regulation may perpetuate monopoly by protecting a monopolist from competitors. Finally, according to the legal cartel theory of regulation, the regulated firms end up "capturing" the regulators, putting into effect a system of rules that creates conditions much like an illegal cartel.

Beginning in the 1970s the problems with regulation led to a backlash of deregulation in many industries. In most cases deregulation led to lower prices and improved efficiency. Deregulation continues in some industries, yet in other industries there are moves towards re-regulation.

Since the 1960s we have seen the proliferation of so-called social regulations aimed at improving health, safety, and environmental conditions. These regulations have improved our quality of life, but at significant cost. There is consensus that we should have social regulation but the appropriate level is controversial. Administrative costs, unintended side effects, and inappropriate uses of social regulation can raise consumer prices, slow the rate of technological innovation, and reduce competition.

Chapter Outline

12.1   Industrial Concentration

◇ What is industrial concentration and how does government combat it?

• Industrial concentration exists when one firm or a few firms control the major portion of the output of an industry. Industrial concentration in this chapter refers to firms that are large in an absolute sense and in relation to their own industry.

• In response to combines (cartels) that began to emerge in various Canadian industries in the 1880s, the Canadian government has implemented anti-combines policy and regulatory

agencies to protect society from harmful effects of monopolization and industrial concentration.
• The goals of this government intervention include promotion of competition and allocative efficiency. As we learned in Chapter 9, monopolies restrict output and raise price above marginal cost, resulting in allocative inefficiency.
• A merger is the joining of two or more firms to form one firm. There are three types of mergers, with horizontal mergers having the most potential to create industrial concentration and monopoly power:
 o A horizontal merger joins firms that are competitors selling similar products in the same market (e.g., two daily newspapers serving the same city).
 o A vertical merger joins firms at different stages of the production process in the same industry (e.g., a magazine publisher and a printing company).
 o A conglomerate merger joins two firms producing unrelated goods in different industries (e.g., a gold mine and a hotel).
• Canadian anti-combines legislation began in 1889. This law and its successor, the Combines Investigation Act of 1910, were enacted to restrain the growth and exploitation of monopoly power. The legislation was periodically amended and updated in the light of court decisions, the emergence of new marketing strategies, and changing perceptions of the benefits and costs of particular business practices.
• The effectiveness of the anti-combines law in preventing monopoly and maintaining competition was questionable, especially in the monopoly and merger areas. Convictions were difficult to obtain because what the law prohibited was fairly vague, and the burden of proof is very heavy under criminal law.
• The Competition Act of 1986 replaced the Combines Investigation Act. The new Act views competition not as an end in itself but as one means to promote efficiency. A quasi-judicial body called the Competition Tribunal replaced the criminal courts for adjudication of prosecutions of mergers and monopolies under the civil law. The conspiracy provisions now provide for larger fines, and allow for prosecutions based on circumstantial evidence.
• Among the most important recent cases dealt with by the Competition Tribunal under the Competition Act are the merger in 1999 of Air Canada and Canadian Airlines (which was allowed), and two bank mergers proposed in 1998. They were denied, but bank mergers were once again before the policy-makers in 2002.
• These cases illustrate the trade-off between the efficiency effects of mergers and the anti-competitive effects of mergers. Government also weighs trade-offs between maximizing competition and maximizing the ability of Canadian producers to export goods (and improve our balance of trade), and between maximizing competition and fostering the implementation of new technologies.

⮌ A thorough understanding of the Canadian economy today requires knowledge of our economic history and of how current laws and policies have been shaped by past cases. For example, the present Competition Act and regulatory framework reflect current economic and legal thinking, but also decades of experience with previous laws and regulatory mechanisms.

Quick Quiz

1. Which is part of the case against industrial concentration? Industrial concentration:
 (a) leads to income inequality
 (b) results in lower per unit costs
 (c) promotes allocative inefficiency
 (d) produces economic profits that are used for R&D

2. A merger between two retailers, Shoppers Rug Mart and London Rugs, would be what kind of merger?
 (a) horizontal
 (b) vertical
 (c) conglomerate
 (d) none of the above

3. Which one was among the legal changes incorporated in the 1986 Competition Act?
 (a) placing uncompetitive mergers under the civil law framework
 (b) the first introduction of laws against price-fixing
 (c) making the laws applicable to banks and crown corporations
 (d) making illegal price-fixing agreements among export consortia

12.2   Industrial Regulation

◈ What is industrial regulation and in what

circumstances does government use it?

◈ What are the problems with industrial regulation?

• In industries where economies of scale are so extensive that efficiency dictates that there be only producer (a natural monopoly), anti-combines is not appropriate. Instead, government often employs a policy of public ownership or of industrial regulation.

• According to the public interest theory of regulation, the goal of regulation is to capture for society some of the cost savings from natural monopoly without suffering the cut in output and rise in price that occurs with unregulated monopoly. Regulators attempt to allow the monopolist to charge a price that will cover production costs and provide a "fair" return.

• Not everyone agrees that industrial regulation is effective. There are least two major criticisms:

    o Regulated monopolists are prone to X-inefficiency. There is little incentive to minimize costs because the regulated price is based on the firm's costs.

    o Regulators often protect firms from competition based on a mistaken diagnosis of natural monopoly. Thus, monopolies can be perpetuated by regulation.

• The legal cartel theory of regulation sees regulation as being "supplied" by politicians to firms who fear competition. Such regulation often works to block entry and divide the market up among existing firms, creating a legal cartel. Unlike illegal cartels, these cartels can be very durable. Occupational licensing is a prime example.

• By the 1970s the problems with industrial regulation had created much pressure for deregulation. Many transportation and utility industries have since been opened to competition, despite considerable controversy, and in some cases, re-regulation.

• Based on numerous studies, economists believe that regulation overall has been beneficial to consumers and the economy by lowering prices and costs, and raising output.

Quick Quiz

4. Legislation designed to regulate natural monopolies would be based on which theory of regulation?
    (a) legal cartel
    (b) public interest
    (c) X-inefficiency
    (d) public ownership

5. Some opponents of industrial regulation argue that:
    (a) many regulated industries are natural monopolies
    (b) regulation tends to promote X-inefficiency in regulated firms
    (c) regulation leads to more mergers
    (d) regulation helps moderate costs and improve efficiency in a regulated industry

6. Critics of the deregulation of industry argue that deregulation leads to:
    (a) lower prices
    (b) increased output
    (c) destructive price wars and ultimate re-monopolization of the industry
    (d) an increase in bureaucratic inefficiencies in the industry

12.3 Social Regulation

◈ What is social regulation and what are its effects?

• In the 1960s Canadian governments began to enact social regulations to improve our quality of life.

• Such regulations govern health and safety conditions in the workplace, environmental impacts of production activities, product quality and safety standards, etc. Many new regulatory agencies were formed. Social regulation usually applies across all industries.

• The aim of social regulation is uncontroversial, but the costs to the economy are high. Critics argue that we are now overregulated: that regulation's marginal cost now exceeds its marginal benefits. They also believe that social regulation tends to be based on inadequate information and administered by overzealous personnel.

• Social regulation raises prices (as costs of compliance are transferred to consumers), slows the rate of innovation (because producers are reluctant to take risks), and reduces competition (because compliance is harder for small firms).

• Supporters of social regulation contend that the benefits outweigh the costs, though the benefits are often underestimated and may only become apparent over time. Supporters believe that many serious and neglected social problems can be attacked only with such regulations.

• The Microsoft case is an enormously important example of government action against a monopoly. U.S. courts ruled that Microsoft acted illegally – not by having a monopoly – but by abusing its monopoly position, using anticompetitive strategies to prevent Netscape from gaining any toehold in the operating system market.

➲ In any discussion of regulation it is important to be clear on the type of regulation. The purposes, methods, and effects of industrial regulation and social regulation are quite different.

Quick Quiz

7. Social regulation might be concerned with:
(a) the price of gasoline
(b) competition in the airline industry
(c) working conditions in factories
(d) profit rates in the telephone industry

8. A main criticism of social regulation is that:
(a) it is pro-competitive
(b) it will decrease the rate of innovation in the economy
(c) it will increase the amount of price-fixing among businesses
(d) it will take too long to achieve its objectives

9. An example of social regulation is:
(a) the Competition Act of 1986
(b) the government's decision to deny the banks' merger application
(c) the decision to ratify the Kyoto Accord
(d) all of the above

Terms and Concepts

anti-combines policy	Competition Act
anti-combines (anti-monopoly) legislation	competition tribunal
horizontal merger	natural monopoly
vertical merger	public interest theory of regulation
conglomerate merger	legal cartel theory of regulation
Combines Investigation Act	social regulation

Fill-In Questions

1. In this chapter the term "_____" refers to industries in which firms are large in absolute terms and in relation to the total market.

2. Canadian anti-combines legislation was initially administered under a (civil, criminal) _____ law framework. Under this legislative framework there were (few, many) _____ successful prosecutions.

3. The Combines Investigation Act was replaced in 1986 by the _____ Act. Under the new law, mergers and monopolies (now called abuse of dominant position) are offenses only where they result in an unacceptable _____ of competition. Mergers that result in gains in _____ may be allowed even though they result in a _____ of competition.

4. Mergers and monopoly (abuse of dominant position) are now adjudicated by the Competition _____, which can issue _____ orders to restore and maintain market competition.

5. Critics claim that social regulation (increases, decreases) _____ product prices, reduces worker _____ by reallocating investment funds, causes a (slower, more rapid) _____ rate of innovation, and (more, less) _____ competition in the economy.

6. (Industrial, Social) _____ regulation tends to cause X-inefficiency because the regulated firm has little incentive to reduce _____.

True-False

Circle T if the statement is true, F if it is false.

1. Since most wheat in Canada is produced on the Prairies, there is a high degree of industrial concentration in the wheat growing industry. **T F**

2. A horizontal merger is a merger between firms selling similar products in the same market. **T F**

3. A merger of the Globe and Mail and the National Post newspapers would be an example of a vertical merger. **T F**

4. A merger of an oil company and a department store would be an example of a conglomerate merger. **T F**

5. The latest major revision to Canada's anti-combines laws was passed in 1986.   **T F**

6. The Competition Act makes some allowances for trade-offs between the goal of competition and other goals.   **T F**

7. Under the Competition Act mergers and monopolies are no longer violations of Canada's Criminal Code.   **T F**

8. Examples of social regulation are health, safety, and environmental laws.   **T F**

9. Those who favour social regulation believe that it is needed in order to improve the quality of life in Canada.   **T F**

10. Economists' overall assessment is that in most industries that have been deregulated, consumers have suffered.   **T F**

Multiple-Choice

Circle the letter that corresponds to the best answer.

1. "Industrial concentration" in this chapter refers to which one of the following?
(a) firms that are absolutely large
(b) firms that are relatively large compared to others in their industry
(c) firms that are either absolutely or relatively large compared to others in their industry
(d) firms that are both absolutely and relatively large compared to others in their industry

2. Which of the following is not a part of the case against industrial concentration?
(a) firms in highly concentrated industries are larger than they need to be to take advantage of economies of scale
(b) firms in highly concentrated industries earn economic profits that they use for research and technological development
(c) monopoly power leads to the misallocation of resources
(d) monopoly power leads to greater income inequality

3. Which kind of merger is anti-combines policy mostly concerned with?
(a) horizontal
(b) vertical
(c) conglomerate
(d) all of the above

4. The Competition Tribunal is a quasi-judicial body that:
(a) has jurisdiction to determine cases on mergers and monopoly
(b) has recommended removal of interprovincial barriers to trade
(c) regulates agricultural marketing boards
(d) was replaced by the Restrictive Trade Practices commission in 1986

5. Suppose only two Canadian firms make furnaces, with each currently producing both large and small furnaces. How would the Competition Tribunal treat an agreement to split the market, with each firm specializing in one size of furnace?
(a) the Tribunal would have no jurisdiction over such an agreement
(b) the Tribunal must deny such an agreement
(c) the Tribunal would not care about such an agreement
(d) the Tribunal might allow such specialization if it allowed the firms to reduce average costs

6. Which one of the following has not tended to reduce competition?
(a) occupational licensing
(b) natural monopoly
(c) legal cartels
(d) the Competition Act

7. Critics of the deregulation of industry argue that (among other things) deregulation can lead to:
(a) higher prices for the products produced by the industry
(b) the monopolization of the industry by a few large firms
(c) a decline in the quantity or the quality of the product produced by the industry
(d) all of the above

8. Which of the following is not a concern of social regulation?
(a) the prices of goods
(b) the physical characteristics of goods

(c) the conditions under which goods are manufactured

(d) the environmental impact of production processes

9. Which of the following is not one of the criticisms levelled against social regulation?
(a) it results in higher prices
(b) it is too slow in achieving its objectives
(c) it slows the rate of innovation in the economy
(d) it is anti-competitive

10. Which theory predicts that regulation will sometimes perpetuate monopoly by creating barriers to entry in the regulated industry?
(a) legal cartel theory
(b) public interest theory of regulation
(c) natural monopoly theory
(d) economies of scale theory

11. Supporters of social regulation believe that:
(a) there is a pressing need to reduce the number of mergers between large businesses in Canada
(b) corporate profits are too high
(c) the benefits of social regulation justify its costs
(d) administrative and compliance costs are usually underestimated

12. Which of the following is not among Canada's main regulatory agencies?
(a) Canadian Wheat Board
(b) National Energy Board
(c) Bank of Canada
(d) Canadian Grain Commission

13. What would the critics of deregulation have predicted would happen when the airline industry was deregulated?
(a) destructive price wars
(b) improved safety
(c) improved customer service
(d) all of the above

14. Opponents of Canada's decision to reduce greenhouse gas emissions as required by the Kyoto Accord are concerned that:
(a) Canadian industries will lose international competitiveness
(b) new technologies will emerge to supply cleaner power sources

(c) jobs will be created in new industries
(d) Canada's provinces will bear an equal burden in meeting the Kyoto targets

Problems and Projects

1. Terminology
Match the item in List A with the item in List B.
List A:
(a) balance of trade versus competition
(b) civil law versus criminal law
(c) "fair" rate of return
(d) perpetuating monopoly
List B
(i) legal cartel theory
(ii) tradeoffs among goals
(iii) burden of proof
(iv) public interest theory of regulation

2. The Competition Act of 1986
Go to your library and find a copy of the Competition Act. Identify the specific section of the Act that applies to each of the following:
(a) a price-fixing agreement among five companies controlling 97 percent of the business of the compressed gas market
(b) the purchase of a controlling interest in a group of 38 community and real estate newspapers in the lower mainland region of British Columbia by a firm that controlled the dominant dailies in that area
(c) the purchase of waste disposal firms so that 87 percent of the waste disposal market in three Vancouver Island areas was brought under the control of one firm
(d) a merger of two major firms in the oil refining industry
(e) misleading representation as to the price at which a product is ordinarily sold

3. Mergers
Magna Carta and Maps for All are two retail chains that sell maps. Cartographica is a company that prints maps. Dogwood & Blandie is a restaurant chain.
(a) If Magna Carta merged with Maps for All it would be a _____ merger.
(b) If Magna Carta merged with Cartographica it would be a _____ merger.
(c) If Magna Carta merged with Dogwood & Blandie it would be a _____ merger.

(d) Of these mergers, the one most likely to be prohibited under the Competition Act is the _____ merger.

Discussion Questions

1. What is the difference between how the term "monopoly" is used in this chapter and how it is used in Chapter 9? What is "industrial concentration"?

2. When and why was Canadian anti-combines policy born?

3. Why was it difficult under the Combines Investigation Act to convict firms for forming a monopoly or a merger?

4. Section 1.1 of the Competition Act begins: "The purpose of this Act is to maintain and encourage competition in Canada in order to promote the efficiency and adaptability of the Canadian economy...." Why might there be a conflict between encouraging competition and efficiency? Which goal is emphasized more in the Act?

5. Find the Competition Act in your library and read Section 45. Now explain why the Ottawa Senators in the NHL had to pay millions of dollars to other NHL teams to be allowed to serve fans willing to pay for hockey entertainment.

6. Explain the role of the Bureau of Competition Policy in a hypothetical merger of Labatt's and Molson's brewing companies.

7. Why is the definition of the market an important issue in the application of anti-combines laws?

8. Give examples of how strict enforcement of anti-combines laws could conflict with other key social goals.

9. How does social regulation differ from industrial regulation? The critics of social regulation argue that it has resulted in excessive regulation. How so? If there is too much regulation, what are the more important implications?

10. Why did industrial regulation give way in many industries to deregulation? What did critics of deregulation fear? What were the results of deregulation?

Answers

Quick Quiz
1. (c) pp. 301-302
2. (a) p. 302
3. (a) p. 304
4. (b) p. 306
5. (b) p. 306
6. (c) p. 308
7. (c) p. 309
8. (d) p. 311
9. (c) p. 310

Fill-in Questions
1. industrial concentration
2. criminal; few
3. Competition; lessening; efficiency, lessening
4. Tribunal, remedial
5. increases, productivity, slower, less
6. Industrial, costs

True-False
1. F   wheat is produced by a larger number of firms
2. T
3. F   horizontal; they compete in the same market
4. T   they produce in unrelated markets
5. T   entitled the Competition Act
6. T
7. T   they are now handled under civil law
8. T
9. T
10. F   in most industries consumers have enjoyed lower prices

Multiple-Choice
1. (d)
2. (b)   this is a defense for industrial concentration
3. (a)   this type of merger increases monopoly power
4. (a)
5. (d)   efficiencies can be a justification for anti-competitive behaviours like specialization agreements
6. (d)
7. (d)

8. (a) prices are the concern of industrial regulation

9. (b) if anything, critics complain that it moves too swiftly (before costs and benefits are understood)

10. (a)

11. (c)

12. (c)

13. (a) the others would have been expected by advocates of deregulation

14. (a) they will have to bear the costs of changing business practices related to energy use

Problems and Projects

1. (a) (ii); (b) (iii); (c) (iv); (d) (i)

2. (a) section 45(1)(b); (b) section 79(1); (c) section 79(1); (d) section 79(1); (e) section 36(1)

3. (a) horizontal; (b) vertical; (c) conglomerate; (d) horizontal.

Chapter 13 — The Demand for Factors of Production

Overview

Chapter 13 studies pricing and employment in resource markets. When a firm chooses how many units of output to produce, it simultaneously chooses how much land, labour, capital and entrepreneurial ability to employ. Resource markets are important because resource prices determine households' incomes, because efficiency in resource markets is vital for overall efficiency of the economy, and because there are many important ethical and policy issues related to these markets.

The demand for inputs is derived from the demand for the firm's product. The chapter deals mostly with the simplest case: a firm selling its product in a purely competitive market, and hiring its inputs in a purely competitive market. The firm is thus a "price taker" in the output market and a "wage taker" in the input market.

Marginal revenue product (MRP) is the change in the firm's total revenue resulting from using one more unit of input. It depends on the productivity of the resource and the price of the output. Marginal factor cost (MFC) is the change in the firm's total cost resulting from hiring one more unit of input. In order to maximize profits, a firm will hire an extra unit of input if the added revenue earned exceeds the added cost (that is, until MRP = MFC). By hiring up to this point, the firm is also choosing the output level where MR = MC. Therefore, the input demand decision and output supply decision are one and the same.

The MRP curve is the firm's resource demand curve. In the short run, the law of diminishing returns guarantees that this curve must eventually slope downward. For firms that are "price makers" in the output market the MRP curve also falls because as more units of the input are hired the firm must lower its output price to sell the increased output. The MRP curve shifts with changes in: demand for the product, productivity of the resource, and prices of substitute or complementary resources. Elasticity of the demand curve depends on: the rate of decline in the marginal productivity of the resource, the ease with which the resource can be substituted for other resources, the elasticity of demand for the product, and the proportion of total production costs accounted for by the resource.

In the long run the firm can vary its employment of all resources. Thus, long-run resource demand decisions depend on the substitutability or complementarity of resources. Two key concepts are the "least-cost rule" and the "profit-maximizing rule."

The marginal productivity theory of income distribution holds that resource owners are paid according to the marginal contribution that their resources contribute to society's output, and that therefore the distribution of income is fair and equitable. This view of economic justice is flawed, however, by the very unequal distribution of resources among society's members, and by the fact that resource markets are far from purely competitive.

Chapter Outline

13.1 Factor Pricing and Demand

◇ How are factor prices determined?

◇ What is marginal revenue product?

• As firms make the output supply decisions discussed in recent chapters they simultaneously make input demand decisions. These decisions are the subject of this chapter. Most of the examples use labour as the input, though land, capital, or entrepreneurial ability could be used equally well.

• The study of resource pricing is important because resource prices: 1) influence households' incomes and the distribution of income, 2) allocate scarce resources and affect the economy's efficiency, 3) affect how firms combine resources to minimize costs and maximize profits, and 4) raise policy issues about the distribution of income.

• The basic analysis assumes the firm's output market is purely competitive, and so is the resource market. Therefore, the firm is both a "price taker" and a "wage taker."

• The demand for a resource is a derived demand because it flows from the demand for the product that the resource helps to produce.

• The demand for a resource depends upon its marginal productivity and the market price of the product it helps to produce. Marginal revenue product (MRP) combines the two factors of marginal product and output price into a single variable that indicates the amount that an extra unit of input adds to the firm's revenue.

• Marginal resource cost (MRC) is the addition to the firm's costs from hiring one more unit of the input. MRC is also known as marginal factor cost (MFC).

• A profit-maximizing firm will hire a resource up to the quantity at which MRP = MRC.

• From a product market perspective, this is also the point where MR = MC.

• The firm's MRP curve is their demand curve for the resource. In the short run this curve is down-sloping because of the law of diminishing returns.

• The MRP curve for an imperfectly competitive producer falls more steeply (is less elastic) than for a purely competitive producer. The firm's MRP curve is down-sloping for two reasons: diminishing returns and the fact that the firm's output price falls as the firm produces more output.

• The market (or total) demand for a resource is found by summing horizontally the individual demands of all firms employing the resource.

⮞ Three terms used frequently in this chapter mean exactly the same thing: resource, factor, and input.

⮞ Recall the production function that related inputs and outputs. Given that relationship, it should come as no surprise that decisions about output levels simultaneously imply decisions about levels of input usage.

⮞ When we view the firm's profit-maximizing decisions from the output perspective, marginal revenue and marginal cost are calculated with respect to changes in output, so we plot output on the horizontal axis of graphs. When the same decisions are viewed from the input perspective, marginal revenue product and marginal resource cost are calculated with respect to changes in input usage, so we plot input on the horizontal axis.

Quick Quiz

1. A firm is considered a "wage taker" if:
   (a)   the price of the firm's product is constant regardless of output
   (b)   the price of the firm's product is constant regardless of their level of resource employment
   (c)   the price of the resource is constant regardless of the firm's level of resource employment
   (d)   the firm is able to exploit their market power in the resource market and exploit the resource suppliers

2. A firm's MRP curve for a resource will increase if:
   (a)   the price of the firm's product rises
   (b)   the marginal productivity of the resource decreases at any given level of employment
   (c)   the price of the resource falls
   (d)   both (a) and (b)

3. The firm's demand curve for a resource is:
   (a)   the MRP curve for the resource
   (b)   the MFC for the resource
   (c)   the marginal product curve for the resource
   (d)   none of the above

13.2   Determinants of Factor Demand

◈ What determinants shift the factor demand curve?

• The demand for a resource will increase if:
   ○   demand for the firm's product increases
   ○   the productivity of the resource increases (whether caused by an increase in the quantity of other resources, technological progress, or improvement in resource quality)
   ○   the price of a substitute resource rises -- if the substitution effect outweighs the output effect. (The substitution effect oc-

curs when a firm uses more of a resource that has become relatively less expensive, and less of resources that have become relatively more expensive. The output effect occurs when a change in the price of a resource leads to a change in output, and therefore, in input usage.)
- o the price of a complementary resource falls. (This is due to the output effect; there is no substitution effect.)
- Many trends in growth of employment in different occupations can be traced to shifting demand for these kinds of labour. For example, rising incomes and an aging population continue to increase the demand for health care workers.

Quick Quiz
4. What would shift to the right the demand curve for bulldozers used in building roads?
- (a) an increase in the wages for road construction workers
- (b) a drop in the price of bulldozers
- (c) an increase in government spending on road construction
- (d) all of the above

5. A firm has some ability to substitute between labour and capital in its production process. If the price of capital rises, the firm's demand curve for labour will:
- (a) decrease because of the substitution effect and the output effect
- (b) increase because of the substitution effect
- (c) decrease because of the output effect
- (d) increase or decrease depending on the relative size of the substitution effect and the output effect

6. Which of the following are complementary inputs for a trucking firm?
- (a) trucks and drivers
- (b) small trucks and large trucks
- (c) gasoline and diesel fuel
- (d) TV advertising and radio advertising

7. Increasing wages for lab technicians in hospitals could be explained by:
- (a) technological improvements that increase the accuracy and value of lab tests
- (b) an increased population of patients
- (c) higher levels of technical qualifications among lab technicians
- (d) all of the above

13.3 Elasticity of Factor Demand
◈ What determines the elasticity of the demand for a factor?
- The elasticity of resource demand measures the sensitivity of the demand to changes in the price of the resource. It is measured as:

$$Erd = \frac{\%\ change\ in\ factor\ quantity}{\%\ change\ in\ factor\ price}$$

- This elasticity depends on three factors:
  - o The easier it is to find other resources to substitute in the production process, the more elastic the demand.
  - o The more elastic the product demand, the more elastic the resource demand.
  - o The larger the proportion of the firm's total cost represented by a resource, the more elastic the resource demand.

➲ Though the context is a bit different this time, the elasticity of demand for a resource is calculated and interpreted exactly the same way as the price elasticity of demand for a product. Therefore, you may wish to review the section of Chapter 5 dealing with this calculation.

Quick Quiz
8. Which kind of factor would have the most inelastic demand, *ceteris paribus*?
- (a) a factor for which there are several very close substitutes available
- (b) a factor producing a product that consumers can readily do without
- (c) a factor producing a product with a very inelastic demand
- (d) a factor that represents a very large percentage of the firm's overall production costs

13.4 Optimal Combination of Factors
◈ What combination of factors will minimize cost at a specified level of output?

◈ What combination of factors will maximize profit?

- Most products can be produced with various combinations of resources, and in the long run the profit-maximizing firm will vary its resource mix in order to find the cost-minimizing combination for producing the chosen level of output.
- The firm is producing a specific output level using the least-cost combination of resources when the last dollar spent on each resource

yields the same marginal product. Expressed another way, the ratio of the marginal product to resource price is the same for all resources.

• The firm is hiring resources in the most profitable combination if it hires resources to the point where the MRP of each factor is equal to the price of that factor.

• A firm that is hiring resources in the most profitable combination is also using a least-cost combination of inputs.

• Some people contend that a competitive market system produces a fair and just distribution of income. The marginal productivity theory is taken to support this claim because each unit of a resource receives a payment equal to its marginal contribution to the firm's revenue. However, the theory has at least two serious faults:

  o The distribution of income is unequal because individuals own radically different amounts of resources in the first place.

  o Incomes of resource suppliers are not based on their marginal productivities if there is monopoly power in resource markets.

➲ The profit-maximizing rule for combining resources is easy enough to remember. Since the price of any resource must equal its marginal revenue product at the profit maximum, the ratio must equal one for every resource.

Quick Quiz

9. A factory's workers each cost $10 per hour, and each machine costs $15 per hour. If the marginal product of a worker is 5 units of output per hour, and the marginal product of a machine is 6 units of output per hour, the firm's current production level could be produced at lower cost by:

(a) using more machines and fewer workers

(b) using fewer machines and more workers

(c) using fewer machines and fewer workers

(d) there is insufficient data to draw a conclusion

10. If at current employment levels for inputs L and K the firm finds that MPK/PK > MPL/PL, then:

(a) a unit of L produces more extra output than a unit of K

(b) a unit of K produces more extra output than a unit of L

(c) a unit of K is more expensive than a unit of L

(d) an extra dollar spent on K will produce more extra output than an extra dollar spent on L

Terms and Concepts

derived demand	elasticity of factor
marginal product (MP)	demand
marginal revenue	least-cost combination
product (MRP)	of factors
marginal factor cost	profit-maximizing
(MFC)	combination of
MRP = MFC rule	factors
substitution effect	marginal productivity
output effect	theory of income
	distribution

Fill-In Questions

1. The demand for a resource is _____ from the demand for the _____ of the resource.

2. The impact of an additional unit of input on the firm's production is called the marginal _____, while the impact on the firm's total revenues is called the marginal _____.

3. The marginal revenue product schedule is obtained by multiplying the _____ of each unit of input by the _____ of the output.

4. The marginal resource cost is the change in the firm's _____ due to the hiring of _____ more unit of a(n) _____.

5. The marginal revenue product of the imperfectly competitive seller falls for two reasons: both _____ and _____ fall as output increases. As a consequence, the MRP (or demand) schedule for the resource is (more, less) _____ elastic than it would be if the output were sold in a purely competitive market.

6. For each event below, indicate whether it would tend to increase (+), decrease (-), or have an uncertain effect (?) upon a manufacturer's demand for conveyor machines.

(a) an increase in the price of the manufacturer's product _____

(b)   a decrease in the number of workers employed to run conveyor machines ____

(c)   an increase in the productivity of conveyor machines ____

(d)   an increase in the price of a substitute resource when the output effect is greater than the substitution effect ____

(e)   a decrease in the price of a complementary resource ____

7. Holding constant the output of the firm, a decrease in the price of resource A will induce the firm to hire (more, less) _____ of resource A and _____ of other resources; this is called the _____ effect. But if the decrease in the price of A results in lower total costs and an increase in output, the firm may hire _____ of both resources; this is called the _____ effect.

8. A firm's demand for labour will be less elastic: 1) the (less, more) _____ elastic is the demand for the product the labour produces, 2) the (more, less) _____ difficult it is to substitute other resources in place of labour, 3) the (larger, smaller) _____ the percentage of the firm's total costs represented by labour costs.

9. Suppose a firm employs resources in purely competitive markets. If the firm wishes to produce any given amount of its product in the least costly way, the ratio of the _____ of each resource to its _____ must be the same for all resources. In order to maximize _____, the firm must not only minimize costs, but also produce the optimal level of output. At this level, the firm employs the combination of resources where the ratio of the _____ of each resource to its _____ is equal to _____ for all resources.

True-False

Circle T if the statement is true, F if it is false.

1. The demand for resources is derived from the demand for the goods and services the resources produce.   **T F**

2. Marginal factor cost is the extra resource cost of producing one more unit of output.   **T F**

3. For a firm that is a "price taker," the marginal revenue product is found by multiplying the marginal product of the extra input by the price of the output.   **T F**

4. Health care occupations are among the fields with the faster growth in labour demand.   **T F**

5. If the productivity of computer programmers rises because they are given faster computers to use, the demand for programmers will shift to the right.   **T F**

6. A firm's demand schedule for a resource will be more elastic if it sells its product in a purely competitive market than it would be if it sold the product in an imperfectly competitive market.   **T F**

7. When two resources are substitutable for each other, both the substitution effect and the output effect of a decrease in the price of one of these resources operate to increase the quantity the firm employs of the other resource.   **T F**

8. Consider two inputs termed i and j. If an increase in the price of j results in a decrease in the use of i, then i and j are called complements.   **T F**

9. If a firm wishes to produce any level of output at least-cost, resources should be combined so that their marginal products are equal.   **T F**

10. *Ceteris paribus*, a construction company that hires hundreds of labourers and only a few supervisors will have a higher elasticity of demand for supervisors than for labourers.   **T F**

11. If there are no close substitutes for haircuts, but many close substitutes for massages, then the demand for hair stylists will be less elastic than the demand for masseurs, *ceteris paribus*.   **T F**

12. If labour is less expensive in India than in Canada, and capital is about equally expensive in India and Canada, the theories of this chapter predict a tendency towards the use of more labour-intensive production methods in India. **T F**

13. If individuals are paid according to the marginal products of their resources, society's income distribution will be fair and equal.   **T   F**

14. The existence of monopoly power helps resource suppliers gain a larger share of the income from their production.   **T   F**

Multiple-Choice

Circle the letter that corresponds to the best answer.

1. The price paid for resources affects:
(a)   the money incomes of households
(b)   the allocation of resources among different firms and industries
(c)   the quantities of different resources employed to produce a particular product
(d)   all of the above

2. The demand for a resource depends on:
(a)   the marginal productivity of the resource and price of the good or service produced from it
(b)   the marginal productivity of the resource and the price of the resource
(c)   the price of the resource and the price of the good or service produced from it
(d)   the price and quantity demanded of the resource

3. The resource demand curve for a competitive firm slopes downward because of:
(a)   the law of down-sloping demand
(b)   the law of diminishing returns
(c)   decreasing returns to scale
(d)   the reduction in output price required to increase sales

4. All but one of the following would shift the demand curve for a resource. Which one?
(a)   a change in technology
(b)   a change in the price of the other inputs used in production
(c)   a change in the price of the resource
(d)   a change in the price of the output

5. Which of the following would increase a firm's demand for a particular resource?
(a)   an increase in the prices of complementary resources used by the firm

(b)   a decrease in the demand for the firm's product
(c)   an increase in the productivity of the resource
(d)   an increase in the productivity of a substitutable resource

6. Marginal factor cost is:
(a)   the price paid for an input
(b)   the slope of the input supply curve
(c)   the increase in total cost when one more unit of the input is hired
(d)   the increase in total cost when one more unit of output is produced

7. A firm is a "wage taker" if:
(a)   it hires so little of a particular type of labour that it has no effect on the price of this labour
(b)   it has all of the power in the employment relationship and can therefore determine the wage
(c)   it earns wage income rather than paying wages
(d)   it sells its output in a purely competitive market

8. A profit-maximizing firm will hire an input up to the point where:
(a)   the law of diminishing returns no longer holds
(b)   average cost of production is minimized
(c)   marginal product begins to fall
(d)   marginal revenue product equals marginal resource cost

9. If a firm hires resources up to where marginal resource cost equals marginal revenue product, then the firm must also be operating where:
(a)   marginal revenue equals marginal cost
(b)   the marginal products of all inputs are equal
(c)   the elasticity of resource demand equals 1
(d)   marginal revenue is greater than the output price

10. As a firm that sells its product in an imperfectly competitive market hires more units of a resource, the marginal revenue product of that resource falls because:
(a)   the price paid for the resource falls
(b)   the marginal product of the resource falls

(c)   the price of the firm's product falls

(d)   both the marginal product and the price at which the firm sells its product fall

11. A firm that is a "price maker" in its output market will, as compared to a firm that is a "price taker":

(a)   employ more labour and produce more output

(b)   employ less labour and produce less output

(c)   employ more labour and produce less output

(d)   employ less labour and produce more output

12. To maximize profits a competitive firm should hire additional units of a resource so long as:

(a)   marginal resource cost is greater than output price

(b)   input price is greater than marginal revenue product

(c)   each successive resource unit adds more to the firm's revenues than to its costs

(d)   the firm is earning economic profits

Using the following schedules showing total product and marginal product for a resource, answer questions 13 through 15. Assume that the firm employs constant quantities of other resources.

Units of Resource	Total Product	Marginal Product
1	8	8
2	14	6
3	18	4
4	21	3
5	23	2

13. If the firm's product sells for a constant $3 per unit, the marginal revenue product of the 4th unit of the resource is:

(a) $3

(b) $6

(c) $9

(d) $12

14. If the firm's product sells for a constant $3 per unit and the price of the resource is a constant $15, how many units of the resource will the firm hire?

(a)   2

(b)   3

(c)   4

(d)   5

15. If the firm can sell 14 units of output at a price of $1 per unit and 18 units of output at a price of $0.90 per unit, the marginal revenue product of the third unit of the resource is:

(a) $4

(b) $3.60

(c) $2.20

(d) $0.40

16. A firm operating in competitive input and output markets pays $6 per unit for a certain input. If the last unit of this input hired produces $16 worth of output, the firm:

(a)   is maximizing profits

(b)   should hire more units of the input

(c)   should reduce employment of the input

(d)   should raise the price paid to the input

17. A computer disk manufacturer is employing resources so that the MRP of the last unit hired for resource X is $240 and the MRP of the last unit hired for resource Y is $150. The price of resource X is $80 and the price of resource Y is $50 and both of these prices are constant. The firm should:

(a)   hire more of resource X and less of resource Y

(b)   hire less of resource X and more of resource Y

(c)   hire less of both resource X and resource Y

(d)   hire more of both resource X and resource Y

18. A firm that hires resources in competitive markets is necessarily maximizing its profits when:

(a)   the marginal revenue product of every resource is equal to 1

(b)   the marginal product of every resource is the same

(c)   the ratio of the marginal revenue product of every resource to its price is equal to 1

(d)   it is minimizing costs of producing the current output level

19. The effect on the employment of a resource when its price or the price of other inputs changes can be broken down into a substitution effect and

an output effect. In finding the substitution effect which of the following is assumed to be constant?
(a) the total output of the firm
(b) the total expenditures of the firm
(c) the employment of all other resources
(d) the marginal products of all resources

20. Suppose resource A and resource B are substitutable and the price of A increases. If the output effect is greater than the substitution effect:
(a) the quantity of A employed by the firm will rise and the quantity of B employed will fall
(b) the quantity of both A and B employed by the firm will fall
(c) the quantity of neither A nor B employed will fall
(d) the quantity of A employed will fall and the quantity of B employed will rise

21. If lower prices for computers have decreased the employment of secretaries in medical clinics, then:
(a) computers and secretaries are complements
(b) there is no substitution effect on the demand for secretaries
(c) there is no output effect on the demand for secretaries
(d) the substitution effect on the demand for secretaries outweighs the output effect

22. Which of the following is the best example of a pair of complementary inputs?
(a) tractors and fertilizer in agriculture
(b) bricks and lumber in house-building
(c) cars and drivers in the taxi business
(d) denim and wool in making jackets

23. A firm is allocating its expenditure on resources so as to minimize the total cost of producing any given output when:
(a) the amount the firm spends on each resource is the same
(b) the marginal revenue product of each resource is the same
(c) the marginal product of each resource is the same
(d) the marginal product per dollar spent on the last unit of each resource is the same

24. A competitive firm is currently using two inputs, A and B, and is producing its output at least

cost. The input prices are $4 and $6 respectively. If the marginal product of A is 12 units, then the marginal product of B must be:
(a) 6 units
(b) 12 units
(c) 18 units
(d) 24 units

25. A business is using inputs such that the MP of labour is 20 and the MP of capital is 45. The price of labour is $10 and the price of capital is $15. If the business wants to minimize cost, then it should:
(a) use more labour and less capital
(b) use less labour and more capital
(c) use less labour and less capital
(d) make no change in resource use

26. At present levels of resource usage, a firm's MP of labour is 4, MP of capital is 12, and the prices are $1 per unit of labour, and $4 per unit of capital. Given this, the firm is:
(a) minimizing cost and maximizing profit
(b) minimizing cost but not maximizing profit
(c) maximizing cost but not minimizing cost
(d) not minimizing cost or maximizing profit

27. When a firm hiring resources in an imperfectly competitive market is at maximize profit, the marginal revenue product of each resource equals:
(a) its marginal product
(b) its marginal resource cost
(c) its price
(d) one

28. A major criticism of the marginal productivity theory of income distribution is that:
(a) markets are subject to imperfect competition
(b) the theory predicts that there will be equality in incomes
(c) the theory does not allow for losses in the short run
(d) in order to maximize profits, firms will pay their inputs as little as possible and not their marginal revenue product

29. Individuals' incomes vary because of differences in:
(a) the amounts of resources they own
(b) the productivity of resources they own
(c) the amounts of market power they have in resource markets

(d)   all of the above

30. The marginal productivity theory of income distribution is consistent with which of the following ethical propositions?
(a)   to each according to what he/she creates
(b)   each person deserves an equal share
(c)   those who work hard should receive their just desserts
(d)   from each according to ability and to each according to need

Problems and Projects

1. Resource Demand and Marginal Revenue Product in a Purely Competitive Firm

The table shows production and input cost data for a firm buying and selling competitively. The firm uses one variable input and has fixed costs of $20. Complete the table and then use the information to answer the fill-in questions.

Input Units	Q	MP	Unit Input Price $	Price of Q $	MRP $	TR $	TC $	Profit $
1	17	__	20	2	__	__	__	__
2	32	__	20	2	__	__	__	__
3	45	__	20	2	__	__	__	__
4	56	__	20	2	__	__	__	__
5	65	__	20	2	__	__	__	__
6	72	__	20	2	__	__	__	__
7	77	__	20	2	__	__	__	__

(a) The firm's marginal resource cost is $____.
(b) For the first unit of input marginal revenue product is $____ and is found by multiplying _____ and _____.
(c) The firm should hire the first unit of input since the _____ is greater than the _____.
(d) For the second unit of input the MRC is $____ and the MRP is $____. The firm should hire the second unit of resource since the _____ is greater than the _____.
(e) To maximize profits the firm should hire ____ units of input and obtain profits of $____.
(f) Suppose the firm was using 4 units of input and was considering using one more unit. For the 5th unit of input the increase in the firm's revenue is $____ and the increase in the firm's

costs is $____. The firm (should, should not) _____ hire the 5th unit of input.
(g) Another way to show whether the firm should hire the 5th unit of input is to compare the marginal revenue and marginal cost of an additional unit of output. Suppose the firm was using 4 units of input and decided to use 5 units. Total output would increase by ____ units and total cost would increase by $____. Marginal cost of the extra output is defined as: (change in total cost/change in output) and equals $____. Since this is a competitive firm, MR is the same as the _____ and equals $____. Since MR of the output is (greater, less) _____ than its MC, the firm (should, should not) _____ undertake the extra production.

2. Resource Demand Schedule and Graph

The table below refers to the same firm as in problem 1 (above).

Unit Input Price	Qd of Input (Output P = $2)	Qd of Input (Output P = $3)
15	_____	_____
20	_____	_____
25	_____	_____
30	_____	_____
35	_____	_____
40	_____	_____

(a) In the first blank column, fill in this firm's short-run input demand schedule if their product sells in a purely competitive market for $2 (the same price as assumed in Problem 1).
(b) In the second blank column, fill in the input demand schedule if the price of their product rises to $3.
(c) Use the graph below to plot two input demand curves for this firm.

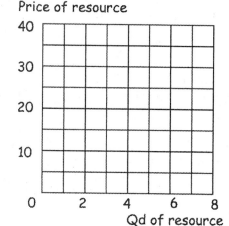

3. A Toy Manufacturer's Resource Demand

A manufacturer of toy wagons uses, among other resources, four wheels and one steel box to make a wagon. If there is an increase in the price of steel boxes, what will happen to the firm's demand for wheels? Is this a result of a substitution effect, an output effect, or both?

4. Substitution and Output Effects for a Soup Maker

A food processing firm combines carrots, corn, and other ingredients to produce tins of soup. The same vegetables are included in every tin, but the proportions can be varied according to cost and availability of specific vegetables. In 1994 the firm paid a lower price for carrots than they did in 1993. The price of corn was the same in both years. The firm participates in competitive markets for inputs and output.

(a) For this firm, are corn and carrots complementary resources or substitute resources?

(b) How would the typical contents of a can of this soup have changed from 1993 to 1994?

(c) How would the firm's output level have changed?

(d) Did the firm buy more or less carrots in total in 1994 than in 1993? Explain in terms of the substitution effect and the output effect.

(e) Did the firm buy more or less corn in total in 1994 than in 1993? Explain in terms of the substitution effect and the output effect.

5. Least-Cost and Profit-Maximizing Input Combinations

The next two tables show the marginal product and marginal revenue product schedules for a firm employing resources C and D. Both resources are variable, and the productivity of one is independent of the level of usage of the other. The price of C is $2 and the price of D is $3.

(a) The least-cost combination of C and D that would enable the firm to produce:

(1) 64 units of output is _____ C and _____ D;

(2) 99 units of output is _____ C and _____ D.

(b) The profit-maximizing combination of C and D is _____ C and _____ D.

(c) If the firm employs the profit-maximizing combination of C and D, this is also the least-cost combination because _____ = _____.

(d) The figures in the table show that the firm sells its product in a _____ competitive market at a price of $_____.

(e) Employing the profit-maximizing combination of C and D, calculate the firm's:
(1) total output: _____
(2) total revenue: $_____
(3) total cost: $_____
(4) total profit: $_____

Units of C Employed	Marginal Product of C	Marginal Revenue Product of C
1	10	$5.00
2	8	4.00
3	6	3.00
4	5	2.50
5	4	2.00
6	3	1.50
7	2	1.00

Units of D Employed	Marginal Product of D	Marginal Revenue Product of D
1	21	$10.50
2	18	9.00
3	15	7.50
4	12	6.00
5	9	4.50
6	6	3.00
7	3	1.50

6. Minimizing Cost and Maximizing Profits

Below are shown three cases of a firm using two inputs and operating in competitive output and input markets. For each case, decide whether or not the firm is:

(a) minimizing costs at current input levels;

(b) maximizing profits at current input levels.

	Case 1	Case 2	Case 3
Output Price	$1	$2	$3
MP of Labour	12	3	6
MP of Capital	8	2	6
Price of Labour	$6	$6	$6
Price of Capital	$4	$4	$4
Cost Minimization ?	Yes	Yes	Yes
	No	No	No
Profit Maximization ?	Yes	Yes	Yes
	No	No	No

Discussion Questions

1. Why is resource pricing an important topic?

2. Why is the demand for a resource a derived demand, and upon what two factors does the strength of this derived demand depend?

3. What constitutes a firm's demand schedule for a resource? Why? What determines the total, or market, demand for a resource?

4. Explain why firms that wish to maximize their profits will follow the MRP = MRC rule.

5. Explain the difference in the derivation of the resource demand curve for a competitive and imperfectly competitive firm.

6. Explain the factors that will cause the demand for a resource to increase or decrease.

7. Suppose that there is an increase in the price of lumber used to build houses. Explain how the "substitution effect" and the "output effect" might affect the total use of lumber, and of bricks.

8. What determines the elasticity of the demand for a resource? Explain the relationship between each of these four determinants and elasticity.

9. Considering the four determinants of elasticity of resource demand, which would be more elastic, a hospital's demand for heart surgeons, or its demand for nurses? Explain.

10. Assuming a firm employs resources in purely competitive markets, explain the rule for combining inputs so that it can produce a given output for the least total cost.

11. If highway engineers in China have the same knowledge and expertise as Canadian engineers, why might they build highways using more labour-intensive methods than are used here?

12. What is the marginal productivity theory of income distribution? What ethical proposition must be accepted if this distribution is to be fair and equitable? What are the two major shortcomings of the theory?

Answers

Quick Quiz
1. (c) p. 317

2. (a) p. 318
3. (a) p. 319
4. (c) p. 323
5. (d) pp. 323-324
6. (a) p. 324
7. (d) p. 325
8. (c) p. 326
9. (b) pp. 327-328
10. (a) pp. 327-328

Fill-in Questions
1. derived, product
2. product, revenue product
3. marginal product, marginal revenue (or price, in pure competition case)
4. total costs, one, input
5. marginal product, output price; less
6. (a) +; (b) -; (c) +; (d) -; (e) +
7. more, less, substitution; more, output
8. 1) less, 2) more, 3) smaller
9. marginal product, price; profits; marginal revenue product, price, one

True-False
1. T
2. T
3. T
4. F   demand will shift right
5. T   increase in marginal productivity increases demand
6. T   the product price does not fall when a purely competitive firm hires more inputs
7. F   the substitution effect will lower the employment of the other resource
8. F   they could be complements, or they could be substitutes with the output effect outweighing the substitution effect
9. F   the ratio MP/P should be equal for each resource
10. F   lower elasticity for supervisors because they represent a smaller share of the firm's total costs
11. T   elasticity of demand for an input is directly related to the elasticity of demand for its product
12. T   due to the least-cost rule
13. F   resources are not equally distributed among individuals
14. T

Multiple-Choice
1. (d)

2. (a) the price of the resource determines the point on the demand curve, but not the position of the whole demand

3. (b)

4. (c) this causes a movement along the resource demand curve, not a shift in the curve

5. (c)

6. (c)

7. (a) so it faces a horizontal supply of labour

8. (d)

9. (a) MRP = MRC implies MR = MC

10. (d)

11. (b) output is restricted; therefore so is the amount of labour hired to produce the output

12. (c)

13. (c) MP x P = 3 x 3

14. (a) MRP > MRC for the first 2 units, after that MRP < MRC

15. (c) (18 x 0.90) – (14 x 1)

16. (b) hire more of an input whenever MRP > MRC

17. (d) the firm is minimizing cost at the current output level, but profits could be increased by producing more

18. (c)

19. (a) the effect of output change is captured in the "output effect"

20. (b) employment of A falls due to both effects; employment of B rises because of substitution effect, but falls due to output effect, and in this case output effect is stronger

21. (d) substitution effect: less secretaries; output effect: more secretaries

22. (c) cars and drivers are used in fixed proportions

23. (d)

24. (c) MPa/Pa = MPb/Pb: 12/4 = 3; 18/6 = 3

25. (b) this will cause MP of L to rise and MP of K to fall, until MP/P is equal for L and K

26. (d)

27. (b) exactly as for firms in purely competitive markets

28. (a) and this distorts relative prices of inputs and incomes of their owners

29. (d)

30. (a)

Problems and Projects

1. MP: 17, 15, 13, 11, 9, 7, 5; MRP: 34, 30, 26, 22, 18, 14, 10; TR: 34, 64, 90, 112, 130, 144, 154; TC: 40, 60, 80, 100, 120, 140, 160; Profit: -6, 4, 10, 12, 10, 4, -6; (a) 20; (b) 34, marginal product, output price; (c) MRP, MRC; (d) 20, 30;

MRP, MRC; (e) 4, 12; (f) 18, 20; should not; (g) 9, 20; 2.22; price, 2.00; less, should not

2. (a) Qd at P = $2: 5, 4, 3, 2, 0, 0; (b) Qd at P = $3: 7, 6, 5, 4, 3, 2. (hire more workers as long as MRP > MRC)

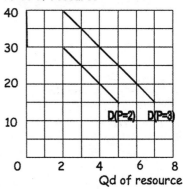

Price of resource

3. output effect leads to decreased demand for wheels; no substitution effect because input proportions are fixed: 4 wheels per 1 box.

4. (a) substitutes; (b) more carrots and less corn in 1994; (c) lower costs lead to increased output; (d) more because of both effects; (e) less due to substitution effect, more due to output effect; net effect on amount of corn used is unknown

5. (a) (1) MP/P = 5 where C=1, D=3 (here output = 10+21+18+15=64); (2) MP/P = 3 where C = 3, D = 5; (b) MRP = P where C = 5, D = 6; (c) MPc/Pc; MPd/Pd; (d) purely, 0.50 because MRP/MP = MR; (e) (1) by summing MP's of C and D: 10+8+6+5+4+21+18+15+12+9+6=114; (2) 114 x 0.50=57; (3) (5x2)+(6x3) =28; (4) 57-28=29

6. Case 1: Yes (MPL/PL=MPK/PK), No (MRPL/PL and MRPK/PK not both = 1); Case 2: Yes, Yes; Case 3: No, No

Chapter 14 — Wage Determination

Overview

Why do wage rates differ between individuals, occupations, regions and nations? This chapter addresses such questions by exploring the interaction of labour demand and labour supply in purely competitive markets, in markets where market power is held by employees (unions) or employers (monopsony), and in markets where government intervenes to modify market outcomes (e.g., minimum wage laws or immigration policy).

In general, real wages are high in markets where the demand for labour is high relative to its supply. Labour demand depends crucially on its productivity. There are many reasons for international variations in productivity and wages.

Earlier chapters showed the importance of market structure for the setting of prices and quantities in product markets. This is equally true in the labour market. The Chapter 8 model of pure competition translates directly to a purely competitive market for labour. Employers and workers are "wage takers," so the equilibrium wage rate is determined where the market supply of labour intersects the market demand for labour. Here, the firm's marginal revenue product is equal to its marginal resource cost.

A monopsony involves market power in labour demand because there is only one employer in the market. A monopsony employer is a "wage maker" because it faces an upsloping labour supply curve and must simultaneously choose the wage rate and the number of workers to employ. The monopsonist restricts employment in order to hold the wage rate down below the marginal revenue product, or competitive wage rate.

When workers are unionized, there is market power in labour supply. The chapter presents three models of unions: (1) in the demand enhancement model the union benefits workers by raising wages and employment; (2) in an exclusive or craft union model wages are raised through supply reduction, and; (3) in an inclu-

sive or industrial union model the union attempts to organize all workers and then impose an above equilibrium wage on the employers. Evidence suggests that unions have managed to raise wages, but at the expense of employment.

A bilateral monopoly occurs when a union and a monopsony exist in the same market. The model alone cannot predict where the equilibrium wage will end up because the outcome depends on relative bargaining power and skill.

The chapter closes with policy issues, controversies, and research relating to labour markets in Canada. These include: (1) the pros and cons of minimum wage legislation; (2) the reasons for wage differentials between different workers; (3) the effects of performance-based compensation schemes; and (4) immigration policy.

Chapter Outline

14.1 Labour, Wages, and Earnings

◈ How are these terms defined: labour, wages, earnings?

- "Labour" refers to workers of all kinds, covering the spectrum from blue-collar to white-collar, and unskilled to highly trained professionals.
- The "wage rate" is the price paid per unit of labour.
  - o A nominal wage is the number of dollars paid per time period.
  - o A real wage is the quantity of goods the worker can buy with the money received per time period.
- Earnings are equal to the wage multiplied by the amount of time worked.

Quick Quiz
1. Manuel's job pays $8.00 per hour. A meal costs him $4.00. He works 2000 hours per year. Which of the following statements is not correct?
   - (a) Manuel's nominal wage is $8.00 per hour
   - (b) Manuel's real wage is 2 meals per hour

(c)   Manuel's earnings are $16,000 per year

(d)   all of these statements are correct

14.2 Productivity and the General Level of Wages

◇ What is the connection between labour productivity and wage rates?

•   In general, wages in Canada are relatively high because the demand for labour in Canada has been strong relative to the supply of labour.

•   Strong demand for labour in Canada results from high labour productivity, which can be traced back to:
   o   plentiful capital for workers to work with
   o   abundant natural resources
   o   advanced technology
   o   high quality labour through investment in training, education, and health
   o   intangible factors related to Canada's strong economic and social institutions

•   The real hourly wage rate in Canada rises at about the same rate as the output per hour of labour input. Rapid productivity growth over the decades has caused the demand curve for labour to grow faster than the supply, leading to secular growth in Canadian real wages.

Quick Quiz

2. Average wage rates in Canada would tend to increase if:
   (a)   education levels drop among our workers
   (b)   our health care system deteriorates
   (c)   our stock of capital equipment shrinks
   (d)   our technology improves

14.3 Wages in a Purely Competitive Labour Market

◇ How are wages and employment determined in a purely competitive labour market?

•   The wage rate earned by any specific type of labour depends on the demand and supply of that labour and on the competitiveness of the markets in which that labour is hired and its output is sold.

•   In a purely competitive labour market:
   o   many firms are in competition to hire a specific type of labour
   o   many equally qualified and skilled workers supply this labour
   o   employers and workers are "wage takers."

•   The market demand curve is the horizontal sum of the marginal revenue product curves for all individual firms.

•   The market supply is the sum of the supply curves from all individual workers. It is upward sloping as higher wage rates draw more workers in from other places or other occupations.

•   At the equilibrium the marginal revenue product of labour is equal to the firm's marginal resource cost.

•   From an individual employer's perspective, the supply of labour is perfectly elastic at the wage rate determined by the market demand and supply.

Quick Quiz

3. The market demand for electricians would increase:
   (a)   the higher the marginal revenue product of electricians
   (b)   the fewer electricians are available for work
   (c)   the lower the wage rate for electricians
   (d)   the fewer the number of firms employing electricians

4. The industry's labour supply curve may be upward sloping because a wage increase will attract workers from:
   (a)   leisure
   (b)   other occupations
   (c)   other regions
   (d)   all of the above

5. In a purely competitive labour market the marginal factor cost is equal to:
   (a)   wage rate
   (b)   marginal revenue product
   (c)   product price
   (d)   marginal revenue

14.4 Monopsony Model

◇ What is a monopsony?

◇ How are wages and employment affected under a monopsony?

•   In a monopsony market power exists on the employer's side of the market because:
   o   there is only a single buyer of a particular type of labour
   o   the labour is immobile

o   the firm is a wage-maker, because the wage rate it must pay depends on the number of workers employed
- The firm faces an upsloping labour supply curve, so the marginal factor cost (MFC) exceeds the wage rate.
- The firm hires the amount of labour at which marginal factor cost and the marginal revenue product of labour are equal.
- The wage rate is set on the labour supply curve at the equilibrium employment level, and this is below the marginal factor cost and the marginal revenue product.
- Both the wage rate and level of employment are less than they would be under purely competitive conditions.

➲ The term marginal resource cost (MRC) is sometimes used instead of marginal factor cost (MFC). They have the same meaning.

Quick Quiz
6. The key feature of the monopsony model is:
   (a)   many buyers and sellers of resources
   (b)   a single seller of resources
   (c)   a single seller of the product of the re-sources
   (d)   a single buyer of the resource

7. The MFC measures the:
   (a)   wage rate
   (b)   total wage bill
   (c)   increase in the total wage bill due to hir-ing an additional worker
   (d)   increase in total revenue produced by hiring an additional worker

8. Compared with a firm that faces a perfectly elastic supply curve of labour, a monopsony has:
   (a)   lower wages and more employees
   (b)   higher wages and more employees
   (c)   lower wages and fewer employees
   (d)   higher wages and fewer employees

14.5 Unions and the Labour Market
◈ How do unions affect wages and employ-ment?
- Where a union represents workers collec-tively, the workers sell their labour collectively.
- In the demand-enhancement model, a union attempts to raise wage rates by increasing the demand for its members by:

o   increasing the demand for the products made by union workers
o   increasing the workers' productivity
o   increasing prices of resources that are substitutes for union labour;
- In the exclusive or craft union model a union attempts to raise wages by reducing the supply of labour by:
   o   forcing employers to hire union members
   o   restricting membership in the union
   o   supporting occupational licensing
- In the inclusive or industrial union model a union attempts to raise wages by organizing as many workers as possible and imposing upon employers wage rates that are higher than the equilibrium wage rate that would prevail in a purely competitive market.
- Union members on average enjoy a 10 to 15 percent wage advantage over nonunion workers. Because of the tradeoff between wage increases and employment for their members unions may limit their demands for higher wages. The unem-ployment effect of higher wages could be lessened by increases in labour productivity or a relatively inelastic demand for labour.
- In a bilateral monopoly market the wage rate depends, within certain limits, on the relative bargaining power of the union and of the em-ployer. Bilateral monopoly may be more socially desirable than a situation of market power on only one side of the market because having mar-ket power on both sides may cancel out the effect of that power, yielding a wage and employment equilibrium near the purely competitive level.

➲ To clarify the differences between the various wage determination models presented in this chapter, note that there are four fundamental scenarios in a labour market:
   o   pure competition in both labour demand and supply
   o   pure competition in labour demand, and market power in supply (union)
   o   pure competition in labour supply, and market power in demand (monopsony)
   o   market power in both demand and sup-ply (bilateral monopoly)

Quick Quiz
9. A strategy by a garment workers union to oppose the importation from Asia of children's pajamas made of flammable materials would be consistent with which union model?

(a)   demand-enhancement model
(b)   exclusive union model
(c)   inclusive union model
(d)   bilateral monopoly model

10. A move by members of a nurses union to require all nurses working in hospitals to have nursing degrees would be consistent with which union model?
(a)   demand-enhancement model
(b)   exclusive union model
(c)   inclusive union model
(d)   bilateral monopoly model

11. The unemployment effect when a union is successful in increasing members' wages may be reduced if:
(a)   general economic growth is increasing the demand for these workers
(b)   the union wins provisions in their collective agreements that make it more difficult for employers to substitute other inputs for labour
(c)   the union wins provisions in their collective agreements that require employers to pay large settlements to laid off workers
(d)   all of the above

14.6 The Minimum-wage Controversy

◇ What are the arguments for and against a minimum-wage law?

• A minimum wage law is normally imposed as a way to provide a "living wage" for less-skilled workers, but may not be effective.
  o   Opponents of minimum wage laws argue that employers are simply pushed back up their demand curves for unskilled labour, causing a loss of employment for these workers. Secondly, many of the workers that benefit from a wage increase are teenagers, most of whom have low incomes for only a few years.
  o   Advocates argue that in monopsonistic firms both wages and employment may be increased by the minimum wage. Also, if forced to pay higher wages, employers may be pushed into using workers more efficiently, therefore improving their productivity.
• Recent evidence suggests that increases in the minimum wages cause small or negligible decreases in employment. At the same time, the

law is not as strong an anti-poverty tool as hoped because many of its benefits go to workers from non-poverty households.
• Minimum wage laws clearly have strong political support. This may be because they help more workers than they harm, and because they are seen as protection against exploitation of vulnerable workers.

Quick Quiz
12. Minimum wage laws:
(a)   mainly benefit individuals from low-income households
(b)   cause large decreases in employment among low-skill workers
(c)   may work to cancel the incentive of monopsonistic employers to pay very low wages
(d)   are opposed by most people

14.7 Wage Differentials

◇ What factors cause wage differentials between workers?

• Wage differentials exist for four main reasons related to supply and demand differences between labour markets.
  o   Workers differ in their marginal revenue productivity for their employers.
  o   Workers are not homogeneous, so they fall into non-competing groups with differences in ability, skill, and in human capital investment through education, training, or work experience.
  o   Compensating differences in wages exist because of differences in non-monetary aspects of jobs (e.g., location, health risks, and working conditions).
  o   Market imperfections impede the mobility of workers due to: (1) lack of job information; (2) geographical immobility; (3) union or government restraints; (4) race or gender discrimination.

Quick Quiz
13. Tom Cruise commands a much higher fee for appearing in a movie than the vast majority of actors. This is best explained by the concept of:
(a)   geographic immobility
(b)   market imperfections
(c)   discrimination
(d)   non-competing groups

14. Average wage differentials in Canada would tend to increase if:

   (a)   inter-provincial barriers to labour mobility are eliminated

   (b)   information about jobs in different occupations and regions become more widely available

   (c)   demand for the most highly skilled workers in society grow faster than the demand for less skilled workers

   (d)   labour market discrimination decreases

14.8 Pay for Performance and the Principal-Agent Problem

◇ What is the principal-agent problem?

◇ How can compensation schemes be designed to control this problem?

• Many workers are not paid on a fixed basis, but have their compensation tied directly to performance.

• In labour markets the principal-agent problem arises when the interests of firms (the principals) do not match the interests of their workers (the agents). The workers may increase their own utility by shirking on the job.

   o   Firms combat shirking by monitoring (supervision), but this is sometimes ineffective, and always costly. Another solution is an incentive pay plan. Examples include: piece rates, commissions or royalties, bonuses, stock options, profit sharing, and efficiency wages.

• Poorly designed incentive pay systems may eliminate shirking but introduce unexpected negative side effects.

Quick Quiz
15. In theory, incentive pay plans can be designed to encourage workers to improve their performance. Depending on how they are structured, such plans may:

   (a)   allow the firm to reduce its expenditures on supervision

   (b)   induce the workers to work faster

   (c)   induce the workers to produce sub-standard products

   (d)   have any of the above effects

14.9 Immigration and Wages

◇ What are the effects of immigration on wages and other economic variables?

• When workers migrate from low-wage nations to a high-wage nation such as Canada, they increase Canada's labour supply, and decrease the labour supply in their original countries. This reduces wage differentials between nations and results in more efficient allocation of the world's labour. It also benefits Canadian businesses that employ immigrant workers, but harms businesses in the low-wage nations.

• Several complications in the real world modify our conclusions somewhat.

   o   Costs of migration (monetary and non-monetary) impede migration to some extent, and prevent immigration from totally eliminating the wage differential between nations.

   o   Remittances by immigrants to their families at home cause some of the benefits to be captured by the nations the migrants have left.

   o   If immigrants were unemployed in their home nations before coming to Canada, then it is possible for both countries to gain from the migration. If the immigrants leave jobs in low-wage nations and become unemployed in Canada, both nations can lose.

• Whether immigration benefits Canada depends on the number of immigrants, the amount and type of human capital they bring, and the ease with which they can be absorbed into Canada's economy and become productive workers here.

⟳ The basic supply and demand model is a powerful tool for understanding the effects of immigration. By the way, have you noticed how much more competent you have become at using supply and demand tools? You should feel real satisfaction in that!

Quick Quiz
16. In a two country model we predict that migration will equalize the wages rates in the two country if it is assumed that:

   (a)   workers can migrate free of cost

   (b)   workers choose where to live strictly on the basis of wage levels

   (c)   migration is completely unimpeded by laws in either country

   (d)   all of the above assumptions are necessary

17. Migration of workers from Mexico (low-wage country) to Canada (high-wage country) tends to:
- (a)   increase the total output of the two countries combined
- (b)   raise wage rates in Canada
- (c)   lower wage rates in Mexico
- (d)   none of the above

Terms and Concepts

wage rate	wage differentials
nominal wage	marginal revenue
real wage	productivity
purely competitive	non-competing groups
labour market	investment in human
monopsony	capital
exclusive unionism	compensating
occupational	differences
licensing	incentive pay plan
inclusive unionism	legal immigrants
bilateral monopoly	illegal immigrants
minimum wage	

Fill-In Questions

1. A nominal wage is an amount of _____ received per time period, while a real wage is an amount of _____ that can be purchased with the nominal wage. The percentage change in real wages is found by subtracting the percentage change in the price level from the percentage change in _____. Thus, a 3.5% increase in the nominal wage over the same period that the price level rose by 2% yields a _____ real wage increase for that period.

2. The general level of wages is (higher, lower) _____ in Canada than in most nations. The demand for labour in Canada is (great, small) _____ relative to its supply. The demand for Canadian labour has been strong because of its high productivity, which results from: (a) plentiful _____; (b) abundant _____; (c) advanced _____; (d) labour _____; and, (e) _____ factors.

3. A monopsonist faces an _____-sloping supply curve of labour and has to pay a _____ wage rate to hire more labour.
(a) The extra cost of hiring an extra input is (greater than, less than) _____ the wage rate

paid to that input. To the monopsonist the _____ is greater than the wage rate.
(b) The monopsonist hires labour up to the point where _____ equals _____.
(c) Other things being equal, the monopsonist hires (more, fewer) _____ workers and pays a (higher, lower) _____ wage than would a competitive employer.

4. The most important economic goal of a labour union is to _____. The union attempts to accomplish this goal either by increasing the _____ for labour, restricting the _____ of labour, or imposing demands for wages _____ their competitive equilibrium value.

5. Craft unions, which are examples of _____ unionism, typically try to increase wages by _____ the supply of labour. Industrial unions, which are examples of _____ unionism, try to increase wages by _____ the demand for labour.

6. A wage difference between two jobs that exists because one job is more hazardous than the other is an example of a _____ differential.

7. The firm is the (agent, principal) _____, and the worker is the _____. The principal-agent problem arises because the objectives of the two are _____. Specifically, it may be in the worker's interest to _____ on the job. To control this problem, the firm may implement some sort of _____ pay plan.

8. Mike sells magazine subscriptions door-to-door and is paid $50 a day. On an average day he sells 10 subscriptions. If Mike was paid by commission instead of a wage, and if his productivity is unchanged, a commission of $_____ per subscription would leave Mike with the same average daily income. However, a commission is an example of an _____ pay plan, and it would probably (decrease, increase) _____ Mike's productivity by reducing his incentive to _____ at his employer's expense.

9. If some workers from India relocate to Canada in search of better job opportunities, the supply of labour in India will (increase, decrease) _____ and the wage rate will _____, whereas in Canada the supply of labour will _____ and the wage rate will _____. National output will increase in _____ and decrease in _____.

True-False

Circle T if the statement is true, F if it is false.

1. The general level of real wages is lower in Canada than in foreign countries because the supply of labour in Canada is great relative to the demand for labour.   **T F**

2. In the long run, the real income per worker can only increase at about the same rate as output per worker.   **T F**

3. Nominal wages measure the purchasing power of wages.   **T F**

4. If the price level falls, a person's real wage could rise even if the nominal wage falls.   **T F**

5. If an individual firm employs labour in a competitive market, its marginal resource cost for labour is equal to the wage rate.   **T F**

6. Both a monopsonist and a firm hiring labour in a competitive market hire labour up to the point where the marginal revenue product of labour and wage rate are equal.   **T F**

7. Most unions consider their most important economic objective to be job security for their members.   **T F**

8. Restricting the supply of labour is a means of increasing wage rates more commonly used by craft unions than by industrial unions.   **T F**

9. Unions attempt to increase the demand for the products their workers produce by lobbying for reduced import quotas and higher tariffs. **T F**

10. Craft unions are composed of members who possess specialized skills.   **T F**

11. Industrial unions are also considered exclusive unions.   **T F**

12. The imposition of an above-equilibrium wage rate will cause employment to drop more when

demand for labour is inelastic than when demand is elastic.   **T F**

13. A bilateral monopoly in a labour market involves a union and a monopsonist.   **T F**

14. In the bilateral monopoly model the market power of the employer and the union are offsetting.   **T F**

15. In a competitive labour market, the imposition of an effective minimum wage will increase the wage rate and decrease employment.   **T F**

16. The labour force is considered to be divided into noncompeting groups of workers because of the differences between workers in their abilities, talents, training, etc.   **T F**

17. The principal-agent problem exists in labour markets because workers do not understand employers' objectives.   **T F**

18. If Zippy's is the only gas station in the city paying its attendants an efficiency wage, Zippy's can expect to have higher employee turnover than other gas stations.   **T F**

Multiple-Choice

Circle the letter that corresponds to the best answer.

1. Real wages would decline if the:
  (a)   prices of goods and services rose more rapidly than nominal wage rates
  (b)   prices of goods and services rose less rapidly than nominal wage rates
  (c)   prices of goods and services fell while nominal wage rates rose
  (d)   prices of goods and services and nominal wage rates both increase by the same percent

2. Which of the following is not among the reasons for the generally high productivity of Canadian workers?
  (a)   the high level of real wage rates in Canada
  (b)   the superior quality of the Canadian labour force

(c) the advanced technology used in Canadian industries

(d) the large quantity of capital available to assist the average worker in Canada

3. The level of the demand curve for a particular kind of labour depends on:
(a) the price of the labour's output
(b) the marginal productivity of the labour
(c) the wage rate for the labour
(d) both (a) and (b)

4. Which of the following is not true of a firm that hires labour in a purely competitive market?
(a) the firm is a "wage taker"
(b) the firm's marginal resource cost equals the wage rate
(c) the firm's marginal resource cost is constant
(d) the firm's labour supply curve is upward sloping

5. Which is the best example of a monopsony employer?
(a) the Sears store in Hamilton in the market for furniture salespeople
(b) Concordia University in Montreal in the market for physics professors
(c) the Vancouver Symphony Orchestra in the market for violinists
(d) NASA in Houston in the market for astronauts

6. A monopsonist employing 4 workers at a wage rate of $80 per day calculates that the marginal revenue product of an additional worker would be $95 per day. To get 5 workers to supply their services, the wage rate would have to be increased to $84 per day. Should the fifth worker be hired?
(a) no, because the MFC is $84, which is above the MRP
(b) yes, because the MFC is $84, which is below the MRP
(c) yes, because the MFC is $100, which is above the MRP
(d) no, because the MFC is $100, which is above the MRP

7. A monopsonist pays a wage rate that is:
(a) above the marginal revenue product of labour
(b) equal to the marginal revenue product of labour

(c) equal to the firm's marginal labour cost
(d) below the marginal revenue product of labour

8. Higher wage rates and a higher level of employment are the usual consequences of:
(a) inclusive unionism
(b) exclusive unionism
(c) an above-equilibrium wage rate
(d) an increase in the productivity of labour

9. A craft union is composed of workers who:
(a) work for the same employer
(b) work in the same industry
(c) possess the same skill
(d) are members of non-competing wage groups

10. Industrial unions typically attempt to increase wage rates by:
(a) imposing an above-equilibrium wage rate upon employers
(b) increasing the demand for labour
(c) decreasing the supply of labour
(d) forming a bilateral monopoly

11. The demand for labour can be increased by all but which one of the following?
(a) increasing labour productivity
(b) increasing the demand for the goods produced by labour
(c) increasing the price of substitute resources
(d) occupational licensing

12. Which policy would be opposed by the Canadian Union of Wooden Hockey Stick Makers?
(a) strict quotas on imported hockey sticks
(b) elimination of federal subsidies to municipal governments to help with construction of hockey rinks
(c) tax deductions for children's hockey registration fees
(d) stringent safety regulations that would apply to hockey sticks made of graphite or new materials

13. Which could not be considered to be a union attempt to restrict the labour supply?
(a) support for tighter immigration laws
(b) long apprenticeships
(c) opposition to compulsory retirement

(d)   seeking to have the employer hire only union members

14. Which of the following has been a consequence of unionization?
(a)   higher wage rates for unionized workers
(b)   greater employment of unionized workers
(c)   greater employment of the workers in the entire labour force
(d)   higher level of real wages in the economy

The next two questions are based on the data in the table below.

Wage Rate	Quantity of Labour Supplied	Marginal Resource Cost	Marginal Revenue Product of Labour
$10	0	---	$18
11	100	$11	17
12	200	13	16
13	300	15	15
14	400	17	14
15	500	19	13
16	600	21	12

15. If the firm employing labour were a monopsonist, the wage rate and the quantity of labour employed would be, respectively:
(a) $15 and 300
(b) $13 and 400
(c) $14 and 400
(d) $13 and 300

16. If the market for this labour were competitive, the wage rate and the quantity of labour employed would be, respectively:
(a) $14 and 300
(b) $13 and 400
(c) $14 and 400
(d) $13 and 300

17. The fact that a star baseball player receives a wage of $15,000,000 a year can best be explained in terms of:
(a)   noncompeting labour groups
(b)   equalizing differences
(c)   labour immobility
(d)   imperfections in the labour market

18. Compensating wage differentials are paid to:
(a)   firefighters because they work in hazardous situations

(b)   garbage collectors because they work under unpleasant conditions
(c)   offshore oilrig workers because they work in isolated locations
(d)   all of the above

19. Which is not an example of an incentive pay plan utilized to overcome shirking on the job?
(a)   piece rates
(b)   commissions and royalties
(c)   a wage premium for overtime work
(d)   bonuses and profit-sharing

20. Efficiency wage theory suggests:
(a)   the most efficient workers prefer to be paid piece rates
(b)   gains in efficiency from using large size plants allow the payment of higher wages
(c)   in any group of workers the more efficient should receive higher wages
(d)   it may be profitable to pay workers a higher wage than they can find elsewhere

21. A principal-agent problem arises if:
(a)   physicians supply more treatments than necessary because patients don't know exactly what is necessary
(b)   patients take more medications than they need because the costs are covered under a drug plan
(c)   the federal government supplies insufficient health-care funding to the provinces
(d)   there are waiting lists for MRI machines

Answer the next three questions based on this graph.

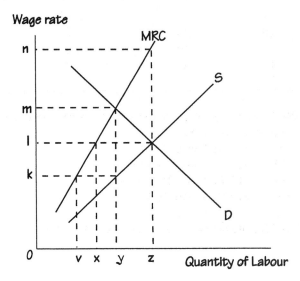

22. If this is a purely competitive labour market, the number of workers hired and the wage rate in equilibrium are:
(a) 0z and 0l
(b) 0z and 0n
(c) 0y and 0m
(d) 0y and 0n

23. If this is a monopsonistic labour market, the employment level and wage rate in equilibrium are:
(a) 0x and 0l
(b) 0v and 0k
(c) 0y and 0m
(d) 0y and 0k

24. If the market is a bilateral monopoly, the number of workers hired and the wage rate in equilibrium are:
(a) 0x and 0l
(b) 0v and 0k
(c) 0y and 0m
(d) indeterminate

The following table shows the number of workers demanded at various wage rates in nation A and nation B and nation B. Assume that workers care about the wage rate and freely able to migrate between A and B. There are currently 40 workers in A and 60 workers in B. Use the data for the two questions that follow.

Wage Rate	Quantity of Labour Demanded A	Quantity of Labour Demanded B
$9	80	60
10	70	50
11	60	40
12	50	30
13	40	20
14	30	10
15	20	0

25. If there is no migration, the current equilibrium wage rates are:
(a) $13 in A and $11 in B
(b) $11 in A and $9 in B
(c) $11 in A and $11 in B
(d) $13 in A and $9 in B

26. Migration will result in an equilibrium with:

(a) employment of 50 workers in each nation, with the wage ending up at $12 in A and $10 in B
(b) 10 workers having moving from B to A, with the wage ending up at $11 in A and B
(c) 20 workers having moved from B to A, with the wage ending up at $11 in A and B
(d) all 60 workers having moved from B to take the higher wage of $13 in A

27. Migration of people from low-wage countries to high-wage countries is associated with:
(a) falling wages in the countries from which people emigrate
(b) rising wages in the countries to which people immigrate
(c) increased output in both high-wage and low-wage nations
(d) an overall increase in world output

Problems and Projects

1. Labour Demand in Agriculture: a Competitive Labour Market

One farm has, for a certain type of labour, the marginal-revenue-product schedule in the first table below.

Units of Labour	MRP of Labour
1	$15
2	14
3	13
4	12
5	11
6	10
7	9

Quantity of Labour Demanded	Wage Rate	Quantity of Labour Supplied
_____	$15	850
_____	14	800
_____	13	750
_____	12	700
_____	11	650
_____	10	600
_____	9	550

(a) Assume there are 100 farms with the same MRP schedules. Compute the total or market demand for this labour by completing the first column of the second table below.

(b) Combining the total demand for labour with the total supply given in the same table, the equilibrium wage rate is $_____, and _____ units of labour will be hired in this market.

Wage Rate

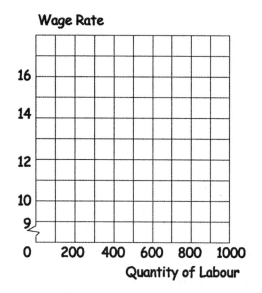

Quantity of Labour

(c) At the equilibrium found in (b), the individual firm will have a marginal labour cost of $_____, will employ _____ units of labour, and will pay a wage of $_____.

(d) On the graph above, plot the market demand and supply curves for labour and indicate the equilibrium wage rate and the total quantity of labour employed.

(e) On the next graph, plot the individual firm's demand for labour, supply of labour, and MRC curve. Indicate the quantity of labour the firm will hire and the wage it will pay.

Wage Rate

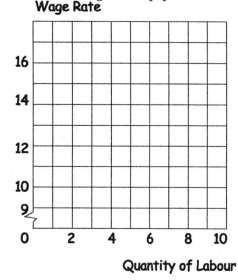

Quantity of Labour

(f) The imposition of a $12 minimum wage rate would change the total amount of labour hired in this market to _____.

2. Monopsony

A monopsonist has the marginal-revenue-product schedule for labour given in columns 1 and 2 of the next table, and faces the labour supply schedule as given in columns 1 and 3.

(1) Units of Labour	(2) MRP of Labour	(3) Wage Rate	(4) Total Labour Cost	(5) Marginal Resource Cost
0		$2	$_____	
1	$36	4	_____	_____
2	32	6	_____	_____
3	28	8	_____	_____
4	24	10	_____	_____
5	20	12	_____	_____
6	16	14	_____	_____
7	12	16	_____	_____
8	8	18	_____	_____

Wage Rate

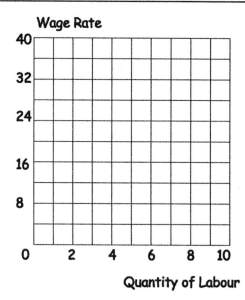

Quantity of Labour

(a) Compute the firm's total labour costs at each level of employment and the marginal resource cost of each unit of labour, and enter these figures in columns 4 and 5 of the table.

(b) The firm will hire _____ units of labour, pay a wage of $ _____, and have a marginal revenue product for labour of $_____ for the last unit of labour employed.

(c) Plot the MRP curve, the supply curve for labour, and the MRC curve on the graph above.

Indicate the quantity of labour the firm will employ and the wage it will pay.
(d) If this firm hired labour in a competitive labour market, it would hire _____ units and pay a wage of $_____.

3. A Bilateral Monopoly: Monopsony and Union

The next graph represents the market for iron miners in an isolated Labrador community. The local iron mine is the only employer, and the miners are not unionized.
(a) If the employer behaves as a monopsonist, _____ miners will be employed at a wage rate of $_____.
(b) Suppose that the miners now unionize and demand a wage rate of $8 per hour. On the graph identify the new supply curve of labour.
(c) Why is the wage rate outcome uncertain when the union deals with the monopsony employer?

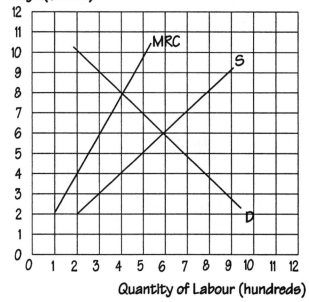

Wage ($/hour)

Quantity of Labour (hundreds)

Discussion Questions

1. Why is the general level of real wages higher in Canada than in most nations? Why has the level of real wages continued to increase even though the supply of labour has continually increased?

2. Explain why the productivity of the Canadian labour force increased in the past to its present high level. And why has productivity stagnated recently? Or has it?

3. In the competitive model, what determines the market demand for labour and the wage rate? What kind of supply situation is faced by all firms as a group? Why? What kind of supply situation does the individual firm face? Why?

4. In the monopsony model, what determines employment and the wage rate? What kind of supply situation does the monopsonist face? Why? How do the equilibrium wage and level of employment compare with what would result if the market were competitive?

5. In what sense is a worker who is hired by a monopsonist "exploited," while one who is employed in a competitive labour market "justly" rewarded? Why does a monopsonist wish to restrict employment?

6. When the supply curve of labour is upward sloping, marginal labour cost is greater than the wage rate. Why?

7. What methods might labour unions employ to increase the demand for labour? If these methods are successful, what effect do they have upon wage rates and employment?

8. What strategies can a labour union use to restrict the supply of labour, and why is it in their interest to do so? Are there circumstances under which supply restriction would be pointless, or even detrimental to members' interests?

9. Both exclusive and inclusive unions are able to raise the wage rates received by their members. Why might unions limit or temper their demands for higher wages?

10. What is bilateral monopoly? Do you know of any examples of bilateral monopoly in labour markets? What determines wage rates in a labour market of this type?

11. What is the effect of minimum wage laws upon wage rates and employment in (a) competitive labour markets, and (b) monopsony labour markets?

12. Peter is a hard rock miner working in Nunavut. Kanti works as a graphic designer in Vancouver. Peter's hourly wage rate is twice as high as Kanti's. What possible reasons are there for this differential?

13. What is the principal-agent problem, as applied to labour markets? How do incentive pay plans help address the problem? Discuss the reasons for, and the drawbacks of, using incentive pay schemes in some jobs that you have held, or that students typically hold (restaurant worker, retail clerk, etc.).

14. In what ways, and under what conditions, will Canada as a whole benefit from increased immigration? What will be the effects on the nations that the immigrants stem from?

15. What is the role of remittances and backflows in understanding the costs and benefits of immigration?

Answers

Quick Quiz
1. (d) p. 336
2. (d) p. 337
3. (a) pp. 339-340
4. (d) p. 339
5. (b) pp. 340-341
6. (d) pp. 341-342
7. (c) pp. 342-343
8. (c) pp. 342-343
9. (a) pp. 344-345
10. (b) p. 346
11. (d) p. 348
12. (c) p. 350
13. (d) p. 351
14. (c) pp. 350-354
15. (d) pp. 354-356
16. (d) pp. 357-358
17. (a) pp. 357-358

Fill-in Questions
1. money, goods and services, nominal wages, 1.5%
2. higher; great; (a) capital; (b) natural resources; (c) technology; (d) quality; (e) intangible
3. upward, higher; (a) greater than; MRC (or MFC); (b) MRP, MRC (or MFC); (c) fewer, lower
4. increase wages, demand, supply, above
5. exclusive, restricting, inclusive, increasing

6. compensating
7. principal, agent, different, shirk, incentive (or performance-based)
8. 5, incentive, increase, shirk
9. decrease, increase, increase, decrease, Canada, India

True-False
1. F   Canadian wages are higher because labour supply is small relative to demand
2. T
3. F   real wages measure purchasing power
4. T   if price level falls by larger percentage than nominal wage
5. T
6. F   the monopsonist ceases hiring additional labour before this point is reached
7. F   increasing wages is the key objective
8. T
9. T   these tactics can help increase demand for domestically produced products as prices of imports rise
10. T   e.g., an electricians' union or steamfitters' union
11. F   they unionize as many members as possible
12. F   employment will fall more if demand is elastic
13. T
14. T
18. T   employers move back up along their demand curve for labour
16. T
17. F   the issue is lack of incentive, not of understanding
18. F   Zippy's will pay more than other stations, and therefore have less turnover

Multiple-Choice
1. (a)
2. (a) real wages are high because of high productivity, not the other way around
3. (d)
4. (d) the firm's labour supply is horizontal (infinitely elastic)
5. (d) there are no other employers of astronauts – at least in the United States
6. (d) the wage bill rises from $320 to $420, so MRC=$100, but MRP is only $95
7. (d) MRP=MRC, but MRP>wage
8. (d) shifting the demand curve to the right
9. (c) such as plumbers or nurses
10. (a)

11. (d) this is a strategy for reducing supply

12. (b) fewer hockey rinks would mean less demand for sticks, and less demand for their labour

13. (c) workers could supply labour past age 65

14. (a)

15. (d) employment is where MRC = MRP, but the wage rate is below this on the labour supply curve

16. (c) where wage = MRP

17. (a) very few workers have comparable skills that his employer could substitute instead

18. (d)

19. (c) the other result in higher pay for higher effort or productivity

20. (d) giving them the incentive to work especially hard to avoid losing the high-paying job

21. (a) such physicians (agents) would be following self-interest instead of the interests of their patients (principals)

22. (a) where supply and demand intersect

23. (d) employment is set where MRC = demand, and the wage is found from supply curve

24. (d)

25. (d) where supply = demand in each nation

26. (c) $11 is the single wage rate at which a total of 100 workers are demanded in A and B taken together (60 in A and 40 in B)

27. (d) the workers move from a place where their marginal productivity was lower to a place where it is higher

Problems and Projects

1. (a) Qd of Labour Demanded: 100, 200, 300, 400, 500, 600, 700; (b) 10, 600; (c) 10, 6, 10; (f) 400 (at market labour demand for W=12)

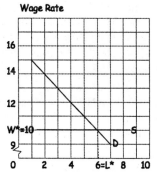

2. (a) Total Labour Cost: 0, 4, 12, 24, 40, 60, 84, 112, 144; MRC: 4, 8, 12, 16, 20, 24, 28, 32; (b) 5, 12, 20; (d) 6, 14

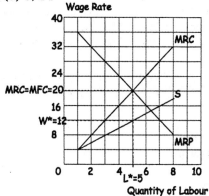

3. (a) 400, 4; (b) horizontal at $8 to 800 miners, and then following the supply curve; (c) equilibrium is uncertain because of countervailing market power

Chapter 15   Rent, Interest, and Profit

Overview

This chapter concludes our study of resource prices by examining the incomes earned from land, capital and entrepreneurial ability. Various concepts from the past two chapters are now applied to the study of rent, interest, and profits.

For land – and any other resources in perfectly *inelastic* supply – economic rent is the term given to its income. Since the same supply will exist no matter what, rent is an unnecessary payment from the perspective of ensuring a supply. Therefore, given the quantity of land available, demand is the only active determinant of rent. Differences in land rents reflect productivity differences between pieces of land. Though land rents serve no purpose in creating an incentive to supply, they do serve an allocative function by determining how the land will be allocated between alternative uses.

Capital, in economic terms, means real capital goods (e.g. machinery and equipment). Is the rate of interest, then, the price paid for the use of capital goods? No; interest is the price paid for the use of money that can be used to invest in real capital goods. The loanable funds theory of interest is a demand and supply explanation of interest rate determination. As the interest rate rises, households find it worthwhile to defer some of their spending, and lend some of their money for a time in exchange for interest income. As the interest rate rises, businesses seeking financing to pay for capital goods will prefer to cut or defer some of their planned capital spending. They decide this by comparing the interest rate with the expected rate of return on their capital spending projects. The equilibrium interest rate balances the supply of loanable funds with the demand, and allocates available funds to those investment projects and R&D ventures expected to produce the highest rate of return.

At any moment there is a range of interest rates to account for differences between loans in the level of risk, term to maturity, loan size, and market imperfections. We also distinguish between the nominal interest rate and the real (or inflation-adjusted) interest rate.

Entrepreneurs earn profit. Part is a "normal" profit covering the opportunity cost of the entrepreneur's time, energy, and ability. This part is necessary to keep the entrepreneur in the current business. Any residual return after the normal profit is called "economic" profit, or pure profit, and this can be positive or negative. Economic profit is a payment for taking uninsurable risks, and for the uncertainty in undertaking innovation. It is also a return on monopoly power. Economic profit is what lures entrepreneurs to take the risks that lead to greater efficiency and progress.

The chapter closes with a brief assessment of how the nation's income is shared between wages, interest, rent, and profit. Perhaps surprisingly, labour's share has been a fairly stable share of about 80% ever since the 1920s.

Chapter Outline

15.1 Economic Rent

◈ What is economic rent, and how is it determined?

• Economic rent is the price paid for the use of land or other natural resources that are completely fixed in supply (perfectly inelastic).

• Demand is the active determinant of economic rent because supply changes cannot occur. Economic rent is, therefore, a surplus payment that is not necessary to ensure that land is available to the economy as a whole. The rent serves no incentive function.

• Rent is not a surplus payment from the viewpoint of a single firm. To the firm, rent is a cost that must be paid to attract the land away from other potential users. Therefore, rent does serve an allocative function in ensuring land is allocated for the most valuable uses.

• Economic rents on different types of land vary because land differs in its productivity. Land of very low productivity may be a free good, attracting no rent at all.

➲ You may be confused by different uses of the term "rent." Usually it applies to income from land, but sometimes it refers to other incomes. In every case, rent pertains to a surplus earned when a resource earns more than it would take to retain that resource in its current use.

Quick Quiz

1. An increased demand for waterfront property on Georgian Bay will:
   (a) increase the supply of waterfront property in existence
   (b) increase the quantity supplied of waterfront property
   (c) increase the rent and the supply of waterfront property
   (d) increase only the rent of waterfront property

2. Which is a reason for differential rents on different pieces of land?
   (a) different levels soil quality for farmland
   (b) different locations for retail land
   (c) different distances from sawmills for timberland
   (d) all of the above

3. All of the income paid to a factor of production will be economic rent if:
   (a) demand for the factor is totally elastic
   (b) demand for the factor is totally inelastic
   (c) supply for the factor is totally elastic
   (d) supply for the factor is totally inelastic

15.2 Interest: The Price of Money

◈ What is interest?

◈ How is the interest rate determined?

• The interest rate is the price paid for the use of money.
   o The interest rate is stated as a percentage annually of the amount borrowed.

   o Money itself is not a resource, but it can be used to buy physical capital resources such as factories, machinery, etc.
• Interest rates are determined by the demand for and supply of loanable funds. Graphically, the interest rate is measured on the vertical axis, and the quantity of loanable funds is measured on the horizontal axis.
   o The supply curve of loanable funds is upward sloping. As interest rates rise, households are more willing to defer present consumption and to save more money, which can then be supplied (through the financial system) as loans to businesses.
   o The demand curve for loans is downward sloping. As interest rates rise, fewer investment projects that firms are considering will have rates of return that exceed the interest rate, hence firms will wish to borrow less funds to finance investment projects.
   o The equilibrium interest rate is where the quantity supplied equals the quantity demanded in the loanable funds market.
   o Shifts in the supply or demand of loanable funds will change the interest rate.
• For convenience we speak as if there is only a single interest rate. In reality, there are numerous interest rates. Rates vary because of four factors:
   o Loans with a higher risk of default carry higher interest rates.
   o Loans with longer terms to maturity usually carry higher interest rates.
   o Loans for smaller amounts carry higher interest rates.
   o Market imperfections, or monopoly power considerations, can also affect interest rates.
• The pure rate of interest is approximated by the interest rate on long-term, virtually risk-free securities, such as 30-year Government of Canada bonds.
• The interest rate plays three roles.
   o Because a lower interest rate will stimulate the demand for capital goods, there is an inverse relationship between the interest rate and the level of total output of the economy.
   o The interest rate rations (allocates) loanable funds, and therefore real capital, among competing firms and industries,

thereby determining what kinds of capital are produced.

   o   The interest rate determines the level and composition of R&D spending.

• When there is inflation we must adjust the nominal interest rate to get the real interest rate, which is expressed in purchasing power terms. The real interest rate, not the nominal rate, affects investment and R&D spending decisions.

Quick Quiz

4. A drop in the real rate of interest would result in:
   (a)   decreased R&D spending
   (b)   an increase in the inflation rate
   (c)   increased spending on capital goods
   (d)   a decreased supply of loanable funds

5. The interest rate would tend to rise if:
   (a)   businesses have fewer profitable investment opportunities
   (b)   households become more impatient to consume goods now instead of later
   (c)   fewer families are buying and financing new homes
   (d)   the government reduces its borrowing

6. To take into account the effects of inflation:
   (a)   subtract the expected inflation rate from the nominal rate of interest
   (b)   subtract the nominal interest rate from the expected inflation rate
   (c)   subtract the expected rate of inflation from the pure rate of interest
   (d)   subtract the expected inflation rate from the real rate of interest

15.3 Economic Profit

◈ What is economic profit?

◈ What are the functions of economic profit in the economy?

• Economic profit (or pure profit) is the residual after all explicit and implicit costs are deducted from a firm's total revenues.

• The entrepreneur's return includes a normal profit that is the minimum payment necessary to keep the entrepreneur in the current business.

• Any return (positive or negative) after allocating the normal profit is economic profit.

• In a static, competitive economy, there is no economic profit. Such profit arises from three sources:
   o   compensation for assuming the uninsurable risks of business that are inherent in a dynamic economy;
   o   compensation for dealing with the uncertainties inherent in innovation; and
   o   surpluses obtained from the exploitation of monopoly power.

• The expectation of economic profits motivates business firms to innovate; and profits (and losses) guide business firms to produce products and to use resources in the ways most desired by society.

➜ To see clearly the difference between normal profit and economic profit, focus on the difference between a static, competitive economy and a dynamic economy with market power. Remember that it is the expectation, not the certainty, of profit that drives the entrepreneur. Except where it derives from monopoly power, economic profit is never certain. In order to generate profit, the entrepreneur must take risks. You should distinguish between risks that are insurable and risks that are uninsurable. Bearing uninsurable risk is a major source of profit in a dynamic and unpredictable market economy.

Quick Quiz

7. Normal profit:
   (a)   compensates entrepreneurs for their opportunity costs
   (b)   is a residual after all opportunity costs are accounted for
   (c)   is a consequence of bearing risk
   (d)   is received by firms with monopoly power

8. Economic profit:
   (a)   is the payment for capital
   (b)   is an opportunity cost
   (c)   does not exist in a static economy
   (d)   can be a compensation for dealing with uncertainty

9. Which is not a source of economic profit?
   (a)   monopoly power
   (b)   insurable risk
   (c)   uninsurable risk
   (d)   innovations

15.4 Income Shares

◇ What share of Canada's income goes to each factor of production?

• Canada's national income is divided between wages, rent, interest, and profit.

• Using a broad definition of labour income that includes net income of farmers and unincorporated businesses, labour's share has been fairly stable around 80%, so the share going to capitalists (through rent, interest, and profits) has been about 20% of national income.

Quick Quiz

10. As relative shares of Canadian domestic income, in 2002 as compared to the 1920s:
   (a)   wages, salaries and supplementary income were roughly the same
   (b)   corporate profits before taxes were nearly double
   (c)   net incomes from farming had fallen dramatically
   (d)   interest income had fallen dramatically

Terms and Concepts

economic rent	explicit costs
incentive function of price	implicit costs
	economic (pure) profit
loanable funds theory of interest	normal profit
	static economy
pure rate of interest	insurable risks
nominal interest rate	uninsurable risks
real interest rate	

Fill-In Questions

1. Rent is the price paid for the use of _____ and other _____ resources with a completely (horizontal, vertical) _____ supply curve. Their supply can also be described as perfectly _____.

2. From society's perspective, rent is a _____, because the supply of land is fixed. From a single firm's perspective, a rent payment is a _____ that must be paid in order to attract land away from alternate uses.

3. Interest is the price paid for the use of _____. Money itself is not an economic resource, but when firms borrow money for in-

vestment they are ultimately purchasing the use of real _____ goods.

4. The individual firm is willing to continue investing in capital, and therefore (lending, borrowing) _____, up to the point where the rate of _____ and the expected rate of _____ on capital are equal.

5. The firm's demand for loanable funds is _____ sloping because lower interest rates mean (higher, lower) _____ investment costs so (more, fewer) _____ investment projects will be profitable.

6. The supply curve of loanable funds is _____-sloping because (higher, lower) _____ interest rates are required to induce households to _____ more.

7. The interest rate helps determine how much _____ will occur in the economy and also _____ financial and real capital among firms.

8. Normal profits are paid to the human resource called _____ ability. This resource performs four functions: combining the other _____ to produce goods and services; making (routine, non-routine) _____ decisions for the firm; (inventing, innovating) _____ products and production processes; and bearing the economic _____ associated with the other three functions.

True-False

Circle T if the statement is true, F if it is false.

1. Rent is a surplus because it does not perform an incentive function. **T F**

2. Demand is the sole active determinant of land rent. **T F**

3. Demand for land, and therefore the rent on land, would increase if there were an increase in the demand for the product obtained from the land. **T F**

4. Rent, which is a surplus from the viewpoint of society, is a cost from the viewpoint of the firm that pays the rent. **T F**

5. If the demand curve for land lies entirely to the left of the supply curve for land, the land will be free. **T F**

6. A decrease in the supply of loanable funds would tend to increase the interest rate and to decrease investment spending and national output and employment. **T F**

7. A borrower at a financial institution is a demander of loanable funds. **T F**

8. The pure rate of interest is the nominal rate of interest minus the rate of inflation. **T F**

9. One reason to oppose a merger of major Canadian banks is that such a merger would increase monopoly power in the lending industry, and possibly raise interest rates. **T F**

10. A normal profit is the return required by the entrepreneur to prevent her from transferring her service to another firm. **T F**

11. Uninsurable risks are the business risks that can be predicted and for which no insurance is required. **T F**

12. The expectation of profits is the basic motive for innovation, while actual profits and losses aid in the efficient allocation of resources. **T F**

13. Economic profits are guaranteed to exist only in a static economy with pure competition. **T F**

14. Growing corporate profits have resulted in a slow but steady growth of capital's share of the national income. **T F**

Multiple-Choice

Circle the letter that corresponds to the best answer.

1. The supply of land to society is:
  (a)   perfectly inelastic
  (b)   of unitary elasticity
  (c)   perfectly elastic
  (d)   elastic but not perfectly elastic

2. From the viewpoint of society, an increase in the demand for land results in:
  (a)   an increase in the supply of land
  (b)   an increase in the quantity supplied of land
  (c)   an increase in rent and an increase in the quantity supplied of land
  (d)   an increase in rent only

3. If an input, such as land, is fixed in supply:
  (a)   rent is supply determined
  (b)   rent is determined by the owner of that fixed supply
  (c)   rent is demand determined
  (d)   in some provinces rent payments are determined by a Rental Review Board

4. The payment to a resource performs an incentive function if:
  (a)   the supply curve of the resource is perfectly inelastic
  (b)   the price of the resource is fixed
  (c)   the demand curve for the resource is downward sloping
  (d)   the supply curve of the resource is upward sloping

5. Economists consider rent to be a surplus because:
  (a)   no matter what the level of rent payment the same quantity of land is available to the economy
  (b)   agricultural products are grown from seeds using land and so a surplus results
  (c)   landowners are monopolists and charge a price greater than the competitive price
  (d)   there is a large quantity effect and little price effect when the demand for land changes

6. Which of the following statements about differential interest rates is true?
  (a)   interest rates tend to be lower on riskier loans
  (b)   interest rates tend to be lower on smaller loans
  (c)   interest rates tend to be lower on shorter-term loans
  (d)   all of the above

7. The supply of loanable funds is provided by all of the following except:
  (a)   borrowers at a commercial bank

(b)   business savings
(c)   buyers of Canada Savings Bonds
(d)   credit creation by financial institutions

8. Which of the following would shift the supply of loanable funds to the right?
(a)   an increase in thriftiness of households
(b)   an increase in tax rates on interest income
(c)   a technological advance
(d)   an increase in consumer demands

9. Usually the lower the rate of interest on a loan:
(a)   the greater the risk involved
(b)   the shorter the length of the loan
(c)   the smaller the amount of the loan
(d)   the greater the imperfections in the money market

10. The rate of interest does all of the following except:
(a)   affect the total amount of investment in the economy
(b)   affect the aggregate level of domestic output and employment
(c)   allocate money and physical capital to those industries in which it will be most productive
(d)   guarantee that there will be full employment in the economy

11. The profit-maximizing amount of financial and real capital an individual firm would employ is the amount at which the interest rate is equal to the:
(a)   expected rate of return
(b)   marginal physical product of capital
(c)   marginal cost of capital
(d)   marginal resource cost of capital

12. If the rate of interest is 12% and a firm expects that a new warehouse investment would yield a rate of return of 14%, the firm would:
(a)   not build the new warehouse
(b)   build the new warehouse
(c)   have to toss a coin to decide whether to build the new warehouse
(d)   not be able to determine, from these figures, whether to build the warehouse

13. The pure rate of interest is the interest rate on:
(a)   a basic Visa card
(b)   a fixed rate mortgage
(c)   a savings account

(d)   long term government bonds

14. Which of the following is an economic cost?
(a)   business profit
(b)   normal profit
(c)   economic profit
(d)   windfall profit

15. Economic profit is the same as:
(a)   normal profit
(b)   accounting profit
(c)   pure profit
(d)   none of the above

16. The residual claimant is:
(a)   the government
(b)   the bank that has provided loans
(c)   bondholders who have provided capital financing
(d)   the entrepreneur

17. Uninsurable risks can stem from:
(a)   changes in the general economic environment
(b)   changes in the structure of the economy
(c)   changes in government policy
(d)   all of the above

18. Identify the uninsurable risk from the following list:
(a)   shoplifting losses
(b)   injuries to employees
(c)   technological change
(d)   fire damage

19. Which of the following is **not** a basic function of the entrepreneur?
(a)   to introduce new products to the market
(b)   to supply loanable funds
(c)   to incur uninsurable risks
(d)   to combine resources to produce a good or service

20. Business firms obtain profits because:
(a)   not all risks are insurable
(b)   not all markets are competitive
(c)   the economy is dynamic
(d)   all of these

21. Capital's share of national income is around 20%, and includes:
(a)   rent
(b)   interest

(c)   profit
(d)   all of the above

22. If the inflation rate is 2% and the nominal rate of interest is 8%, then the real rate of interest is:
(a)   -6%
(b)   4%
(c)   6%
(d)   10%

Problems and Projects

1. Supply and Demand for Land

Assume that there are 300,000 hectares available of a certain type of farmland, which has no other use but farming. The demand for this land is given in the following table:

Land Rent ($/hectare)	Land Demanded (hectares)
$125	100,000
100	200,000
75	300,000
50	400,000
25	500,000

(a) _____ hectares will be rented.
(b) The rent will be $____ per hectare.
(c) If there was a $50 per hectare tax on this farmland, there would be ____ hectares available.
(d) A tax of $50 per hectare would reduce the landowners' net income to $____ per hectare.

2. Land Productivity and Rents

Wheat is grown on three grades of land (A, B, and C). Assume no other inputs are used but labour. The table gives the output for various amounts of labour applied.

Labour	Output by Land Grade (bushels)		
	Grade A	Grade B	Grade C
1	50	45	20
2	90	75	30
3	120	95	37
4	140	105	41
5	150	110	43
6	155	112	44

If the price is a constant $1 per bushel, complete the following table showing the marginal revenue product for the various levels of labour input.

Labour	Marginal Revenue Product ($)		
	Grade A	Grade B	Grade C
1	_____	_____	_____
2	_____	_____	_____
3	_____	_____	_____
4	_____	_____	_____
5	_____	_____	_____
6	_____	_____	_____

Labour costs $20 per unit and is purchased in a perfectly competitive input market.
(a) A profit-maximizing firm would employ _____ units of labour on Grade A land; _____ units of labour on Grade B land; and ____ units of labour on Grade C land.
(b) The net income earned: on Grade A land is $____; on Grade B land is $____; and on Grade C land is $____.
(c) In a competitive market for land, Grade A land would rent for up to $____, Grade B land for $____, and Grade C land for $____.
(d) Suppose the price of wheat rose to $2/bushel. The rent on Grade A land becomes $____; on Grade B land $____; on Grade C land $____.
(e) If the price of wheat stays at $1 per bushel, Grade B land would command no rent whatsoever if the price of labour rises to at least $____.

3. Real and Nominal Interest Rates

A farmer takes out a one-year loan. The farmer and the bank are both willing to make this loan agreement at a real interest rate of 5%. At the time the loan is made they both expect the inflation rate for the year to be 2%. The inflation rate turns out to 3%.
(a) The nominal interest rate agreeable to both parties when the loan is agreed to is ____%.
(b) The actual real interest rate ends up being ____%.
(c) The higher than expected inflation rate benefit the (farmer, bank) _____ and harms the _____.

Discussion Questions

1. Explain what determines the economic rent paid for the use of land. What is unique about the supply of land?
2. Even though land rent is an economic surplus, it is also an economic cost for the individual user of land. How can it be both an economic surplus and an economic cost?

3. How would a decrease in the supply of loanable funds affect: (a) the interest rate; (b) investment spending; (c) national output and employment?

4. Why are there many different interest rates in the economy at any given time?

5. What is the pure rate of interest and how does it differ from the real rate of interest?

6. Why does the amount of business investment increase when the interest rate falls?

7. What two important functions does the rate of interest perform in the economy?

8. What are economic profits? Why would there be no economic profits in a purely competitive static economy?

9. "The risks an entrepreneur assumes arise because of uncertainties that are external to the firm and because of uncertainties that are developed by the initiative of the firm itself." Explain.

10. What two important functions do profits or the expectations of profits perform in the economy? Why could monopoly power, such as that created by a patent, both impede and enhance the effective performance of these functions?

11. What part of Canada's national income is wages and salaries and what part is labour income? Why do your answers to these two questions differ? What part of the national income do capitalists receive? What kinds of income is capitalist income?

Answers

Quick Quiz
1. (d) p. 367
2. (d) pp. 367-368
3. (d) p. 367
4. (d) p. 369
5. (b) p. 369
6. (a) pp. 373-374
7. (a) p. 374
8. (d) p. 375
9. (b) p. 375
10. (a) pp. 377-378

Fill-in Questions
1. land, natural, vertical, inelastic
2. surplus, cost
3. money, capital
4. borrowing, interest, return
5. downward, lower, more
6. upward, higher, save
7. investment, allocates
8. entrepreneurial, resources, nonroutine, innovating, risks

True-False
1. T
2. T
3. T   the MRP of the land rises
4. T
5. T   the equilibrium price is zero
6. T
7. T
8. F   this describes the real rate of interest, not the pure rate
9. T   monopoly power does tend to raise interest rates
10. T
11. F   profits pertain to uninsurable risks, not insurable risks
12. T
13. F   in such an economy there would be no economic profits
14. F   capital's share has remained fairly stable at about 20%

Multiple-Choice
1. (a)   supply is vertical
2. (d)
3. (c)
4. (d)   an upward sloping supply means quantity supplied responds to price changes
5. (a)
6. (c)
7. (a)   borrowers are demanders of loanable funds
8. (a)   increased thriftiness means more savings available to lend
9. (b)
10. (d)   a flexible interest rate helps, but does not guarantee the economy will maintain full employment
11. (a)
12. (b)   the return exceeds the opportunity cost of the interest, so the warehouse would be profitable

13. (d)

14. (b) this covers the opportunity cost of the entrepreneurial input

15. (c)

16. (d)

17. (d)

18. (c) frequencies of shoplifting, injuries, and fires are predictable, so these risks are insurable

19. (b)

20. (d)

21. (d)

22. (c) in purchasing power terms, the return is 6%

Problems and Projects

1. (a) 300,000; (b) 75; (c) 300,000; (d) 25

2. Grade A: 50, 40, 30, 20, 10, 5; Grade B: 45, 30, 20, 10, 5, 2; Grade C: 20, 10, 7, 4, 2, 1; (a) employing labour up to where MRP = MRC: 4, 3, 1; (b) (P x Q) – (wage x L) = 60, 35, 0; (c) 60, 35, 0; (d) 200, 130, 20; (e) 45, because this is the MRP of the first unit of labour

3. (a) 5+2=7%; (b) 7-3=4%; (c) farmer, banker

Chapter 16 — Income Inequality, Poverty, and Discrimination

Overview

This chapter deals with the facts about income inequality, poverty and discrimination in Canada, including how these variables are measured and interpreted, and some discussion of policies designed to make incomes more equal. There is significant and growing inequality of incomes between Canadian households, and a substantial percentage of Canadians live in poverty. To some extent, these important problems are inherent to any market economy, but in Canada there is a consensus that government should play a role in modifying the distribution of income.

The Lorenz curve, which plots the percent of the nation's income versus the percent of Canadian families, is a useful device to show that the distribution of income is unequal. There are many causes of inequality, ranging from very individual circumstances (including life cycle effects), to social trends, and policies.

How much our governments should redistribute incomes, and what the effects are of present income redistribution mechanisms, are both highly controversial. The basic case for an equal distribution of income — and therefore for income taxes and transfer payments — is that income equality is necessary for consumer utility to be maximized for society as a whole. The case for inequality is based on the idea that the potential of earning higher incomes provides people with an incentive to work hard, save, invest, and take risks — and thereby contribute to the nation's output. Therefore, there is a tradeoff between equality and efficiency because redistribution of income reduces incentives and productivity.

The definition of poverty is necessarily subjective. Nevertheless, no matter where the line is drawn, and no matter whether one considers absolute poverty or relative poverty, poverty is not randomly distributed. For example, unattached individuals, households headed by women, and households with more children are much more likely to live in poverty.

Canada's income maintenance system consists of many component programs including social insurance elements and public assistance (welfare) elements. Important tradeoffs exist in these programs.

Chapter Outline

16.1 Facts About Income Inequality

◈ How is income inequality measured?

◈ How unequal are incomes in Canada?

• Considerable inequality of household incomes is a persistent state of affairs in Canada.

  o A table of distribution of personal incomes by families shows the extent of the inequality.

  o The Lorenz curve is a geometric device for portraying the extent of inequality at a particular point in time.

  o The Gini coefficient measures the ratio of the area between the Lorenz curve and the diagonal and the total area below the diagonal. The bigger this ratio the more unequal is the distribution of income.

• Several factors must be considered when interpreting the data on income inequality.

  o Due to income mobility the degree of income inequality is less if viewed over a lifetime. Earnings for most workers start at a low level in youth, peak during middle age, and then decline, meaning that most people move between income quintiles over the life cycle.

  o Government redistribution through taxes and transfer payments serves to reduce – modestly – the degree of income of inequality in Canada. Transfers have more impact than taxes in this regard.

➥ Given how strongly people feel about income distribution issues, and given the current political turmoil over the overhaul of Canada's income maintenance programs, it is easy to lose track of the distinction between positive and normative statements. It is important that you keep the positive vs. normative distinction in mind in order to get the most out of this chapter.

Quick Quiz

1. A quintile refers to:
    (a)   a measure of income inequality
    (b)   one fifth of the population
    (c)   the top income group in the population
    (d)   the distance from the diagonal in the Lorenz curve

2. The Lorenz curve plots:
    (a)   the Gini coefficient vs. the number of families
    (b)   the Gini coefficient vs. the percent of families
    (c)   the percent of income vs. the number of families
    (d)   the percent of families vs. the percent of income

3. Which would be consistent with decreasing inequality of income:
    (a)   a higher percent of income going to members of the top quintile
    (b)   the Lorenz curve falling farther away from the diagonal
    (c)   a falling Gini coefficient
    (d)   none of the above

16.2   Causes of Income Inequality

✧ What are the causes of income inequality in Canada?

✧ What are the trends in income inequality in Canada?

• The impersonal market system does not necessarily result in a distribution of income that we would consider just. Income inequality can be explained by individual differences in at least seven areas:
    o   ability
    o   education and training
    o   discrimination
    o   preferences and risk
    o   unequal distribution of wealth

    o   market power
    o   luck, connections, and misfortune

• Over the years, absolute incomes in Canada have risen across the whole distribution of income.

• However, Canada's income distribution has become somewhat more unequal in the last fifty years. The percentage of income going to members of the lowest three quintiles has decreased and the percentage going to members of the highest two quintiles has increased.

• Several factors are contributing to the growing inequality of incomes over the last three decades.
    o   Demand is shifting strongly towards the more highly skilled and educated workers. The "superstar" phenomenon among CEOs and entertainers is an example.
    o   Demographic changes can produce higher proportions of less skilled and less experienced workers, higher proportions of households headed by unmarried or divorced mothers, and a growing tendency for men and women with high earnings to marry each other.
    o   Wages in certain Canadian industries are suffering because of growing competition from imports produced in low-wage countries, and a decline in unionism.

Quick Quiz

4. Reasons for income inequality include individual differences in:
    (a)   education
    (b)   luck
    (c)   ability
    (d)   all of the above

5. Income inequality would tend to decrease if:
    (a)   female workers begin to experience more job market discrimination
    (b)   post-secondary education becomes more difficult to afford
    (c)   the government introduces new taxes on inherited wealth
    (d)   the percentage of workers belonging to unions decreases

16.3   Equality versus Efficiency

✧ What is the tradeoff between income equality and efficiency of the economy?

- It is important for society to decide what degree of income inequality to aim for, given the tradeoff between equality and efficiency.
  - o A case for equality is made on the basis of maximizing total utility for all consumers. Given diminishing marginal utility to income, redistributing some income from a higher-income individual to a lower-income individual will increase the amount of utility produced by that amount of income.
  - o A case for inequality is based on the argument that if all income were distributed equally, individuals would lack incentive to work hard, take risks, etc., in order to produce more income. Therefore, society would have much less income to distribute.

➲ The concept of the equality-efficiency tradeoff is at the centre of many public policy debates about our income maintenance programs. Politicians on the right typically believe strongly in this tradeoff, while politicians on the left tend to minimize its importance.

Quick Quiz

6. Suppose Alanis has $8 million, and Sarah has $2 million. If Alanis and Sarah have identical marginal-utility-of-income curves, their combined total utility will be maximized if:
  (a) $2 million is redistributed from Alanis to Sarah
  (b) $3 million is redistributed from Alanis to Sarah
  (c) $6 million is redistributed from Alanis to Sarah
  (d) they maintain the current distribution of income

7. Which statement is correct?
  (a) income redistribution to reduce income inequality has no effect on total consumer utility
  (b) income redistribution to reduce income inequality has no effect on the amount of output produced by society
  (c) income redistribution to reduce income inequality makes sense only if all individuals have identical marginal-utility-of-income curves

  (d) income redistribution to reduce income inequality tends to reduce incentives to work, save and invest

16.4 The Nature of Poverty

◈ How is poverty defined?

◈ What is the profile of Canada's poor?

- Poverty is a significant and persistent problem in Canadian society.
  - o Absolute poverty exists when basic material needs (food, clothing, and shelter) of a household are not met. Relative poverty exists when a household's income is low relative to others in the society.
  - o Statistics Canada defines poverty by a "low income cut-off" (revised in 1992, defined as a family spending more than about 53% of their income on food, shelter, and clothing. In 2000, nearly 11% of Canadians were considered to be living in poverty. Among unattached individuals the ratio was closer to 29%.
- While the poor are found in all regions, age groups, ethnic groups, and rural and urban populations, poverty is far from randomly distributed. Unattached individuals, households with children, and households headed by women, younger people, or the unemployed are much more likely to be low income.
- Poverty in Canada tends to be invisible because there is significant income mobility, because the "permanent poor" are increasingly isolated geographically, and because the poor lack political voice or organization.
- About half of federal government spending is on transfer payments, but the bulk of these expenditures are not targeted at the poor. Major programs in Canada's income-maintenance system include:
  - o The Canada Pension Plan (CPP) and Quebec Pension Plan (QPP), payable at age 65 based on employer and employee contributions.
  - o The Old Age Security (OAS) Pension, payable to everyone reaching the age of 65, and the Guaranteed Income Supplement (GIS), for those over 65 and with incomes below a certain level.
  - o Employment Insurance (EI) benefits, paid as temporary support to unemployed

workers on the basis of previous contributions.

Quick Quiz

8. How does Statistics Canada define the income level below which Canadian families are living in poverty?

(a) based on an absolute income cutoff

(b) based on the assumption that a certain predetermined percentage of families will always be counted as living in poverty

(c) based on a certain predetermined percentage of income spent on food, clothing and shelter

(d) based on what percentage of income is spent on food, clothing and shelter compared to the percentage spent by an average family

9. Which statement about Canada's poverty situation in 2000 is false?

(a) a woman is more likely to be among the poor than a man

(b) an unattached individual is more likely to be among the poor than a person who lives in a household with others

(c) a person over the age of 65 is more likely to be among the poor than a person in the 18-64 age group

(d) the percentage of Canadians living in poverty differs considerably from province to province

10. Irma retires at age 65, after working since high school as a sales clerk in the Bay in Winnipeg. From which program will she be eligible to receive benefits?

(a) CPP

(b) OAS

(c) GIS, if her income is low enough

(d) all three, if her income is low enough

16.5 Welfare Policy: Goals and Conflicts

◇ What are the goals in designing welfare policy?

◇ What conflicts exists between the goals of welfare policy?

• An ideal public assistance (welfare) program should achieve three goals:

  o It should get people out of poverty.

  o It should provide adequate incentives for able-bodied, non-retired people to work.

  o It should have a reasonable cost.

• Conflicts of the three goals are illustrated in a comparison of three hypothetical welfare plans. All have a minimum annual income, and a benefit-reduction rate (the rate at which recipients' benefits are reduced as a result of earned income).

  o Lower minimum annual incomes keep costs down but reduce the ability of the plan to move people out of poverty.

  o Lower benefit-reduction rates protect the incentive to work but raise the cost of the plan.

Quick Quiz

11. The break-even income level is:

(a) the level of earned income at which the transfer payments become zero

(b) the level of income at which the recipient is able to avoid poverty

(c) the level of earned income at which the recipient has no incentive to work

(d) the level at which earned income equals transfer payments

12. The disadvantage of a higher benefit-reduction rate is that:

(a) it tends to make a public assistance program more expensive

(b) it tends to increase the number of people eligible for the program

(c) it tends to reduce incentives to work

(d) it does all of the above

16.6 Labour Market Discrimination

◇ What are the types of labour market discrimination?

◇ What are the effects of labour market discrimination?

• Labour market discrimination occurs when equivalent labour resources are paid or treated differently even though their productive contributions are equal. Discrimination may be based on gender, race, ethnicity, or other minority status, and takes four main forms.

  o Wage discrimination occurs when members of one group receive lower wages than members of another group doing the same work.

o Employment discrimination occurs when one group experiences inferior treatment in hiring, promotion, layoffs, etc.

o Occupational discrimination occurs when members of one group are arbitrarily restricted from entering certain desirable occupations.

o Human capital discrimination occurs when members of one group enjoy less access to investments in education and training.

• Labour market discrimination imposes a cost on its victims, but also on society as a whole. Because some labour resources are not allocated to their most productive uses, our nation's output ends up below its potential (inside our production possibilities curve).

• Several models of discrimination are presented.

o In the taste-for-discrimination model, prejudiced employers behave as if employing visible minority workers involves an extra cost (captured in the concept of the discrimination coefficient). In equilibrium, minority workers are employed by prejudiced employers only if their wage rate is lower than the wage for other workers. Competition should eventually work to reduce this type of discrimination, but the results to date are not encouraging.

o Statistical discrimination occurs when workers are judged on the basis of average characteristics of the group with which they are associated, rather than on their individual characteristics or productivity. This sort of discrimination causes undesirable effects even though it is not malicious. Because it is also profitable it tends to persist.

o In the crowding model, or occupational segregation model, members of one group are segregated into less desirable occupations, which also end up lower-paying because of the large supply of labour crowded there.

• Each of these models appears to explain some of the labour market discrimination faced by women and visible minorities in Canada, and some of the inefficiency in our economy due to misallocation of labour resources.

Quick Quiz

13. The term "labour market discrimination" refers to a situation where two groups of workers with identical productivity in their jobs experience:
  (a) unequal wage levels
  (b) unequal opportunities for promotion
  (c) unequal opportunities for training and professional development
  (d) any of the above

14. The fact that most nurses are women and most engineers are men may suggest:
  (a) wage discrimination
  (b) employment discrimination
  (c) occupational discrimination
  (d) human capital discrimination

15. In which model of discrimination is it predicted that competition should eventually reduce discrimination?
  (a) taste-for-discrimination
  (b) crowding
  (c) occupational segregation
  (d) statistical discrimination

Terms and Concepts

income inequality
Lorenz curve
Gini ratio
income mobility
non-cash transfer
equality-efficiency trade-off
absolute poverty
relative poverty
Canada Pension Plan (CPP)
Old Age Security (OAS)
Guaranteed Income Supplement (GIS)
Employment Insurance (EI)

wage discrimination
employment discrimination
occupational discrimination
human capital discrimination
taste-for-discrimination model
discrimination coefficient
statistical discrimination
occupational segregation

Fill-In Questions

1. Over time, household incomes in Canada have risen in (absolute, relative) _____ terms, but the _____ distribution has been roughly stable since 1951.

2. Income inequality can be portrayed graphically by drawing a _____ curve.

(a) When such a curve is plotted, the cumulative percentage of (income, families) _____ is plotted on the horizontal axis and the cumulative percentage of _____ is plotted on the vertical axis.

(b) A curve that would show a completely equal distribution of income is a diagonal line, which would run from the (lower, upper) _____ left to the _____ right corner of the graph.

(c) The more unequal the distribution of income, the (less, more) _____ the curve "sags" below the diagonal. Thus, the degree of income inequality is measured by the area that lies between the curve and the _____.

3. Those who argue for:

(a) equal distribution of income contend that it results in the maximization of total (income, utility) _____ in the economy;

(b) unequal distribution of income believe income distribution is an important determinant of _____.

4. There is an important tradeoff between _____ and _____. This means that:

(a) less income inequality leads to a (greater, smaller) _____ total output; and

(b) a larger total output requires (more, less) _____ income inequality.

5. Poverty tends to be concentrated:

(a) among the (young, old) _____;

(b) among (families, unattached individuals) _____;

(c) in families headed by _____;

(d) among those who are poorly _____;

(e) in (large, small) _____ families.

6. What do the following abbreviations stand for?

(a) OAS: _____

(b) GIS: _____

(c) CPP: _____

(d) EI: _____

7. The two critical elements of any welfare, or public assistance, program are a _____ income below which a family's income would not be allowed to fall, and a _____ rate that specifies the rate at which the subsidy would be reduced if earned income increases.

True-False

Circle T if the statement is true, F if it is false.

1. The long-run trend has been for family incomes in Canada to rise in absolute terms.   **T F**

2. In Canada there is considerable mobility between income classes from one year to the next.   **T F**

3. The progressive tax system in Canada has made the after-tax income distribution much more equal than the before-tax income distribution.   **T F**

4. In Canada the "low income cutoff" for defining poverty is set by Statistics Canada on a relative rather than an absolute basis.   **T F**

5. In Canada, the top quintile of the population earns about 10 times as much as the bottom quintile of the population.   **T F**

6. The argument that redistributing income will increase society's well-being is based on the assumption of diminishing marginal utility of income.   **T F**

7. The lower is the benefit-loss rate in an income assistance plan, the smaller are the incentives to earn additional income.   **T F**

8. All Canadians over the age of 65 are eligible to receive OAS and GIS benefits.   **T F**

9. In the taste-for-discrimination model, if employers discriminate against women, then the higher the employer's discrimination coefficient, the higher women's wages relative to men's wages.   **T F**

10. An employer using statistical discrimination is probably sacrificing profits as a result of his prejudice.   **T F**

11. Women suffer human capital discrimination if they must have higher grades than men in order to be admitted to the same university programs.   **T F**

Multiple-Choice

Circle the letter that corresponds to the best answer.

1. In 2000, roughly what percentage of Canadian families had annual incomes of at least $60,000?
(a)   5%
(b)   11%
(c)   22%
(d)   35%

2. In 2000, approximately what percentage of all Canadian families had annual incomes below $10,000?
(a)   1%
(b)   6%
(c)   18%
(d)   32%

3. Which of the following applies to how the Canadian distribution of income has changed over time?
(a)   incomes have fallen in absolute terms
(b)   inequality has decreased in relative terms
(c)   the relative distribution of income has been fairly stable since 1951
(d)   income mobility has decreased

4. Which of the following would be evidence of a decrease in relative income inequality in Canada?
(a)   a decrease in the percentage of total income received by the lowest quintile
(b)   an increase in the percentage of total income received by the highest quintile
(c)   an increase in the percentage of total income received by the four lowest quintiles
(d)   a decrease in the percentage of total income received by the four lowest quintiles

5. When a Lorenz curve has been drawn, the degree of income inequality in an economy is measured by:
(a)   the slope of the diagonal that runs from the southwest to the northeast corner of the diagram
(b)   the slope of the Lorenz curve
(c)   the area between the Lorenz curve and the axes of the graph
(d)   the area between the Lorenz curve and the southwest-northeast diagonal

6. Which of the following is **not** one of the causes of the unequal distribution of income in Canada?

(a)   the unequal distribution of property
(b)   the income tax system
(c)   the inability of the poor to invest in human capital
(d)   luck and the unequal distribution of misfortune

7. The case for income inequality is primarily made on the basis that income inequality:
(a)   is reduced by the transfer payment programs for the poor
(b)   is necessary to maintain incentives to work and produce output
(c)   depends on luck and chance, which cannot be corrected by government action
(d)   is created by education and training programs that distort the distribution of income

8. The debate over income redistribution focuses on the tradeoff between equality and:
(a)   efficiency
(b)   unemployment
(c)   economic growth
(d)   economic freedom

9. Carla and Robert have identical marginal-utility-from-income curves. Carla obtains 5 units of utility from the last dollar of income received by her and that Robert obtains 8 units of utility from the last dollar of his income. Therefore: Those who favour an equal distribution of income would:
(a)   Carla's income is less than Robert's
(b)   redistributing income from Carla to Robert would raise total utility
(c)   redistributing income from Carla to Robert would raise Robert's marginal utility more than it would reduce Carla's marginal utility
(d)   both (b) and (c)

10. Which of the following measures would tend to reduce income inequality?
(a)   eliminating the Employment Insurance program
(b)   increasing tax deductions for making financial investments
(c)   taxing all personal income at a flat rate
(d)   levying large taxes on inheritances

11. Which of the following is a major part of the Canadian income-maintenance system?
(a)   public housing

(b)   agricultural subsidies
(c)   Employment Insurance
(d)   minimum-wage laws

12. Under Canada's income maintenance system, basic material needs can be met for almost everyone. Given this, in Canada the poverty problem:
(a)   is one of relative poverty rather than absolute poverty
(b)   is one of both absolute poverty rather than relative poverty
(c)   is one of both absolute poverty and relative poverty
(d)   does not exist

13. Which of the following is designed to provide a nationwide income for all those aged 65 and over?
(a)   Canada Pension Plan
(b)   Guaranteed Income Supplement
(c)   Canada Assistance Plan
(d)   Old Age Security

14. Which of the following programs is most specifically targeted at alleviating poverty?
(a)   Canada Pension Plan
(b)   Guaranteed Income Supplement
(c)   Canada Assistance Plan
(d)   Old Age Security

15. A public assistance plan guarantees a minimum income of $6000 and has a 25% benefit reduction rate. What is the break-even income level?
(a) $18,000
(b) $24,000
(c) $30,000
(d)   none of the above

16. Which is not included among the three goals of any public assistance (welfare) program?
(a)   getting families out of poverty
(b)   providing incentives to work
(c)   assuring the costs of the program are reasonable.
(d)   all of these are included in the goals

17. Under a public assistance (welfare) plan the break-even income is:
(a)   the level of income at which income and consumption expenditure are equal
(b)   the level of income at which income tax payments equal zero

(c)   the level of income equal to the low income cutoff as calculated by Statistics Canada
(d)   the level of income at which the transfer payment equals zero

18. Which of the following is not among the reasons that the poor are invisible in Canada?
(a)   the poor are increasingly isolated in ghettos, slums, and depressed regions
(b)   the poor are politically weak
(c)   many of the poor are able to escape poverty for only a year or two
(d)   there are relatively few poor people

19. According to the crowding hypothesis, the crowding of women into certain occupations:
(a)   is the result of occupational discrimination
(b)   results in the misallocation of resources
(c)   causes lower wage rates for women relative to men
(d)   all of the above

20. If a retailer prefers to hire people from a certain ethnic group because they are more polite, he is engaging in:
(a)   statistical discrimination
(b)   a taste for discrimination
(c)   occupational segregation
(d)   human capital discrimination

21. The discrimination coefficient is a factor in which model?
(a)   taste-for-discrimination
(b)   occupational discrimination
(c)   statistical discrimination
(d)   all of the above

22. If women are rarely sent to training seminars, whereas the men they work with are often sent to the seminars, the women are experiencing:
(a)   statistical discrimination
(b)   occupational segregation
(c)   human capital discrimination
(d)   employment discrimination

23. A defining characteristic of the taste-for-discrimination model is that the employer:
(a)   selects employees on the basis of average group characteristics
(b)   behaves as if employing minority workers adds a cost

(c)   denies minority workers access to certain categories of jobs

(d)   will not hire minority workers

Problems and Projects

1. Lorenz Curve

The distribution of household incomes in a hypothetical economy is shown in the table below.

(a) Complete the table by computing, beginning with the lowest income families:

(1) the percentage of all families in each income class and all lower classes. Enter these figures in column 4.

(2) the percentage of total income received by each income class and all lower classes. Enter these figures in column 5.

(1) Personal Income Class	(2) % of All Families in This Class	(3) % of Total Income Received by This Class	(4) % of All Families in This and All Lower Classes	(5) % of Total Income Received by This and All Lower Classes
Under $10,000	18	4	___	___
$10,000-14,999	12	6	___	___
$15,000-24,999	14	12	___	___
$25,000-34,999	17	14	___	___
$35,000-49,999	19	15	___	___
$50,000-74,999	11	20	___	___
$75,000 and over	9	29	___	___

(b) From the distribution of income data in columns 4 and 5 it can be seen that:

(1) families earning less than $15,000 a year constitute the lowest ____% of all families and receive ____% of the total income.

(2) families earning at least $50,000 a year constitute the highest ____% of all families and receive ____% of the total income.

(c) Use your figures in columns 4 and 5 to draw a Lorenz curve on the graph below. (Plot the seven points and the zero-zero point and connect them with a smooth curve.)

(d) On the same graph draw a diagonal line that would indicate complete equality in the distribution of income.

(e) Label as "A" the area of the graph that shows the degree of income inequality.

(f) Label as "B" the area on the other side of the Lorenz curve.

(g) Given the areas you have labeled, the formula for calculating the Gini coefficient is:_____

(h) Assuming the same percentage distribution of families, but the second highest income group earned 22% of income instead of 20%, and the highest income group earned 27% instead of 29%, then area A would become (bigger, smaller) _____, area B would become _____, and the Gini coefficient value would become _____, indicating (more, less) _____ income inequality.

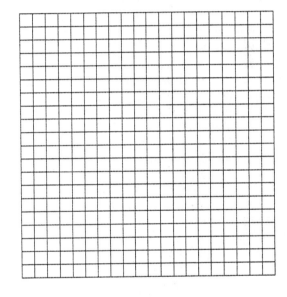

2. Welfare Plans

Following is a table containing different possible earned incomes for a family of a certain size.

Earned Income	Transfer Payment	Total Income
$0	$5,000	$5,000
5,000	___	___
10,000	___	___
15,000	___	___
20,000	___	___
25,000	___	___

(a) Assume that $5,000 is the minimum annual income per family and that the benefit-loss rate is 20%. Enter the transfer payment and the total income at each of the five remaining earned-income levels.

    (1) This welfare program retains strong incentives to work because whenever the family earns an additional $5,000, its total income increases by $_____.

    (2) The family receives a transfer payment until its earned income equals the break-even income of $_____.

(b) To reduce the break-even income, the government raises the benefit-loss rate to 50%. Complete the next table.

Earned Income	Transfer Payment	Total Income
$0	$5,000	$5,000
2,500	_____	_____
5,000	_____	_____
7,500	_____	_____
10,000	_____	_____

    (1) This program is less costly than the previous one because the family receives a transfer payment only until it earns the break-even income of $_____.

    (2) But the incentives to work are less because, whenever the family earns an additional $5,000, its total income increases by only $_____.

(c) Both of the previous two welfare programs guaranteed an income of only $5,000. Assume the minimum annual income is raised to $7,500 and that the benefit-loss rate is kept at 50%. Complete the table below.

Earned Income	Transfer Payment	Total Income
$0	$7,500	$7,500
3,000	_____	_____
6,000	_____	_____
9,000	_____	_____
12,000	_____	_____
15,000	_____	_____

    (1) This program is more costly than the previous one because the break-even income has risen to $_____.

    (2) The incentives to earn additional income are no better in this program than in the previous one. But to improve these incentives by reducing the benefit-loss rate to 40% would raise the break-even income to $_____.

(Hint: Divide guaranteed income by the benefit-loss rate.)

(d) To summarize:

    (1) given the guaranteed income, the lower the benefit-loss rate, the (greater, less) _____ is the incentive to earn additional income and the (greater, less) _____ is the break-even income and the cost of the welfare program;

    (2) and given the benefit-loss rate, the greater the minimum annual income, the (greater, less) _____ is the break-even income and the cost of the program;

    (3) but to reduce the break-even income and the cost of the program requires either a(n) (increase, decrease) _____ in the benefit-loss rate or a(n) _____ in the minimum annual income.

3. Labour Market Discrimination Models

Match each example in the first list with the appropriate model or concept in the second list.

List 1

(a) hospital workers earn a higher hourly wage on night shift than on the day shift

(b) a chemical company hires women for secretarial positions and men for technical and engineering positions

(c) a university promotes male professors more readily than female professors with similar academic qualifications, teaching performance, and research productivity

(d) a law firm hires male lawyers over female lawyers because females are more likely to go on parental leave

List 2

(i) statistical discrimination

(ii) employment discrimination

(iii) compensating differentials

(iv) occupational discrimination

4. Occupational Segregation by Gender

Suppose the economy consists of two industries with purely competitive labour markets: A and B. Labour is more productive in A, as shown by the MRP curves in the two diagrams below. There are 100 workers; 50 men and 50 women. They supply their labour no matter what the wage level is. Men and women are equally productive workers, but at present the groups are completely segregated with the men working in A and the women in B.

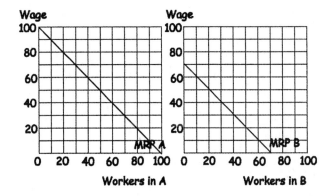

(a) Show the (vertical) supply curves of labour in A and B on the graph.

(b) The wage rate for men will be $_____, and the wage rate for women will be $_____ in this complete segregation situation.

(c) If the causes of segregation are eliminated, and men and women are both free to work in either sector, then (men, women) _____ will move into sector (A, B) ___. The result will be a (rise, drop) _____ in the wage rate in A, and a _____ in the wage rate in B, until wages are equalized in both sectors.

(d) Show the equilibrium (vertical) supply curves of labour for A and B given that labour is fully mobile between the two sectors.

(e) In equilibrium there will be _____ workers employed in A, and _____ workers employed in B. The wage rate will be $_____ in both sector A and sector B.

(f) This question is an example of the _____ model which shows that immobility of workers can lead to job _____ and lower wages for the group concentrated in a sector with lower productivity.

(g) On the graph, show as "+A" the area showing increased output in the industry gaining workers, and "-B" the area showing decreased output in the industry losing workers.

(h) Does total output from both industries combined end up larger or smaller by eliminating segregation?

Discussion Questions

1. How does the degree of income inequality in Canada compare with other nations, such as the United States, South Africa, or Norway? What factors do you think explain the differences?

2. Has the distribution of income changed much in Canada during the past 40 years? What does this imply about the efficiency of Canada's schemes for income redistribution?

3. If a nation's Lorenz curve becomes more sharply bowed over time, what does that indicate? What happens to the Gini coefficient in this case?

4. In your view, is there any difference between a 19-year-old college student being below the low income cutoff, and a 39-year-old retail clerk, working full-time, and parent of three, being below the cutoff? Do these cases present different implications for policy-makers attempting to combat poverty?

5. State the case for an equal distribution of income and the case for an unequal distribution. What are the assumptions underlying each point of view?

6. How is poverty currently defined in Canada? What are the reasons for defining poverty in this way? What are the problems with this definition?

7. What characteristics — other than the small incomes they have to spend — do the greatest concentrations of the poor families of the nation tend to have?

8. Why does poverty in Canada tend to be invisible or hidden?

9. What are the three goals or objectives of any welfare plan? Explain why these goals are in conflict.

10. Suggest some policies that the Canadian government might adopt to significantly reduce income inequality. For each of your suggestions, would you support such a change? Are your reasons normative or positive?

11. What are the aspects or forms of discrimination that contribute to a substantial earnings gap when comparing Canadian women and men? Other than discrimination, what factors might explain the gap?

Answers

Quick Quiz
1. (b) p. 382
2. (c) pp. 382-383
3. (c) p. 383
4. (d) p. 384-386
5. (c) pp. 385-386
6. (b) p. 389
7. (d) pp. 389-390
8. (c) p. 390
9. (c) p. 391
10. (d) p. 392
11. (a) p. 393
12. (c) p. 394
13. (d) p. 394
14. (c) p. 395
15. (a) pp. 397-398

Fill-in Questions
1. absolute, relative
2. Lorenz; (a) families, income; (b) lower, upper; (c) more; diagonal
3. (a) utility; (b) output (or income)
4. equality, efficiency (either order); (a) smaller; (b) more
5. (a) young; (b) unattached individuals; (c) females; (d) educated; (e) large
6. (a) Old Age Security; (b) Guaranteed Income Supplement; (c) Canada Pension Plan; (d) Employment Insurance
7. minimum annual, benefit-loss

True-False
1. T
2. F there is significant income mobility, but over periods longer than one year
3. F somewhat more equal, but not much more
4. T it is based on a percentage of income spent on food, clothing, and shelter
5. T in before tax income, this is about the correct ratio
6. T
7. F a low benefit-loss ratio means that a small percentage of the benefit is deducted when additional income is earned
8. F OAS is universal whereas GIS is received only by those with lower incomes
9. F the lower women's wages will be
10. F statistical discrimination is often profitable
11. T thus, they have poorer opportunities to create acquire human capital

Multiple-Choice
1. (d) see Table 16-1
2. (b) see Table 16-1
3. (c) considering that 50 years have passed, the data is remarkably stable
4. (c) this would also imply lower share of income for top quintile
5. (d)
6. (b) the income tax system (moderately) reduces income inequality
7. (b)
8. (a)
9. (b) the last dollar taken from Carla and given to Robert would change utility in the society by (+8) + (− 5)=+3
10. (d) inherited wealth is a source of inequality, so taxing such wealth would reduce one advantage
11. (c)
12. (a)
13. (d) the others are not universal
14. (b) because it is subject to a means test
15. (b) 6,000/.25 = 24,000
16. (d)
17. (d) because of the benefit reduction as a function of earned income
18. (d) about 10.9% of the population was below the low income cutoff in 2000
19. (d)
20. (a) he is using a stereotype as a predictor (based on group characteristics rather than the actual characteristics of the individual)
21. (a) the bigger this coefficient is, the stronger the taste for discrimination
22. (c) training seminars build human capital
23. (b) the size of this cost determines the discrimination coefficient

Problems and Projects
1. (a) (1) Column 4: 18, 30, 44, 61, 80, 91, 100;
(2) Column 5: 4, 10, 22, 36, 51, 71, 100; (b) (1)
30, 10; (2) 20, 49; (g) A/(A+B); (h) smaller, bigger,
smaller, less

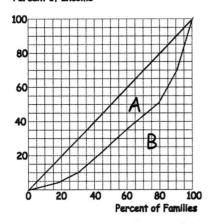

2. (a) Transfer payment: 4,000, 3,000, 2,000,
1,000, 0; Total Income: 9,000, 13,000, 17,000,
21,000, 25,000; (1) 4,000, (2) 25,000; (b) Transfer
payment: 3,750, 2,500, 1250, 0; Total Income:
6,250, 7,500, 8,750, 10,000; (1) 10,000, (2)
2,500; (c) (1) 15,000; (2) 18,750; (d) (1) greater,
greater; (2) greater; (3) increase, decrease
3. (a) (iii); (b) (iv); (c) (ii); (d) (i)
4. (b) 50; 20; (c) women, A; drop, rise; (e) 65, 35,
35; (d) crowding, segregation; (e) larger, because
area A is bigger than area B

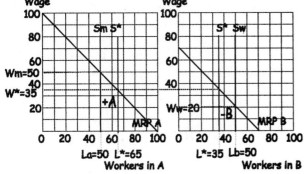

Chapter 17 Government and Market Failure

Overview

Market failure is said to occur when private markets do not generate the socially optimal allocation of resources. In such cases, there may be a role for government intervention to improve upon market outcomes. This chapter covers three types of market failure (public goods, externalities, and information asymmetries) as well as the economics of solid-waste disposal and recycling.

Whereas a private good is characterized by rivalry and excludability, a public good is the opposite: it is non-rivalrous and non-excludable. Because of the free rider problem created by these characteristics, markets will underproduce public goods unless government is directly involved in supplying the product or otherwise encouraging its production. Using benefit-cost analysis, government can determine which public goods to provide, and what level to provide.

An externality, or spillover effect, occurs when a benefit or cost accrues to a third party that is external to a market transaction. Spillover costs lead to overproduction and overallocation of resources, whereas spillover benefits cause underproduction and underallocation of resources. There are several solutions, depending on the circumstances. The Coase theorem suggests that individual bargaining can settle externality problems if property rights are clearly defined, few people are involved, and bargaining costs are negligible. In other situations, lawsuits, trade in externality rights, or government intervention via direct controls, taxes, and subsidies are the best solutions. The discussion emphasizes our worst externality problem – that of pollution – and how it arises in a "tragedy of the commons" situation.

Solid-waste disposal creates significant negative externalities which have led governments to encourage recycling through incentives to supply recycled material, and to demand recycled inputs for use in manufacturing. We hope Canada and other nations can harness market incentives to achieve the reductions in greenhouse emissions negotiated in the Kyoto Protocol.

The third class of market failure is asymmetric information. A market will not function efficiently if the sellers have critical information unavailable to buyers, or vice versa. For example, consumers may be cheated on the quality of products if sellers are dishonest and exploit their information advantage. The consequences range from complete collapse of markets (e.g. the gasoline case), to outright life-threatening situations (e.g. the surgery case). Sometimes it is sellers that are vulnerable to being cheated; for example, sellers of insurance are subject to adverse selection and moral hazard, and workers (suppliers of labour) are vulnerable to working under unsafe conditions. Consequences can range from collapse of insurance markets to unacceptable risks of workplace injuries and deaths. Government solutions to these problems include regulation of quality and safety standards, information disclosure rules, measurement standards, etc.

The common message throughout this chapter is that – for a variety of reasons – markets can fail to operate efficiently and in the best interests of society unless government plays some strategic role.

Chapter Outline

17.1 Public Goods

◇ What is a public good?

◇ How is the optimal quantity of a public good determined?

◇ Why are public goods prone to market failure?

• A public good is non-rivalrous and non-excludable — once it is provided for one person it is available for all.

• The demand for a public good is found by adding the prices that all individuals are willing to pay for the good.

• The supply of a supply of a public good is its marginal-cost curve.

• Individuals have an incentive to conceal their preferences for public goods, since they can be "free riders" (enjoying the benefits if someone else pays to provide the good. Thus, the market demand curve will understate the collective benefit from provision of the good.

• Therefore, private firms cannot profit from supplying public goods, so the market system will underproduce public goods.

• If the true demand by each individual for the public good is known, a collective demand schedule is found by adding the prices that people are willing to pay for the last unit of the public good at each possible quantity demanded. Another way of expressing this is to vertically sum the demand curves (or willingness to pay curves) for all individual consumers.

• The optimal production of a public good is given at the intersection of the collective demand (or marginal benefit) curve and the supply (or marginal cost) curve.

• If the marginal benefit exceeds the marginal cost, there is an underallocation of resources to the public good. This is likely to be the case in the absence of government intervention.

• Government may use cost-benefit analysis to decide whether a project is worth undertaking, and if so, to what extent. Additional resources should be allocated only so long as the marginal benefit to society from using the additional resources for the project exceeds the marginal cost to society of the additional resources.

➲ As you work with this chapter, think carefully about the role of government. One lesson here is that one should not underestimate the market's ability to provide private solutions to market failures, but another lesson is clearly that market failure problems create very important roles for government.

Quick Quiz

1. Which of the following is most clearly non-rivalrous in consumption?
  (a)   a fishing rod
  (b)   a haircut
  (c)   a milkshake
  (d)   a television program

2. If some people do not bother to vote, relying instead on others to vote for the best candidates for government office, this is an example of:
  (a)   the free rider effect
  (b)   an external cost
  (c)   a spillover cost
  (d)   a government failure

3. In deciding how much wilderness land to protect, the government of British Columbia should protect land up to the point where:
  (a)   the net benefit is maximized
  (b)   the marginal social benefit is maximized
  (c)   the marginal social benefit equals the marginal social cost
  (d)   both (a) and (c)

17.2   Externalities Revisited

◇ What is an externality?

◇ Why do externalities often lead to market failure?

◇ What are some ways to deal with externalities?

• Market failure can arise from externalities or spillovers, where a benefit or cost accrues to some third party that is external to a market transaction.

• Negative externalities, such as pollution, cause external (or spillover) costs.
  o   The producer's supply curve lies to the right of the "full-cost" supply curve because the producer ignores the spillover cost. Therefore too many resources are devoted to the production activity, and there is overproduction.

• Positive externalities, such as inoculations against communicable diseases, cause external (or spillover) benefits.
  o   The consumers' demand curve lies to the left of the "full-benefit" demand curve because the buyers ignore the spillover benefits. Therefore too few resources are allocated to the activity, resulting in underproduction.

• Various approaches are used to solve externality problems. Some of these solutions do not directly involve government.
  o   Individual bargaining can be used to correct externalities. The Coase theorem suggests that private bargaining can overcome the externality problem where

(1) property rights are clearly defined, (2) the number of people involved in bargaining is small, and (3) costs of bargaining are negligible. For many important externalities (e.g. global warming), these conditions are not met, so this approach will not work.

o Clearly specified property rights specifying liability rules and allowing for lawsuits by injured parties can induce firms to limit activities that cause negative externalities. Given that legal action can be expensive, slow and of uncertain outcome, this solution is not practical in all situations, and is certainly not a perfect solution.

• When externalities affect many people, or there are significant community interests at stake, direct government intervention may be the best approach.

o Direct controls can ban or limit activities that produce negative externalities. The goal is to reduce the supply of an externality-creating product to the level of allocative efficiency.

o Specific taxes can curb activities that produce negative externalities. By increasing the cost per unit of production, taxes can decrease supply so that equilibrium output occurs at the level of allocative efficiency.

o In the case of large spillover benefits spread over many people government actions may correct for the underallocation of resources by: (1) offering subsidies to buyers to encourage consumption of a good, or (2) offering subsidies to producers to encourage production of a good, or (3) government may itself produce a good.

• The problem known as the "tragedy of the commons" occurs when a resource that we own in common is ruined or wasted because the lack of private ownership gives people an incentive to abuse or neglect the resource. Prime examples are pollution of common property such as air and water, and overuse of fishing grounds and parks.

• One solution to the pollution problem is to create a market for externality rights.

o Government might set a maximum permitted amount of pollution, and then allocate rights or permits based on willingness to pay.

o The permitted amount of pollution would be rationed to those polluters who are willing to pay the most.

• It is not economically efficient to eliminate totally a negative externality such as pollution. For society the optimal reduction occurs where the marginal cost to society and the marginal benefit of reducing the externality are equal (MB = MC).

➲ Table 17-3 is a useful summary of methods of dealing with externality problems. Note the variety of interventions available to government, including imaginative ways to harness market incentives.

Quick Quiz

4. Private markets would tend to produce too much output for goods whose production involves:
(a) external benefits
(b) external costs
(c) either external costs or benefits
(d) both external costs and external benefits

5. In order to reduce the level of activity of a factory that produces noise pollution, government might:
(a) tax the product of the factory
(b) subsidize the consumers of the factory's product
(c) subsidize the factory's production
(d) any of the above

6. The solution to externalities proposed by Coase may be rendered impractical in situations where:
(a) only a few people are involved
(b) property rights are clearly specified
(c) bargaining costs are significant
(d) any of the above

7. Of the following, the best example of a common property resource that is prone to the "tragedy of the commons" problem is:
(a) the ozone layer
(b) a car
(c) a book
(d) a house

17.3   The Economics of Solid-waste Disposal

⬦ How do economic incentives influence recycling behaviour?

◈ How could economic incentives be applied under the Kyoto Protocol?

• Solid waste disposal is a large and growing problem because of the high opportunity costs of land and the negative externalities created by dumps.

• Government can use a variety of taxes or subsidies as demand or supply incentives to stimulate the market for recycled products and thereby encourage recycling.

• Global warming due to excessive carbon dioxide and other gas emissions led industrially advanced nations to agree to the 1997 Kyoto Protocol to cut greenhouse gas emissions. The plan includes a system of tradable emissions credits.

• Though Canada ratified the agreement in 2002, the Kyoto Protocol faces many challenges yet, not the least of which is the fact that the United States has chosen not to sign, and the large developing economies of India and China are exempt from the limits.

• Economists stress that even measures to fight global warming should be weighed in terms of costs and benefits to society. The market system will be able to respond to many changes in the structure of the economy resulting from global warming, but there would be many transition costs.

Quick Quiz

8. To encourage recycling of newspapers, the government could:

 (a) tax the cutting of trees

 (b) subsidize newspaper companies that use recycled paper

 (c) subsidize companies that collect and process used newspapers

 (d) any of the above

9. Which statement concerning the Kyoto Protocol is correct?

 (a) all major developed nations have agreed to follow its provisions

 (b) some developing countries are exempt from its emission restrictions

 (c) its goal is to cap greenhouse gas emissions by industrial nations at their 1997 level,

 (d) none of the above

17.4 Information Failures

◈ What is asymmetric information?

◈ What kinds of market failures result from asymmetric information?

• Market failure can occur because of asymmetric information — unequal knowledge possessed by the parties to a market transaction.

• When information about sellers is incomplete, inaccurate, or very costly, then there will be market failure.

 o For example, consumers need accurate information about product quality of automobiles and assurance about the credentials of surgeon. The cost would be prohibitive if each buyer had to verify the claims made by auto manufacturers and alleged surgeons, so the market economy would be much less effective.

 o Government can remedy such information failures by establishing measurement standards, testing requirements, and licensing bureaus.

• Markets can also fail if sellers have inadequate information about buyers.

 o For example, insurance providers are vulnerable to problems of moral hazard and adverse selection, and workers are vulnerable to injury and other workplace hazards because they lack information about the risks.

 o Governments can address such problems by requiring information disclosure, by implementing regulations, and by defining standards that are legally enforced.

• Government intervention is not the sole solution to information problems. Businesses have devised strategies to overcome the lack of information. Franchising is a technique to help consumers overcome their lack of information. And businesses such as credit bureaus and consumer product testing agencies exist specifically to profit from providing information to other businesses.

Quick Quiz

10. Franchising is at least a partial solution to the problem of:

 (a) asymmetric information problems faced by consumers

 (b) asymmetric information problems faced by producers

 (c) free rider problems

(d)   the tragedy of the commons

11. Which is not an example of adverse selection?
  (a)   employers that provide disability insurance attract more employees with poor health
  (b)   automobile insurance companies who don't factor age into their premiums attract more very young drivers
  (c)   restaurants offering "all you can eat" attract many patrons with unusually large appetites
  (d)   all are examples of adverse selection

12. Requiring all Canadians to be covered under our health care insurance system keeps the cost per person lower by avoiding which problem that would exist under voluntary insurance?
  (a)   tragedy of the commons
  (b)   a public good
  (c)   adverse selection
  (d)   moral hazard

Terms and Concepts

cost-benefit analysis	market for externality rights
marginal cost = marginal benefit (MC = MB rule)	optimal reduction of an externality
externalities	asymmetric information
Coase theorem	moral hazard problem
tragedy of the commons	adverse selection problem

Fill-In Questions

1. A public good has the characteristics of _____ and _____. Once a public good is produced, the benefits flowing from the good cannot be confined to the purchaser and result in a _____ effect. Because benefits can be obtained if someone else purchases the good, buyers (will, will not) _____ reveal their true preferences. The market demand curve for a public good will be significantly _____.

2. The collective demand curve for a public good indicates the combined willingness to _____ by all the individuals consuming an extra unit of the public good, and is constructed as a (horizontal, vertical) _____ sum of all the individual demand curves.

3. Spillovers occur when benefits or costs associated with the production or consumption of a good impact on a _____ party. Spillovers are also called _____.

4. The Coase theorem suggests that when there are externalities in situations where _____ are clearly defined, the number of people involved is _____, and bargaining costs are _____, then government intervention (is, is not) _____ required because the parties involved can _____ privately.

5. The legal system is important for settling externality disputes between parties because it specifies _____ rights and specifies _____ rules that can be used for lawsuits.

6. One method to remedy a negative externality such as pollution is to create a market for _____ .

7. A specific tax on a pollution-producing substance would shift its supply curve to the (left, right) _____, raise equilibrium _____, and _____ the equilibrium output.

8. Government can encourage recycling by stimulating the market for recycled inputs by (subsidizing, taxing) _____ the use of recycled inputs, and _____ the use of original inputs.

9. Markets can produce information failures when information about sellers is incomplete or obtaining the information is very _____. To overcome these deficiencies, government establishes _____ for measurement or quality. In the medical market, the government protects consumers by _____ physicians.

10. Inadequate information about buyers can lead to two problems. First, after a contract is signed, if a buyer alters her or his behaviour in a way that is costly to the seller, then a _____ problem has arisen. Second, if buyers withhold information from sellers that would impose a large cost on sellers, then an _____ problem has been created.

11. The _____ problem eliminates the pooling of high and low risk, which is the basis for profitable _____. Governments overcome this problem by requiring _____ participation in social insurance schemes.

12. Another example of information failure occurs in labour markets where there is incomplete or inadequate information about workplace _____. The government will intervene in these situations to publish _____ or to enforce _____.

True-False

Circle T if the statement is true, F if it is false.

1. For public goods the free-rider problem occurs when people can receive the benefits of a good without contributing to the cost of providing it. **T F**

2. When determining the demand for a public good, we add the prices various individuals are willing to pay for the last unit at each quantity demanded. **T F**

3. When spillover costs exist, private costs do not fully reflect all the costs flowing from the transaction. **T F**

4. In private markets, resources are overallocated to the production of goods that confer spillover benefits. **T F**

5. The Coase theorem states that as long as private property rights exist, the market system will correct for the presence of externalities without government interference. **T F**

6. The optimal amount of pollution abatement occurs when the marginal benefit from further pollution reduction is zero. **T F**

7. The market system penalizes the socially conscious firm in comparison to its polluting competitors. **T F**

8. Taxes imposed on products that create pollution will lower the marginal cost of production and increase supply. **T F**

9. The "tragedy of the commons" results from an incentive problem when private property rights do not exist. **T F**

10. In the market for pollution rights, if a government sets a fixed level for pollution, the supply curve of pollution rights will be perfectly elastic. **T F**

11. The economically efficient level of pollution is zero, so the government is pursuing an inefficient solution when it issues pollution rights. **T F**

12. If the government mandates that newsprint must be made up of 50% recycled products, the price of a newspaper would rise, other things being equal. **T F**

13. Quality inspection of beef by the government may be justified on the grounds that it reduces the costs of obtaining information in the marketplace. **T F**

14. If the provision of deposit insurance encourages banks to invest in more risky business ventures, then it has created a moral hazard. **T F**

Multiple-Choice

Circle the letter that corresponds to the best answer.

1. A spillover cost exists when:
 (a) a part of the cost of a transaction is placed on an uninvolved third party
 (b) a part of the cost of a transaction is paid for by the government
 (c) the private and social costs of production are equal
 (d) marginal cost is above average cost

2. If external benefits accompany the production of a good:
 (a) resources will be overallocated to the production of the good
 (b) resources will be underallocated to the production of the good
 (c) a tax on the production of the good will result in the optimum production of the good
 (d) the market demand curve overstates the total benefits from consuming the good

3. Government could promote the optimal output of a good whose production causes pollution by:
- (a) banning production of the good
- (b) taxing the production of the good
- (c) subsidizing consumers of the good
- (d) subsidizing producers of the good

4. According to the Coase theorem:
- (a) government intervention is required to overcome the misallocation of resources when spillovers are present
- (b) the best way to remedy negative externalities is to create pollution rights
- (c) public goods should be financed by the government with tax revenue generated by a progressive tax
- (d) negative externalities can be solved through bargaining if one party to the dispute has clearly defined property rights, affected parties are few, and bargaining costs are small.

5. An emission fee levied against polluters will:
- (a) encourage the use of pollution-abatement equipment
- (b) eliminate pollution
- (c) reduce the revenues of governments that levy the fee
- (d) externalize the internal costs of pollution

6. An increase in the demand for a fixed quantity of pollution rights will:
- (a) increase both the quantity of pollutants discharged and the market price of pollution rights
- (b) increase the quantity discharged and have no effect on the market price
- (c) have no effect on the quantity discharged and increase the market price
- (d) have no effect on either the quantity discharged or the market price

7. User charges imposed on those who drive on urban expressways would tend to:
- (a) relieve congestion on the expressways
- (b) discourage the use of public transportation facilities
- (c) reduce the funds available for the expansion of the expressway system
- (d) do all of the above

8. Public goods differ from private goods in that public goods are characterized by:

- (a) non-rivalry in consumption
- (b) non-excludability
- (c) both (b) and (c)
- (d) none of the above

Answer the next three questions on the basis of the following information for a public good. Qd1 and Qd2 represent the quantities of the public good demanded at each price by individuals 1 and 2, the only two people in society. Qs represents society's supply curve for the public good.

Price	Q_{d1}	Q_{d2}	Q_s
$7	0	0	6
6	0	1	5
5	1	2	4
4	2	3	3
3	3	4	2
2	4	5	1
1	5	6	0

9. This society is willing to pay what amount for the third unit of the public good?
- (a) $7
- (b) $6
- (c) $5
- (d) $4

10. Given the supply Q_s, the optimal price and quantity of the public good in this society will be:
- (a) $7 and 5 units
- (b) $5 and 4 units
- (c) $4 and 3 units
- (d) $3 and 2 units

11. If this good were a private good instead of a public good, the total quantity demanded at the $2 price would be:
- (a) 9 units
- (b) 8 units
- (c) 7 units
- (d) 6 units

12. The "tragedy of the commons" applies to what situation?
- (a) where individuals overuse and abuse common resources
- (b) where individuals tend to "free ride" on public goods
- (c) where the harm from externalities tends to affect common people rather than wealthy people
- (d) none of the above

13. The Kyoto Protocol deals with what problem?
(a)   global warming
(b)   oil spills
(c)   endangered species
(d)   nuclear power

14. The optimal amount of pollution control occurs where:
(a)   pollution is eliminated
(b)   the marginal benefit from pollution control equals zero
(c)   the marginal benefit from pollution control is maximized
(d)   the marginal benefit from pollution control equals the marginal cost of the controls

15. If the government places a $40 tax on each unit of pollution produced by a firm, all of the following hold with the exception of:
(a)   the firm saves $40 for each unit of pollution it eliminates
(b)   the tax creates an incentive to reduce the amount of pollution produced
(c)   the firm will eliminate pollution completely if the cost of eliminating the last unit is less than $40
(d)   the profits of the firm will decrease

16. The result of government legislation requiring newsprint producers to use a more costly production technique to reduce pollution will be:
(a)   an increase in production and the price of newsprint
(b)   a reduction in production and the price of newsprint
(c)   increased employment in the industries supplying inputs for newsprint
(d)   a reduction in production and an increase in the price of newsprint

17. Which of the following would tend to increase the demand for recycled glass?
(a)   an increase in the price of new glass
(b)   an increase in taxes on glass production
(c)   a decrease in interest in protecting the environment
(d)   a decrease in the price of raw materials used in the production of new glass

18. In order to encourage recycling instead of the use of landfill sites, government could do all of the following except:

(a)   place specific taxes on the inputs substitutable for the recycled input
(b)   legislate the use of recycled inputs in the production process
(c)   subsidize garbage pickup
(d)   shift its purchases toward goods produced with recycled inputs

19. In insurance, the moral hazard problem arises because:
(a)   people tend to be untruthful when asked about their medical history
(b)   large insurance payouts may prompt some people to act in an immoral manner
(c)   people who have insurance coverage tend to alter their behaviour in a way that is costly to the seller of insurance
(d)   of the random nature of accidents

20. The inclusion of a deductible clause (for example, the insured must pay for the first $250 of an accident claim) will:
(a)   decrease the problems arising out of adverse selection
(b)   decrease the moral hazard problem
(c)   increase insurance premiums
(d)   none of the above

21. If the government mandates that deposit insurance on deposits at financial institutions be increased to $240,000 for each depositor, this action would create a moral hazard problem because it may:
(a)   lead to careful screening of depositors and the source of their funds
(b)   reduce the amount of deposits made by customers
(c)   encourage the making of riskier loans
(d)   reduce bank investments in real estate

22. Based on the theory of asymmetric information, for which of the following products would the seller's reputation and brand name recognition be most important to consumers?
(a)   loose-leaf paper
(b)   shoelaces
(c)   parachutes
(d)   mystery novels

23. Which is not an example of moral hazard?
(a)   taking longer showers if the landlord pays the hot water bill
(b)   driving a car harder if it is rented

(c)   slacking off at work if eligible for EI benefits

(d)   all are examples of moral hazard

Problems and Projects

1. The Demand for a Public Good: Mosquito Control

Given below are schedules of three individuals' willingness to pay for mosquito control (a public good). Assume these three people are the only ones in society.

(a) Fill in the collective willingness to pay schedule in column (5).

(b) Given the marginal cost schedule (6), would any of the individuals buy any mosquito control on their own? _____

(c) The optimal quantity of mosquito control is _____.

(d) The total net gain to this society is $_____ if the optimal quantity of mosquito control is undertaken.

(1) Quantity	(2) Pa	(3) Pb	(4) Pc	(5) Price	(6) MC
1	$15	$8	$10	$____	$16
2	12	7	8	____	18
3	8	6	6	____	20
4	6	5	4	____	22
5	5	4	3	____	24
6	4	3	2	____	26

2. Demand for a Public Facility

Imagine that the city of Moose Jaw is considering the construction of a new arena for its Junior A hockey team. The city's estimate of the total costs and the total benefits of arenas with various different seating capacities are shown below. (All figures are in millions of dollars.)

Seats	Total Cost	MC	Total Benefit	MB	Total Net Benefit
No arena	$0	- -	$0	- -	$0
3000	12	$____	20	$____	____
4000	15	____	26	____	____
5000	17	____	29	____	____
6000	20	____	31	____	____

(a) Fill in the marginal cost, marginal benefit, and total net benefit of 3000, 4000, 5000, and 6000 seat arenas.

(b) Will it benefit the city to allocate resources to construct an arena? _____

(c) If Moose Jaw builds an arena:
(1) it should be the _____ seat version
(2) the total cost will be $_____
(3) the total benefit will be $_____
(4) the net benefit to the city will be $_____.

3. Air Pollution

Assume the atmosphere of Metropolitan Toronto is unable to reabsorb more than 1,500 tonnes of pollutants per year. The following schedule shows the price polluters would be willing to pay for the right to dispose of various quantities of pollutants.

Price (per tonne of pollution rights)	Total Quantity of Pollution Rights Demanded (tonnes)
$ 0	4,000
1,000	3,500
2,000	3,000
3,000	2,500
4,000	2,000
5,000	1,500
6,000	1,000
7,000	500

(a) If there were no emission fee, polluters would put ____ tonnes of pollutants in the air each year; this amount of pollutants would exceed the ability of nature to reabsorb them by ____ tonnes.

(b) To reduce pollution to the capacity of the atmosphere to recycle pollutants, an emission fee of $____ per tonne should be set.

(c) Were the quantity of pollution rights demanded at each price to increase by 500 tonnes, the emission fee could be increased to $____.

4.   Optimal Pollution Abatement

The marginal cost of pollution abatement differs between two industrial firms. The data for the Acrid Acid Co. and the Smoky Smelter Ltd. are shown below:

Acrid Acid		Smoky Smelter	
Unit of Abatement	MC	Unit of Abatement	MC
1	$1	1	$1
2	3	2	2
3	7	3	3
4	12	4	4
5	18	5	5
6	25	6	6

Suppose the government decides to reduce pollution by 6 units and demands a 3-unit reduction by both firms:

(a)   the total cost to Acrid will be $_____,

(b)   the total cost to Smoky will be $_____,

(c)   the total cost of the 6-unit reduction will be $_____.

Instead of the above division, suppose that Acrid was required to reduce pollution by 2 units and Smoky by 4 units:

(d)   the total cost to Acrid will be $_____

(e)   the total cost to Smoky will be $_____

(f)   the total cost of the 6-unit reduction will be $_____. By requiring equal reductions by both firms, the cost of pollution reduction (will, will not) _____ be minimized.

Suppose the government, instead of demanding a 6-unit reduction in pollution, placed a tax of $3.50 on each unit of pollution:

(g)   Acrid would reduce pollution by _____ units.

(h)   Smoky would reduce pollution by _____ units.

(i)   With the tax each firm (will, will not) _____ reduce pollution by the same amount. The firm with the highest marginal cost of pollution abatement will reduce pollution the (most, least) _____, and this (is, is not) _____ socially efficient.

5.   Trading Pollution Permits

In question 4, suppose each firm was causing 6 units of pollution and the government wanted to reduce pollution to a total of 6 units by issuing 3 transferable pollution rights to each firm.

(a)   Without trading, Acrid must abate pollution by _____ units. If it obtained one more pollution right, it would have to abate pollution by _____ units and would save $_____. If Acrid could get a pollution right for less than $_____, it would (increase, decrease) _____ net income.

(b)   Without trading, Smoky must abate pollution by _____ units. By giving up one of its pollution rights, Smoky will have to abate pollution by _____ units at an extra cost of $_____. If Smoky could get more than $_____ for a pollution right, it would (increase, decrease) _____ its net income.

(c)   Both firms would benefit if the pollution unit sold for more than $_____ but less than $_____.

(d)   Explain why only one pollution right would be exchanged between the two profit-maximizing firms.

6.   Coase Theorem

Singh has a tree that blocks Cohen's view of English Bay. The only way to clear the view is to fall the tree.

(a)   What would the Coase theorem suggest as a way to determine whether the tree should be cut down or not? Does the Coase theorem seem applicable in this case?

(b)   Why would the Coase theorem be less useful if Singh's tree obstructs the angle of view for 10 or 15 different houses in the neighbourhood?

7.   Cigarette Smoking Externality

The graph below shows the demand for cigarettes (D), the cigarette producers' supply curve (S), and the full-cost curve (St) that includes external cost to people who incur the nuisance and health risks of second-hand smoke.

(a)   If cigarette producers and consumers ignore the external costs of this product, the output of cigarettes will be _____ million packages per year.

(b)   However, this equilibrium represents an (underallocation, overallocation) _____ of resources to cigarettes, because the optimal output is _____ million pkgs/yr.

(c)   Use the graph to determine what amount of tax per package levied on producers would change the quantity to the social optimum and prevent the misallocation of resources. (Hint: show a shift in S.)

(d)   Could the same effect be achieved by taxing cigarette consumers directly?

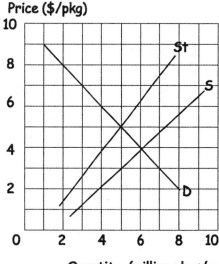

8.   Automobile Safety Externality

The next graph shows the market for an automobile safety features (perhaps anti-lock brakes) which benefits not only the driver who pays for them on his/her vehicle, but also for other drivers who are made less likely to collide with cars that have such equipment. D represents the vehicle owners' demand, and Dt is the full-benefit demand curve.

(a) What type of externality is illustrated here?

(b) On the graph show the level of output that the market will produce, and label this Qe.

(c) On the graph show the socially optimal amount of output, and label this Qo.

(d) The discrepancy between Qe and Qo indicates that the market will (overallocate, underallocate) _____ resources to auto safety features.

(e) What policies could be used to solve this misallocation?

Price

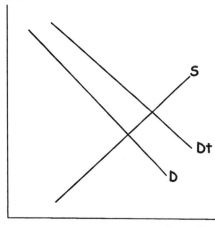

Quantity

Discussion Questions

1. What is "market failure" and what are the three major kinds of such failures?

2. What basic method does government employ in Canada to reallocate resources away from the production of private goods and toward the production of public goods?

3. Describe cost-benefit analysis and state the rules used to make a decision from a marginal and total perspective.

4. What rules can society use to determine the optimal level of pollution abatement? What are the problems with this approach?

5. Explain the "tragedy of the commons" and how this problem relates to property rights. How does the depletion of the stock of Pacific salmon or Atlantic cod relate to property rights?

6. Suppose the Canadian government decided to issue pollution rights and asked your advice on the following. What would be your advice?

(a) What volume of pollution rights should be created? Why shouldn't all pollution be eliminated?

(b) How should the pollution rights be distributed among firms and/or individuals?

(c) Should rights, once created, be purchased and sold on a "pollution rights market"?

7. The government can control pollution directly by setting pollution standards or indirectly by taxing pollution. List the advantages and problems with both methods.

8. From an economic perspective, what do the problems of global warming and your roommate's annoying music have in common? What similarities and differences are there in the types of solutions that might work?

9. Explain what is meant by the "moral hazard problem" and describe how it affects sellers. Should an insurance company be allowed to refuse insurance to a driver with numerous accident claims on his/her record? Before you answer, remember there is an externality involved (insurance not only protects the insured but also other members of the travelling public).

10. How does workplace safety become an informational problem? How might this problem be resolved by government or business?

11. From a social perspective, why is the Lojack car retrieval system better than most car alarm systems (e.g., those with blinking red lights)?

Answers

Quick Quiz

1. (d) p. 409
2. (a) p. 409
3. (c) pp. 410-412
4. (b) pp. 413-414
5. (a) pp. 415-416
6. (c) p. 414
7. (a) p. 418
8. (d) p. 423
9. (b) pp. 423-424
10. (a) pp. 425-426

11. (d) pp. 427-428
12. (c) pp. 427-428

Fill-in Questions
1. buyers, sellers (either order)
2. ceteris paribus
1. non-rivalry, non-excludability, free rider, will not, understated
2. pay, vertical
3. third, externalities
4. property rights, small, negligible, is not, bargain (or contract)
5. property, liability
6. externality rights
7. left, price, decrease
8. subsidizing, taxing
9. expensive, standards, licensing
10. moral hazard, adverse selection
11. adverse selection, insurance, universal
12. safety, information, standards

True-False
1. T
2. T
3. T
4. F underallocated
5. F there are two other conditions: small number of parties affected, and negligible bargaining costs
6. F where marginal benefit of further abatement equals marginal cost
7. T this firm will incur extra costs, and lower profits, in an attempt to deal with pollution
8. F increase marginal cost and reduce supply
9. T people selfishly exploit the resource and have no incentive to conserve or maintain it
10. F perfectly inelastic
11. F efficient level is where MB = MC for abatement; this is most likely not where pollution is zero
12. T if newspaper producers are forced to produce papers in a different way from normal, it will raise their costs
13. T consumers are less well informed about meat quality than suppliers are
14. T the existence of the insurance causes them to behave in a way that places greater risk on the insurer

Multiple-Choice
1. (a)
2. (b)
3. (b) the output should be reduced; not to zero, but to the point where society's MC = MB

4. (d)
5. (a) to the extent that abatement is cheaper than paying the emission fee
6. (c) the total amount that can be discharged is fixed but the rights
7. (a) less cars would use these expressways
8. (c)
9. (a) 4+3
10. (b) MB for the 4th unit = 2+3 = 5; this is also price at which Qs = 4
11. (a)
12. (a)
13. (a)
14. (d)
15. (a) the firm saves $40 less the MC of pollution abatement
16. (d) the firm's MC will shift upward
17. (a) new and recycled glass are substitutes
18. (c) subsidizing garbage pickup would increase the amount of waste going to landfill sites
19. (c) once insured against a loss the person may take chances that raise the risk of that loss occurring
20. (b) with a deductible there is still some incentive for the insured party to take care to prevent a loss
21. (c) banks would be able to risk lending money to riskier borrowers knowing that depositors now have more insurance protection in case the bank can't meet its obligations
22. (c) the quality of a parachute is difficult to judge until one uses it; if it turns out to be defective the consequences are dire
23. (d) being insured or otherwise protected from the cost of an action creates incentive to take less care or put in less effort

Problems and Projects
1. (a) $33, 27, 20, 15, 12, 9; (b) no, MB < MC for every individual; (c) 3, where collective MB = MC; (d) (33+27+20)-(16+18+20) = 26.
2. (a) MC: $12, 3, 2, 3; MB: $20, 6, 3, 2; (b) Yes; (c) (1) 5000, (2) $17 million, (3) $29 million, (4) $12 million.
3. (a) 4,000, 2,500; (b) 5,000; (c) 6,000
4. (a) $11; (b) $6; (c) $17; (d) $4, (e) $10; (f) $14; will not; (g) 2; (h) 3; (i) will not; least, is.
5. (a) 3, 2, $7; $7, increase (b) 3, 4, $4; $4, increase (c) $4, $7 (d) For the next pollution right Smoky would have to charge at least $5 to cover the opportunity cost, whereas Acrid would only be willing to pay $3, so the trade is not mutually beneficial.

6. (a) bargaining between the individuals; if property rights are specified, then yes, since numbers are few and transactions costs seem to be low; (b) the increased numbers raise transactions costs

7. (a) 6; (b) overallocation, 5; (c) the S curve will shift upwards to S+tax; this is a tax of $2 per package; (d) yes: a $2/pkg tax on consumers will shift the D curve down by $2, causing it to intersect S at Q_o.

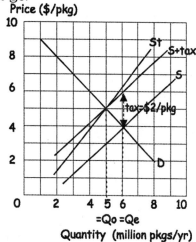

8. (a) spillover benefit: (b) Q_e is where S=D; (c) Q_o is where S=Dt; (d) underallocate; (c) give a subsidy to producers or consumers of the safety feature, have government provide the good directly, or have minimum safety equipment standards for all cars

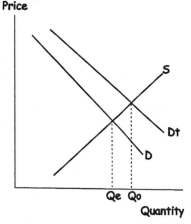

Chapter 18

Public Choice Theory and the Economics of Taxation

Overview

Chapter 17 discussed market failure problems and made the case for government intervention to correct the resulting resource misallocations. Chapter 18 takes the opposite perspective, examining instances of government failure or inefficiency. The explanation is based on public choice theory, which is the economic analysis of public decision-making. The chapter also presents some basic concepts of public finance, including the principles of taxation and the effects of particular kinds of taxes. The chapter ends with a look at recent Canadian tax reforms.

Government decision-making in Canada depends on democratic processes that rely heavily on a majority-voting rule. Even though democracy is probably the best system, a majority-voting rule can produce inefficient or inconsistent results because majority voting does not reflect the intensity of individual's preferences. Action by interest groups and political logrolling can overcome the inefficiencies of majority voting but these tactics themselves may create different inefficiencies. Other problems with voting outcomes are shown in the paradox of voting and the median voter model.

There are several reasons for the failure of the public sector: (1) the special-interest effect and rent-seeking behaviour result in decisions and programs that are not in the interest of society as a whole; (2) politicians opt for programs that provide clear-cut benefits and hidden costs; (3) public choices are limited and inflexible because they tend to entail voting on "bundles" of programs; and (4) bureaucratic inefficiencies arise from a lack of the economic incentives and competitive pressures in the public sector.

A basic issue in public finance is how the burden of taxes is apportioned among members of society. Taxes can be levied based on the bene-

fits-received principle or the ability-to-pay principle. The relationship between tax burden and taxpayer incomes is also important. We learn that taxes are can be progressive, proportional, or regressive.

Supply and demand analysis reveals that those on whom a tax is levied do not necessarily pay the tax, or at least not all of it. The incidence of an excise tax for buyers and sellers depends on the elasticity of demand and supply. The model also shows how a tax creates an efficiency loss for society by reducing the production of a good that is taxed.

Chapter Outline

18.1 Revealing Preferences Through Majority Voting

◇ How are public preferences revealed through majority voting?

◇ Does majority voting lead to efficient and consistent outcomes?

• Majority voting can result in inefficient decisions. Following the majority can result in accepting projects for which total costs outweigh the benefits, or rejecting projects for which benefits outweigh the costs. The problem is that the voting mechanism – in contrast to a market mechanism – does not incorporate the strength of individual preferences.

• Interest groups and political logrolling likely offset some of the inefficiencies of majority voting.

• The paradox of voting shows that situations can arise in which the public may not be able to rank its preferences consistently through pairwise choices put to a majority vote.

• The median voter (or person holding the middle position on an issue) can determine the outcome of an election. Public decisions reflect the median view. Health care resource allocation decisions are a good example.

Quick Quiz

1. Three friends are considering buying a tent that they would share. The cost of the tent is $600 and would be shared equally. Niels values the tent $225, Will values it $210 and Tom values it $100.

   (a)   buying the tent is efficient but would not be supported under majority voting

   (b)   buying the tent is efficient and would be supported under majority voting

   (c)   buying the tent is inefficient and would not be supported under majority voting

   (d)   buying the tent is inefficient but would be supported under majority voting

2. Suppose that MPs from British Columbia agree to vote for a bill providing crop insurance for Prairie farmers in exchange for Saskatchewan MPs voting for a bill subsidizing ferries to Vancouver Island. This is an example of

   (a)   rent-seeking behaviour

   (b)   special-interest effect

   (c)   due process

   (d)   logrolling

3. The paradox of voting describes the phenomenon whereby:

   (a)   logrolling can lead to consistent choices

   (b)   paired-choice comparison of alternatives in a majority voting system may not generate decisions consistently reflecting society's preferences

   (c)   majority voting methods usually lead to results favoured by the minority of the population rather than the majority

   (d)   the majority of the votes in a democracy are cast by a minority of the voters

18.2   Government Failure

◈ What is government failure, and in what circumstances does it occur?

• The theory of public choice suggests that government failure stems from flawed incentives and decision-making processes. A government that makes decisions to maximize its chances of remaining in office will make some decisions that lead to an inefficient allocation of resources.

• Public sector decision makers are subject to pressure from special-interest groups. The power of the government to create and allocate property rights encourages rent-seeking behaviour. Since benefits are often concentrated and costs are widely distributed and not easily identified, politicians tend to support programs demanded by special-interest groups, even though the programs' costs may exceed their benefits

• Politicians tend to favour programs with clear and immediate benefits and vague costs that can be deferred.

• The political process forces voters to choose among limited and bundled choices. When the voters support one party they are accepting a whole set of programs, perhaps including some that have low priority for the voters.

• Public sector employees do not usually face the same competitive pressures to perform that prevail in the market sector. Criteria for measuring success are not easily identified for the public sector.

• The relevant comparison is not between a perfect market and a flawed government sector, or flawed market and perfect government. Instead, we should compare actual market and government institutions, taking into account their inevitable imperfections.

➲ See if you can apply the ideas from these first two sections dealing with political decision making to current events and politics in Canada. The median-voter model, logrolling, the influence of special-interest groups, rent-seeking behaviour, and limited and bundled choices are important concepts. Real world examples are plentiful.

Quick Quiz

4. If politicians favour policies that will maximize the number of votes they receive, then most likely they are:

   (a)   logrolling

   (b)   catering to special interest groups

   (c)   making decisions that maximize society's best interests

   (d)   choosing policies that benefit most citizens

5. Government is most likely to institute an economically inefficient new program if:

   (a)   its benefits are received in large amounts by a few people, and its costs are paid in small amounts by many people

(b) its benefits are received in small amounts by many people, and its costs are paid in small amounts by many people

(c) its benefits are received in small amounts by many people, and its costs are paid in large amounts by a few people

(d) its benefits are received in large amounts by a few people, and its costs are paid in large amounts by a few people

18.3 Apportioning the Tax Burden

◇ By what different principles can the burden of a tax be distributed?

• The need to finance public programs raises questions about how to distribute the tax burden. Taxes can be apportioned based on two alternative principles, both of which are subject to difficulties of measurement:

    o according to the benefits-received principle, beneficiaries of a public program should bear the cost;

    o according to the ability-to-pay principle, public programs should be financed in direct relation to one's income and wealth.

• In Canada there seems to be a social consensus in favour of universal access to health care. According to this view, it would not be acceptable to pay for health care by charging users of the system according to use (i.e. by the benefits-received-principle)

• Taxes are classified as progressive, proportional, or regressive according to whether the average tax rate increases, stays the same, or decreases as income increases.

• Canada's personal income tax is progressive, sales taxes and property taxes are regressive, and the corporate tax nominally proportional (with this tax becoming regressive if the tax is passed onto consumers).

Quick Quiz

6. Which is the best example of a scheme for paying for public goods according to the benefits-received principle is:

(a) property taxes to pay for public schools

(b) GST on movie theatre tickets to pay for general government services

(c) charging all citizens a standard monthly premium for health care insurance

(d) gasoline taxes to pay for highway construction and repair

7. Suppose a nation's income tax system produces the following results: A pays $10,000 income tax on $30,000 of income, B pays $50,000 tax on $200,000 of income, and C pays $$2 million income tax on income of $20 million. This income tax system is:

(a) progressive

(b) regressive

(c) proportional

(d) efficient

8. What is the economic argument for funding Canada's health care system more along the lines of the benefits-received principle?

(a) people who receive the benefits can also afford to pay for the services

(b) this would reduce the bureaucratic costs associated with billing and collecting

(c) universal access to health care is an inappropriate value to hold

(d) this would tend to reduce inefficient usage of the system

18.4 Tax Incidence and Efficiency Loss

◇ How do taxes affect the allocative efficiency of economy?

◇ How do the efficiency effects of taxes depend on price elasticities of demand and supply?

◇ What is the probable incidence of some of Canada's main taxes?

• The incidence of a tax refers to who ultimately pays the tax. A tax could be levied on one party, but then shifted onto someone else. Price elasticities of demand and supply determine the incidence of a sales or an excise tax. An excise tax shifts the supply curve upward by the amount of the tax and increases the price of the product. The price increase is generally less than the tax and indicates the portion of the tax paid by the buyer; the seller pays the rest.

    o Given supply, the more elastic the demand for the commodity, the greater the portion of the tax borne by the seller.

    o Given demand, the more inelastic the supply, the greater the portion of the tax borne by the seller.

• A sales or excise tax causes an efficiency loss because the tax pushes output below the optimal level reached in a competitive market.

• The burden of the tax suffered by consumers and producers is partially captured by the government as tax revenue, but some is also lost. This portion is called the deadweight loss.

• The greater the elasticities of demand and supply, the greater is the efficiency loss. Thus society's total tax burden may differ, even though two different taxes bring in the same amount of revenue.

• However, some taxes are designed to correct other problems. In such cases the efficiency loss should be weighted against other benefits of taxes (e.g. improved income redistribution, reduction of negative externalities).

• The incidence of taxes in Canada depends on the type of tax:

   o Personal income taxes are borne almost exclusively by the individuals being taxed.

   o Corporate income taxes are borne mostly by the shareholders because dividend payments drop, but firms with sufficient market power may be able to shift some of the tax (to consumers in higher prices or to resource suppliers in lower prices).

   o A sales tax such as the GST (levied on a wide range of consumer goods) will be borne mostly by consumers in higher product prices. An excise tax, levied on a particular product, is more likely to be borne only partly by the consumer because the consumer can shift spending to other goods instead.

   o Property taxes are generally borne by the property owner, except in the case of rented and business property where some of the burden can be shifted to tenants or business customers.

• Since 1987, Canada has undergone some major tax reforms.

   o In 1987 the income tax system was revamped to reduce the number of different marginal tax rates, to reduce the highest marginal tax rate, and to change the tax treatment of some transfer payments.

   o In 1991 the Goods and Services Tax (GST) replaced the federal sales tax (which applied mostly to manufactured goods). The GST is levied on the difference between the value of a firm's sales and the value of its purchases from other firms (so it is a type of value-added tax).

   o In 2000 income taxes were cut significantly through a combination of measures including: full indexation to inflation, reductions in some marginal tax rates, and reduction of the capital gains tax.

➲ The technical part of the chapter is the portion dealing with tax incidence. If elasticity is no longer clear in your mind, review Chapter 5.

Quick Quiz

9. An excise tax will:
    (a)   lower the price for consumers
    (b)   raise the price for suppliers
    (c)   create a deadweight loss
    (d)   increase output

10. The consumers bear a relatively large portion of the burden of an excise tax if:
    (a)   demand is elastic
    (b)   supply is inelastic
    (c)   both supply and demand are elastic
    (d)   none of the above: the consumer always pays the whole tax

11. Which tax did the government implement at least partly to help Canadian producers better compete with foreign producers for sales in Canada?
    (a)   the corporate income tax
    (b)   the personal income tax
    (c)   the GST
    (d)   the surtax on high incomes

Terms and Concepts

public choice theory	ability-to-pay principle
logrolling	progressive tax
paradox of voting	regressive tax
median-voter model	proportional tax
government failure	tax incidence
special-interest effect	efficiency loss of a tax
rent seeking	Goods and Services
benefits-received principle	Tax (GST)
	value-added tax (VAT)

Fill-In Questions

1. Many public decisions are made on the basis of majority voting, but:
    (a)   this procedure can produce outcomes that are _____, because projects can be accepted when public benefits are (greater than, less than) _____ total

cost, or projects defeated where total benefits are _____ than total costs.

(1) The inefficiencies of majority voting may be offset by political pressure exerted by _____ groups or by political _____.

(2) Majority voting can lead to inefficient outcomes because it fails to incorporate the strength of _____ of individual voters.

(b) Another difficulty that can result from majority voting is an _____ ranking of preferences and is called the _____ of _____.

(c) Under a majority voting rule the _____ voter is likely to determine the outcome of a vote.

2. Several possible reasons for public sector failure are that:

(a) political considerations may lead to the support of projects that maximize the probability of getting _____;

(b) instead of promoting the general interests (or welfare) of its citizens, government may promote the _____ interests of small groups;

(c) the benefits from a program or project are often (clear, hidden) _____ while its costs are frequently _____;

(d) individual voters are unable to _____ the particular quantities of each public good and service they wish the public sector to provide;

(e) there are weak _____ to be efficient in the public sector and no way to _____ the efficiency of the public sector.

3. With a progressive tax, the tax rate _____ as income increases; the tax rate decreases with increasing income for a _____ tax; and with a proportional tax the _____ stays the same as income increases.

4. When a sales tax is levied on a commodity, the amount of the tax borne by the buyers of the commodity is equal to the amount the _____ of the commodity rises as a result of the tax. The incidence of the tax depends upon the price _____ of _____ and _____.

(a) The buyer's portion of the tax is larger the (more, less) _____ elastic the demand and the _____ elastic the supply.

(b) The seller's portion of the tax is larger, the _____ elastic the demand and the _____ elastic the supply.

5. The Goods and Services Tax (GST) is a type of _____-added tax. The tax rate is applied to the _____ between the value of a firm's sales and the value of its _____ from other firms.

True-False

Circle T if the statement is true, F if it is false.

1. Certain characteristics of the public sector hinder the government's efforts to achieve an efficient allocation of resources. **T F**

2. Since majority voting reveals the demand of the electorate, choices based on majority voting consistently lead to efficient use of society's resources. **T F**

3. Logrolling can improve economic efficiency of government decisions. **T F**

4. The paradox of voting refers to the idea that, in a majority rule election, the median voter will likely determine the outcome. **T F**

5. Even though the market economy may not always result in an efficient allocation, it does not follow that the political process will necessarily yield superior results. **T F**

6. According to the median-voter model, people will have an incentive to move to political jurisdictions where the median voter's preferences are similar to their own. **T F**

7. Rent-seeking behaviour occurs when one group seeks the transfer of wealth from others with the assistance of the government. **T F**

8. The limited-choice, bundled-goods problem refers to the inability of individual voters to select the precise bundle of public goods and services that best satisfies the citizen's wants. **T F**

9. According to the benefits-received principle, all users of services should pay equally for them. **T F**

10. According to the ability-to-pay principle, people should be taxed according to their income or wealth. **T F**

11. Applying the benefits-received principle to funding health care would compromise the goal of universal access to health care.   **T F**

12. For a tax to be regressive, the amount paid in taxes represents a smaller percentage of income as income increases.   **T F**

13. An excise tax causes an efficiency loss because the equilibrium quantity is reduced from the competitive market equilibrium quantity. **T F**

Multiple-Choice

Circle the letter that corresponds to the best answer.

1. Deficiencies in the processes used to make collective decisions and economic inefficiencies caused by government are the primary focus of:
(a)   public finance
(b)   public choice theory
(c)   the study of tax incidence
(d)   the study of tax shifting

2. Majority voting may produce inefficient economic outcomes because:
(a)   of poor voter turnout
(b)   different voters have different preferences about the proposals they are voting on
(c)   majority voting fails to incorporate the intensity of preferences of individuals
(d)   politicians do not keep election promises

3. Three friends are considering buying a camping stove that they will share. The cost of the stove is $300 and would be shared equally between them. Alison values the stove $150, Kate values it $80 and Kristy values it $90.
(a)   buying the stove is efficient, but would not be supported under majority voting
(b)   buying the stove is efficient, and would be supported under majority voting
(c)   buying the stove is inefficient, and would not be supported under majority voting
(d)   buying the stove is inefficient, and would be supported under majority voting

Questions 4 through 7 are based on the following table, which shows the ranking of three public goods by three voters A, B, and C.

Public Good	Voter A	Voter B	Voter C
Pool	2	3	1
Road	3	1	2
Daycare	1	2	3

4. In a choice between a pool and a road:
(a)   a majority of voters favour the pool
(b)   a majority of voters favour the road
(c)   a majority of voters favour both the pool and the road
(d)   there is not a majority of voters for either good

5. In a choice between a road and daycare:
(a)   a majority of voters favour the road
(b)   a majority of voters favour daycare
(c)   a majority of voters favour both the road and daycare
(d)   there is not a majority of voters for either good

6. In a choice between daycare and a pool:
(a)   a majority of voters favour the pool
(b)   a majority of voters favour daycare
(c)   a majority of voters favour both daycare and the pool
(d)   there is not a majority of voters for either good

7. What do the rankings in the table indicate about choices made under majority rule? Majority voting:
(a)   reflects irrational preferences
(b)   can produce inconsistent choices
(c)   can produce consistent choices in spite of irrational preferences
(d)   results in economically efficient outcomes since everyone had a vote to indicate their preferences

8. The suggestion that the middle position will be chosen under majority voting is called:
(a)   the paradox of voting
(b)   the special-interest effect
(c)   logrolling
(d)   the median voter model

9. All of the following can be considered rent-seeking behaviour except:
(a)   political pressure by farm groups to set an effective floor price for an agricultural good

(b) actions aimed at increasing subsidies for the Canadian book publishing industry

(c) actions aimed at eliminating tariffs on foreign automobiles

(d) all are examples of rent-seeking

10. A government seeking to support initiatives that have clear benefits and hidden costs might support:

(a) eliminating a tariff on industrial chemicals

(b) make tuition free for all post-secondary students

(c) institute a gun registry program with gun owners responsible for paying the registration costs

(d) ban fishing for Atlantic cod to allow the fish stocks to replenish themselves over a period of decades

11. Which of the following is **not** among the reasons given in the textbook for the alleged greater efficiency of the private sector?

(a) the least efficient workers in the economy gravitate to the public sector

(b) strong incentives to be efficient are largely absent in the public sector

(c) there is no simple way to measure or test efficiency in the public sector

(d) public sector agencies tend to be rewarded with larger budgets if they perform inefficiently

12. Which of the following would **not** be observed if society established taxes strictly on the benefits-received principle?

(a) the beneficiaries of public programs would pay for them

(b) families with more children would pay higher school taxes

(c) income would be redistributed from the wealthy to the poor

(d) there would be user charges for services provided by governments

13. Taxing people according to the ability-to-pay principle would be most characteristic of:

(a) a sales or excise tax

(b) a progressive income tax

(c) the GST

(d) property taxes

14. In Canada, which tax is actually progressive:

(a) GST

(b) personal income tax

(c) corporate income tax

(d) property taxes

15. A tax that collects a greater amount of revenue the higher the taxpayer's income is called:

(a) progressive

(b) proportional

(c) regressive

(d) may be any of the above

16. In a competitive market the portion of a sales tax borne by the buyer is:

(a) equal to the amount of the tax

(b) equal to 50% of the amount of the tax

(c) equal to the rise in the price of the product

(d) any of the above is possible

17. The final resting place of an excise tax is the:

(a) incidence of the tax

(b) burden of the tax

(c) destination of the tax

(d) efficiency of the tax

Answer questions 18 through 22 based on this graph showing the imposition of a per unit tax.

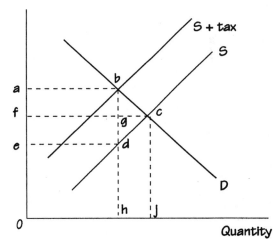

18. Before the tax is levied, the equilibrium price is:

(a) 0e

(b) 0a

(c) 0f

(d) 0b

19. The tax per unit of output is:

(a) 0a

(b) af

(c)   ef
(d)   ae

20. The consumer's burden of the tax, per unit, is:
(a)   0a
(b)   af
(c)   ef
(d)   ae

21. The tax revenue for the government is:
(a)   abgf
(b)   abde
(c)   fged
(d)   bcd

22. The efficiency loss of the tax is the area:
(a)   bgc
(b)   bdc
(c)   bcjh
(d)   abfc

23. A value-added tax would tax a firm's:
(a)   revenues from the sale of a product
(b)   revenue from sales less input costs
(c)   purchases of inputs
(d)   revenues from sales less purchases from other firms

24. The GST was introduced as a replacement for:
(a)   the federal sales tax
(b)   import duties
(c)   excise taxes on tobacco and alcohol
(d)   royalties on oil and gas production

25. The GST most closely resembles:
(a)   a personal income tax
(b)   a corporate profits tax
(c)   a consumption tax
(d)   a property tax

26. Which tax reform was among the measures taken in the February 2000 federal budget?
(a)   a reduction in the GST
(b)   the introduction of a flat tax
(c)   a new surtax on high-income earners
(d)   a reduction in the middle-income tax rate

Problems and Projects

1. Paradox of Voting
Preferences are consistent if when Project A is preferred to Project B and Project B is preferred to Project C, then Project A is preferred to Project C. The tables below illustrate two cases where the preferences of the individual voters are consistent, but majority voting on pairs of alternatives yields consistent choices in one case and inconsistent choices in the other.

Case 1	Preference Rankings		
Public Project	Voter A	Voter B	Voter C
Park	1	3	3
School	2	2	1
Dam	3	1	2

(a) In an election determined by majority vote, which project would win each of the following contests?
School vs. Dam_____
Dam vs. Park _____
School vs. Park_____

Case 2	Preference Rankings		
Public Project	Voter A	Voter B	Voter C
Park	1	2	3
School	2	3	1
Dam	3	1	2

(b) In an election determined by majority vote, which project would win each of the following contests?
School vs. Dam_____
Dam vs. Park _____
School vs. Park_____
(c) Majority voting has led to inconsistent public preferences in Case _____.

2. Comparing Tax Systems
In the table below are five levels of income and the amount of tax to be paid under two different tax systems: A and B.
(a) Compute for each tax system the average rate of taxation at each income level.
(b) Tax A is (regressive, progressive, proportional) _____ up to income level $_____ and then becomes _____. Tax B is consistently _____.

Income	Tax A		Tax B	
	Tax Paid	Average Tax Rate	Tax Paid	Average Tax Rate
$1500	$150	_____%	$300	_____%
3000	300	_____	390	_____
5000	500	_____	600	_____
7500	750	_____	825	_____
10,000	2,000	_____	1,000	_____

3. Majority Voting on Public Projects

Three small towns stand to benefit from the construction of a shared regional airport in a central location. The costs of the airport would be $60 million per year, shared equally by the three towns. Whether or not the airport is built depends on the votes cast at the regional district meeting. Each town has one vote, which it will cast simply based on whether the airport produces enough benefit for their town to cover the cost.

Case	Benefits (million $ per year)		
	Ellis	Nevin	Selby
1	17	22	27
2	8	22	27
3	17	19	27

(a) In which case(s) would the majority voting rule lead to an outcome that is efficient for the region?

(b) In which case(s) would the majority voting rule lead to an inefficient outcome, and why?

4. The Effects of an Excise Tax on Wine Producers

The graph below shows the wine market before and after the imposition of a new production tax.

(a) Which of the two supply curves is the "before tax" supply curve? _____

(b) Before the tax, the price of wine was $_____ per bottle and the quantity produced was _____ bottles per week.

(c) The amount of the tax is $_____ per bottle.

(d) After the tax, the price of wine becomes $_____ per bottle and the quantity produced becomes _____ bottles per week.

(e) The government's tax revenue is $_____ per bottle times _____ bottles per week, for a total of $_____ per week.

(f) On the graph, shade in the area of tax revenue.

(g) Of the total tax per bottle, the consumers' burden is $_____, and the producers' burden is $_____. The consumers bear a (larger, smaller) _____ share relative to the producers because the demand curve is relatively _____ and the supply curve is relatively _____.

(h) On the graph shade in the area of efficiency loss due to the tax.

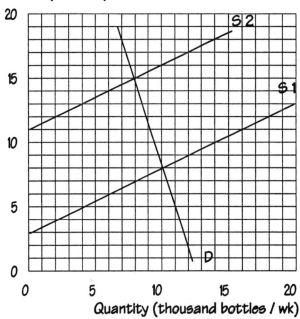

Discussion Questions

1. How do special-interest groups or the use of logrolling influence the efficiency of outcomes in the public sector? Construct an example to show that logrolling could result in an improvement in the efficiency of resource allocation.

2. What are consistent preferences? Why can there be a paradox with majority voting?

3. Describe how the median voter influences the results of majority rule elections on public issues.

4. The theory of public choice suggests that there are a number of possible causes of public sector failures. What are these causes? Explain how each would tend to result in the inefficient allocation of the economy's resources.

5. It is generally agreed that the government best provides a judicial system while beer is best provided by the private sector. Why is there disagreement on which sector should provide so many other goods and services?

6. Explain the two basic philosophies for apportioning the tax burden. What difficulties can be encountered when these two philosophies are put into practice?

7. Explain the difference between progressive, proportional, and regressive taxes. Which Canadian taxes fall into each category?

8. Define the *incidence* of a tax. Explain how the incidence of a sales or excise tax depends upon the elasticities of supply and demand.

9. Why does a firm not simply pass an excise tax on to consumers by increasing the price of the taxed item by the full amount of the tax?

10. If government wishes to raise revenue from an excise tax, should they tax a commodity that has elastic supply and demand or a commodity that has inelastic supply and demand?

11. How does an excise or sales tax produce an efficiency loss for society? How is this loss affected by the elasticity of supply or demand?

Answers

Quick Quiz
1. (d) p. 434
2. (d) p. 435
3. (b) p. 436
4. (b) p. 438
5. (a) p. 440
6. (d) pp.441-442
7. (b) pp. 442-443
8. (d) p. 442
9. (c) p. 446
10. (b) p. 445
11. (c) p. 450

Fill-in Questions
1. (a) inefficient, less than, greater than; (1) special-interest, logrolling; (2) preferences; (b) inconsistent, paradox, voting; (c) median
2. (a) re-elected; (b) special; (c) clear, hidden; (d) select; (e) incentives, test (measure)
3. increases, regressive, tax rate
4. price, elasticity, demand, supply; (a) less, more; (b) more, less
5. value, difference, purchases

True-False
1. T   these characteristics are the subject of public choice theory
2. F   for example, such voting fails to reflect the relative intensity of different individuals' preferences
3. T   sometimes, definitely not always
4. F   paradox of voting refers to potential inconsistency problem
5. T   the public sector is also subject to failure
6. T   since the median voter determines voting outcome, there is incentive to live where median voter has similar preferences to one's own
7. T
8. T
9. F   users should pay in proportion to the benefits they receive, which may not be equal
10. T
11. T   some users couldn't afford to pay
12. T
13. T   the competitive quantity maximizes the net benefits to consumers and producers

Multiple-Choice
1. (b)
2. (c)   the vote of a person with strong feelings about a proposal counts the same as the vote of person who is indifferent to the proposal
3. (a)   the camp stove is valued at $320, but two of the voters would have to pay more than their personal value
4. (a)   A and C vote for the pool
5. (a)   B and C vote for the road
6. (b)   A and B vote for daycare
7. (b)
8. (d)
9. (d)   a certain group or industry is lobbying government for a targeted benefit
10. (b)   tuition savings are a clear benefit to students, but who will bear the cost of replacing that revenue?
11. (a)   it's not the quality of the workers; it's the incentives and structures under which they work
12. (c)
13. (b)   the others are known to be regressive, which generally suggests higher taxes on those with lower ability to pay
14. (c)
15. (d)   the key is the percentage that the tax represents of income
16. (d)   depending on the elasticities of supply and demand
17. (a)
18. (c)   at the intersection of S and D
19. (d)   the vertical shift from S to S + tax
20. (b)   the increase in price to the consumer

21. (b)   tax per unit x number of units sold
22. (b)
23. (d)   a tax on the value that the firm adds to resources it buys from other firms
24. (a)
25. (c)
26. (d) this rate was to come down from 26% to 23% over five years

Problems and Projects

1.   (a) CASE 1; Winner: School; Dam; School; (b) CASE 2; Winner: School; Dam; Park; (c) CASE 2 (because for consistency the School should be preferred to the Park)
2.   (a) Tax A: 10, 10, 10, 10, 20; Tax B: 20, 13, 12, 11, 10; (b) proportional, 7500, progressive; regressive.
3.   (a) Case 1: benefits exceed costs (66 > 60) and airport approved as Nevin and Selby vote in favour; (b) Case 2: benefits are less than costs (57 < 60) but airport is approved as Nevin and Selby vote in favour; Also Case 3: benefits exceed costs (63 > 60), but Ellis and Nevin vote against.
4.   (a) S1; (b) P*=8, Q*=10,000; (c) $8, since the S curve shifts upwards by this amount; (d) P'=15, Q'=8,000; (e) 8, 8,000, 64,000; (f) shaded rectangle on graph; (g) 7, 1, larger, inelastic, elastic; (h) the triangle labeled E.

Price ($/bottle)

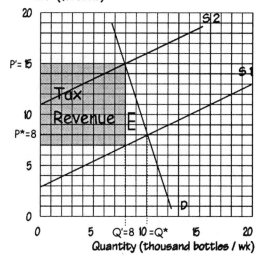

Quantity (thousand bottles / wk)

Answers to the Key Questions

Chapter 1

1-4 (Key Question) Use the economic perspective to explain why someone who is normally a light eater at a standard restaurant may become somewhat of a glutton at a buffet-style restaurant which charges a single price for all you can eat.

This behaviour can be explained in terms of marginal costs and marginal benefits. At a standard restaurant, items are priced individually—they have a positive marginal cost. If you order more, it will cost you more. You order until the marginal benefit from the extra food no longer exceeds the marginal cost. At a buffet you pay a flat fee no matter how much you eat. Once the fee is paid, additional food items have a zero marginal cost. You therefore continue to eat until your marginal benefit becomes zero.

1-8 (Key Question) Explain in detail the interrelationships between economic facts, theory, and policy. Critically evaluate this statement: "The trouble with economic theory is that it is not practical. It is detached from the real world."

Economic theory consists of factually supported generalizations about economic behaviour that can be used to formulate economic policies. Economic theory enables policymakers to formulate economic policies that are relevant to real-world goals and problems that are based upon carefully observed facts.

1-10 (Key Question) Indicate whether each of the following statements applies to microeconomics or macroeconomics:
(a), (d), and (f) are macro; (b), (c), and (e) are micro.

1-11 (Key Question) Identify each of the following as either a positive or a normative statement:
a. The high temperature today was 30 degrees.
b. It was too hot today.

c. Other things being equal, higher interest rates reduce the total amount of borrowing.
d. Interest rates are too high.
(a) and (c) are positive; (b) and (d) are normative..

1-12 (Key Question) Explain and give an illustration of (a) the fallacy of composition; and (b) the "after this, therefore because of this" fallacy. Why are cause-and-effect relationships difficult to isolate in the social sciences?
(a) The fallacy of composition is the mistake of believing that something true for an individual part is necessarily true for the whole. Example: A single auto producer can increase its profits by lowering its price and taking business away from its competitors. But matched price cuts by all auto manufacturers will not necessarily yield higher industry profits.
(b) The "after this, therefore because of this" fallacy is incorrectly reasoning that when one event precedes another, the first even necessarily caused the second. Example: Interest rates rise, followed by an increase in the rate of inflation, leading to the erroneous conclusion that the rise in interest rates caused the inflation. Actually higher interest rates slow inflation. Cause-and-effect relationships are difficult to isolate because "other things" are continually changing.

Chapter 1 - Appendix

A1-2 (Key Appendix Question) Indicate how each of the following might affect the data shown in Table A1-2 and Figure A1-2 of this appendix:
a. IU's athletic director schedules higher-quality opponents.
b. An NBA team locates in the city where IU plays.
c. IU contracts to have all its home games televised.

236

(a) More tickets are bought at each price; the line shifts to the right.

(b) Fewer tickets are bought at each price, the line shifts to the left.

(c) Fewer tickets are bought at each price, the line shifts to the left.

A1-3 (Key Appendix Question) The following table contains data on the relationship between saving and income. Rearrange these data into a meaningful order and graph them on the accompanying grid. What is the slope of the line? The vertical intercept? Interpret the meaning of both the slope and the intercept. Write the equation which represents this line. What would you predict saving to be at the $12,500 level of income?

Income (per year)`	Saving (per year)
$15,000	$1,000
0	-500
10,000	500
5,000	0
20,000	1,500

Income column: $0; $5,000; $10,000, $15,000; $20,000. Saving column: $-500; 0; $500; $1,000; $1,500. Slope = 0.1 (= $1,000 - $500)/($15,000 - $10,000). Vertical intercept = $-500. The slope shows the amount saving will increase for every $1 increase in income; the intercept shows the amount of saving (dissaving) occurring when income is zero. Equation: $S = \$-500 + 0.1Y$ (where S is saving and Y is income). Saving will be $750 at the $12,500 income level.

A1-7 (Key Appendix Question) The accompanying graph shows curve XX' and tangents at points A, B, and C. Calculate the slope of the curve at these three points.

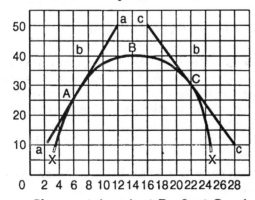

Slopes: at A = +4; at B = 0; at C = -4.

Chapter 2

2-4 (Key Graph) Classify the following Microsoft factors of production as labour, land, capital, or entrepreneurial ability: code writers for software; Bill Gates; production facility for Window CD-ROMs; "campus" on which Microsoft buildings sit; grounds crew at Microsoft campus; Microsoft corporate jet.

Labour: code writers, grounds crew; land: campus; capital: CD production facility, corporate jet; entrepreneurial ability: Bill Gates.

2-5 (Key Question) Distinguish between full employment and full production as they relate to production possibilities analysis. Distinguish between productive efficiency and allocative efficiency. Give an illustration of achieving productive efficiency, but not allocative efficiency.

Full employment occurs when all available resources are utilized; full production means that all employed resources are used to provide the maximum possible satisfaction of material wants. Both are required for an economy to be producing on the production possibilities curve. An economy that is employing all available resources but which allocates labour to unproductive tasks will operate inside the curve. Likewise, putting resources to their most productive uses but failing to employ all resources will result in an economy producing inside the curve.

Allocative efficiency means that resources are being used to produce the goods and services most wanted by society. The economy is then located at the optimal point on its production possibilities curve where marginal benefit equals marginal cost for each good. Productive efficiency means the least costly production techniques are being used to produce wanted goods and services. Examples: manual typewriters produced using the least-cost techniques but for which there is no demand; cigarettes produced using least-cost techniques but for which there are "bads" created that are not accounted for by the market.

2-6 (Key Question) Here is a production possibilities table for war goods and civilian goods:

Type of Production	Production Alternatives				
	A	B	C	D	E
Automobiles	0	2	4	6	8
Rockets	30	27	21	12	0

a. Show these data graphically. Upon what specific assumptions is this production possibilities curve based?

b. If the economy is at point C, what is the cost of one more automobile? One more rocket? Explain how this curve reflects increasing opportunity costs.

c. What must the economy do to operate at some point on the production possibilities curve?

(a) See curve EDCBA. The assumptions are full employment and productive efficiency, fixed supplies of factors, and fixed technology.

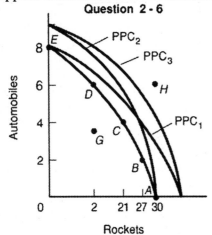

Question 2 - 6

(b) 4.5 rockets; .33 automobiles, as determined from the table. Increasing opportunity costs are

reflected in the concave-from-the-origin shape of the curve. This means the economy must give up larger and larger amounts of rockets to get constant added amounts of automobiles—and vice versa.

(c) It must obtain full employment and productive efficiency.

2-9   (Key Question) Specify and explain the shapes of the marginal-benefit and marginal-cost curves and use these curves to determine the optimal allocation of resources to a particular product. If current output is such that marginal cost exceeds marginal benefit, should more or less resources be allocated to this product? Explain.

The marginal benefit curve is downward sloping, MB falls as more of a product is consumed because additional units of a good yield less satisfaction than previous units. The marginal cost curve is upward sloping, MC increases as more of

a product is produced since additional units require the use of increasingly unsuitable factor. The optimal amount of a particular product occurs where MB equals MC. If MC exceeds MB, fewer resources should be allocated to this use. The resources are more valuable in some alternative use (as reflected in the higher MC) than in this use (as reflected in the lower MB).

2-10   (Key Question) Label point G inside the production possibilities curve you have drawn for question 6. What does it indicate? Label point H outside the curve. What does this point indicate? What must occur before the economy can attain the level of production indicated by point H?

G indicated unemployment, productive inefficiency, or both. H is at present unattainable. Economic growth—through more inputs, better inputs, improved technology—must be achieved to attain H.

2-11   (Key Question) Referring again to question 6, suppose improvement occurs in the technology of producing rockets but not in the production of automobiles. Draw the new production possibilities curve. Now assume that a technological advance occurs in producing automobiles but not in producing rockets. Draw the new production possibilities curve. Now draw a production possibilities curve that reflects technological improvement in the production of both products.

See the graph for question 2-6. PPC$_1$ shows improved rocket technology. PPC$_2$ shows improved auto technology. PPC$_3$ shows improved technology in producing both products.

Chapter 3

3-2   (Key Question) What effect will each of the following have on the demand for product B?

a. Product B becomes more fashionable.

b. The price of substitute product C falls.

c. Income declines and product B is an inferior good.

d. Consumers anticipate the price of B will be lower in the near future.

e. The price of complementary product D falls.

Demand increases in (a), (c), and (e); decreases in (b) and (d).

3-5   (Key Question) What effect will each of the following have on the supply of product B?

a. A technological advance in the methods of producing B.
b. A decline in the number of firms in industry B.
c. An increase in the price of factors required in the production of B.
d. The expectation that the equilibrium price of B will be lower in the future than it is currently.
e. A decline in the price of product A, a good whose production requires substantially the same techniques as does the production of B.
f. The levying of a specific sales tax upon B.
g. The granting of a 50-cent per unit subsidy for each unit of B produced.

Supply increases in (a), (d), (e), and (g); decreases in (b), (c), and (f).

3-7   (Key Question) Suppose the total demand for wheat and the total supply of wheat per month in the Kansas City grain market are as follows:

Thousands of bushels demanded	Price per bushel	Thousand of bushels supplied	Surplus (+) or shortage (-)
85	$3.40	72	_____
80	3.70	73	_____
75	4.00	75	_____
70	4.30	77	_____
65	4.60	79	_____
60	4.90	81	_____

a. What will be the market or equilibrium price? What is the equilibrium quantity? Using the surplus-shortage column, explain why your answers are correct.
b. Graph the demand for wheat and the supply of wheat. Be sure to label the axes of your graph correctly. Label equilibrium price "P" and the equilibrium quantity "Q."
c. Why will $3.40 not be the equilibrium price in this market? Why not $4.90? "Surpluses drive prices up; shortages drive them down." Do you agree?
d. Now suppose that the government establishes a ceiling price of, say, $3.70 for wheat. Explain carefully the effects of this ceiling price. Demonstrate your answer

graphically. What might prompt the government to establish a ceiling price?

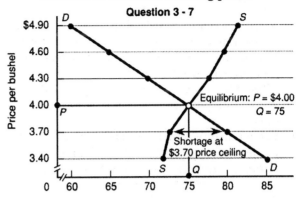

Question 3 - 7

Quantity (thousands) of bushels

Data from top to bottom: -13; -7; 0; +7; +14; and +21.

(a) P_e = $4.00; Q_e = 75,000. Equilibrium occurs where there is neither a shortage nor surplus of wheat. At the immediately lower price of $3.70, there is a shortage of 7,000 bushels. At the immediately higher price of $4.30, there is a surplus of 7,000 bushels. (See Graph top of next page.

(b) Quantity (thousands) of bushels.

(c) Because at $3.40 there will be a 13,000 bushel shortage which will drive price up. Because at $4.90 there will be a 21,000 bushel surplus which will drive the price down. Quotation is incorrect; just the opposite is true.

[d] A $3.70 ceiling causes a persistent shortage. This product may be a necessity and the government is concerned that some consumers might not being able to afford it.

3-8   (Key Question) How will each of the following changes in demand and/or supply affect equilibrium price and equilibrium quantity in a competitive market; that is do price and quantity rise, fall, remain unchanged, or are the answers indeterminate, depending on the magnitudes of the shifts in supply and demand? You should rely on a supply and demand diagram to verify answers.
a. Supply decreases and demand remains constant.
b. Demand decreases and supply remains constant.
c. Supply increases and demand is constant.
d. Demand increases and supply increases.
e. Demand increases and supply is constant.
f. Supply increases and demand decreases.
g. Demand increases and supply decreases.

h. Demand decreases and supply decreases.
(a) Price up; quantity down;
(b) Price down; quantity down;
(c) Price down; quantity up;
(d) Price indeterminate; quantity up;
(e) Price up; quantity up;
(f) Price down; quantity indeterminate;
(g) Price up, quantity indeterminate;
(h) Price indeterminate and quantity down.

3-12 *(Key Question)* What do economists mean when they say that "price floors and ceilings stifle the rationing function of prices and distort resource allocation?"

Price floors can lead to surpluses and price ceilings can lead to shortages, thus stifling the rationing function of prices, and leading to a distortion of resource allocation.

Chapter 4

4-9 *(Key Question)* Some large hardware stores such as Canadian Tire boast of carrying as many as 20,000 different products in each store. What motivated the producers of those products—everything from screwdrivers to ladders to water heaters—to make them and offer them for sale? How did producers decide on the best combinations of factors to use? Who made these factors available, and why? Who decides whether these particular hardware products should continue to get produced and offered for sale?

The quest for profit led firms to produce these goods. Producers looked for and found the least-cost combination of factors in producing their output. Factor suppliers, seeking income, made these factors available. Consumers, through their dollar votes, ultimately decide on what will continue to be produced.

4-12 *(Key Question)* What are the two characteristics of public goods? Explain the significance of each for public provision as opposed to private provision. What is the free-rider problem as it relates to public goods?

Public goods are non-rival (one person's consumption does not prevent consumption by another) and non-excludable (once the goods are produced nobody—including free riders—can be excluded from the goods' benefits). If goods are non-rival, there is less incentive for private firms to produce them – those purchasing the good could simply allow others their

the good could simply allow others their use without compensation. Similarly, if goods are non-excludable, private firms are unlikely to produce them as the potential for profit is low. The free-rider problem occurs when people benefit from the public good without contributing to the cost (tax revenue proportionate to the benefit received).

4-13 *(Key Question)* Draw a production possibilities curve with public goods on the vertical axis and private goods on the horizontal axis. Assuming the economy is initially operating on the curve, indicate the means by which the production of public goods might be increased. How might output of public goods be increased if the economy is initially functioning at a point inside the curve?

On the curve, the only way to obtain more public goods is to reduce the production of private goods (from *C* to *B*).

An economy operating inside the curve can expand the production of public goods without sacrificing private goods (say, from *A* to *B*) by making use of unemployed resources.

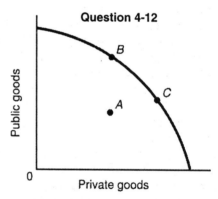

Question 4-12

4-16 *(Key Question)* The following are production possibilities tables for South Korea and Canada. Assume that before specialization and trade the optimal product mix for South Korea is alternative B and for Canada alternative D.

Product	South Korea's production possibilities					
	A	B	C	D	E	F
Radios (in 1000s)	30	24	18	12	6	0
Chemicals (tons)	0	6	12	18	24	30
Product	Canada's production possibilities					
	R	S	T	U	V	W
Radios (in 1000s)	10	8	6	4	2	0
Chemicals (tons)	0	4	8	12	16	20

a. Are comparative cost conditions such that the two areas should specialize? If so, what product should each produce?
b. What is the total gain in radio and chemical output which results from this specialization?
c. What are the limits of the terms of trade? Suppose actual terms of trade are 1 unit of radios for 1-1/2 units of chemicals and that 4 units of radios are exchanged for 6 units of chemicals. What are the gains from specialization and trade for each area?
d. Can you conclude from this illustration that specialization according to comparative advantage results in more efficient use of world resources? Explain.

(a) Yes, because the opportunity cost of radios is less (1R = 1C) in South Korea than in Canada (1R = 2C). South Korea should produce radios and Canada should produce chemicals.

(b) If they specialize, Canada can produce 20 tons of chemicals and South Korea can produce 30,000 radios. Before specialization South Korea produced alternative B and Canada alternative U for a total of 28,000 radios (24,000 + 4,000) and 18 tons of chemicals (6 tons + 12 tons). The gain is 2,000 radios and 2 tons of chemicals.

(c) The limits of the terms of trade are determined by the comparative cost conditions in each country before trade: 1R = 1C in South Korea and 1R = 2C in Canada. The terms of trade must be somewhere between these two ratios for trade to occur.
If the terms of trade are 1R = 1-1/2C, South Korea would end up with 26,000 radios (= 30,000 - 4,000) and 6 tons of chemicals. Canada would have 4,000 radios and 14 tons of chemicals (= 20 - 6). South Korea has gained 2,000 radios. Canada has gained 2 tons of chemicals.

(d) Yes, the world is obtaining more output from its fixed resources.

Chapter 5

5-2 (**Key Question**) Graph the accompanying demand data and then use the midpoints formula for Ed to determine price elasticity of demand for each of the four possible $1 price changes. What can you conclude about the relationship between the slope of a curve and its elasticity? Explain in a nontechnical way why demand is elastic in the northwest segment of the demand curve and inelastic in the southeast segment.

Product price	Quantity demanded
$5	1
4	2
3	3
2	4
1	5

See the graph accompanying the answer to 6-4. Elasticities, top to bottom: 3; 1.4; .714; .333. Slope does not measure elasticity. This demand curve has a constant slope of -1 (= -1/1), but elasticity declines as we move down the curve. When the initial price is high and initial quantity is low, a unit change in price is a *low* percentage while a unit change in quantity is a *high* percentage change. The percentage change in quantity exceeds the percentage change in price, making demand elastic. When the initial price is low and initial quantity is high, a unit change in price is a *high* percentage change while a unit change in quantity is a *low* percentage change. The percentage change in quantity is less than the percentage change in price, making demand inelastic.

5-4 (**Key Question**) Calculate total-revenue data from the demand schedule in question 2. Graph total revenue below your demand curve. Generalize on the relationship between price elasticity and total revenue.

See the graph. Total revenue data, top to bottom: $5; $8; $9; $8; $5. When demand is elastic, price and total revenue move in the opposite direction. When demand is inelastic, price and total revenue move in the same direction.

Question 5-4

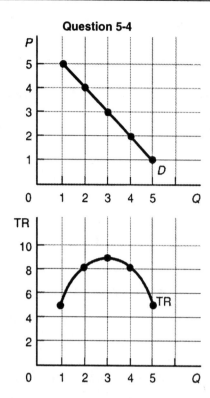

5-5   **(Key Question)** How would the following changes in price affect total revenue. That is, would total revenue increase, decline, or remain unchanged?
  a. Price falls and demand is inelastic.
  b. Price rises and demand is elastic.
  c. Price rises and supply is elastic.
  d. Price rises and supply is inelastic.
  e. Price rises and demand is inelastic.
  f. Price falls and demand is elastic.
  g. Price falls and demand is of unit elasticity.
       Total revenue would increase in (c), (d), (e), and (f); decrease in (a) and (b); and remain the same in (g).

5-6   **(Key Question)** What are the major determinants of price elasticity of demand? Use these determinants and your own reasoning in judging whether demand for each of the following products is elastic or inelastic:

(a) bottled water, (b) tooth paste; (c) Crest toothpaste; (d) ketchup, (e) diamond bracelets; (f) Microsoft Windows operating system.

Substitutability, proportion of income; luxury versus necessity, and time. Elastic: (a), (c), (e). Inelastic: (b), (d), and (f).

5-10   **(Key Question)** In November 1998 Vincent van Gogh's self-portrait sold at auction for $71.5 million. Portray this sale in a demand and supply diagram and comment on the elasticity of supply. Comedian George Carlin once mused, "If a painting can be forged well enough to fool some experts, why is the original so valuable?" Provide an answer.

The supply is perfectly inelastic—vertical—at a quantity of 1 unit. The $71.5 million price is determined where the downward sloping demand curve intersected this supply curve.

If more than one picture where available (all but one having to be a copy), the demand would likely decrease enormously.

5-12   **(Key Question)** Suppose the cross elasticity of demand for products A and B is +3.6 and for products C and D it is -5.4. What can you conclude about how products A and B are related? Products C and D?

A and B are substitutes; C and D are complements.

5-13   **(Key Question)** The income elasticities of demand for movies, dental services, and clothing have been estimated to be +3.4, +1.0, and +0.5 respectively. Interpret these coefficients. What does it mean if the income elasticity coefficient is negative?

All are normal goods—income and quantity demanded move in the same direction. These coefficients reveal that a 1 percent increase in income will increase the quantity of movies demanded by 3.4 percent, of dental services by 1.0 percent, and of clothing by 0.5 percent. A negative coefficient indicates an inferior good—income and quantity demanded move in the opposite direction.

5-15   **(Key Question)** What is the incidence of an excise tax when demand is highly inelastic? Elastic? What effect does the elasticity have on the incidence of an excise tax? The incidence of an excise tax is likely to be primarily on consumers when demand is highly inelastic and primarily on producers when demand is elastic. The more elastic the supply, the greater the incidence of an excise tax on consumers and less on producers.

5-16 (**Key Question**) Why is it desirable for ceiling prices to be accompanied by government rationing? And for price floors to be accompanied by programs that purchase surpluses, restrict output, or increase demand? Show graphically why price ceilings entail shortages and price floors result in surpluses. What effect, if any, does elasticity of demand and supply have on the size of these shortages and surpluses? Explain.

A ceiling price that is set below the equilibrium price necessarily results in the quantity demanded being greater than the quantity supplied. This creates a shortage. To ensure that the restricted supply may be shared fairly among all those desiring it, government rationing is necessary.

A floor price that is set above the equilibrium price necessarily results in the quantity supplied being greater than the quantity demanded. This creates a surplus The government must purchase the surplus (and store it and/or sell it abroad), or restrict supply to the quantity that will be bought at the floor price, or develop new uses for the product.

If the elasticity of demand and/or supply were inelastic, the shortage or surplus created by the government-set price will be less than if the demand and/or supply were elastic.

5-17 (**Key Question**) Can insurance cause over-consumption? How does insurance relate to the Canadian health care system?

Insurance removes or greatly lessens a person's budget constraint at the time the insurance is purchased, causing an over-consumption of the insured product or service. Applying this generalization to the Canadian health care system, we see in Figure 5-9b, insurance reduces the price of health care at the time of purchase from P_u to P_i, increasing the quantity consumed from Q_u to Q_i. At Q_i the marginal cost of health care is represented by point b and exceeds the marginal benefit represented by c, indicating an overallocation of resources. The efficiency loss is area cab. However, effiency is not the only criteria on which to base a society's decision to adopt, or maintain a national healthcare system; equity consideration is just as vital.

Chapter 6

6-2 (**Key Question**) Complete the following table and answer the questions below:

Units consumed	Total utility	Marginal utility
0	0	—
1	10	10
2	—	8
3	25	—
4	30	—
5	—	3
6	34	—

a. At which rate is total utility increasing: a constant rate, a decreasing rate, or an increasing rate? How do you know?

b. "A rational consumer will purchase only 1 unit of the product represented by these data, since that amount maximizes marginal utility." Do you agree? Explain why or why not.

c. "It is possible that a rational consumer will not purchase any units of the product represented by these data." Do you agree? Explain why or why not.

Missing total utility data top – bottom: 18; 33. Missing marginal utility data, top – bottom: 7; 5; 1.

(a) A decreasing rate; because marginal utility is declining.

(b) Disagree. The marginal utility of a unit beyond the first may be sufficiently great (relative to product price) to make it a worthwhile purchase.

(c) Agree. This product's price could be so high relative to the first unit's marginal utility that the consumer would buy none of it.

6-4 (**Key Question**) Columns 1 through 4 of the accompanying table show the marginal utility, measured in terms of utils, which Ricardo would get by purchasing various amounts of products A, B, C, and D. Column 5 shows the marginal utility Ricardo gets from saving. Assume that the prices of A, B, C, and D are $18, $6, $4, and $24, respectively, and that Ricardo has a money income of $106.

Column 1 Units of A	MU	Column 2 Units of B	MU	Column 3 Units of C	MU	Column 4 Units of D	MU	Column 5 No. of $ saved	MU
1	72	1	24	1	15	1	36	1	5
2	54	2	15	2	12	2	30	2	4
3	45	3	12	3	8	3	24	3	3
4	36	4	9	4	7	4	18	4	2
5	27	5	7	5	5	5	13	5	1
6	18	6	5	6	4	6	7	6	1/2
7	15	7	2	7	3.5	7	4	7	1/4
8	12	8	1	8	3	8	2	8	1/8

a. What quantities of A, B, C, and D will Ricardo purchase in maximizing his utility?

b. How many dollars will Ricardo choose to save?

c. Check your answers by substituting them into the algebraic statement of the utility-maximizing rule.

(a) 4 units of A; 3 units of B; 3 units of C, and 0 units of D.

(b) Save $4.

(c) $36/\$18 = 12/\$6 = 8/\$4 = 2/\$1$. The marginal utility per dollar of the last unit of each product purchased is 2.

6-5 **(Key Question)** You are choosing between two goods, X and Y, and your marginal utility from each is as shown below. If your income is $9 and the prices of X and Y are $2 and $1, respectively, what quantities of each will you purchase in maximizing utility? What total utility will you realize? Assume that, other things remaining unchanged, the price of X falls to $1. What quantities of X and Y will you now purchase? Using the two prices and quantities for X, derive a demand schedule (price-quantity-demanded table) for X.

Units of X	MU_x	Units of Y	MU_y
1	10	1	8
2	8	2	7
3	6	3	6
4	4	4	5
5	3	5	4
6	2	6	3

Buy 2 units of X and 5 units of Y. Marginal utility of last dollar spent will be equal at 4 (= 8/$2 for X and 4/$1 for Y) and the $9 income will be spent. Total utility = 48 (= 10 + 8 for X plus 8 + 7 + 6 + 5 + 4 for Y). When the price of X falls to $1, the quantity of X demanded increases from 2 to 4. Total utility is now 58 (= 10 + 8 + 6 + 4 for X plus 8 + 7 + 6 + 5 + 4 for Y).

Demand schedule: $P = \$2; Q = 2. P = \$1; Q = 4.$

Chapter 6-Appendix Questions

A6-3 **(Appendix Key Question)** Using Figure A6-4, explain why the point of tangency of the budget line with an indifference curve is the consumer's equilibrium position. Explain why any point where the budget line intersects an indifference curve will not be equilibrium. Explain: "The consumer is in equilibrium where MRS = P_B/P_A."

The tangency point places the consumer on the highest attainable indifference curve; it identifies the combination of goods yielding the highest total utility. All intersection points place the consumer on a lower indifference curve. MRS is the slope of the indifference curve; PB/PA is the slope of the budge line. Only at the tangency point are these two slopes equal. If MRS > P_B/P_A or MRS < P_B/P_A, adjustments in the combination of products can be made to increase total utility (get to a higher indifference curve).

Chapter 7

7-2 **(Key Question)** What are the major legal forms of business organization? Briefly state the advantages and disadvantages of each. How do you account for the dominant role of corporations in the Canadian economy?

The legal forms of business organizations are: sole proprietorship, partnership, and corporation.

Proprietorship advantages: easy to start and provides maximum freedom for the proprietor to do what she/he thinks best. Proprietorship disadvantages: limited financial resources; the owner must be a Jack-or-Jill-of-all-trades; unlimited liability.

Partnership advantages: easy to organize; greater specialization of management; and greater financial resources. Disadvantages: financial resources are still limited; unlimited liability; possibility of disagreement among the partners; and precarious continuity.

Corporation advantages: can raise large amounts of money by issuing stocks and bonds; limited liability; continuity.

Corporation disadvantages: red tape and expense in incorporating; potential for abuse of stockholder and bondholder funds; double taxation of profits; separation of ownership and control.

The dominant role of corporations stems from the advantages cited, particularly unlimited liability and the ability to raise money.

7-4   (*Key Question*) Gomez runs a small pottery firm. He hires one helper at $12,000 per year, pays annual rent of $5,000 for his shop, and materials cost $20,000 per year. Gomez has $40,000 of his own funds invested in equipment (pottery wheels, kilns, and so forth) that could earn him $4,000 per year if alternatively invested. Gomez has been offered $15,000 per year to work as a potter for a competitor. He estimates his entrepreneurial talents are worth $3,000 per year. Total annual revenue from pottery sales is $72,000. Calculate accounting profits and economic profits for Gomez's pottery.

Explicit costs: $37,000 (= $12,000 for the helper + $5,000 of rent + $20,000 of materials). Implicit costs: $22,000 (= $4,000 of forgone interest + $15,000 of forgone salary + $3,000 of entreprenuership).

Accounting profit = $35,000 (= $72,000 of revenue - $37,000 of explicit costs); Economic profit = $13,000 (= $72,000 - $37,000 of explicit costs - $22,000 of implicit costs).

7-6 (*Key Question*) Complete the following table by calculating marginal product and average product from the data given. Plot total, marginal, and average product and explain in detail the relationship between each pair of curves. Explain why marginal product first rises, then declines, and ultimately becomes negative. What bearing does the law of diminishing returns have on short-run costs? Be specific. "When marginal product is rising, marginal cost is falling. And when marginal product is diminishing, marginal cost is rising." Illustrate and explain graphically.

Inputs of labour	Total product	Marginal product	Average product
0	0	___	___
1	15	___	___
2	34	___	___
3	51	___	___
4	65	___	___
5	74	___	___
6	80	___	___
7	83	___	___
8	82	___	___

Marginal product data, top to bottom: 15; 19; 17; 14; 9; 6; 3; -1. Average product data, top to bottom: 15; 17; 17; 16.25; 14.8; 13.33; 11.86; 10.25. Your diagram should have the same general characteristics as text Figure 8-2.

MP is the slope—the rate of change—of the TP curve. When TP is rising at an increasing rate, MP is positive and rising. When TP is rising at a diminishing rate, MP is positive but falling. When TP is falling, MP is negative and falling. AP rises when MP is above it; AP falls when MP is below it.

MP first rises because the fixed capital gets used more productively as added workers are employed. Each added worker contributes more to output than the previous worker because the firm is better able to use its fixed plant and equipment. As still more labour is added, the law of diminishing returns takes hold. Labour becomes so abundant relative to the fixed capital that congestion occurs and marginal product falls. At the extreme, the addition of labour so overcrowds the plant that the marginal product of still more labour is negative—total output falls.

Illustrated by Figure 7-6. Because labour is the only variable input and its price (its wage rate) is constant, MC is found by dividing the wage rate by MP. When MP is rising, MC is falling; when MP reaches its maximum, MC is at its minimum; when MP is falling, MC is rising.

7-9   **(Key Question)** A firm has fixed costs of $60 and variable costs as indicated in the table below. Complete the table. When finished, check your calculations by referring to question 4 at the end of Chapter 8.

Total product	Total fixed cost	Total variable cost	Total cost	Average fixed cost	Average variable cost	Average total cost	Marginal cost
0	$____	$ 0	$____	$____	$____	$____	
1	____	45	____	____	____	____	____
2	____	85	____	____	____	____	____
3	____	120	____	____	____	____	____
4	____	150	____	____	____	____	____
5	____	185	____	____	____	____	____
6	____	225	____	____	____	____	____
7	____	270	____	____	____	____	____
8	____	325	____	____	____	____	____
9	____	390	____	____	____	____	____
10	____	465	____	____	____	____	____

a. Graph total fixed cost, total variable cost, and total cost. Explain how the law of diminishing returns influences the shapes of the total variable-cost and total-cost curves.
b. Graph AFC, AVC, ATC, and MC. Explain the derivation and shape of each of these four curves and their relationships to one another. Specifically, explain in non-technical terms why the MC curve intersects both the AVC and ATC curves at their minimum points.
c. Explain how the locations of each of the four curves graphed in question 7b would be altered if (1) total fixed cost had been $100 rather than $60, and (2) total variable cost had been $10 less at each level of output.

The total fixed costs are all $60. The total costs are all $60 more than the total variable cost. The other columns are shown in Question 4 in Chapter 8.

[a] See the graph. Over the 0 to 4 range of output, the TVC and TC curves slope upward at a decreasing rate because of increasing marginal returns. The slopes of the curves then increase at an increasing rate as diminishing marginal returns occur.

[b] See the graph. AFC (= TFC/Q) falls continuously since a fixed amount of capital cost is spread over more units of output. The MC (= change in TC/change in Q), AVC (= TVC/Q), and ATC (= TC/Q) curves are U-shaped, reflecting the influence of first increasing and then diminishing returns. The ATC curve sums AFC and AVC vertically. The ATC curve falls when the MC curve is below it; the ATC curve rises when the MC curve is above it. This means the MC curve must intersect the ATC curve at its lowest point. The same logic holds for the minimum point of the AVC curve.

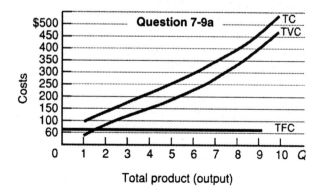

Question 7-9a

Costs / Total product (output)

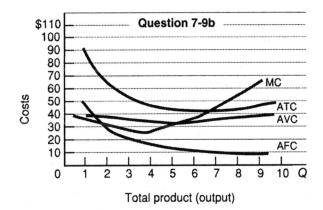

Question 7-9b

Costs

Total product (output)

(c1) If TFC has been $100 instead of $60, the AFC and ATC curves would be higher—by an amount equal to $40 divided by the specific output. Example: at 4 units, AVC = $25.00 [= ($60 + $40)/4]; and ATC = $62.50 [= ($210 + $40)/4]. The AVC and MC curves are not affected by changes in fixed costs.

(c2) If TVC has been $10 less at each output, MC would be $10 lower for the first unit of output but remain the same for the remaining output. The AVC and ATC curves would also be lower—by an amount equal to $10 divided by the specific output. Example: at 4 units of output, AVC = $35.00 [= $150 - $10)/4], ATC = $50 [= ($210 - $10)/4]. The AFC curve would not be affected by the change in variable costs.

7-12 (Key Question) Use the concepts of economies and diseconomies of scale to explain the shape of a firm's long-run ATC curve. What is the concept of minimum efficient scale? What bearing may the exact shape of the long-run ATC curve have on the structure of an industry?

The long-run ATC curve is U-shaped. At first, long-run ATC falls as the firm expands and realizes economies of scale from labour and managerial specialization and the use of more efficient capital. The long-run ATC curve later turns upward when the enlarged firm experiences diseconomies of scale, usually resulting from managerial inefficiencies.

The MES (minimum efficient scale) is the smallest level of output needed to attain all economies of scale and minimum long-run ATC.

If long-run ATC drops quickly to its minimum cost which then extends over a long range of output, the industry will likely be composed of both large and small firms. If long-run ATC descends slowly to its minimum cost over a long range of output, the industry will likely be composed of a few large firms. If long-run ATC drops quickly to its minimum point and then rises abruptly, the industry will likely be composed of many small firms.

Chapter 8

8-3 (Key Question) Use the following demand schedule to determine total and marginal revenues for each possible level of sales:

Product Price ($)	Quantity Demanded	Total Revenue ($)	Marginal Revenue ($)
2	0		
2	1		
2	2		
2	3		
2	4		
2	5		

a. What can you conclude about the structure of the industry in which this firm is operating? Explain.

b. Graph the demand, total-revenue, and marginal-revenue curves for this firm.

c. Why do the demand and marginal-revenue curves coincide?

d. "Marginal revenue is the change in total revenue." Explain verbally and graphically, using the data in the table.

Total revenue, top to bottom: 0; $2; $4; $6; $8; $10. Marginal revenue, top to bottom: $2, throughout.

(a) The industry is purely competitive—this firm is a "price taker." The firm is so small relative to the size of the market that it can change its level of output without affecting the market price.

[b] See graph.

(c) The firm's demand curve is perfectly elastic; MR is constant and equal to *P*.

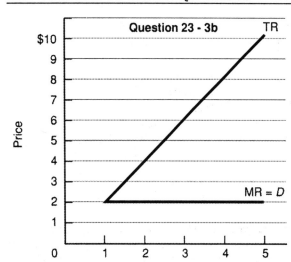

Question 23 - 3b

(d) Yes. Table: When output (quantity demanded) increases by 1 unit, total revenue increases by $2. This $2 increase is the marginal revenue. Figure: The change in TR is measured by the slope of the TR line, 2 (= $2/1 unit).

8-4 (Key Question) Assume the following unit-cost data are for a purely competitive producer:

Total Product	Average fixed cost	Average variable cost	Average total cost	Marginal cost
0				
1	$60.00	$45.00	$105.00	$45
2	30.00	42.50	72.50	40
3	20.00	40.00	60.00	35
4	15.00	37.50	52.50	30
5	12.00	37.00	49.00	35
6	10.00	37.50	47.50	40
7	8.57	38.57	47.14	45
8	7.50	40.63	48.13	55
9	6.67	43.33	50.00	65
10	6.00	46.50	52.50	75

a. At a product price of $56, will this firm produce in the short run? Why, or why not? If it does produce, what will be the profit-maximizing or loss-minimizing output? Explain. What economic profit or loss will the firm realize per unit of output.

b. Answer the questions of 4a assuming that product price is $41.

c. Answer the questions of 4a assuming that product price is $32.

d. In the table below, complete the short-run supply schedule for the firm (columns 1 to 3) and indicate the profit or loss incurred at each output (column 3).

(1) Price	(2) Quantity supplied, single firm	(3) Profit (+) or loss (l)	(4) Quantity supplied, 1500 firms
$26	___	$___	___
32	___	___	___
38	___	___	___
41	___	___	___
46	___	___	___
56	___	___	___
66	___	___	___

e. Explain: "That segment of a competitive firm's marginal-cost curve which lies above its average-variable-cost curve constitutes the short-run supply curve for the firm." Illustrate graphically.

f. Now assume there are 1500 identical firms in this competitive industry; that is, there are 1500 firms, each of which has the same cost data as shown here. Calculate the industry supply schedule (column 4).

g. Suppose the market demand data for the product are as follows:

Price	Total quantity demanded
$26	17,000
32	15,000
38	13,500
41	12,000
41	10,500
56	9,500
66	8,000

What will equilibrium price be? What will equilibrium output be for the industry? For each firm? What will profit or loss be per unit? Per firm? Will this industry expand or contract in the long run?

(a) Yes, $56 exceeds AVC (and ATC) at the loss—minimizing output. Using the MR =

MC rule it will produce 8 units. Profits per unit = $7.87 (= $56 - $48.13); total profit = $62.96.

(b) Yes, $41 exceeds AVC at the loss—minimizing output. Using the MR = MC rule it will produce 6 units. Loss per unit or output is $6.50 (= $41 - $47.50). Total loss = $39 (= 6 ⊚ $6.50), which is less than its total fixed cost of $60.

(c) No, because $32 is always less than AVC. If it did produce, its output would be 4— found by expanding output until MR no longer exceeds MC. By producing 4 units, it would lose $82 [= 4 ($32 - $52.50)]. By not producing, it would lose only its total fixed cost of $60.

(d) Column (2) data, top to bottom: 0; 0; 5; 6; 7; 8; 9, Column (3) data, top to bottom in dollars: -60; -60; -55; -39; -8; +63; +144.

(e) The firm will not produce if P < AVC. When P > AVC, the firm will produce in the short run at the quantity where P (= MR) is equal to its increasing MC. Therefore, the MC curve above the AVC curve is the firm's short-run supply curve, it shows the quantity of output the firm will supply at each price level. See Figure 9-6 for a graphical illustration.

(f) Column (4) data, top to bottom: 0; 0; 7,500; 9,000; 10,500; 12,000; 13,500.

(g) Equilibrium price = $46; equilibrium output = 10,500. Each firm will produce 7 units. Loss per unit = $1.14, or $8 per firm. The industry will contract in the long run.

8-6 (Key Question) Using diagrams for both the industry and representative firm, illustrate competitive long-run equilibrium. Assuming constant costs, employ these diagrams to show how (a) an increase and (b) a decrease in market demand will upset this long-run equilibrium. Trace graphically and describe verbally the adjustment processes by which long-run equilibrium is restored. Now rework your analysis for increasing- and decreasing-cost industries and compare the three long-run supply curves.

See Figures 8-8 and 8-9 and their legends. See figure 8-11 for the supply curve for an increasing cost industry. The supply curve for a decreasing cost industry is below.

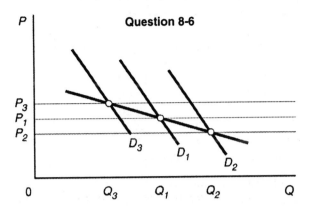

Question 8-6

8-7 (Key Question) In long-run equilibrium, P = minimum ATC = MC. Of what significance for economic efficiency is the equality of P and minimum ATC? The equality of P and MC? Distinguish between productive efficiency and allocative efficiency in your answer.

The equality of P and minimum ATC means the firms is achieving *productive efficiency*; it is using the most efficient technology and employing the least costly combination of factors of production. The equality of P and MC means the firms is achieving *allocative efficienc*;, the industry is producing the right product in the right amount based on society's valuation of that product and other

Chapter 9

9-4 (Key Question) Use the demand schedule that follows to calculate total revenue and marginal revenue at each quantity. Plot the demand, total-revenue, and marginal-revenue curves and explain the relationships between them. Explain why the marginal revenue of the fourth unit of output is $3.50, even though its price is $5.00. Use Chapter 5's total-revenue test for price elasticity to designate the elastic and inelastic segments of your graphed demand curve. What generalization can you make regarding the relationship between marginal revenue and elasticity of demand? Suppose that somehow the marginal cost of successive units of output were zero. What output would the profit-seeking firm produce? Finally, use your analysis to explain why a monopolist would never produce in the inelastic region of demand.

Price	Quantity Demanded	Price	Quantity Demanded
$7.00	0	$4.50	5
6.50	1	4.00	6
6.00	2	3.50	7
5.50	3	3.00	8
5.00	4	2.50	9

Total revenue, in order from Q = 0: 0; $6.50; $12.00; $16.50; $20.00; $22.50; $10-00; $10-50; $10-00; $22.50. Marginal revenue in order from Q = 1: $6.50; $5.50; $4.50; $3.50; $2.50; $1.50; $.50; -$1.50. See the accompanying graph. Because TR is increasing at a diminishing rate, MR is declining. When TR turns downward, MR becomes negative. Marginal revenue is below D because to sell an extra unit, the monopolist must lower the price on the marginal unit as well as on each of the preceding units sold. Four units sell for $5.00 each, but three of these four could have been sold for $5.50 had the monopolist been satisfied to sell only three. Having decided to sell four, the monopolist had to lower the price of the first three from $5.50 to $5.00, sacrificing $.50 on each for a total of $1.50. This "loss" of $1.50 explains the difference between the $5.00 price obtained on the fourth unit of output and its marginal revenue of $3.50. Demand is elastic from P = $6.50 to P = $3.50, a range where TR is rising. The curve is of unitary elasticity at P = $3.50, where TR is at its maximum. The curve is inelastic from then on as the price continues to decrease and TR is falling. When MR is positive, demand is elastic. When MR is zero, demand is of unitary elasticity. When MR is negative, demand is inelastic. If MC is zero, the monopolist should produce 7 units where MR is also zero. It would never produce where demand is inelastic because MR is negative there while MC is positive.

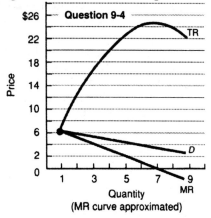

(MR curve approximated)

9-5   **(Key Question)** Suppose a pure monopolist is faced with the demand schedule shown below and the same cost data as the competitive producer discussed in question 4 at the end of Chapter 9. Calculate the missing total- and marginal-revenue amounts, and determine the profit-maximizing price and output for this monopolist. What is the monopolist's profit? Verify your answer graphically and by comparing total revenue and total cost.

Price	Quantity demanded	total revenue	Marginal revenue
$115	0	$___	
100	1	$___	$___
83	2	$___	$___
71	3	$___	$___
63	4	$___	$___
55	5	$___	$___
48	6	$___	$___
42	7	$___	$___
37	8	$___	$___
33	9	$___	$___
29	10	$___	

Total revenue data, top to bottom, in dollars: 0: 100; 166; 213; 252; 275; 288; 294; 296; 297; 290. Marginal revenue data, top to bottom, in dollars: 100; 66; 47; 39; 23; 13; 6; 2; 1; -7.

Price = $63; output = 4; profit = $42 [= 4($63 - 52.50)]. Your graph should have the same general appearance as Figure 10-4. At Q =4, TR = $252 and TC = $210 [= 4($52.50)].

9-6   **(Key Question)** If the firm described in question 5 could engage in perfect price discrimination, what would be the level of output? Of profits? Draw a diagram showing the relevant demand, marginal-revenue, average-total-cost, and marginal-cost curves and the equilibrium price and output for a non-discriminating monopolist. Use the same diagram to show the equilibrium position of a monopolist that is able to practice perfect price discrimination. Compare equilibrium outputs, total revenues, economic profits, and consumer prices in the two cases. Comment on the economic desirability of price discrimination.

Perfect price discrimination: Output = 6. TR would be $420 (= $100 + $83 + $71 + $63 + $55

+ $48). TC would be $285 [= 6(47.50)]. Profit would be $135 (= $420 -$285).

Your single diagram should combine Figure 9-8a and 9-8b in the chapter. The discriminating monopolist faces a demand curve that is also its MR curve. It will sell the first unit at f in Figure 9-8b and then sell each successive unit at lower prices (as shown on the demand curve) as it moves to Q_2 units, where D (= MR) = MC. Discriminating monopolist: Greater output; total revenue, and profits. Some consumers will pay a higher price under discriminating monopoly than with non-discriminating monopoly; others, a lower price. Good features: greater output and improved allocative efficiency. Bad feature: More income is transferred from consumers to the monopolist.

9-11 (**Key Question**) It has been proposed that natural monopolists should be allowed to determine their profit-maximizing outputs and prices and government should tax their profits away and distribute them to consumers in proportion to their purchases from the monopoly. Is this proposal as socially desirable as requiring monopolists to equate price with marginal cost or average total cost?

No, the proposal does not consider that the output of the natural monopolist would still be at the suboptimal level where P > MC. Too little would be produced and there would be an under-allocation of resources. Theoretically, it would be more desirable to force the natural monopolist to charge a price equal to marginal cost and subsidize any losses. Even setting price equal to ATC would be an improvement over this proposal. This fair-return pricing would allow for a normal profit and ensure greater production than the proposal would.

Chapter 10

10-2 (**Key Question**) Compare the elasticity of the monopolistically competitor's demand curve with that of a pure competitor and a pure monopolist. Assuming identical long-run costs, compare graphically the prices and output that would result in the long run under pure competition and under monopolistic competition. Contrast the two market structures in terms of productive and allocative efficiency. Explain: "Monopolistically competitive industries are characterized by too many firms, each of which produces too little."

Less elastic than a pure competitor and more elastic than a pure monopolist. Your graphs should look like Figures 8.12 and 10-1 in the chapters. Price is higher and output lower for the monopolistic competitor. Pure competition: P = MC (allocative efficiency); P = minimum ATC (productive efficiency). Monopolistic competition: P > MC (allocative efficiency) and P > minimum ATC (productive inefficiency). Monopolistic competitors have excess capacity; meaning that fewer firms operate at capacity (where P = minimum ATC) could supply the industry output.

10-7 (**Key Question**) Answer the following questions, which relate to measures of concentration:.
a. What is the meaning of a four-firm concentration ratio of 60 percent? 90 percent? What are the shortcomings of concentration ratios as measures of monopoly power?
b. Suppose that the five firms in industry A have annual sales of 30, 30, 20, 10, and 10 percent of total industry sales. For the five firms in industry B the figures are 60, 25, 5, 5, and 5 percent. Calculate the Herfindahl index for each industry and compare their likely competitiveness.

A four-firm concentration ration of 60 % means the largest four firms in an industry account for 60 % of sales; a four-firm concentration ratio of 90 % means the largest four firms account for 90 percent of sales. Shortcomings: (1) they pertain to the whole nation, though relevant markets may be localized; (2) they do not account for interindustry competition; (3) the data are for Canadian products, not imports; and (4) they don't reveal the dispersion of size among the top four firms.

Herfindahl index for A: 2,400 (= 900 + 900 + 400 + 100 + 100). For B: 4,300 (= 3,600 + 625 + 25 + 25 +25). We would expect industry A to be more competitive than Industry B, where one firm dominates and two firms control 85 percent of the market.

10-9 (**Key Question**) Explain the general meaning of the following profit payoff matrix for oligopolists C and D. All profit figures are in thousands.
a. Use the payoff matrix to explain mutual interdependence of oligopolistic industries.

b. Assuming no collusion between C and D, what is the likely pricing outcome?

c. In view of your answer to 9b, explain why price collusion is mutually profitable. Why might there be a temptation to chat on the collusive agreement?

C's possible prices

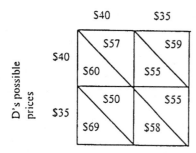

The matrix shows 4 possible profit outcomes for two firms following two different price strategies. Example: If C sets price at $35 and D at $40, C's profits are $59,000, and D's $55,000.

(a) C and D are interdependent because their profits depend not just on their own price, but also on the other firm's price.

(b) Likely outcome: Both firms will set price at $35. If either charged $40, it would be concerned the other would undercut the price and its profit by charging $35. At $35 for both; C's profit is $55,000, D's, $58,000.

(c) Through price collusion—agreeing to charge $40—each firm would achieve higher profits (C = $57,000; D = $60,000). But once both firms agree on $40, each sees it can increase its profit even more by secretly charging $35 while its rival charges $40.

10-10 (Key Question) What assumptions about a rival's response to price changes underlie the kinked-demand curve for oligopolists? Why is there a gap in the oligopolist's marginal-revenue curve? How does kinked demand curve explain price rigidity in oligopoly? What are model weaknesses?

Assumptions: (1) Rivals will match price cuts: (2) Rivals will ignore price increases. The gap in the MR curve results from the abrupt change in the slope of the demand curve at the going price. Firms will not change their price because they fear that if they do their total revenue and profits will fall. Shortcomings of the model: (1) It does not explain how the going price evolved in the

first place; (2) it does not allow for price leadership and other forms of collusion.

10-12 (Key Question) Why is there so much advertising in monopolistic competition and oligopoly? How does such advertising help consumers and promote efficiency? Why might it be excessive at times?

Monopolistically competitive firms maintain economic profits through product development and advertising. Advertising can increase demand for a firm's product. An oligopolist would rather not compete on a basis of price. Oligopolists can increase market share through advertising financed with economic profits from past advertising campaigns. Advertising can act as a barrier to entry.

Advertising provides information about new products and product improvements to the consumer. It may result in an increase in competition by promoting new products and product improvements. Advertising may result in manipulation and persuasion rather than information. An increase in brand loyalty through advertising will increase the producer's monopoly power. Excessive advertising may create barriers to entry into the industry.

Chapter 11

11-4 (Key Question) Suppose a firm expects that a $20 million expenditure on R&D will result in a new product which will increase its revenue by a total of $30 million 1 year from now. The firm estimates that the production cost of the new product will be $29 million.

a. What is the expected rate of return on this R&D expenditure?

b. Suppose the firm can get a bank loan at 6 percent interest to finance its $20 million R&D project. Will the firm undertake the project? Explain why or why not.

c. Now suppose the interest-rate cost of borrowing, in effect, falls to 4 percent because the firm decides to use its own retained earnings to finance the R&D. Will this lower interest rate change the firm's R&D decision? Explain.

(a) 5 percent;

(b) No, because the 5 percent rate of return is less than the 6 percent interest rate;

(c) Yes, because the 5 percent the rate of return is now greater than the 4 percent interest rate.

11-5 **(Key Question)** Answer the lettered questions below on the basis of the information in this table:

Amount of R&D, millions	Expected rate of return on R&D, %
$10	16
20	14
30	12
40	10
50	8
60	6

a. If the interest-rate cost of funds is 8 percent, what will be the optimal amount of R&D spending for this firm?

b. Explain why $20 million of R&D spending will not be optimal.

c. Why won't $60 million be optimal either?

(a) $50 million, where the interest-rate cost of funds (i) equals the expected rate of return (r);

(b) at $20 million in R&D, r of 14 percent exceeds i of 8 percent, thus there would be an under-allocation of R&D funds;

(c) at $60 million, r of 6 percent is less than i of 8 percent, thus there would be an over-allocation of R&D funds.

11-6 **(Key Question)** Refer to Table 11-1 and suppose the price of new product C is $2 instead of $4. How does this affect the optimal combination of products A, B, and C for the person represented by the data? Explain: "The success of a new product depends not only on its marginal utility but also on its price."

(a) The person would now buy 5 units of product C and zero units of A and B;

(b) The MU/price ratio is what counts; a new product can be successful by having a high MU, a low price, or both relative to existing products.

11-8 **(Key Question)** Answer the following questions on the basis of this information for a single firm: total cost of capital = $1,000; price paid for labour = $12 per labour unit; price paid for raw materials = $4 per raw-material unit.

a. Suppose the firm can produce 5,000 units of output by combining its fixed capital with 100 units of labour and 450 units of raw materials. What are the total cost and average total cost of producing the 5,000 units of output?

b. Now assume the firm improves its production process so that it can produce 6,000 units of output by combining its fixed capital with 100 units of labour and 45 units of raw materials. What are the total cost and average cost of producing the 6,000 units of output?

c. In view of your answers to 8a and 8b, explain how process innovation can improve economic efficiency.

(a) Total cost = $4,000; average total cost = $.80 (= $4,000/5,000 units);

(b) Total cost = $4,000, average total cost = $.667 (= $4,000/6,000 units);

(c) Process innovation can lower the average total cost of producing a particular output, meaning that society uses fewer resources in producing that output. Resources are freed from this production to produce more of other desirable goods. Society realizes extra output through a gain in efficiency.

Chapter 12

12-2 **(Key Question)** Explain how strict enforcement of the anti-combines laws might conflict with (a) promoting exports to achieve a balance of trade, and (b) encouraging new technologies. Do you see any dangers of using selective anti-combines enforcement as part of an industrial policy?

Strict enforcement of the anti-combines laws could mean that a merger of two large firms would be prohibited or a dominant manufacturer in an industry might be broken up. (a) The targeted firms could be weakened, which might reduce their ability to compete successfully with strong foreign firms in sales abroad. This in turn conflicts with the goal of expanding Canadian exports. (b) Major mergers involving companies in banking, telecommunications, computer manufacturers, and software producers have led to questions of how strict anti-combines enforcement should be in these industries, where emerging technology may benefit from industry restructuring. Hastening the development of the "information superhighway" could also benefit Canadian exports of these services, which would strengthen our trade balance.

Selective enforcement of anti-combines laws is a type of government industrial policy that interferes with the market process to the extent that it favours some industries by easing the way for concentration in some industries and strictly limiting consolidation in others. Such a selective policy can be dangerous when one considers the opportunities for public sector failure discussed in Chapter 18. Selective enforcement encourages rent seeking and self-interest lobbying efforts, which may dictate policy more than the technological merits warrant.

12-3 (Key Question) How would you expect anti-combines authorities to react to (a) a proposed merger of Ford and General Motors ? (b) evidence of secret meetings by contractors to rig bids for highway construction projects? (c) a proposed merger of a large shoe manufacturer and a chain of retail shoe stores? and (d) a proposed merger of a small life insurance company and a regional candy manufacturer?

(a) They would block this horizontal merger. (b) They would charge these firms with price fixing. (c) They would allow this vertical merger, unless both firms had very large market shares. (d) They would allow this conglomerate merger.

12-8 (Key Question) What types of industries, if any, should be subjected to industrial regulation? What specific problems does industrial regulation entail?

Industries composed of firms with natural monopolies conditions are most likely to be sub-

jected to industrial regulation. Regulation based on "fair-return" prices creates disincentives for firms to minimize costs since cost reductions lead regulators to force firms to change a lower price. Regulated firms may also use "creative" accounting to boost costs and hide profits. Because regulatory commissions depend on information provided by the firms themselves and commission members are often recruited from the industry, the agencies may in effect be controlled by the firms they are supposed to oversee. Also, industrial regulation sometimes is applied to industries that are not, or no longer are, natural monopolies. Regulation may lead to the conditions of a cartel, conditions that are illegal in an unregulated industry.

12-10 (Key Question) How does social regulation differ from industrial regulation? What types of costs and benefits are associated with social regulation?

Industrial regulation is concerned with prices, output, and profits specific industries, whereas social regulation deals with the broader impact of business on consumers, workers, and third parties. Benefits: increased worker and product safety, less environmental damage, reduced economic discrimination. Two types of costs: administrative costs, because regulations must be administered by costly government agencies, compliance costs, because firms must increase spending to comply with regulations.

Chapter 13

13-2 (Key Question) Complete the following labour demand table for a firm that is hiring labour competitively and selling its product in a competitive market.

Units of labour	Total product	Marginal product	Product price	Total revenue	Marginal revenue product
0	0	____	$2	$____	
1	17	____	$2	$____	$____
2	31	____	2	____	____
3	43	____	2	____	____
4	53	____	2	____	____
5	60	____	2	____	____
6	65	____	2	____	____

a. How many workers will the firm hire if the going wage rate is $27.95? $19.95? Explain why the firm will not hire a larger or smaller number of workers at each of these wage rates.

b. Show in schedule form and graphically the labour demand curve of this firm.

c. Now re-determine the firm's demand curve for labour, assuming that it is selling in an imperfectly competitive market and that, although it can sell 17 units at $2.20 per unit, it must lower product price by 5 cents in order to sell the marginal product of each successive worker. Compare this demand curve with that derived in question 2b. Which curve is more elastic? Explain.

Marginal product data, top to bottom: 17; 14; 12; 10; 7; 5. Total revenue data, top to bottom: $0, $34; $62; $86; $106; $120; $130. Marginal revenue product data, top to bottom: $34; $28; $24; $20; $14; $10.

(a) Two workers at $27.95 because the MRP of the first worker is $34 and the MRP of the second worker is $28, both exceeding the $27.985 wage. Four workers at $19.95 because workers 1 through 4 have MRPs exceeding the $19.95 wage. The fifth worker's MRP is only $14 so he or she will not be hired.

[b] The demand schedule consists of the first and last columns of the table:

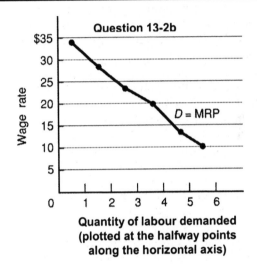

Question 13-2b

Wage rate ($35, 30, 25, 20, 15, 10, 5)

D = MRP

Quantity of labour demanded
(plotted at the halfway points
along the horizontal axis)

(c) Reconstruct the table. New product price data, top to bottom: $2.20; $2.15; $2.10; $2.05; $2.00; $1.95. New total revenue data, top to bottom: $0; $37.40; $66.65; $90.30; $108.65; $120.00; $126.75. New marginal revenue product data, top to bottom: $37.40; $29.25; $23.65; $18.35; $11.35; $6.75. The new labour demand is less elastic. Here, MRP falls because of diminishing returns *and* because product price declines as output increases. A decrease in the wage rate will produce less of an increase in the quantity of labour demanded, because the output from the added labour will reduce product price and thus MRP.

13-5 (*Key Question*) What are the determinants of the elasticity of factor demand? What effect will each of the following have on the elasticity or the location of the demand for factor C, which is being used to produce commodity X? Where there is an uncertainty as to the outcome, specify the causes of that uncertainty.

a. An increase in the demand for product X.
b. An increase in the price of substitute factor D.
c. An increase in the number of factors substitutable for C in producing X.
d. A technological improvement in the capital equipment with which factor C is combined.
e. A decline in the price of complementary factor E.
f. A decline in the elasticity of demand for product X due to a decline in the competitiveness of the product market.

Four determinants: the rate at which the factor's MP declines; the ease of substituting other factors; elasticity of product demand; and the ratio of the factor cost to the total cost of production.

(a) Increase in demand C.
(b) The price increase for D will increase the demand for C through the *substitution effect*, but decrease the demand for all factors—including C—through the *output effect*. The net effect is uncertain; it depends on which effect outweighs the other.
(c) Increases the elasticity of demand for C.
(d) Increases the demand for C.
(e) Increases the demand for C through the output effect. There is no substitution effect.
(f) Reduces the elasticity of demand for C.

13-6 (Key Question) Suppose the productivity of labour and capital are as shown below. The output of these factors sells in a purely competitive market for $1 per unit. Both labour and capital are hired under purely competitive conditions at $1 and $3 respectively.

Units of capital	MP of capital	Units of labour	MP of labour
1	24	1	11
2	21	2	9
3	18	3	8
4	15	4	7
5	9	5	6
6	6	6	4
7	3	7	1
8	1	8	1/2

a. What is the least-cost combination of labour and capital to employ in producing 80 units of output? Explain.
b. What is the profit-maximizing combination of labour/ capital the firm should use? Explain. What is the resulting level of output? What is the economic profit? Is this the least costly way of producing the profit-maximizing output?

(a) 2 capital; 4 labour.
$MP_L/P_L = 7/1; MP_C/P_C = 21/3 = 7/1.$
(b) 7 capital and 7 labour.
$MRP_L/_L = 1 (= 1/1) = MRP_C/P_C = 1(= 3/3).$
Output is 142 (= 96 from capital + 46 from labour). Economic profit is $114 (= $142 - $38). Yes, least-cost production is part of maximizing profits; the profit-maximizing rule includes the least-cost rule.

13-7 (Key Question) In each of the following four cases, MRP_L and MRP_C refer to the marginal revenue products of labour and capital, respectively, and P_L and P_C refer to their prices. Indicate in each case whether the conditions are consistent with maximum profits for the firm. If not, state which factor(s) should be used in larger amounts and which factor(s) should be used in smaller amounts.

a. $MRP_L = \$8; P_L = \$4; MRP_C = \$8; P_C = \$4$.
b. $MRP_L = \$10; P_L = \$12; MRP_C = \$14; P_C = \$9$.
c. $MRP_L = \$6; P_L = \$6; MRP_C = \$12; P_C = \$12$.
d. $MRP_L = \$22; P_L = \$26; MRP_C = \$16; P_C = \$19$.

(a) Use more of both.
(b) Use less labour and more capital.
(c) Maximum profits obtained.
(d) Use less of both.

Chapter 14

14-3 (Key Question) Describe wage determination in a labour market in which workers are unorganized and many firms actively compete for the services of labour. Show this situation graphically, using W_1 to indicate the equilibrium wage rate and Q_1 to show the number of workers hired by the firms as a group. Compare the labour supply curve of the individual firm with that of the total market and explain any differences. In the firm's diagram, identify total revenue, total wage cost, and revenue available for the payment of nonlabour resources.

See Figure 14-3 and its legend.

14-4 **(Key Question)** Complete the accompanying labour supply table for a firm hiring labour competitively.

Units of labour	Wage rate	Total labour cost (wage bill)	Marginal resource (labour) cost
0	$14	$____	
1	14	____	$____
2	14	____	____
3	14	____	____
4	14	____	____
5	14	____	____
6	14	____	____

a. Show graphically the labour supply and marginal resource (labour) cost curves for this firm. Explain the relationships of these curves to one another.

b. Compare these data with the labour demand data of question 2 in Chapter 14. What will the equilibrium wage rate and level of employment be? Explain.

Total labour cost data, top to bottom: $0; $14; $28; $42; $56; $70; $84. Marginal resource cost data: $14, throughout.

(a) The labour supply curve and MRC curve coincide as a single horizontal line at the market wage rate of $14. The firm can employ as much labour as it wants, each unit costing $14; wage rate = MRC because the wage rate is constant to the firm.

(b) Graph: equilibrium is at the intersection of the MRP and MRC curves. Equilibrium wage rate = $14; equilibrium level of employment = 4 units of labour. Explanation: From the tables: MRP exceeds MRC for each of the first four units of labour, but MRP is less than MRC for the fifth unit.

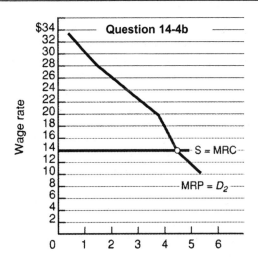

Quantity of labour
(MRP is plotted at the halfway points on the horizontal axis)

14-6 **(Key Question)** Assume a firm is a monopsonist that can hire the first worker for $6, but must increase the wage rate by $3 to attract each successive worker. Show the labour supply and marginal labour cost curves graphically and explain their relationships to one another. Compare these data with the labour demand data of question 2 for Chapter 14. What will be the equilibrium wage rate and the level of employment? Why do these differ from your answer to question 4?

The monopsonist faces the market labour supply curve S—it is the only firm hiring this labour. MRC lies above S and rises more rapidly than S because all workers get the higher wage rate that is needed to attract each added worker. Equilibrium wage rate = $12; equilibrium employment = 3 (where MRP = MRC). The monopsonist can pay a below competitive wage rate by restricting its employment.

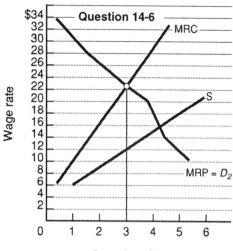

Question 14-6

Quantity of labour
(MRP is plotted at the halfway points
on the horizontal axis)

14-7 (Key Question) Assume a monopsonistic employer is paying a wage rate of W_m and hiring Q_m workers, as indicated in Figure 14-8. Now suppose that an industrial union is formed and that it forces the employer to accept a wage rate of W_c. Explain verbally and graphically why in this instance the higher wage rate will be accompanied by an increase in the number of workers hired.

The union wage rate W_c becomes the firm's MRC, which we would show as a horizontal line to the left of S. Each unit of labour now adds only its own wage rate to the firm's costs. The firm will employ Q_c workers, the quantity of labour where MRP = MRC (= W_c); Q_c is greater than the Q_m workers it would employ if there were no union.

14-12 (Key Question) Use graphical analysis to show the gains and losses resulting from the migration of population from a low-income country to a high-income country. Explain how your conclusions are affected by (a) unemployment, (b) remittances to the home country, (c) backflows of migrants to their home country, and (d) the personal characteristics of the migrants. If the migrants are highly skilled workers, is there any justification for the sending country to levy a "brain drain" tax on emigrants?

See Figure 14-10. Migration of labour from the low- to high-income country increases labour supply in the high-income country and decreases it in the low-income country. Wages are equalized at We. Output and business income increase in

the receiving country; decline in the sending country. World output increases: The output gain in the receiving country exceeds the output loss in the sending country.

(a) The gains to the receiving country will not materialize if the migrants are unemployed after they arrive; there may be gains in the low-income country if the immigrant had been unemployed prior to moving. (b) Remittances to the home country will decrease the income gain in the receiving country and reduce the income loss in the sending country. (c) If migrants who return to their home country have enhanced their skills, their temporary departure might be to the long-run advantage of the home country. (d) Young, skilled migrants will increase output and likely be the net taxpayers in the receiving country, but the sending country will experience a "brain drain." Older or less skilled workers who are not so easily assimilated could be net recipients of government services.

In view of the sometimes large investments which sending countries have made in providing education and skills, there is a justification for levying a departure tax on such migrants. But if this tax were too high, it would infringe on a basic human right: the right to emigrate.

Chapter 15

15-2 (Key Question) Explain why economic rent is a surplus to the economy as a whole but a cost of production from the standpoint of individual firms and industries. Explain: "Rent performs no incentive function in the economy."

Land is completely fixed in total supply. As population expands and the demand for land increases, rent first appears and then grows. From society's perspective, this rent is a surplus payment unnecessary for ensuring that the land is available to the economy as a whole. If rent declined or disappeared, the same amount of land would be available. If it increased, no more land would be forthcoming. Thus, rent does not function as an incentive for adding land to the economy.

But land does have alternative uses. To get it to its most productive use, individuals and firms compete and the winners are those who pay the highest rent. To the high bidders, rent is a cost of production that must be covered by the revenue gained through the sale of the commodities produced on that land.

15-5 (Key Question) Why is the supply of loanable funds upsloping? Why is the demand for loanable funds downsloping? Explain the equilibrium interest rate. List some factors that might cause it to change.

Supply is upsloping because households prefer present consumption to future consumption and must be enticed through higher interest rates to save more (consume less) now. The higher the interest rate, the greater the saving and the amount of money made available to the loanable funds market. Demand is downsloping because more business investment projects become profitable as the cost of borrowing (the interest rate) falls. The equilibrium interest rate is the rate at which the quantities of funds supplied and demanded in the loanable funds market are equal. Anything that changes the supply of loanable funds or the demand for loanable funds will change the equilibrium interest rate. Two examples: Higher taxes on interest income would reduce the supply of loanable funds and increase the equilibrium interest rate; a decrease in business optimism would reduce the expected return on investment, decrease the demand for loanable funds, and reduce the equilibrium interest rate.

15-7 (Key Question) Distinguish between nominal and real interest rates. Which is more relevant in making investment and R&D decisions? If the nominal interest rate is 12 percent and the inflation rate is 8 percent, what is the real rate of interest?

The nominal interest rate is the interest rate stated in dollars of current value (unadjusted for inflation). The real interest rate is the nominal interest rate adjusted for inflation (or deflation). The real interest rate is more relevant for making investment decisions—it reflects the true cost of borrowing money. It is compared to the expected return on the investment in the decision process. Real interest rate = 4 percent (= 12 percent - 8 percent).

15-8 (Key Question) How do the concepts of accounting profits and economic profits differ? Why are economic profits smaller than accounting profits? What are the three basic sources of economic profits? Classify each of the following in accordance with these sources:

a. A firm's profits from developing and patenting a ball-point pen containing a permanent ink cartridge.
b. A restaurant's profit that results from construction of a new highway past its door.
c. The profit received by a firm benefiting from an unanticipated change in consumer tastes.

Accounting profit is what remains of a firm's total revenues after it has paid for all the factors of production employed by the firm (its explicit costs) but not for the use of the resources owned by the business itself. Economists also take into consideration implicit costs—the payment the owners could have received by using the resources they own in some other way. The economist adds these implicit costs to the accountant's explicit costs to arrive at total cost. Subtracting the total cost from total revenue results in a smaller profit (the economic profit) than the accountant's profit.

Sources of economic profit: (1) uninsurable risks; (2) innovations; and (3) monopoly.

(a) Profit from assuming the uncertainities of innovation, as well as monopoly profit from the patent.
(b) Monopoly profit arising from its locational advantage.
(c) Profit from bearing the uninsurable risk of a change in demand (the change could have been unfavourable).

Chapter 16

16-2 (Key Question) Assume Al, Beth, Carol, David, and Ed receive incomes of $500, $250, $125, $75, and $50 respectively. Construct and interpret a Lorenz curve for this five-person economy. What percentage of total income is received by the richest and by the poorest quintiles?

See the figure below. In this simple economy each person represents a complete income quintile—20 percent of the total population. The richest quintile (Al) receives 50 percent of total income; the poorest quintile (Ed) receives 5 percent.

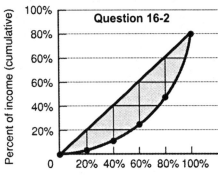

Percent of income (cumulative) [y-axis: 100%, 80%, 60%, 60%, 40%, 20%]
Question 16-2
Percent of individuals (cumulative) [x-axis: 0 20% 40% 60% 80% 100%]

16-4 (*Key Question*) Briefly discuss the major causes of income inequality. With respect to income inequality, is there any difference between inheriting property and inheriting a high IQ? Explain.

The reasons for income inequality may be grouped into three broad categories: unequal personal endowments, differences in individual character, and external social factors. The first is largely a matter of luck—some people possess high intelligence, particular talents, or physical dexterity that allow them to earn high incomes. Also, they may inherit property or be aided by the social status and financial resources of their parents. The second reason involves personal initiative—individuals may be willing to undergo costly training, accept risk, or tolerate unpleasant working conditions in the expectation of higher pay. They may also show high personal initiative on the job. The third factor relates to society as a whole. Market power and discrimination are two important social determinants of income inequality.

A high IQ normally does not lead to high income unless it is combined with personal initiative and favourable social circumstances. Inherited property—as long as it is competently managed—provides income irrespective of one's character and personal attributes. Both factors are largely a matter of luck to the recipient.

16-9 (*Key Question*) The table shown below contains three hypothetical public assistance plans.

Plan One			Plan Two			Plan Three		
Earned income	NIT subsidy	Total income	Earned income	NIT subsidy	Total income	Earned income	NIT subsidy	Total income
$ 0	$4,000	$4,000	$ 0	$4,000	$ 4,000	$ 0	$8,000	$ 8,000
2,000	3,000	5,000	4,000	3,000	7,000	4,000	6,000	10,000
4,000	2,000	6,000	8,000	2,000	10,000	8,000	4,000	12,000
6,000	1,000	7,000	12,000	1,000	13,000	12,000	2,000	14,000

a. Determine the basic benefit, the benefit reduction rate, and the break-even income for each plan.
b. Which plan is the most costly? The least costly? Which plan is most effective in reducing poverty? The least effective? Which plan embodies the strongest disincentive to work? The weakest disincentive to work?
c. Use your answers in part (b) to explain the following statement: "The dilemma of the negative income tax is that you cannot bring families up to the poverty level and simultaneously preserve work incentives and minimize program costs."
(a) Plan 1: Minimum income = $4,000; benefit reduction rate = 50 percent; break-even income = $8,000 (= $4,000/.5). Plan 2: Minimum income = $4,000; benefit reduction rate = 25 percent; break-even income = $16,000 (= $4,000/.25). Plan 3: Minimum income = $8,000; benefit reduction rate = 50 percent; break-even income = $16,000 (= $8,000/.5).
(b) Plan 3 is the most costly. Plan 1 is the least costly. Plan 3 is most effective in reducing poverty (although it has a higher benefit reduction rate than Plan 2, its minimum income is higher). Plan 1 is least effective in reducing poverty. Plan 3 has the strongest disincentive to work (although it has the same benefit reduction rate as Plan 1, its higher minimum income discourages work more). Plan 2 has the weakest disincentives

to work (its minimum income and benefit reduction rates are low).

(c) The only way to eliminate poverty is to provide a minimum income high enough to lift everyone from poverty, including people who cannot work or choose not to work. But this large minimum income reduces the incentive to work, expands the number of people receiving transfer payments, and substantially boosts overall program costs.

16-12 (Key Question) Use a demand and supply model to explain the impact of occupational segregation or "crowding" on the relative wage rates and earnings of men and women. Who gains and who loses from the elimination of occupational segregation? Is there a net gain or net loss to society? Explain.

See Figure 16-5. Discrimination against women in two of the three occupations will crowd women into the third occupation. Labour supply in the "men's occupations" (X and Y) decreases, making them high-wage occupations. Labour supply in the "women's occupation" (Z) increases creating a low-wage occupation.

Eliminating occupational segregation would entice women into the high-wage occupations, increasing labour supply there and reducing it in the low-wage occupation. The wage rates in the three occupations would converge to B. Women would gain, men would lose. Society would gain because the increase in output in the expanding occupations would exceed the loss of output in the contracting occupation.

Chapter 17

17-1 (Key Question) Based on the following three individual demand schedules for a particular good, and assuming these three people are the only ones in the society, determine (a) the market demand schedule on the assumption that the good is a private good, and (b) the collective demand schedule on the assumption that the good is a public good. Explain the differences, if any, in your schedules.

Individual #1		Individual #2		Individual #3	
Price	Q_d	Price	Q_d	Price	Q_d
$8	0	$8	1	$8	0
7	0	7	2	7	0
6	0	6	3	6	1
5	1	5	4	5	2
4	2	4	5	4	3
3	3	3	6	3	4
2	4	2	7	2	5
1	5	1	8	1	6

(a) Private good, top to bottom: P = $8, Q = 1; P = $7, Q = 2; P = $6, Q = 4; P = $5, Q = 7; P = $4, Q = 10; P = $3, Q = 13; P = $2, Q = 16; P = $1, Q = 19. (b) Public good, top to bottom: P = $19, Q = 1; P = $16, Q = 2; P = $13, Q = 3; P = $10, Q = 4; P = $7, Q = 5; P = $4, Q = 6; P = $2, Q = 7; P = $1, Q = 8. The first schedule represents a horizontal summation of the individual demand curves; the second schedule represents a vertical summation of these curves. The market demand curve for the private good will determine—in combination with market supply—an actual price–quantity outcome in the marketplace. Because potential buyers of public goods do not reveal their individual preferences in the market, the collective demand curve for the public good is hypothetical or needs to be determined through "willingness to pay" studies.

17-2 (Key Question) Use your demand schedule for a public good determined in question 1 and the following supply schedule to ascertain the optimal quantity of this public good. Why is this the optimal quantity?

P	Q_s
$19	10
16	8
13	6
10	4
7	2
4	0

Optimal quantity = 4. It is optimal because at 4 units the collective willingness to pay for the final unit of the good (= $10) matches the marginal cost of production (= $10).

17-3 (**Key Question**) The following table shows the total costs and total benefits in billions for four different antipollution programs of increasing scope. Which program should be undertaken? Why?

Program	Total Cost	Total Benefit
A	$ 3	$ 7
B	7	12
C	12	16
D	18	19

Program B, since the marginal benefit no longer exceeds marginal cost for programs which are larger in scope. Plan B is where net benefits—the excess of total benefits over total costs—are maximized.

17-4 (**Key Question**) Why are spillover costs and spillover benefits also called negative and positive "externalities"? Show graphically how a tax can correct for a spillover cost and a subsidy to producers can correct for a spillover benefit. How does a subsidy to consumers differ from a subsidy to producers in correcting for a spillover benefit?

Spillover costs are called negative externalities because they are *external* to the participants in the transaction and *reduce* the utility of affected third parties (thus "negative"). Spillover benefits are called positive externalities because they are *external* to the participants in the transaction and *increase* the utility of affected third parties (thus "positive"). See Figures 17-3 and 17-4. Compare (b) and (c) in Figure 17-4.

17-7 (**Key Question**) Explain the following statement, using the MB curve in Figure 17-6 to illustrate: "The optimal amount of pollution abatement for some substances, say, water from storm drains, is very low; the optimal amount of abatement for other substances, say, cyanide poison, is close to 100 percent."

Reducing water flow from storm drains has a low marginal benefit, meaning the MB curve would be located far to the left of where it is in the text diagram. It will intersect the MC curve at a low amount of pollution abatement, indicating the optimal amount of pollution abatement (where

MB = MC) is low. Any cyanide in public water sources could be deadly. Therefore, the marginal benefit of reducing cyanide is extremely high and the MB curve in the figure would be located to the extreme right where it would intersect the MC curve at or near 100 percent.

17-12 (**Key Question**) Place an M beside the items in the following list that describe a moral hazard problem; place an A beside those which describe an adverse selection problem.
  a. A person with a terminal illness buys several life insurance policies through the mail.
  b. A person drives carelessly because he or she has insurance.
  c. A person who intends to "torch" his warehouse takes out a large fire insurance policy.
  d. A professional athlete who has a guaranteed contract fails to stay in shape during the off-season.
  e. A woman anticipating having a large family takes a job with a firm that offers exceptional child care benefits.

Moral hazard problem: (b) and (d). Adverse selection problem: (a), (c), and (e).

Chapter 18

18-2 (**Key Question**) Explain the paradox of voting through reference to the accompanying table, which shows the ranking of three public goods by voters Larry, Curley, and Moe.

Public Good	Larry	Curley	Moe
Courthouse	2d choice	1st choice	3d choice
School	3d choice	2d choice	1st choice
Park	1st choice	3d choice	2d choice

The paradox is that majority voting does not always provide a clear and consistent picture of the public's preferences. Here the courthouse is preferred to the school and the park is preferred to the courthouse, so we would surmise that the park is preferred to the school. But paired-choice voting would show that the school is preferred to the park.

18-3 (*Key Question*) Suppose that there are only five people in a society and that each favours one of the five highway construction options shown in Table 17-2 (include "no protection" as one of the options). Explain which of these highway options will be selected using a majority rule. Will this option be the optimal size of the project from an economic perspective?

Project B (small reservoir) wins using a paired choice vote. There is no "paradox of voting" problem here and B is the preference of the median voter. The two voters favouring No Reservoir and Levees, respectively, will prefer Small Reservoir—project B—to Medium or Large Reservoir. The two voters preferring Large Reservoir or Medium Reservoir will prefer Small Reservoir to Levees or No Reservoir. The median voter's preference for B will prevail. However, the optimal size of the project from an economic perspective is C—it would provide a greater net benefit to society than B.

18-4 (*Key Question*) How do the problems of limited and bundled choices in the public sector relate to economic efficiency? Why are public bureaucracies alleged to be less efficient than private enterprises?

The electorate is faced with a small number of candidates, each of whom offers a broad range or "bundle" of proposed policies. Voters are then forced to choose the individual candidate whose bundle of policies most resembles their own. The chances of a perfect identity between a particular candidate's preferences and those of any voter are quite slim. As a result, the voter must purchase some unwanted public goods and services. This represents an inefficient allocation of resources.

Government bureaucracies do not function on the basis of profit, so the incentive for holding down costs is less than in the private sector. Also, because there is no profit-and-loss test of efficiency, it is difficult to determine whether public agencies are operating efficiently. Nor is there entry of competing entities to stimulate efficiency and develop improved public goods and services. Furthermore, wasteful expenditures can be maintained through the self-seeking lobbying of bureaucrats themselves, and the public budgetary process can reward rather than penalize inefficiency.

18-7 (*Key Question*) Suppose a tax is such that an individual with an income of $10,000 pays $2,000 of tax, a person with an income of $20,000 pays $3,000 of tax, a person with an income of $30,000 pays $4,000 of tax, and so forth. What is each person's average tax rate? Is this tax regressive, proportional, or progressive?

Average tax rates: 20; 15; and 13.3 percent. Regressive.

18-9 (*Key Question*) What is the incidence of an excise tax when demand is highly inelastic? Elastic? What effect does the elasticity of supply have on the incidence of an excise tax? What is the efficiency loss of a tax, and how does it relate to elasticity of demand and supply?

The incidence of an excise tax is likely to be primarily on consumers when demand is highly inelastic and primarily on producers when demand is elastic. The more elastic the supply, the greater the incidence of an excise tax on consumers and the less on producers.

The efficiency loss of a sales or excise tax is the net benefit society sacrifices because consumption and production of the taxed product are reduced below the level of allocative efficiency that would occur without the tax. Other things equal, the greater the elasticities of demand and supply, the greater the efficiency loss of a particular tax.

Chapter 19W

19W-1 (*Key Question*) Carefully evaluate: "The supply and demand for agricultural products are such that small changes in agricultural supply will result in drastic changes in prices. However, large changes in farm prices have modest effects on agricultural output." (*Hint*: A brief review of the distinction between supply and quantity supplied may be of assistance.) Do exports increase or reduce the instability of demand for farm products? Explain.

First sentence: Shifts in the supply curve of agricultural goods (*changes in supply*) relative to fixed inelastic demand curves produce large changes in equilibrium prices. Second sentence: But these drastic changes in prices produce only small changes in equilibrium outputs (where *quantities demanded* equals *quantities supplied*) because demands are inelastic.

Because exports are volatile from one year to the next, they increase the instability of demand for farm products.

19W-3 (Key Question) Explain how each of the following contributes to the farm problem: (a) the inelasticity of the demand for farm products, (b) rapid technological progress in farming, (c) the modest long-run growth in the demand for farm commodities, and (d) the competitiveness of agriculture.

(a) Because the demand for most farm products is inelastic, the frequent fluctuations in supply brought about by weather and other factors have relatively small effects on quantity demanded, but large effects on equilibrium prices of farm products. Farmers' sales revenues and incomes therefore are unstable. (b) Technological innovations have decreased production costs, increased long-run supply for most agricultural goods, and reduced the prices of farm output. These declines in prices have put a downward pressure on farm income. (c) The modest long-run growth in the demand for farm products has not been sufficient to offset the expansion of supply, resulting in stagnant farm income. (d) Because the number of producers in most agricultural markets is high, it is difficult if not impossible for producers to collude as a way to limit supply and lessen fluctuations in prices and incomes or halt their long-run declines.

19W-7 (Key Question) Explain the economic effects of price supports. Explicitly include environmental and global impacts in your answer. On what grounds do economists contend that price supports cause a misallocation of resources?

Price supports benefit farmers, harm consumers, impose costs on society, and contribute to problems in world agriculture. Farmers benefit because the prices they receive and the output they produce both increase, expanding their gross incomes. Consumers lose because the prices they pay for farm products rise and quantities purchased decline. Society as a whole bears several costs. Surpluses of farm products will have to be bought and stored, leading to a greater burden on taxpayers. Domestic economic efficiency is lessened as the artificially high prices of farm products lead to an overallocation of resources to agriculture. the environment suffers: the greater use of pesticides and fertilizers contributes to water pollution; farm policies discourage crop rotation; and price supports encourage farming of environmentally sensitive land. The efficient use of world resources is also distorted because of the import tariffs or quotas which such programs often require. Finally, domestic overproduction leads to supply increases in international markets, decreasing prices and causing a declined in the gross incomes of foreign producers.

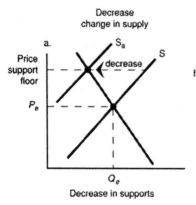

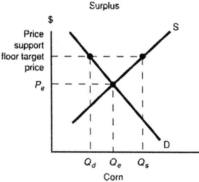

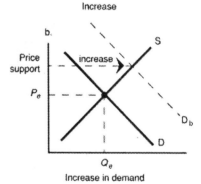